PROPHECY
AND
INSPIRED
SPEECH

*In Early Christianity
and its Hellenistic
Environment*

CHRISTOPHER FORBES

D1548196

HENDRICKSON
PUBLISHERS

Hendrickson Publishers, Inc.
P. O. Box 3473
Peabody, Massachusetts 01961-3473

ISBN 1–56563–269–9

Hendrickson Publishers' edition published by arrangement with J. C. B. Mohr (Paul Siebeck), Tübingen.

PROPHECY, AND INSPIRED SPEECH IN EARLY CHRISTIANITY AND ITS HELLENISTIC ENVIRONMENT, by Christopher Forbes © 1995 J. C. B. Mohr (Paul Siebeck), P.O. Box 2040, D-72010 Tübingen, Germany.

First printing —March 1997

Printed in the United States of America

Library of Congress Cataloging-in-Publication Data

Forbes, Christopher.
    Prophecy and inspired speech in early Christianity and its Hellenistic environment / Christopher Forbes.
    Originally published: Tübingen: J.C.B. Mohr (Paul Siebeck), c1995.
    Originally presented as the author's thesis (Ph. D.)—Macquarie University, 1987.
    Includes bibliographical references and indexes.
    ISBN 1–56563–269–9 (paper)
    1. Glossolalia—History of doctrines—Early church, ca. 30–600.
2. Prophecy—Christianity—History of doctrines—Early church, ca. 30–600.
3. Christianity and other religions—Greek. 4. Christianity and other religions—Roman. 5. Glossolalia—History. 6. Prophecy—History.
7. Greece—Religion. 8. Rome—Religion. I. Title.
BT122.5.F67   1997
234'.132'09015—dc21   97–2499
                                                         CIP

Contents

Synopsis.

This book, originally a thesis submitted for a Ph.D. in Ancient History at Macquarie University in 1987, examines the hypothesis that the dispute between Paul and his converts in Corinth over inspired speech is best explained in terms of the pre-Christian religious experience of some of the Corinthians. That hypothesis suggests that Hellenistic enthusiastic religion involved its participants in experiences of inspired speech which closely resembled early Christian glossolalia and prophecy, either phenomenologically, conceptually, or both. It argues that some among the Corinthians brought with them from their pre-Christian background a view of the nature and status of inspired speech with which Paul found himself in conflict. The hypothesis is grounded, in the modern scholarly debate, in exegetical detail drawn largely from 1 Corinthians chapters 12-14 (and to a lesser extent the book of Acts), and in comparative studies in Hellenistic religion.

It is my contention that the hypothesis is false. A close examination of the Hellenistic evidence presented by scholars for phenomena similar to early Christian glossolalia and prophecy produces no compelling parallels, either at the level of phenomena, or at the level of theological concepts. Those exegetical details which have been interpreted in the light of the hypothesis therefore require re-examination.

Chapter 2 surveys the contributions of scholars to this hypothesis since the publication, in 1959, of the relevant articles in Kittel's *Wörterbuch*. In Chapters 3 and 4 the early Christian phenomenon of glossolalia is analysed in detail. In Chapters 5, 6 and 7 the evidence for proposed Hellenistic parallels is examined and found wanting. Chapter 7 then draws conclusions for the exegesis of 1 Corinthians 12-14. An appendix surveys some related Jewish evidence.

Chapters 8 to 10 deal with early Christian prophecy. In Chapter 8 questions of definition appropriate to the drawing of cross-cultural parallels are dealt with, and several recent scholarly contributions treated. Chapters 9 and 10 are concerned with prophecy in Acts and the Letters of Paul, with particular emphasis on 1 Corinthians. Chapter 11 surveys prophecy and divination in the Hellenistic environment of the New Testament, and suggests several contrasts between Christian prophecy and prophecy in that Hellenistic world. A summary and conclusions follow.

Acknowledgements

In the case of any book such as this there are always people who have been of great assistance, whose patience and kindness cannot go without thanks. In my case these include Dr. David Aune, Dr. Paul Barnett, Dr. Don Carson, Mr. Jeff Cayzer, Prof. James Dunn, Prof. Earle Ellis, Dr. Bruce Harris, Dr. Greg Horsley, Dr. Ros Kearsley (who beat me to finishing by six months), Prof. Ken Kitchen, Mrs. Catherine Kroeger, Dr. John Lee, Prof. Bruce Malina, Dr. Peter O'Brien, Dr. Boyo Ockinga, Prof. W.D. Smith and Dr. R.P. Spittler. Without their various contributions the writing of this book would have been much more difficult.

My heartfelt thanks must also go to all those friends, first at St. James', and now at St. Matthew's, who have prayed for me and my work over the years. They know that without their support it would all have been immeasurably harder.

For more than ten years Gordon Garner and Piers Crocker of the Australian Institute of Archaeology helped to keep butter on the bread. The Institute also paid for the computer on which most of this work was originally written. I could not have hoped for a more understanding employer or more prayerful friends. Prof. M.K. Hopkins of King's College insisted I think about something else while I was in Cambridge, and then gave me plenty of other things to think about. He might not recognise his influence, but it's here! The late Dr. Colin Hemer and the residents and staff of Tyndale House took this Antipodean to their hearts for a term, and made that term a most enjoyable and productive time.

My mother and father have spent years listening to me talking about subjects of the utmost obscurity without ever betraying any trace of discontent at my choice of career. Many years ago they said that they didn't mind what their children did, or how well they did it, so long as they did their best. They have never shown any regret at signing this blank cheque. Mum and Dad: here it is. And Dad, thanks for your help with the Index.

Seven years in composition and as many again in revision is a long time to spend on one topic. It remains a matter of wonder to me that two people in particular, other than myself, have managed to maintain their interest in this work. One is Professor E.A. Judge, my Ph.D. supervisor, who has been lavish of his time and skills in ways I could neither have predicted nor required of him. The other is my wife, Jan. She has shared it all, from the first gropings for a topic to the final form. She knows what that has meant to me. She also knows I could not have done it without her.

Many others have contributed in many ways. The essential concept and structure, however, are mine, as are the mistakes. It may be true that Teiresias prophesied about the past as well as the future, and that History is the prophet of truth. But "to know all things", as W.C. van Unnik points out, is the mark of a prophet, and I am not one, nor even the son of one.

Becky and Joey, it's for you, too. I'm glad you were too young to remember the last six months of getting it finished. I am also very glad that your generation is unlikely to grow up in a church where prophecy is as unfamiliar as it was for Jan and myself.

Abbreviations

Aune, *Prophecy*

D.E. Aune, Prophecy in Early Christianity and the Ancient Mediterranean World, Grand Rapids, 1983.

Boring, *Sayings*

M.E. Boring, *Sayings of the Risen Jesus: Christian Prophecy in the Synoptic Tradition*, Cambridge, 1982.

Carson, *Showing the Spirit*

D.A. Carson, *Showing the Spirit: a Theological Exposition of 1 Corinthians 12-14*, Sydney, 1987.

Crone, *Prophecy*

T.M. Crone, *Early Christian Prophecy: a Study of its Origin and Function*, St. Mary's University Press, Baltimore, Maryland, 1973.

Currie, "Early Evidence"

S.D. Currie, "'Speaking in Tongues': Early Evidence Outside the New Testament Bearing on *'Glōssais Lalein'*", Interpretation, vol. 19, 1965, pp. 274-294.

Dautzenberg, "Glossolalie"

G. Dautzenberg, "Glossolalie", *Reallexikon für Antike und Christentum*, vol. 11, 1981, cols. 225-246.

Didyma Inscriptions

Didyma Inscriptions; Texts and List, D.F. McCabe and M.A. Plunkett, eds., Princeton, 1985.

Engelsen, *Glossolalia*

N.I.J. Engelsen, *Glossolalia and Other Forms of Prophetic Speech According to 1 Corinthians 12-14*, unpublished Ph.D thesis, Yale, 1970.

Fascher, *Prophetes*

E. Fascher, *Prophetes: Eine sprach- und religionsgeschichtliche Untersuchung*, Giessen, 1927.

Gillespie, *Prophecy and Tongues*   T.W. Gillespie, *Prophecy and Tongues: the Concept of Christian Prophecy in the Pauline Theology.*, unpublished Ph.D. thesis, Claremont Graduate School and University Centre, 1971.

Gillespie, "A Pattern"   T.W. Gillespie, "A Pattern of Prophetic Speech in 1 Corinthians", *J.B.L.* vol. 97, no. 1, 1978, pp. 74-95.

Grudem, *Gift*   W. Grudem, *The Gift of Prophecy in 1 Corinthians*, Washington, 1982

Hart, *Tongues And Prophecy*   M.E. Hart, *Speaking in Tongues and Prophecy as Understood by Paul and at Corinth, with reference to early Christian usage*, unpublished Ph.D. thesis, Durham, 1975.

Hill, *Prophecy*   *New Testament Prophecy*, London, 1979

Horsley, "Spiritual Elitism"   R.A. Horsley, " 'How can some of you say there is no resurrection of the dead?' Spiritual Elitism in Corinth", *Novum Testamentum*, vol. 20, 1978, pp. 202-231.

Johanson, "Tongues"   B.C. Johanson, "Tongues, A Sign for Unbelievers?: a Structural and Exegetical Study of 1 Corinthians XIV. 20-25", *N.T.S.*, vol. 25, 1978-79, pp. 180-203.

Panagopoulos, *Vocation*   J. Panagopoulos, ed., *Prophetic Vocation in the New Testament and Today*, Leiden, 1977.

Thiselton, "Interpretation"   A.C. Thiselton, "The 'Interpretation' of Tongues: a New Suggestion in the Light of Greek Usage in Philo and Josephus", *J.Th.S.*, vol. 30, 1979, pp. 15-36.

Wire, *Women Prophets*   A.C. Wire, *The Corinthian Women Prophets: a Reconstruction through Paul's Rhetoric*, Minneapolis, 1990.

Chapter 1

Introduction

This book began as a fairly straightforward attempt to investigate Hellenistic culture for phenomena that might be enlightening as parallels to New Testament prophecy and other forms of inspired speech within first-century Christianity. The original conception was suggested to me by the fact that, among the recent outpouring of scholarly research on early Christian prophecy, a great deal of attention had been paid to the Old Testament background. Relatively little attention had been given to the understanding of prophecy in first-century Judaism, and very little systematic work at all had been done (or so it seemed at first), on the relevant Hellenistic phenomena. This appeared to be so despite the fact that our single most explicit source of information about early Christian prophecy, 1 Corinthians chapters 12-14, comes from a predominantly Hellenistic environment where the particular problems in view appear to many to have a distinctly Hellenistic basis.

This original conception has both grown and contracted. It has grown for one primary reason. As I set myself to master the views of the secondary authorities on the subject it rapidly became clear the most promising lines of inquiry all pointed in one general direction. They noted the odd variety of issues to which Paul addresses himself in 1 Corinthians, and tried to relate them, usually in combinations, to the Hellenistic culture of their environment. Taken together, these studies suggested that the issues of dress and deportment in 1 Corinthians ch. 10, and the not always carefully distinguished issues of charismatic outcry, glossolalia, prophecy and the teaching role of women in chs. 11-14 ought to be investigated as related issues. Though I have not been able to investigate all of these issues in the same depth, the above suggestion is one I have set out to put to the test.

The conception has contracted as well. Reading the primary sources quickly showed me that the Hellenistic concept of "inspiration" was one that spread far beyond the boundaries of those matters related to early Christian prophecy and inspiration. The whole body of Greek poetry, for example, is widely conceived of as being "inspired" in a sense closely related to the more strictly religious sense. I have therefore sought to limit my investigation to those forms of Hellenistic inspiration that have to do with strictly religious phenomena: primarily those to do with oracular practice, and "charismatic" and "enthusiastic" religion. Where this practice has been abandoned for a wider view, this has been noted in the text. There are, of course, other ways in which modern, ancient Hellenistic and New Testament conceptions of prophecy and inspiration fail to overlap or to mesh smoothly, but these need to be dealt with in detail.

The second way in which the conception has contracted is that it has been necessary to limit the area of study within early Christianity. In his recent major contribution to the study of early Christian prophecy, David Aune has forcefully argued that the preoccupation of scholarship with the canonical evidence for prophecy, over against any other forms of evidence, has seriously distorted our understanding of the subject.[1] I am in full agreement with him. Unfortunately the constraints placed on a thesis such as this mean that only a relatively small body of evidence can be meaningfully treated. Virtually all our explicit evidence as to the nature of early Christian prophecy in the first century is to be found in 1 Corinthians and the Acts of the Apostles. I have restricted the main thrust of my investigation to those sources, not because they are canonical, but because they are our earliest evidence. My conclusions, therefore, relate not to early Christian prophecy and inspired speech more widely, but to prophecy and inspired speech as they were conceived of by Paul and Luke.

The greatest single weakness of most recent attempts to relate early Christian prophecy to its Hellenistic environment has been the willingness to collect "parallel" material almost indiscriminately from Greek sources ranging over more than eight hundred years - from classical Greek literature of the fifth and fourth centuries B.C. to writers like Iamblichus, and the Greek Magical Papyri of the third and fourth centuries A.D. This tendency is especially to be deplored when we consider that it appears to be a matter of consensus among scholars that between the middle of the first and the end of the second century A.D. several fairly basic changes occurred in beliefs related to our area of interest. Central to these changes was a widespread rise in the credibility of the miraculous, and an increasing fascination with occult and ecstatic phenomena, especially as evidence of divine powers or

---

[1]   D.E. Aune, *Prophecy*, pp. 13-16.

divine activity. This phenomenon has been described by Dannemann in the following words:

As far as the educated and literary stratum of Greco-Roman culture is concerned, in the first century A.D. Plutarch and Seneca still confidently portray the divine sage Socrates, and his moral courage in the face of death, in order to dismiss attempts to authenticate figures as divine by their power to work miracles. But in the second century Lucian fights bitterly on several fronts trying to maintain this criterion; however, as the growth of the cults of such figures as Peregrinus and Alexander shows, he does not succeed. Philostratus and Porphyry give in; although still aware of the philosophical standards, they describe Apollonius and Pythagoras as both divine sages and miracle workers."[2]

To extend the point, in the first century Philo positively plays down the miraculous element in his interpretative recasting of the Moses traditions of the Old Testament, in favour of the "philosopher-king" motif. In the early third century, however, Philostratus' "Life of Apollonius" interweaves the two threads of philosophy and magic in a way that would have been unthinkable in Philo's time.[3] In other words, the credibility of the supernatural and the miraculous was on the increase over the period under discussion, and the New Testament material dates from the early stage of the development. It is true that we can know very little of attitudes at the popular level, as opposed to the educated level referred to above, from which the vast bulk of our evidence comes. The same development may not occur there. But insofar as evidence contemporary with the New Testament is available, it is most unwise to base an argument on parallels which date

---

[2] Ruth Dannemann, *J.B.L.*, vol. 93, 1974, p. 130, in a review of D. L. Tiede, *The Charismatic Figure as Miracle Worker*. See also Ramsay MacMullen, *Enemies of the Roman Order*, Cambridge, Mass., 1966, p. 109, "The mind, in fact, from the second century on, comes under increasingly open, angry, and exasperated attack." See also p. 111 : "It is instructive to compare the philosopher of an Augustan painting . . ., a face and pose to remember, surely, but no more than a man, or to compare the self-comfortable ordinariness of Seneca's appearance . . . with the later fourth or fifth century bust of a philosopher . . . He is shown at the moment of gnosis, head tilted back, long locks flying, mouth slack. His eyes above all focus attention. They are enormous and visionary." "So much for the changing attitudes of the aristocracy over the first four centuries A.D. They were willing to grant the importance of portents in the first century, of oracles in the second, of apparitions in the third and later, though to put the matter so shortly and schematically is no doubt a little misleading . . ." (p. 120.) A similar position is taken up by D.E. Aune, in "The Problem of the Genre of the Gospels", in *Gospel Perspectives*, vol. 2, ed. R.T. France and D. Wenham, Sheffield, 1981, p. 34, and H.W. Parke, *The Oracles of Apollo in Asia Minor*, London, 1985, p. 74, p. 82.

[3] For this issue generally see also Ramsay MacMullen, *Paganism in the Roman Empire*, New Haven, 1967, pp. 72ff. He also notes the important place of Apuleius' "Apology" in this on-going development.

from the later stages of the development. I have chosen, therefore, to begin my selection of material with writers working within a century of the main New Testament authors. They cover the period from about 50 B.C. to about 150 A.D., and form the basis of my study. This period may reasonably be described as "the immediate environment" of the New Testament, though even across this relatively brief span, changes in attitude are notable. The ancient authors on whom I have especially concentrated are Diodorus Siculus, Dionysius of Halicarnassus, Philo, Josephus, Dio Chrysostom, and Plutarch (the Moralia). Together they form a substantial corpus of literature reflecting attitudes and beliefs in these centuries.

Scholarly attention to the topic of early Christian prophecy and inspired speech has two major focusses. The first of these is on the phenomena themselves, as they are described, and as information about them may be inferred, from the various New Testament and other early Christian documents.[4] The second is on the attempt to detect the literary remains of early Christian prophecy within those documents, and hence to trace the influence of prophecy and inspired speech on the theological growth of the early Christian movement.[5] Though it ought to be clear that the first of these two endeavours is logically prior to the second, perhaps the bulk of scholarly research has been directed to the second. My interest, for the purposes of this study, however, is in the first. This study will be concerned to elucidate the phenomena of early Christian inspired speech, and the relationship between these and inspired-speech phenomena in the Graeco-Roman world.

The range of evidence within the New Testament on the topic of early Christian prophecy is wide, indeed too wide to be properly dealt with in such a study as this. I have decided to concentrate on only two aspects within this topic. I will be concerned primarily with the reports of prophecy

---

[4] Works focussing on this aspect of the topic include, notably, J.D.G. Dunn, *Jesus and the Spirit*, London, 1975, for our purposes especially chapters 6-9, and D. Hill, *Prophecy*, esp. chapters 4-5.

[5] The two most notable works on this aspect of the topic of the past few years both came to print while this study was in progress. They are M.E. Boring, *Sayings of the Risen Jesus: Christian Prophecy in the Synoptic Tradition*, London, 1982, and D.E. Aune, *Prophecy in Early Christianity and the Ancient Mediterranean World*, Grand Rapids, 1983. Naturally, both these works include substantial contributions to the study of the phenomena of early Christian prophecy, but they are both concerned with these issues fundamentally as a prelude to the task of detecting and isolating prophetic material preserved in other contexts.

and other inspired speech-forms from the Pauline correspondence and the Book of Acts, with a lesser interest in related phenomena drawn from Luke's Gospel. These two aspects have been selected because they constitute the most accessible body of explicit evidence about the topic. I am therefore concerned with prophecy within the early churches in the first fifty years or so of their existence. The self-understanding of Jesus as a prophet, the place of John the Baptist, and similar issues, will not be treated here. Nor, for other reasons, will the Revelation to John, or the Epistle to the Hebrews, though both of these have much to tell us about early Christian prophecy. The addition of these two bodies of source material would simply expand the project beyond the bounds of manageability.

Over the last thirty years and more a consensus has arisen within the work of those scholars who have set out to examine the Hellenistic evidence for parallels to the New Testament phenomena. This consensus, broadly stated, is that the inspired speech phenomena that we find within the New Testament, and the terminology that is used to describe them, can be, in many respects, closely paralleled within the world of Hellenistic popular religion. These parallels, it is suggested, help us to solve several otherwise extremely difficult exegetical puzzles within the text of the New Testament itself. The main form that this general argument takes centres on 1 Corinthians chapters 12-14, and suggests that in these chapters Paul sets out to correct ideas about the nature of glossolalia and prophecy that have their origins in the pre-Christian religious experience of the Corinthian congregation.

As I worked through the literature on this matter I became more and more convinced, on exegetical grounds, that this consensus was basically correct. However, as I turned to the primary Hellenistic evidence I began to have doubts, and these grew as my reading continued. I have now become convinced that the consensus is based on only the flimsiest of evidence, and must be abandoned, at least in its present form. It is extremely difficult to parallel many of the features of early Christian enthusiasm *at all* within Hellenistic religion and culture. Some features are, so far as I have been able to determine, unique. Certainly the differences between the two groups of phenomena are greater than the similarities. I have tried at all times to avoid overstressing the differences, and to note when they have to do with wider concerns than the "prophetic" or "inspired" phenomena themselves. For example, the differing roles of "the prophet" within Hellenistic culture and early Christianity seem to me to have far more to do with the differences between the wider structures of those different "cultures" than with the prophetic phenomena themselves. None the less, these two sets of phenomena themselves are fundamentally different, and ought not to be confused.

1. A Note on the Evaluation of "Unique" Phenomena.

As mentioned above, at several important points in this book, the claim will be made that certain phenomena or conceptions are unique in their historical context. Such claims are not as popular as they once were among Biblical scholars. In the heady days of the "Biblical Theology" movement the claim that such and such a feature of the Biblical tradition was "unique" was often seen to imply that the feature in question, whether it were a particular view of the nature of time or of the value of historical events, or the relationship between humanity and the divine, was therefore particularly important, and likely to be of abiding value for modern questions. "Uniquely" Biblical points of view were therefore to be defended against extra-Biblical parallels, and their "loss" in the inter-Testamental period under the onslaught of Hellenisation (or earlier, under the pervasive influence of Canaanite, Mesopotamian or Iranian ideas), was to be deplored.[6] In some cases this defence was justifiable on historical grounds (though in others it smacked of theological polemic). But is it necessarily the case that the unique is the important or the characteristic? Or that "unique" features of a phenomenon should automatically be treated as its "defining" features?

Scholars do not seem to be sure how to treat "unique" phenomena. For one thing, they are particularly vulnerable: they are the positive side of the "argument from silence", and a single clear counter-example refutes their claim. For another, the temptation to base interpretative judgements on them is strong, and the judgements may work either "for" or "against" the credibility of the phenomenon in question. As another example, we may cite the use of the "criterion of dissimilarity" in research into the question of the

---

[6] Samuel Sandmel, "Palestinian and Hellenistic Judaism and Christianity: The Question of the Comfortable Theory", *H.U.C.A.*, vol. 50, 1979, pp. 137-148, is one who has been severely critical of such tendencies, and though I cannot agree with many of his examples, particularly those drawn from more recent research, his principal point seems to me to be well made.

reliability of the Gospel tradition.[7] Put simply, the logical basis of this criterion is as follows: we can be more certain that a saying attributed to Jesus is actually from him if it contains ideas that are unique in their environment: that is, which cannot be found in first-century Judaism, or in the beliefs of the early churches. Put thus positively, the principle is unexceptionable. The unique becomes the (knowably) authentic. But the rigorous application of the method produces an unbalanced picture of the sayings of Jesus, which must of necessity emphasise his originality, and his lack of affinities with his environment.

On the other hand, scholars can easily treat unique phenomena only so as to do away with them, or to treat them as aberrant. At the risk of prejudicing my own case, I offer the following example: Joseph Fontenrose and others clearly distinguish between the "mantic" or prophetic frenzy and Bacchanalian frenzy.[8] Yet in two cases known to me it is claimed that Bacchants in their frenzy give prophecies. However, since one of these cases is the highly coloured account in Livy of the suppression of the "Bacchanalian Conspiracy", and the other uses the prophecies of the Maenads simply as proof that Dionysus shares attributes with other recognised gods, and since in neither case is the prophetic side of Bacchanalian frenzy developed in any detail at all, I feel myself free to argue, along the same lines as Fontenrose, that prophetic phenomena were not a significant aspect of Dionysiac experience.[9] In other words, the rare or unique becomes the inauthentic or the unimportant.

Too often the interpretation scholars have drawn from the claim that a phenomenon is unique has been based on personal bias rather than

---

[7] For a recent critique of the use of this criterion with particular reference to the question of isolating the sayings of Christian prophets in the Synoptic tradition see J.D.G. Dunn, "Prophetic 'I'-Sayings and the Jesus tradition: The importance of testing prophetic utterances within early Christianity", *N.T.S.*, vol. 24, 1977-78, N.B. pp. 197-198.

[8] J. Fontenrose, *The Delphic Oracle*, University of California Press, Berkeley, 1978, p. 207; K. Latte, "The Coming of the Pythia", *H.Th.R.*, vol. 33, 1940, pp. 9-18.

[9] For the full development of this case, see Chapter 6, "Glossolalia and the Cults of Dionysus and Cybele". A similar, though more clear-cut example is the one and only case known to me where the inspired speech of the Delphic prophetess is described as resembling another language. This case may be treated as exceptional and aberrant because it is so clearly treated as such by the ancient authors. See Herodotus 8.135, Plutarch, Mor. 412 a, Life of Aristides 19.1-2, Pausanias, 23.6. Again, for a full treatment of this case see Chapter 5, "Glossolalia and Hellenistic Inspiration: Delphic and Delian Apollo."

inferential logic. Let us recognise, then, that "unique" events or phenomena are, quite simply, unique. The importance of each case cannot be decided on that criterion alone. Each case will need to be judged carefully, with due regard for the limits of current knowledge (and in this study, the limits of the evidence being surveyed), and, most importantly, each case will have to be judged on its own particular merits.

2. A Note on the Evaluation of Parallels.

The enormous scholarly output of the "History of Religions School", which attempted to understand early Christianity within the broad context of the tradition of ancient religion, has often been criticised for its over-use of parallels drawn from a wide historical and cultural range.[10] Yet few historians articulate the distinctions between the possible purposes of comparison, or what the proper way to use cross-cultural parallels might be. Of course the distinction between merely formal parallels and genetic parallels is usually observed,[11] but direct or indirect borrowing, or common origins, are not the only relationships that can lead to parallels in cultural phenomena.

The use of cultural parallels changes according to the question being asked by the historian. The historian who is inquiring about the links between early Christianity and its environment will use comparisons differently from the historian who is asking about the factors which distinguish it from that environment.[12] It is our task to avoid the effects of this problem by asking: precisely how strong are the parallels between early

---

[10] See, for example, the comments of C.H. Dodd on the work of Reitzenstein: " . . . it depends on too many arbitrary assumptions. It is not too much to say that in Reitzenstein's later work much of ancient literature became one vast jig-saw puzzle, to be dissected and reassembled by methods which often had too little regard for the maxim that a chain is as strong as its weakest link." (*The Interpretation of the Fourth Gospel*, 1953, p. 121, note 3.)

[11] Compare the judicious comments of B.M. Metzger, "Methodology in the Study of the Mystery Religions and Early Christianity", *Historical and Literary Studies, Pagan, Jewish and Christian*, Leiden, 1968, pp. 9-10.

[12] Gerd Theissen describes these two styles as "contrasting" and "analogizing" comparison, *The Social Setting of Pauline Christianity*, Edinburgh, 1982, p. 194. He emphasises that they are the opposing sides of the same comparative method, as no comparison can be exclusively "analogizing" (as that would indicate identity, not comparability) or exclusively "contrasting" (as that would exclude comparability altogether).

Christianity and its environment with regard to inspired speech? And if the parallels are strong, what do they mean?

The next question, of necessity, is: what constitutes a strong parallel? In general the following points apply. In the study of cultural phenomena, one ought to study parallels not of isolated phenomena or concepts, but of complexes of phenomena or concepts.[13] At the level of artefacts, for example, the fact that two tribes both use a particular style of working to sharpen stone may or may not be significant. It may, for example, be dependent purely on the physical properties of the best available stone. But if both tribes use this method of stone-working on only one particular type of tool, and always in association with another particular style of decoration, then the parallel is infinitely more likely to have cultural and historical significance. At the level of concepts rather than artefacts, we should look not merely for parallel terminology, but for parallel *complexes* of terminology, and even more importantly, for parallel complexes of ideas and phenomena related to this terminology. In our particular case a close parallel in terms of inspired speech would be not merely the use of the terms for "prophecy", but the fact of similar prophetic phenomena, recognisable to members of both cultures as similar, performing similar social functions, and perhaps even understood by way of similar conceptual frameworks. The more the features of the complex of concepts and phenomena we call "prophecy" are similar, the stronger the parallel. Naturally, the value of the parallel is also affected by its proximity to the New Testament phenomena in time and space. But granting that we have a parallel, the next question must be, what does the parallel mean?

There at least three possibilities. Strong parallels can indicate that a custom or concept in two cultures has a common origin, or is borrowed by one from the other: these are genetic parallels. For very strong parallels, with, say, parallel phenomena, terminology and concepts, this is the most likely case. Alternatively, parallels can indicate common underlying patterns, otherwise obscure. Parallels in political organisation, for example, can be related to parallels in family organisation, obscured by differing terminology. In our case, parallels in inspired speech might be related to parallels at the religious level more generally. These parallels themselves would then need investigation. Finally, parallels could indicate independent

---

[13] Cf. D.E. Aune, *Prophecy*, p. 17: "What must be compared are not isolated features but features considered within their structural framework."

responses to similar environmental factors, whether that environmental factor is a physical one (as in the hypothetical stone-working case above) or a cultural one. For example, the fact that different client states rebelling against the Romans tended to organise their armies according to the Roman model is not evidence of common origins. It is evidence of independent borrowing brought on by a common cultural environment, in which the success of Roman military methods was a clearly observable fact.

What we need to ask, then, is: if we do find parallels, into which of these categories (if any) do they fall? Naturally, if our parallels are judged to have failed, this will not exclude the possibility that one of the above types of relationship existed. It will merely fail to provide evidence for it.

In the survey that follows I have attempted to outline the development of scholarly views on the relationship between early Christian inspired speech and its suggested Hellenistic parallels. The aim of the survey is to show how various threads of evidence, some derived exegetically from the New Testament alone, others drawn directly from the Hellenistic context, have been combined to form a coherent hypothesis about the nature of early Christian inspired speech and, more particularly, about the dispute over inspired speech between St. Paul and his Corinthian converts. Though the major conclusions of my research are occasionally foreshadowed, I have made no attempt within the survey itself to interact with every detail of the cases presented. They are extensively treated in the chapters that follow. Issues that do require critical comment within the survey are dealt with immediately.

3. Final Note.

The portion of Chapter 5 that deals with the cult of Delphic Apollo has appeared in an earlier form in the journal *Novum Testamentum*, vol. 28, part 3, 1986, pp. 257-270, under the title "Early Christian Inspired Speech and Hellenistic Popular Religion".

In the later stages of the preparation of this thesis for presentation the major work of D.E. Aune, *Prophecy in Early Christianity and the Ancient Mediterranean World*, came to my attention. At this point chapters 3-7 were already in virtually final form. Naturally, however, so major a contribution to the scholarly discussion could not be ignored, and I have done my best to take account of Aune's views. However, the main lines of my own research were already clear to me, and Aune's work has not affected the overall emphasis or results of my work significantly. This situation has not altered in the revision of the work for publication. I have taken particular care to make sure that references both ancient and modern gained from Aune are acknowledged. In areas where our work overlaps our conclusions are often similar, though mostly independent.

Between the finalisation of the thesis and the preparation of the final version for publication, in mid 1994, the two most significant contributions to the field have probably been G.D. Fee's *The First Epistle to the Corinthians*, Grand Rapids, 1987, and Antoinette Clark Wire's *The Corinthian Women Prophets: a Reconstruction through Paul's Rhetoric*, Minneapolis, 1990. I have resisted the temptation to go through my footnotes adding the phrase "and Fee thinks so too" (or the opposite) where appropriate, and limited my citation of his commentary largely to points of significant disagreement. This ought not to be taken as indicating my view of his work, with which I am in whole-hearted agreement on many points. I regret that it has not been possible to take full account of the work of Antoinette Clark Wire. However, on a number of significant points I do interact with Wire's position, including cases when she draws on the evidence of the Graeco-Roman world.

All translations of ancient works, unless otherwise noted, are from the Loeb Classical Library edition. Likewise, unless otherwise noted, the Biblical translation used is the New International Version.

Chapter 2

Literature Survey: Theme and Variations

What was the problem over inspired speech in Corinth? Answers abound. Surprisingly, nobody has recently dealt with the suggestion of John Chrysostom, that glossolalia was especially prized in Corinth and in the other early congregations because it was known to be the gift given to the apostles, in highly spectacular circumstances, at Pentecost.[1] Those who take seriously Luke's reports of glossolalia in the earliest Jewish-Christian churches sometimes suggest that Jewish-Christian pressure for converts to manifest glossolalia, or "Palestinian piety", was behind the problem encountered by Paul in Corinth.[2] Naturally, those who doubt that there is a connection between the Lukan and Pauline reports of glossolalia doubt that the problem can have a Jewish origin.[3] But few modern scholars enquire deeply into the question of causation. It is one of the strengths of the "Hellenistic cult background" hypothesis that it at least attempts to find distinctively Corinthian reasons for what seems to have been a distinctively Corinthian issue.

Most scholars attempt, instead, merely an accurate description of the problem. Yet even so there is a range of views. Most simplistically, F.W. Beare argues that the occurrence of glossolalia itself is the problem: "There

---

[1]   John Chrysostom, Homilies on 1 Corinthians 29.1 and 35.1. A similar view is taken by J.C. Hurd, *The Origins of 1 Corinthians*, London, 1965, pp. 281 and 194-5, who suggests that it was Paul's early use of glossolalia, as against his later teaching about it, that so impressed the Corinthians with the importance of the gift. My own view, as will become apparent in Chapter 7, is similar to Chrysostom's, though I only discovered so after reaching my conclusions, and by accident.

[2]   J.P.M. Sweet, "A Sign for Unbelievers: Paul's Attitude to Glossolalia", *N.T.S.*, vol. 13, 1966-67, p. 246, following T.W. Manson, doubts that is a superabundance of glossolalia that is the problem, and suggests that it was the insistence (in Peter's name) on glossolalia.

[3]   See, for example, Hart, *Tongues And Prophecy*, p. 146. Hart is, however, correct to rule out the possibility that Apollos himself is the cause of the problem (pp. 148-9). Paul never refers to him at all negatively: see the further discussion below.

can be no doubt, then, that the main purpose of Paul is to discourage the practice of speaking with tongues among Christians."[4] Others argue that the problem is not the *practice* of glossolalia, but the inordinately high value attached to the practice by (some of) the Corinthians.[5] G. Dautzenberg suggests that in Paul's view the problem is the Corinthian preference for tongues over prophecy, and a number of scholars take up basically similar positions.[6] For others still, the problems can be linked together under headings such as "misdirected individualism", without the attempt to ask where this attitude originated.[7] Most recently, W.C. van Unnik has argued that scholarship overestimates the problem. Paul wishes to encourage the

---

[4] F.W. Beare, "Speaking with Tongues, a Critical Survey of the New Testament Evidence", *J.B.L.*, vol. 83, 1964, p. 244. C.D. Isbell agrees ("Glossolalia and Propheteialalia: a Study of 1 Corinthians 14", pp. 16-17, *Wesleyan Theological Journal*, vol. 10, 1975, p. 17): "by telling his readers to exchange their ability at glossolalia for powers of interpretation, (Paul) has very clearly told them to choose that other way of speaking, the way that produces understandability."

[5] D.M. Smith, "Glossolalia and Other Spiritual Gifts in New Testament Perspective", *Interpretation*, vol. 28, 1974, p. 312, suggests that "these Corinthian Christians put a high premium specifically on glossolalia". J.W. MacGorman, "Glossolalic Error and Its Correction: 1 Corinthians 12-14", *Review and Expositor*, vol. 80, 1983, p. 394, argues that the Corinthian glossolalists thought glossolalia the highest gift, the criterion of spirituality: an over-reaction with attempts to forbid it resulted. K. Stendahl, "Glossolalia and the Charismatic Movement", *God's Christ and His People*, ed. J. Jervell and W. Meeks, Oslo, 1977, p. 123, thought that glossolalia had "fired the imaginations of the Corinthian Christians" so that they were more than willing to use it in situations where it brought them contempt and mockery. Hart summarises the problem as "obsession with the spectacular", especially with regard to speech (*Tongues And Prophecy*, p. 154). W.A. Meeks, *The First Urban Christians*, Yale, 1983, pp. 119-121, has a good brief discussion of glossolalia as a source of prestige in Corinth, though his analysis of the phenomenon itself is far too dependent on only one or two modern psychological studies of glossolalia.

[6] G. Dautzenberg, "Glossolalie", cols. 228, 238-9. B.A. Pearson, *The Pneumatikos-Psychikos Terminology in 1 Corinthians*, Missoula, 1973, pp. 44-50, argues that the Corinthian preference for glossolalia, which he thinks they identified as prophecy, was based on a view of inspiration similar to that expressed in Philo, Quis Rerum Divinarum Heres 263-266, which he postulates was common in the Hellenistic world. In anticipation of the fuller discussion of Philo in Chapter 6 it ought simply to be said that this is a risky suggestion on two counts: nothing in the Philo passage is similar to what 1 Corinthians tells us about glossolalia, and any attempt to reconstruct "the Corinthian view of inspiration" must remain speculative. B.C. Johanson, "Tongues", thinks the problem arose out of competition between glossolalists and prophets for influence in Corinth. In his view the prophets were the natural leaders once Paul and Apollos had left, and the glossolalists within the congregation wanted influence. They and the prophets competed with each other for attention in the assembly.

[7] Thus Engelsen, *Glossolalia*, pp. 127-132.

Corinthians to practise their gifts of inspired speech with all zeal: he merely wishes to fine-tune their priorities.[8]

Other issues prevalent in the Corinthian congregation are sometimes used to explain the problem. Here there are three main views. The first, now very much out of favour, is that identified with the work of W. Schmithals, which suggests that many or most of the various points at issue between Paul and his churches in Corinth (and elsewhere) can be related to disputes over Gnosticism.[9] The second view is exemplified by the recent survey of Thiselton,[10] who analyses "the problem in Corinth" as a case of "over-realised eschatology". Such an approach comes closer to a true causal explanation of the problem than most of those cited above, but does not go all the way, because it tells us little about why that problem might have developed in Corinth rather than elsewhere. Its second weakness, which is more significant for the Corinthian situation, is that while it convincingly links several issues in the Corinthian correspondence, it is very unconvincing when it comes to matters of inspired speech.[11] The third view is that "the problem" in Corinth has to do with the influence of Hellenistic-Jewish speculation about σοφία. This case has been most fully developed in recent times by R.A. Horsley.[12] Horsley's hypothesis seems to

---

[8] W.C. van Unnik, "The Meaning of 1 Corinthians 12.31", *Nov.T.* vol. 35, part 2, 1993, pp. 142-159. The article was published posthumously by P.W. van der Horst, though its existence was reported by Jannes Reiling in 1977, in his essay "Prophecy, the Spirit and the Church", in J. Panagopoulos, *Vocation*, pp. 58-76.

[9] W. Schmithals, *Gnosticism in Corinth*, trans. J.E. Steely, Nashville, 1971, and *Paul and the Gnostics*, trans J.E. Steely, Nashville, 1972.

[10] A.C. Thiselton, "Realised Eschatology at Corinth", *N.T.S.*, vol. 24, 1977-78, pp. 510-526, and the works of Barrett, Bruce and Käsemann cited there. Compare R.P. Martin, *The Spirit and the Congregation*, Grand Rapids, 1984, where a sustained exegesis of 1 Corinthians 12-14 is based on this hypothesis. The strictures of D.J. Doughty, "The Presence and Future of Salvation in Corinth", *Z.N.W.*, vol. 66, 1975, pp. 61-90, ought not to be ignored, but in my view Thiselton's survey still produces a coherence between many of the issues in 1 Corinthians.

[11] Thiselton, *art.cit.*, especially p. 512: "an over-realised eschatology leads to an 'enthusiastic' view of the Spirit". How is such a generalisation to be made to apply to questions of inspired speech? In my view the only argument in its favour is the suggestion that glossolalia was understood as being the language of heaven, available to believers now. We will see, however, that such a position is based on the slenderest of evidence. R.P. Martin, *op.cit.*, p. 88, suggests that the Corinthian enthusiasts saw themselves as already some kind of angelic beings, and that their glossolalia was thus viewed as the language of the angels. This is sheer speculation, unsupported by any evidence of which I am aware.

[12] See most recently "Spiritual Elitism", pp. 203ff. The hypothesis was developed in

me to be an advance on that proposed by Thiselton, as it more adequately explains the question why the resurrection of the dead became problematic.[13] It likewise provides a genuine causal link in the person of Apollos, whose "Alexandrine" style Horsley suggests as the origin of many Corinthian ideas. But again the point at which the hypothesis is weakest is the question of inspired speech. Horsley can provide no convincing background whatever to suggest that Hellenistic-Jewish wisdom speculation knew of glossolalic phenomena.[14] Chapter 12 of 1 Corinthians begins the discussion of τὰ πνευματικά, but Horsley admits that for this term he can find no useful parallel.[15]

Horsley's earlier articles, "Pneumatikos vs. Psychikos: Distinctions of Spiritual Status among the Corinthians", *H.Th.R.*, vol. 69, 1976, pp. 269-288, and "Wisdom of Word and Words of Wisdom in Corinth", *C.B.Q.*, vol. 39, 1977, pp. 224-239, and touched on briefly by B.A. Pearson, *op.cit.*, p. 15. Horsley is careful not to argue that Hellenistic philosophical speculations similar to Philo's are actually the problem in Corinth: his case is that the striking similarities in vocabulary and concept help us to explain what the problem may have been. ("Spiritual Elitism", p. 207.)

[13] It is, of course, quite possible that a synthesis of the two views could be made that would account more adequately than either view alone for the group of issues in 1 Corinthians. Pearson points the way towards one possible synthesis, *op.cit.*, pp. 24-25.

[14] The development of Horsley's work by J.A. Davis, *Wisdom and Spirit: an Investigation of 1 Corinthians 1.18-3.20 Against the Background of Jewish Sapiental Traditions in the Greco-Roman Period*, Lanham, 1984, comes closer to providing a true background by showing that wisdom traditions stressed the role of the Spirit of God in the gaining of wisdom. This might well explain the problem over the use and abuse of prophecy, but certainly gets us no further with glossolalia. Compare E.E. Ellis, "Wisdom and Knowledge in 1 Corinthians", *Tyndale Bulletin*, vol. 25, 1974, pp. 82-98, and G. Dautzenberg, "Glossolalie", col. 238.

[15] For Apollos as the causal agent see B.A. Pearson, *op.cit.*, p. 18 and note 23, with the references cited there, Horsley, "Wisdom of Word", p. 231, and, more cautiously, "Spiritual Elitism", p. 207. Here Horsley seems to be suggesting that it is the Corinthian appropriation of Apollos' ideas and style that Paul sees as the problem, not the direct influence of Apollos himself. This seems much more likely to me. On glossolalic phenomena see Pearson, *op.cit.*, pp. 44-46, Horsley, "Spiritual Elitism", p. 228 and note 54. While it is true that prophetic ecstasy features in Philo's philosophy, I can find no evidence for glossolalia whatsoever. On this matter see, in detail, Chapter 6. The closest we come to an explicit link is probably Philo's discussion of the kinds of gifts (δωρεα) given by God to different categories of mankind, in Migrations of Abraham 46, 53, 70-106. But the parallel is far from close: the terminology is only vaguely similar, and the issue under discussion in each case is different (see Pearson, *op.cit.*, p. 29). On the term πνευματικός Horsley says: "there is no convincing terminological parallel whatsoever in contemporary comparative material . . . the term πνευματικός occurs by itself very few times in Philo, and then with little or no religious significance." ("Pneumatikos vs. Psychikos", pp. 270-271.)

While either or both of the two major schools of thought, represented by Thiselton and Horsley, outlined above, might explain the status-seeking and the elitism of the Corinthians, I contend that neither gives us any particular understanding of the relationship of these wide problems to that of inspired speech. Certainly the Corinthian use (or misuse) of inspired speech was related to their problems with individual status and elitism. But did those give rise to the problems over inspired speech? (They may have exacerbated them, of course.) Neither approach explains the origin of the use of inspired speech of the type we see Paul objecting to in Corinth.

The hypothesis that the "problem in Corinth" is the result of the importation by some of the Corinthians of values drawn from their pre-Christian religious experience, on the other hand, has the very considerable virtue that it does explicitly set out to relate the inspired speech phenomena at Corinth to the general background. The hypothesis can take varied forms. Perhaps the most common is simply that the Corinthian over-valuation of glossolalia derives from the experience of glossolalia, or similar phenomena, in Hellenistic religion.[16] In its more developed form, this hypothesis then attempts to relate other features of Paul's language (and, by implication, that of the Corinthians), to a similar background. More sophisticated versions of the hypothesis argue that it is not merely with the high value placed on glossolalia that Paul takes issue, but with the Corinthian preference for glossolalia over prophecy. It is then argued that, in Hellenistic religion generally, prophecy normally took a form analogous to glossolalia. We will now briefly examine the ways in which this hypothesis has been developed in the literature of approximately the last thirty years, before turning to a detailed study of the New Testament and Hellenistic evidence on which such an hypothesis might be based.

As noted in Chapter 1, the articles on γλῶσσα, πνεῦμα and προφήτης from Kittel's and Friedrich's *Wörterbuch* form the baseline of our discussion.

---

[16] Such a view is often based on the argument that ecstatic practices were foreign to early Christianity, but common within Hellenistic Religion. See, for example, W.C. Klein, who says that "St. Paul here addresses a congregation of recently converted pagans who are still behaving like pagans in a number of respects . . . They do not realize how much of the paganism in which they were bred has survived their adoption of Christianity. The first thing they have to learn is that a Christian cannot abandon himself uncritically to religious emotion. Whatever the intensity of the ecstatic experience they had as pagans, they were then idolaters. They let themselves go in those days." ("The Church and its Prophets", *Anglican Theological Review*, vol. 44 no. 1, 1962, p. 7.)

We begin with the article on γλῶσσα by J. Behm. Under "glossolalia" he argues as follows:

Parallels may be found for this phenomenon in various forms and at various places in religious history.

In Gk. religion there is a series of comparable phenomena from the enthusiastic cult of the Thracian Dionysus with its γλῶττης βακχεῖα . . . to the divinatory manticism of the Delphic Phrygia (*sic*), of the Bacides, the Sibyls etc . . . Cf. also Plato on μάντις and προφήτης in Tim., 71e-72a . . . Paul is aware of a similarity between Hellenism and Christianity in respect of these mystical and ecstatic phenomena. The distinguishing feature as he sees it is to be found in the religious content . . . Higher than the gift of tongues, which in view of their pagan background the Corinthians are inclined to view as the spiritual gift par excellence (1 C. 14:37; →πνευματικός), is the gift of prophecy . . .[17]

A very similar point of view is to be found in Kleinknecht's treatment of the term πνεῦμα. Discussing the use of the term in manticism, he argues that

The religious view of pneuma takes on special significance at the pt. where it is most ancient, namely, in Apollonian inspiration-manticism . . . It evokes physical effects as the wind may also do: streaming hair, panting breath, violent filling or seizing or snatching away in a Bacchantic frenzy of ἔκστασις or μανία . . . The longest list of traditional effects of the spirit, which includes fiery phenomena, is to be found in Lucan *De Bello Civili* V, 169-174 . . . The supreme and (historically) most important result of the spirit's working is the giving of oracles . . . Theologically significant is the idea that πνεῦμα is the cause and source of ecstatic speech . . . From the standpoint of religious phenomenology the NT bears witness to the same original combination when it constantly links πνεῦμα and προφητεύειν . . . or when it refers to speaking in tongues as a gift of the Spirit (a reflection of Pythian prophesying in Corinth, 1 C. 12-14) . . .

In Kleinknecht's view the parallel with Delphi may be extended:

Plato is alluding to the historically developed cultic usage as a result of which the words of the Pythia, burbled out in ecstasy, are normally taken up, supplemented, clarified and made into valid oracles . . . The criticism to which Plato here subjects the manifestations of μαντική ἔνθεος καὶ ἀληθής (Tim., 71e) is basically akin to the διακρίσεις πνευμάτων of 1 C. 12:10 . . . whereby Paul steers into the right channels the ecstatic glossolalia of the church in Corinth . . . the γλῶσσαι of the Christian ecstatic also need ἑρμηνεία . . .[18]

---

[17] J. Behm, "Γλῶσσα", in Kittel, ed., *T.D.N.T.*, vol. 1, 1932, E.T. 1964, pp. 722-724. It should be noted that Behm does not exclude possible Jewish parallels for glossolalia (see p. 723), but he does argue that the Hellenistic parallels are the critical ones for understanding 1 Corinthians 12-14.

[18] H. Kleinknecht, "Πνεῦμα", in G. Friedrich, ed., *T.D.N.T.*, vol. 6, 1959, E.T. 1968, pp. 345-346, 348. He also notes (p. 346, note 50) that G. Delling prefers the parallel with Dionysiac enthusiasm to that with Delphic manticism.

H. Krämer and G. Friedrich, on the other hand, in their treatments for the *Wörterbuch* of prophets and prophecy in the Greek world, and early Christian prophecy, though they cover similar ground, make no mention of the suggested parallels between Christianity and its environment. Indeed, they make virtually no use of parallels between Christianity and its environment at all, being content to outline the differing usages of terminology without speculating about wider phenomena.

In 1965 S.D. Currie published an important article on the non-canonical evidence bearing on the nature of glossolalia. In it he raised several issues related to our question. The first had to do with the Delphic parallel noted above. Commenting on Paul's statement that the response of an unbeliever to uninterpreted glossolalia would be "μαίνεσθε", he suggests that "The observer might not be able to decide whether the utterances are lunatic or mantic, frenzied or oracular."[19] The presumption that oracles spoke in some form analogous to glossolalia is clear. The reverse possibility, that glossolalia was unintelligible in the way some recorded oracles are, is canvassed in his suggestion that glossolalia may be "dark sayings", "something oracular in character which needs to be interpreted."[20] His final suggestion has to do with prophecy rather than glossolalia. He argues, in line with many other scholars, that one major distinction between Christian prophecy and Graeco-Roman oracles is that it is spontaneous rather than being a matter of responses. He comments: "Some early Christians thought it might be possible to be guided by a simple test: Oracular *answers* are to be distrusted: the Holy Spirit speaks of his own initiative, not in response to interrogation."[21]

In 1965 W.D. Smith published a little-noted article on the differing ways in which the Classical and Hellenistic world, and early Christianity, conceived of "the ways in which gods and δαίμονες affected mortals".[22] He argued that the belief that the gods actually entered into their prophets and spoke through them was not to be found in pre-Christian Greek literature, and that the Greek world uniformly believed that inspiration, μανία and related states were brought on, not by what we might call possession, i.e.

---

[19] S.D. Currie, " 'Speaking in Tongues', Early Evidence Outside the New Testament bearing on '*Glōssais Lalein*' ", *Interpretation*, vol. 19, 1965, p. 275.

[20] S.D. Currie, "Early Evidence", p. 285.

[21] S.D. Currie, "Early Evidence", p. 286.

[22] W.D. Smith, "So-called Possession in Pre-Christian Greece", *T.A.Ph.A.*, vol. 96, 1965, pp. 403-426, esp. p. 404.

influence from within, but by influence from *outside* the person. In support of his contention he argued that the ways in which such daimonic influence is countered are diagnostic: unwanted daemonic influence from without is cured by way of purifications, incantations, and the use of foods with special properties. Possession is cured by exorcism, and the first exorcism in secular Greek literature is to be found in Lucian. Even there the exorcist is a Palestinian.[23]

Insofar as I am aware, Smith's article completely escaped the attention of New Testament scholars until the brief comment of D.E. Aune.[24] Aune agrees that Smith's general case has been made out, but suggests two exceptions: Longinus' Peri Hypsous 13.2, and those persons known as "Eurycleis". Peri Hypsous speaks of many (like the Pythia) being inspired to prophesy by the entry into their person of an ἀλλότριον πνεῦμα, but it must be noted that these πνεύματα are not δαίμονες: they are impersonal vapours, influences, rather than possessing "spirits" in any personal sense. Aune is correct, however, to point to Eurycleis as evidence that some form of possession was not unknown, and Smith's contention that such people were quite atypical of purely Greek ideas of enthusiasm becomes harder to maintain. The evidence to do with Eurycles will be examined in Chapter 11.

One of the very few writers to object strenuously to the proposition that Christian glossolalia was phenomenologically similar to inspired speech in Hellenistic religion is R.H. Gundry. In his important short article, " 'Ecstatic Utterance' (N.E.B.)?", he argues that

> The effectiveness of glossolalia as an authenticating sign . . . depended on its *difference* from the ecstatic gobbledegook in Hellenistic religion . . . The fear that unbelievers will think glossolalists are mad stems solely from the Corinthian failure to require accompanying translation at all times, with the result that what Paul regarded as genuine human languages sounded to unbelievers like meaningless successions of syllables similar to the ecstatic speech in Hellenistic religions familiar to the hearers . . . Even if it were admitted that ecstatic utterance such as was practised in Hellenistic religion was invading Corinthian church meetings, Paul would be condemning it by presenting normative Christian glossolalia as something radically different in style as well as in content . . .

> We have good reasons, then, to doubt that either Paul or Luke meant 'ecstatic utterance' when referring to speaking in tongues. Indeed, their apparent attempt to distinguish it from ecstatic utterance should make us hesitate to compare Christian glossolalia with ecstatic utterance in Hellenistic religion . . .[25]

---

[23] W.D. Smith, *art.cit.*, pp. 407-409.
[24] D.E. Aune, *Prophecy*, 1983, p. 354, notes 123-5.
[25] R.H. Gundry, " 'Ecstatic Utterance' (N.E.B.)?", *J.Th.S.*, vol. 17, part 2, 1966, pp. 299-307, esp. pp. 303, 305 and 307.

While Gundry's major point, that it is mistaken to argue that the New Testament writers believe glossolalia to be ecstatic, is well taken, other questions remain unanswered. His concession that "Even if it were admitted that ecstatic utterance such as was practised in Hellenistic religion was invading Corinthian church meetings, Paul would be condemning it" does leave the way open for such a case to be made. The question must remain: were forms of inspired speech in early Christianity and its environment sufficiently similar for an outsider or a recent convert to confuse them?

In an important article published the next year, J.P.M. Sweet argued that Paul's problem with his Corinthian converts over glossolalia (and other issues) had its origins, not in Hellenistic enthusiasm, but in the "demand . . . from the leaders of the Cephas party . . . to instil Palestinian piety and orthodoxy into the Corinthian church."[26] Despite this, he argues that certain aspects of Paul's polemic suggest a 'pagan connection'. Specifically, he approves of J. Héring's reading of 1 Corinthians 12.2, to the effect that the Corinthians believed that "when they were pagans" they had been transported to the heavens, whereas in Paul's view they had been led away (ἀπαγόμενοι) to evil forces (the "dumb idols" of v.2). Further, Sweet thinks that the mention of gongs and cymbals in chapter 13.1, and the use of μαίνεσθε in 14.23 and εὐσχημόνως in 14.40, suggest (in different ways) some link with enthusiastic Hellenistic religion. All these points are highly suggestive, but they are only mentioned in passing: it is left to later scholars to develop what Sweet only hints at.[27]

The thesis of N.I.J. Engelsen, *Glossolalia and Other Forms of Prophetic Speech According to 1 Corinthians 12-14*, completed in 1970, is the first full-scale study of which I am aware (within the time confines of this survey) which sets out to place Christian forms of inspired speech firmly within the context of such phenomena in the Graeco-Roman world. This Engelsen does with an extensive survey of prophetic phenomena in that world, including both the Jewish and Hellenistic traditions. His central thesis is that, in the Graeco-Roman world,

---

[26] J.P.M. Sweet, "A Sign for Unbelievers: Paul's Attitude to Glossolalia", *N.T.S.*, vol. 13, 1966-67, pp. 240-257, esp. p. 246.

[27] J.P.M. Sweet, *art.cit.*, p. 252, note 5. On the "gongs and cymbals" see also H. Riesenfeld, "Note supplémentaire sur I Cor. XIII", in *Coniectanea Neotestamentica*, vol. 12, Uppsala, 1948, pp. 50-53. He cites Athenaeus 14, p. 636a, 8 361 e, Anthologia Graeca 6.51, 6.94 1-3, 6, and Herodian 5.5.9. On this matter see also the fuller discussion in chapter 6, note 31.

in no place (sc. in pre-Christian literature) does a particular term for unintelligible speech appear, the reason being that unintelligible utterances were envisioned as an inherent feature of (ecstatic) prophetic speech . . . Paul offers the first evidence of a separation of intelligible and unintelligible speech by his separation of prophecy and speaking in tongues."[28]

In other words, for Engelsen, Graeco-Roman prophetic speech is characteristically ecstatic and unintelligible, requiring interpretation before it can be understood at all, and Paul is the first (with the exception of Plato, who is treated in the body of the argument as an exceptional case), to make the distinction between intelligible and unintelligible forms of inspired speech. He sets out to justify this proposition by surveying evidence from classical Greece, first-century Judaism, and "late pre-Christian and early Christian era" evidence from outside the New Testament.

Engelsen's case is largely based on the account of Cassandra in Aeschylus' Agamemnon, the story of the visit of Mys of Caria to the oracle of Ptoan Apollo recorded in Herodotus, Plutarch and Pausanias, the kinds of terminology used by the Greeks to describe the obscurity of oracles, a reference to "Bacchic tongues" in Aristophanes, and Plato's treatment of inspiration and prophecy in his Timaeus. But on the methodological level it is very disappointing to find that by far the greatest emphasis is given to the classical Greek evidence, which is treated in some detail. The conclusions drawn from this evidence are then made definitive for the later evidence, and a pattern is extracted from this 'consensus'. Conspicuous by its absence is any real treatment of pre-Christian Hellenistic material.[29]

Dealing with the fact that prophecy is widely described in our sources as unintelligible, Engelsen summarises the section of his case that deals with the Classical Greek evidence as follows:

It is not because the mantic purposely spoke in riddles or used archaic words. What he mediated in his frenzy was more or less unintelligible, and not related to any particular situation . . . The sources demonstrate beyond doubt the occurrence of involuntary or automatic speech within the Greek oracle cult. It is referred to by Plato in Timaeus as a recognised fact, and Aeschylus presupposes it in "Agamemnon" and uses it as a motif. He dramatises two features which characterise prophetic ecstasy. One is the strange

---

[28] Engelsen, *Glossolalia*, p. ii.
[29] Each of the points mentioned above, making up the core of Engelsen's argument, is treated in detail in chapters 5-7, below. My critical comments on Engelsen's overall case here are made because Engelsen's conclusions, which are in my view largely erroneous, have begun to find their way into the footnotes of others (see the comments in the last stages of this survey). His views seem likely to become part of the "received wisdom" of our subject, rather than being scrutinised in detail.

presentiment or "tremendum", the feeling of terror and inner pain which accompanies a special kind of ecstasy. The other is the unintelligibility of the frenzied utterances.[30]

Engelsen's case, then, is that unintelligible speech was a commonplace form of prophecy in the classical world. He turns next to the evidence from the first and second centuries A.D. In Josephus, first of all, he is concerned with reports of "ecstatic prophecy", especially in the period of crisis leading up to the Jewish revolt. He discusses the well-known description by Lucian of the foundation, by Alexander "the false prophet", of his cult of Glykon/Asclepius at Abonouteichos, and the report in Origen's reply to Celsus of prophetism in the late second century. Finally he treats the reports of the nature of Montanist prophecy, and beliefs about inspired speech and angelic languages in Gnosticism. In each case, he argues, there is clear evidence that, as in the classical period, phenomena akin to glossolalia were believed to be characteristic of inspired speech.

We do not pretend that the collected material is exhaustive, but hopefully it is representative, and forms a dependable basis for the conclusion that unintelligible speech was a peculiarity inherent in prophecy. Ecstatic speech has a tendency to relapse into inarticulate ejaculations and rapturous speech flows, or it may have this character only . . .

As a result, Engelsen argues,

A special term for unintelligible speech is simply not available, because this kind of speech was not singled out as a category in its own right.[31]

Paul made such a distinction, however, as part of his polemic against the "misdirected individualism" of the Corinthians, who preferred glossolalia to the more communally-orientated prophecy.[32]

This conclusion, naturally, is only as convincing as Engelsen's collection of parallels for glossolalia. If, as I will be arguing, "ecstatic speech" of the kind Engelsen is discussing is (a) not actually phenomenologically or theologically similar to glossolalia, and (b) not at all common anyway, then a simple alternative presents itself: a special term for unintelligible speech was not available because it was not needed.

The second feature of Engelsen's case that requires comment here has been touched on briefly above. Between Plato in the early fourth century B.C. and Lucian in the mid-second century A.D. are more than five hundred

---

[30] Engelsen, *Glossolalia*, p. 20.
[31] Engelsen, *Glossolalia*, p. 60.
[32] Engelsen, *Glossolalia*, pp. 127-130.

years. I have argued in the previous chapter that between the mid-first and mid-second centuries our evidence attests to an important change in attitudes to the paranormal. Yet the only evidence cited by Engelsen which is even close to contemporary with the New Testament is that of Josephus, where, significantly, he can suggest no single case of ecstatic unintelligibility. If "inarticulate ejaculations and rapturous speech flows" were a commonplace form of inspired speech in this period, it ought to be possible to document them. Yet the task appears to have hardly been attempted.

In the year following the completion of Engelsen's work a second important Ph.D. thesis was submitted which deals (independently) with much similar material. This is the work of T.W. Gillespie, "Prophecy and Tongues: the Concept of Christian Prophecy in the Pauline Theology". One important aspect of his work was elaborated further in his article of 1978, "A Pattern of Prophetic Speech in 1 Corinthians."[33] Since the two are integrally related, they will be dealt with together.

From our point of view Gillespie's most important contribution is twofold. First, at an exegetical level, he sets out to analyse Paul's comments on inspired speech in 1 Corinthians 12-14 as relating to one central issue. Second, he relates this issue to an understanding of the nature of inspired speech in Hellenistic religion. Gillespie sets out to understand how the opening words of ch. 12, "Now about spiritual things / people", relate to the stated problem in v.3, that of the statement "Anathema Iesous". The statement is attributed to a prophet within the Corinthian congregation.[34] Gillespie's suggestion is as follows.

The prophetism at work in the Corinthian congregation has taken a form strongly influenced by the "pre-Christian encounter of the Gentiles of the congregation with the religious ecstasy of Hellenistic enthusiasm".[35] For the Corinthians, prophecy, which according to Gillespie they called interchangeably either "word of knowledge" or "word of wisdom", was intelligible utterance under inspiration, which was then vindicated and legitimated by being *immediately followed* with ecstatic, unintelligible

---

[33] T.W. Gillespie, *Prophecy and Tongues*, and "A Pattern". On the question of whether πνευματικῶν is masculine or neuter see *Prophecy and Tongues*, pp. 35ff, p. 44. On the link between the "anathema" question, prophetic speech and glossolalia, see *Prophecy and Tongues*, pp. 57ff.

[34] Gillespie, *Prophecy and Tongues*, pp. 57ff.

[35] Gillespie, *Prophecy and Tongues*, p. 37.

speech: glossolalia. This glossolalia was understood as the sure proof of inspiration. However,

The cursing of the earthly Jesus by a recognised prophet within the congregation has rendered the prophetic word problematic. How is the authenticity of the prophet's claim to Spirit-inspiration to be determined? Until now the practice has been to look for an ecstatic sign of their divine possession, specifically that expression of inspired utterance which Paul designates as "tongues". In response, the apostle points up the deceptiveness of such ecstatic signs (12:2), and calls for the critical discernment of the spirits (12:10c) on the basis of the church's confession that "Jesus is Lord" (12:3). In creating a theological context for the ensuing discussion (12:4-31), he effectively separates the charisma of "tongues" from the Corinthian "word of wisdom" (="word of knowledge") in his enumeration of the Spirit's distribution of the charismata to each member of the congregation (12:8-10). By this means "tongues" is not only severed from all proclaimers of the word (apostles, prophets, teachers, 12:29-30), but is devalued as such as the least of the gifts . . .

. . . The subordination of "tongues" as the least of the gifts involves, therefore, not only its devaluation but its separation from that very form of charismatic speech with which it was essentially associated in Corinthian practice. The hidden polemical point of the first enumeration in 12:8-10 is thus more than a confirmation of the spiritual endowment of the entire congregation . . . the distribution of these particular gifts to different members of the community effectively separates them, and thus eliminates the sign value of "tongues" in relation to the prophetic "word of wisdom" by creating an independent status for "tongues" among the charismata . . . Paul's insistence that "tongues" must become intelligible through "translation" in order to be legitimate within the assembled community (14:5, 13, 27-28) in effect gives it a new function and thus an independent status among the charismata.[36]

This is clearly a subtle and ingenious reconstruction of the Corinthian situation, and exegetically speaking it has much to recommend it. It has the virtue of linking together the problems in chapters 1-3 of 1 Corinthians with those in chapters 12-14, and also of making very good sense of the relationships between the various sections of Paul's argument. It is not Gillespie's intention in his thesis to provide a detailed justification of his view of "Hellenistic enthusiasm", since it seems to him to be well entrenched in the literature on the topic. He is satisfied to briefly cite Origen's Contra Celsum and Lucian's Alexander the False Prophet, as well as Irenaeus' Against Heresies, to establish the point. He takes up the Origen reference in more detail in his 1978 article.

In this article he is at pains to show that the kind of prophecy described by Celsus for the late second century has clear links with the prophetic phenomena he has postulated within the Corinthian congregation. He takes

---

[36] Gillespie, *Prophecy and Tongues*, pp. 70-71, and cf. p. 67.

up the three parts of Celsus' characterisation of the prophets of his day, and describes them as comprising (a) a prophetic claim, based on the ἐγώ…εἰμι formula well known in antiquity, (b) the prophetic message, beginning with a ἥκω formula, and (c) a "prophetic legitimation", which took the form of glossolalia or a closely related phenomenon.[37] He is well aware of the problems associated with the Celsus passage, especially the possibility of Origen's having worked over the material he presents, thus making it unreliable for the reconstruction of the ideas of the Palestinian prophets it describes. None the less, he believes that most especially in the third element, the legitimation by glossolalia, we have evidence for a widespread pattern in antiquity.

What Celsus (and Lucian) understood as the nonsense born of madness was accepted at the level of *Volksreligion* as the sure sign that a prophet was genuinely inspired by the god for whom he spoke. By lifting the prophet to this high level of ecstasy, the deity thereby authenticated the message delivered previously in understandable language. Put simply, among the common people "tongues" was recognised as the divine legitimation of prophecy in the Hellenistic age . . .[38]

There are two problems with this reconstruction that need to be noted here. The first is that the evidence of Lucian does not exactly follow the pattern suggested by Gillespie. Alexander does not normally follow his oracles with frenzied ravings at all. On the *one* occasion of his dramatic entry into Abonouteichos he *precedes* them this way - and it is to be noted that his gibberish is accompanied by what are (I will argue below) far clearer signs of divine inspiration: violent tossings of the head and foaming at the mouth, for example. The second is that the passage of the Contra Celsum from which this understanding is drawn is quite clearly the most violently polemical part of Celsus' portrayal of the "prophets", being loaded with emotive terminology. It is thus the most likely to be distorted.

Leaving these matters aside, however, we return to Gillespie's thesis. Continuing his case, he argues that it is not only the Corinthian understanding of prophecy that is influenced by Hellenistic religion; so is Paul's reply.

In thus differentiating between prophecy and "tongues", Paul appears to be drawing upon the distinction in antiquity between two types of Spirit-inspiration. In both the human subject is believed to be filled with the divine presence (ἔνθεος, ἐνθουσιασμός), thus altering his normal psychic condition (ἐν ἔκστασις) (*sic*). The difference is that in

---

[37] Gillespie, "A Pattern", pp. 75-77.
[38] Gillespie, "A Pattern", p. 82.

one instance the subject's normal rational powers are not neutralised, clear thinking remains, while in the other the νοῦς is overcome, clear consciousness being subverted.[39]

If Gillespie is arguing that Paul is distinguishing between "ecstatic" glossolalia and "non-ecstatic" prophecy, he needs to show that this was the distinction that Paul was drawing between the two forms of inspired speech. To me this seems most unlikely. The instructions he gives as to how glossolalia and prophecy are to be managed within the assembly are too similar, and presume in both cases that the practitioners were capable of following his instructions. This could hardly be so if glossolalia took place in a frame of mind in which "νοῦς is overcome, clear consciousness being subverted". But the question of ecstasy will be dealt with in detail in Chapter 3, below. The related question, as to whether the "distinction in antiquity between two types of Spirit-inspiration" has been correctly understood, will be taken up in Chapter 5.

Gillespie's exegesis of the "sign-character" of tongues is thoroughly consistent with his overall position. Paul's statements about tongues as a sign reflect a Corinthian slogan to the effect that tongues are a sign for believers, based on what Gillespie has argued is the common view of the time. Given Paul's generally negative attitude to "signs and wonders", he argues, it is Paul's point that

It is only unbelievers who hold such ecstatic manifestations to be signs of the Spirit's presence in the word of the prophet (cf. 1 Cor. 12.2). For the believer, no such sign is required in that he recognises the understandable message of the prophet as its own sign.[40]

Thus he interprets the response of the unbeliever in vv. 24-5 of 1 Cor. 14, "μαίνεσθε", as meaning "you are possessed". This, for Paul, is not sufficient. Not only does such a response fail to do justice to Christian monotheism (for who knows what divinity may be the cause of this possession?), but it also focuses attention on the believers, rather than on their God.

If "tongues" produces the response "*You* are possessed [by God]", prophecy brings forth the confession, "*God* is surely present among you."[41]

---

[39] Gillespie, *Prophecy and Tongues*, p. 77. In support of this conclusion Gillespie cites F. Pfister, "Ekstase", *R.A.C.*, vol. 4, Stuttgart, 1959, cols. 944-987, but I do not see that anything Pfister has said supports his argument.

[40] Gillespie, *Prophecy and Tongues*, p. 124.

[41] Gillespie, *Prophecy and Tongues*, p. 126.

Gillespie has thus produced a sophisticated reconstruction of the background and details of Paul's dispute with his Corinthian converts. Both the evidence related to Hellenistic religion and inspired speech, and several other issues raised by Gillespie's work, will be consider in the chapters which follow, but for now one important exegetical problem needs to be touched upon. For the problem in these verses is not quite as Gillespie outlines it. If his understanding of the link between prophecy and tongues were correct, and glossolalia normally followed each episode of prophecy, it would be rare for an unbeliever to hear tongues unaccompanied by prophecy. Thus Paul's counter-suggestion "but if you all prophesy" as an *alternative* to "if you are all speaking in tongues" would make no sense, if directed to the problem Gillespie has outlined. If they were all speaking in tongues, they *would* all have been prophesying. But the unbeliever's "μαίνεσθε" is clearly a response to tongues alone. That is the point of Paul's rejoinder: he requires intelligibility. We must argue, then, that whatever the merits of Gillespie's discussion of the Hellenistic evidence, his solution appears not to fit the problem in Corinth insofar as we can deduce it from Paul's rejoinder.[42]

In the same year, 1971, L.T. Johnson published a short article entitled "Norms for True and False Prophecy in First Corinthians". His essential point is that

Paul's concern is that both the Christians of Corinth and their pagan neighbours will equate Christian prophecy with the ecstatic, frenzied prophecy which was well known in the Hellenistic world. Since of all the gifts that of tongues seemed most like these ecstatic ravings, Paul is especially concerned to separate the charism of prophecy from any identification with this gift and consequently remove it from any danger of being mistaken for pagan prophecy.[43]

On this basis Johnson then argues that glossolalia is ecstatic, but prophecy is not. Like Sweet and Héring, he argues that 1 Corinthians 12.2 refers to the pre-Christian experience of members of the congregation. Again, like Gillespie, he argues that the "μαίνεσθε" in 1 Corinthians 14.23 means that "Paul has the unbeliever mistake the Christian prayer meeting as just one more enthusiastic Hellenistic cult."[44] But Johnson goes beyond the

---

[42] For a brief critique along similar lines see A.C. Wire, *Women Prophets*, p. 140.

[43] L.T. Johnson, "Norms for True and False Prophecy in First Corinthians", *The American Benedictine Review*, vol. 22, 1971, pp. 29-45.

[44] L.T. Johnson, *art.cit.*, p. 41.

previously cited scholars by considering Hellenistic prophecy in its own right, not only insofar as it can be argued that it resembles glossolalia.

Here he makes five major points. He claims that

1) Inspiration was possession in the strictest sense. The prophet lost his own consciousness . . . He was only the passive instrument of the god, and could neither know nor control what he said . . . 2) Prophecy was usually expressed in the mantic frenzy, which included loud shouts and unintelligible ravings . . . 3) The prophetic experience was more or less dependent on material means of arousal, ranging from the playing of musical instruments to the sniffing of chthonic fumes . . . 4) The initiative for inspiration therefore lay in a real way with man. The prophet could induce his state of possession, even though once it came, he experienced the state as coming from "outside" . . . 5) The content of the prophecies corresponded to the mode of delivery. They were rarely clear, and they dealt more with ambiguous predictions concerning the future of men, than with communicating God's will to them. The prophet was less a spokesman for God than a medium of supernatural and morally neutral knowledge.[45]

In all this Johnson summarises and develops the views of a number of earlier scholars, notably E. Fascher, K. Prümm and H. Bacht. In each of these five cases his conclusions will be subject to detailed treatment in Chapter 11. For the moment it is sufficient to note that his contribution extends the range of the debate by treating Hellenistic prophecy seriously both where it does, and where it does not, resemble glossolalia.

While the 1973 monograph of Jannes Reiling, *Hermas and Christian Prophecy*, subtitled "A Study of the Eleventh Mandate", deals almost exclusively with the post-apostolic period, it is an important example of precisely the kind of research that this study sets out to undertake. At the methodological level, Reiling argues that

it is not only commendable to look for Hellenistic parallels, but even necessary. Unless we are prepared to take into account the meaning of those parallels, and to interpret them in terms of their function in the thought of the writer which we study, we shall be unable to penetrate the deepest level of his thoughts.[46]

With this principle I can only agree, and I cannot see that it is any less applicable to Paul and Luke than to Hermas.

The central thrust of Reiling's work is that the picture of true and false prophecy given in the Eleventh Mandate of Hermas shows us clearly that Hellenistic forms of divination were finding their way into the second-century church. In Reiling's view, the "false prophet" in Hermas is in

---

[45] L.T. Johnson, *art.cit.*, p. 33. Clearly point 1) here is at variance with W.D. Smith's view of inspiration.

[46] Jannes Reiling, *Hermas and Christian Prophecy*, subtitled "A Study of the Eleventh Mandate", *Supplements to Novum Testamentum*, vol. 37, Leiden, 1973, p. 169.

fact a semi-Christianised diviner, operating within or on the borders of the church. Hermas sets himself to combat this phenomenon, and his description of the false prophet and his tests for distinguishing him from the true prophet form the evidence on which Reiling draws.

In second-century Christianity generally, criteria for detecting false prophecy were varied. The Didache, for example, specifically rules out any testing of a prophet while he is speaking, and insists on moral guidelines for discernment. While Hermas also suggests such tests, his main emphasis is elsewhere. For him the main characteristics of the false prophet are as follows. He prophesies in response to enquiries, not spontaneously; he prophesies to individuals, not to the gathered congregation; and he charges a fee. He prophesies according to what they want to hear.[47] He occasionally tells the truth in order to trap people: or rather, the devil does, through him. The true prophet can be detected by the qualities of his life. He is filled with the divine spirit when Christians gather, and prophesies to them there. The false prophet, on the other hand, can be detected by his ambition, his shamelessness and talkativeness, and the luxury of his life. He avoids the gathering of Christians, and if he does come among them, his (diabolical) spirit leaves him, and he is revealed to all as helpless.

So far this material can simply be read off from the Eleventh Mandate. Reiling goes on to correlate it with what we know of divinatory practice. The diviner prophesies in response to enquiries, and charges a fee. He tends to do this publicly, for the sake of publicity: Hermas' diviners operate covertly through fear of condemnation within the church. There is no evidence that they are Gnostics, and doctrinal issues play no part in Hermas' polemic against them. They cannot be Montanists, for they are much too early, and most of the criteria would be of no value in detecting Montanism. Rather they are to be seen as semi-Christianised μάντεις such as Peregrinus Proteus seems to have been for one period of his career.

Reiling then sets out to find a convincing background from the Hellenistic world against which to place these diviners.

It is tempting to compare the false prophet in Hermas with the 'theioi andres' of that time, such as Alexander of Abonuteichos or Apollonius of Tyana; but the Christian

---

[47] On this particular point see the critical note of D.E. Aune, "Herm. Man. 11.2: Christian False Prophets Who Say What People Wish to Hear", *J.B.L.*, vol. 97, 1978, pp. 103-4.

'mantis' operates on a much smaller scale. . . A very striking and illuminating parallel, however, is found in Apuleius' description of a Chaldaean diviner, operating in Corinth.[48]

Reiling is correct to prefer his Diophanes to the better known "prophets" he cites: they are even less appropriate when we are dealing with N.T. prophetic phenomena, as we shall see.

Turning to the true prophet, or rather "the prophet" used absolutely, he sketches Hermas' characterisation. Here the picture becomes complex, but let it suffice to say that Reiling is able to show convincingly that Hermas' "prophet", with his attendant "angel of the prophetic spirit", is a composite of Jewish, Christian and Hellenistic elements.[49] There are several subtle problems of terminology to do with the "inspiration event", in which a man "full of the divine spirit" is "filled with the prophetic spirit". Reiling believes these phrases can be understood in terms of what I would call a "modal" understanding of the spirit: the "prophetic spirit" is the latent power of the Holy Spirit, and "having the divine Spirit" is the base experience on which all else depends. "A man must have the divine spirit in him if the prophetic spirit is to speak through him."[50]

Reiling also distinguishes very clearly between apostles, prophets and teachers, and argues that "ecstasy" in the sense of total loss of consciousness is not to be seen as a defining characteristic of either Hellenistic or Christian forms of prophecy.[51]

We turn now to one of the most important works in this field: T.M. Crone's *Early Christian Prophecy: a Study of its Origin and Function*.[52] This Tübingen dissertation attempts to situate early Christian prophecy in its Hellenistic environment. Crone sets out to survey the phenomenon of prophecy in the Graeco-Roman world. This he does under two major headings. The first is Oracle Prophets. He briefly discusses what is known about the functioning of the major oracular shrines in Greece, and their personnel. The terminology used to describe the various functionaries is described. Firstly, the person actually inspired by the god in question can, at Delphi at least, be called both a πρόμαντις and a προφῆτις. There are also separate persons, in this case priests, whose job he argues it is to interpret

---

[48] J. Reiling, *op.cit.*, p. 81.

[49] J. Reiling, *op.cit.*, pp. 110-111.

[50] J. Reiling, *op.cit.*, p. 119.

[51] J. Reiling, *op.cit.*, p. 17.

[52] T.M. Crone, *Early Christian Prophecy: a Study of its Origin and Function*, St. Mary's University Press, Baltimore, Maryland, 1973.

the oracle to the enquirer. They are specifically called προφῆται. However, it ought not to be assumed that because the oracle needed interpreting, it was totally unintelligible. Crone points out that a reference in Plutarch seems to suggest that the oracle was intelligible, and that the task of the προφήτης was more to put it into polished form than into plain Greek.[53] The term προφήτης, in his view, is neutral with regard to both inspiration and ecstasy: it can imply either or both, but it need not. Crone can cite one case from Herodotus where a prophet speaks to an enquirer in a language unknown to himself, but known to the enquirer,[54] but beyond this example "xenoglossy" does not seem to him to be associated with prophecy.

Crone's treatment of oracular prophecy in the Greek world shows a far greater awareness of the technicalities of the subject than those of previous writers. The second major heading under which he examines possible parallels to Christian prophetism is "The Hellenistic Wandering Preacher". He suggests that "they offer the closest comparison in the Hellenistic world to the Christian prophets".[55] Crone's treatment of his four chosen examples, Apollonius of Tyana, Alexander of Abonouteichos, Pythagoras and Peregrinus Proteus, is examined in detail in Chapter 8, below. For the present we should note that the criteria by which he believes a comparison is possible are as follows. Both Christian prophets and Hellenistic wandering teachers are said to exhibit the following: wandering and teaching activities, gathering of followers, moral and civic virtue as the content of teaching, wonder-working, second sight and prediction, and inspiration or divination.

It is not until the concluding chapter of his work that he himself evaluates his "parallels" in any detail. Though he believes that his second-century "prophets" have first-century antecedents, he admits that there is insufficient evidence to demonstrate a real parallel between the Hellenistic phenomena he has been discussing and first-century Christian prophecy. Summarising his case, he says:

we have compared him [sc. the Christian prophet] to the popular eschatological preacher in Palestinian Judaism and to the wandering preacher of contemporary Hellenistic religion . . . the Jewish counterpart offers points of comparison in terms of the eschatological nature of his message and the inspired enthusiasm with which he proclaimed it. The Greek counterpart represents a broad category of religious propagandist who in certain areas of the church influenced the Christian prophet in his

---

[53] Crone, *Prophecy*, pp. 33-34, citing Plutarch, de Def. Orac. 51, Mor. 438b.
[54] Herodotus 8.135: the prophet answers Mys the Carian in his native language, Crone, *Prophecy*, p. 36. For a detailed examination of this incident see chapter 5.
[55] Crone, *Prophecy*, p. 39.

life- style and the understanding of his function . . . there are sufficient indications to conclude that this Hellenistic counterpart exercised an influence on the Christian prophet already in the first century . . . [nonetheless] Christian prophecy cannot be explained by an appeal to the Hellenistic wandering preacher and philosopher . . . we have been able to explain first-century Christian prophecy in light of its Jewish origins with some influence from the Hellenistic wandering preacher . . .[56]

Since Crone had argued earlier that Paul's congregations did not know of wandering prophets and that the earliest mention of such itinerants is in Matthew and the Didache,[57] and since he gives no details as to what the "indications" that "this Hellenistic counterpart exercised an influence on the Christian prophet already in the first century" might be, I believe we are free to argue that he has not shown any substantial parallel between Christian prophecy in the churches of Luke and Paul and Hellenistic wandering teachers. When we add to this the caveat expressed by Reiling above about the scale of the activities of Hellenistic teachers and wonder-workers, the care needed in making use of such parallels becomes even greater. Crone is aware of these problems, and it seems to me he really makes use his parallels only with respect to the second century Christian phenomena.[58] He comments that "all our evidence points to contemporary Judaism as the origin of early Christian prophecy" and the fact that Peregrinus became for a period a Christian prophet is "the only *direct* link between the wandering preacher and the Christian prophet, and the reference is too late to draw any conclusions for the first century."[59]

In Part II of his thesis Crone sets out to interpret early Christian prophecy against the background he has sketched for it. As we have noted above, he does not feel that the case for Hellenistic parallels for first-century phenomena has been made out. It is therefore not surprising that he argues

---

[56] Crone, *Prophecy*, pp. 290, 286, 289.

[57] Crone, *Prophecy*, pp. 218, 285.

[58] Crone, *Prophecy*, p. 286. Of Crone's picture of early Christian prophets, Aune, *Prophecy*, p. 9 says: "his conception of the early Christian prophet is a blend of the eschatological orientation and inspired prophetic consciousness of the prophets of the Jewish liberation movement combined with the hortatory and admonitory emphases and even peripatetic life-style of the wandering Hellenistic moral philosophers." But this seems to me to fail to take account of Crone's proper caution. Aune's comment might well apply as a statement of Crone's conception of prophecy according to the Didache, but it certainly does not apply in the cases of Luke and Paul, where Crone does not believe that Christian prophets exhibit a "peripatetic life-style". However, it must be admitted that Crone's final conclusions are not totally clear as to how influential he thinks Hellenistic factors were in the first century.

[59] Crone, *Prophecy*, pp. 281, 286.

that the origin of Christian prophecy must be sought in its Judaic background. But here there is no need for us to follow him further.

Between 1973 and 1978 a number of articles and monographs took up aspects of the relationship between early Christian and Hellenistic inspired speech without breaking any essentially new ground. M.E. Boring suggested a program of research into the background of early Christian prophecy, "to explore the phenomenon of prophecy in the Hellenistic world prior to and apart from its manifestation in early Christianity."[60] U.B. Müller found himself confident enough of the essentially Hellenistic nature of glossolalia to argue that, since the closest known parallel to glossolalia is to be found in the Testament of Job, that document must be regarded as a product of Hellenistic Judaism.[61] Both James Dunn, in his important work *Jesus and the Spirit*, and M.E. Hart, in a Durham Ph.D. thesis, argued that any real understanding of Paul's view of glossolalia and its interpretation must take into account the closely parallel understanding of prophecy and its interpretation at Delphi, and in the thought of Plato.[62] Hart developed the point further, arguing (correctly, in my view, at least in terms of her negative point) that "interpretation" at Delphi was not a matter of "translation" (because Delphic utterances were not gibberish), but rather a matter of "explanation". She also argued, with Behm and Engelsen, that glossolalia was paralleled in the "Bacchic tongues" of the Dionysiac cult, in inspired speech in Gnosticism, and in the "new prophecy" of the Montanists. Finally, in line with all these parallels, she argued that the μαίνεσθε of 1 Corinthians 14.23, attributed by Paul to the outsider overhearing glossolalia, was a statement of recognition of divine activity: "you are inspired" rather than "you are insane".[63] Likewise in 1975, H.J. Tschiedel published an article in which he argued that a miracle very similar to that recorded by Luke of Pentecost was a regular feature of the cult of Delian Apollo, as recorded in the "Homeric" Hymn to Apollo.[64] R.A. Harrisville, in a very thorough survey

---

[60] M.E. Boring, " 'What Are We Looking For?' Toward a Definition of the Term 'Christian prophet' ", *S.B.L. Seminar Papers, 1973*, Missoula, 1973, p. 142.

[61] U.B. Müller, *Prophetie und Predigt im Neuen Testament*, Gütersloh, 1975, pp. 31-37.

[62] J.D.G. Dunn, *Jesus and the Spirit*, London, 1975, pp. 228 and 247, and Hart, *Tongues And Prophecy*, pp. 6-12 and p. 256.

[63] Hart, *Tongues And Prophecy*: Dionysiac cult and "Bacchic tongues", pp. 10-12, p. 111 note 17, Gnosticism, p. 19, Montanism, pp. 105-6, μαίνεσθε, p. 240. Hart's case, though very similar in many points to that of Engelsen, appears to be quite independent.

[64] H.J. Tschiedel, "Ein Pfingstwunder im Apollonhymnus", *Zeitschrift für Religions-*

of the problem of the terminology of glossolalia, supported the view of Nils Engelsen that in all likelihood the reason that the pre-Christian world had no special terms for glossolalia was that it had not previously been considered a separate category of ecstatic speech. Harrisville, however, was not interested in the Hellenistic parallels.[65] Finally, F.F. Bruce, in his major survey of Paul's career and theology, argued briefly that the dispute between Paul and the Corinthians over inspired speech had its background in Pythian practice and/or Dionysiac cult, both prominent in the proximity of Corinth.[66]

The next major development in the attempt to link together the various issues addressed by Paul in 1 Corinthians 12-14 came with the publication by R. and C.C. Kroeger of a short paper entitled "An Inquiry into Evidence of Maenadism in the Corinthian Congregation".[67] The hypothesis put forward provocatively links the issue of inspired speech and the issue of disorder among the women into one complex of Hellenistic influence: Dionysiac religion. The Kroegers argue that

The Apostle specifically complains that the congregation gives the impression of ritual madness (14:23) . . . women were the recipients *par excellence* [sc. of divine frenzy] and thereby earned the title "mad women" or maenads . . . The city of Corinth was a major center of Dionysiac cult . . . Even a cursory reading of the first Corinthian Epistle reveals the affinity of the new converts for their former pagan modes . . . They were asked . . . to refrain from attending pagan feasts -- a notable feature of Dionysiac cult during the Roman period. Formerly they served dumb idols, wrote Paul, and were "carried away" (ἤγεσθε ἀπαγόμενοι) apparently a reference to ecstatic mystery religion. Significantly, there was drunkenness (another Dionysiac attribute) at the Lord's Supper. Rather than bemoan the presence of fornication in their midst, the Corinthians were complacent and indeed "puffed up." It is hard to understand their satisfaction apart from a cultic background which represented certain extramarital sex acts as sacramental in nature.[68]

They then argue that the complex of issues - inspired speech, propriety of hairstyle and gender-role reversal - found in 1 Corinthians 11-14 is particularly suggestive of a Dionysiac cult background, where inspired frenzy, wildly flying hair (and shorn heads) and ritual transvestitism were commonplace. They likewise argue that what Paul rejects about Corinthian glossolalia and prophecy is the uncontrolled *clamor* that results when many

und Geistesgeschichte, vol. 27, 1975, pp. 22-39. This case is dealt with in detail in Chapter 5.

[65] R.A. Harrisville, "Speaking in Tongues: a Lexicographical Study", *C.B.Q.*, vol. 38, 1976, pp. 35-48, esp. pp. 37 and 41.

[66] F.F. Bruce, *Paul: Apostle of the Free Spirit*, Exeter, 1977, p. 260.

[67] "An Inquiry into Evidence of Maenadism in the Corinthian Congregation", *S.B.L. Seminar Papers*, 1978, Missoula, 1978, pp. 331-338.

[68] R. and C.C. Kroeger, *art.cit.*, p. 331-332.

speak at once, reminiscent of the din of the cults where trumpets and stringed instruments likewise gave forth inarticulate sounds in the general tumult. In this context, they argue, Paul forbids, not any speech by women, but specifically the ecstatic shouts of converted maenads, the ὀλολυγμός. He commands instead the silence that characterised other phases of Dionysiac cult: "A gentle and quiet phase of worship was surely far more in accord with Christian κοινωνία than frenzy . . . therefore women were asked to subdue themselves in compliance with the law."[69] The Kroegers argue that since no particular Jewish law on the submission of women can be produced, it is plausible to argue that the law in question is one of the common Hellenistic-Roman laws regulating the involvement of women in ecstatic cults.

Clearly what is involved here is a thorough-going reinterpretation of Paul's problem in 1 Corinthians, though it is presented only in outline. In later material, privately circulated, the Kroegers have listed what they consider to be no less than thirty-nine distinct points of contact between 1 Corinthians and Hellenistic ecstatic religion. While some of them are doubtless only common metaphors - the concept of offering metaphorical milk to neophytes, not solid food, is too commonplace a notion to indicate any particular background - the cumulative case is impressive. Two questions, however, must be asked. At an exegetical level, we must ask: how compelling is the suggestion that it is ritual outcry and clamour (as opposed to, say, glossolalia without interpretation) to which Paul is objecting? Especially among women? Can the two concepts be so easily equated? At the level of Hellenistic religious practice, however, the critical question must be: how similar was inspired speech within Christianity to that practised in Dionysiac circles?

With the contribution of the Kroegers the main lines of the scholarly "consensus" are set. Writers since have, in the main, accepted various features of the outline presented above, and developed its implications. P. Roberts, in a short article in the *Expository Times*, argued that

ecstatic religious experience . . . was a part of the fabric of life for the common man in many parts of the ancient world. He met it in many of his religious cults and mysteries. Ecstatic experience, in fact, is a part of the common religious heritage of mankind and was no stranger in the first-century Mediterranean world . . .[70]

---

[69] R. and C.C. Kroeger, *art.cit.*, p. 336.

[70] P. Roberts, "A Sign - Christian or Pagan?", *Expository Times*, vol. 90, no. 7, April 1979, pp. 199-203.

Paul's language in describing tongues as "a sign for unbelievers" is thus thoroughly explicable. Tongues (by implication a common feature of such "ecstatic experience") are a sign that unbelievers will recognise as evidence of some divine activity or other. Paul's objection is that they will communicate nothing explicitly Christian, for the same reason. David Hill suggested, without detailed argument, that the tension between Paul and the Corinthians was caused by a cross-cultural disagreement about the nature of prophecy. In his essay, "Christian Prophets as Teachers or Instructors in the Church" he argues that

It is most likely that Paul derived his view of προφητεία from Old Testament-Jewish models and possibly from contact with prophets (as portrayed in Acts) influenced by such models, whereas the Corinthians' understanding reflects the Greek ecstatic model: its practitioners were employed in the Mystery cults and these activities and experiences were described by terms like μαίνομαι, μάντις and ἐνθουσιασμός - terms not used of Christian prophets.

In his *New Testament Prophecy* Hill again speaks of the Corinthians being influenced by the "Greek ecstatic model" of prophecy, but since his discussion does not distinguish between glossolalia and prophecy at this point, his view is unclear.[71]

Here at least one comment must be made: it seems most unlikely that any "Greek model" of prophecy ought to be derived from the mystery cults: oracles and mysteries were different things altogether, and practitioners of prophecy were *not* employed by the cults, as far as we know. Prophetic and "telestic" μανία were distinguished even in antiquity, at the level of theory,[72] and at the level of cult were very different phenomena. We need only note that oracles were among the most publicly accessible institutions of Hellenistic religion, whereas the Mysteries were the most relentlessly private and secretive. Hill's blending of two such different religious phenomena seems to me to be a symptom of the strength of the "consensus" view that he here articulates: so entrenched is it that it no longer even requires close attention to the evidence.

In 1980 Morton Smith argued that glossolalia - and many other features of Pauline congregational practice - closely reflect contemporary magical practice. He argued that

---

[71] D. Hill, "Christian Prophets as Teachers or Instructors in the Church", in Panagopoulos, *Vocation*, p. 110, note 6, and *Prophecy*, p. 121.

[72] See, for example, Plato, Phaedrus, 265b.

Invocation of spirits to prophesy was perhaps the commonest of ancient magical practices. It regularly led to revelations . . . Such pronouncements often culminated in inarticulate utterances which seem to have resembled very closely the noises the Christians made when they "spoke in tongues.[73]

Though it can certainly be argued that the formulae by which spirits were *invoked* in order to produce revelations resembled glossolalia, I am not aware of any evidence to support Smith's view that magical revelations ever *culminated in* inarticulate utterances. Certainly he does not cite any. We should also note that in the Magical papyri "there is very little evidence for the phenomenon of possession trance. In an era when possession trance was regarded as a typical way of understanding oracular inspiration, the emphasis in the magical papyri is decidedly on the vision trance."[74] The case for a relationship between magical ritual and glossolalia is discussed in detail in Chapter 7.

The major work of M.E. Boring, *Sayings of the Risen Jesus*, likewise maintains the consensus view. He draws heavily on what Hill describes as "the Greek ecstatic model" of prophecy, and explains Paul's clash with his Corinthian converts with the suggestion that they were heavily influenced by "the common Hellenistic view that prophetic speech is validated by glossolalia".[75] For this, of course, he cites Gillespie. Drawing on the presumed Dionysiac parallels, he also argues that

For Paul, μαίνεσθαι (*sic*) (14.23) is a stinging rebuke, not a goal to be sought after, as it was in the Bacchic experience of the Dionysian cult . . . the prophet, like the speaker in tongues, is in control of himself and can be silent - though he may have to be reminded that this is the case . . . Paul's understanding of the prophetic experience is to be seen against the Old Testament-Jewish-Rabbinic background, rather than as a reflection of the Hellenistic enthusiastic view of prophecy.[76]

Approaching the topic from the terminological end, J. Painter argues that Paul's problem with the "Pneumatikoi" in Corinth can only fully be understood when we realise that "The constellation of terms used by the self-styled πνευματικοί, to which attention has been drawn, was also used by certain Gnostic sects and in the mystery cults." In support of this conclusion he cites Reitzenstein and W. Scott. "Either this is the source of the Corinthian *terminology* or no source is known to us . . . the problem of

---

[73] M. Smith, "Pauline Worship as seen by Pagans", *H.Th.R.*, vol. 73, 1980, p. 241-249, esp. p. 246.
[74] Thus Aune, *Prophecy*, p. 45.
[75] M.E. Boring, *Sayings*, pp. 82-84.
[76] Boring, *Sayings*, p. 85.

the πνευματικοί is to be understood in the context of pagan ecstatic religion."[77]

The classic consensus case was extensively presented at a more popular level in 1983 by H.W. House, in an article entitled "Tongues and the Mystery Religions of Corinth". He argued that in Corinth

Religious ecstasy, particularly glossolalia, is found in the mystery religions or the religion of Apollo . . . The slave girl that Paul encountered on the way to Corinth had a spirit of Python, or one inspired by Apollo. The ecstatic tongues-speaking of the oracle and the subsequent interpretation by the priest at Delphi are widely known. The cult of Apollo was widespread in Achaia, but especially around the temple of Delphi across from Corinth. This religion easily could have provided the kind of impetus for spiritual experience found in the Corinthian church . . . With the ecstaticism of Dionysianism and the emphasis on tongues-speaking and oracles in the religion of Apollo, it is not surprising that the Corinthians carried these pagan ideas in the church at Corinth, especially the practice of glossolalia for which both of these religions are known (though the Dionysian cult did not include interpretation of the glossolalia as did that of Apollo) . . . The very phrase γλώσσαις λαλεῖν, 'to speak in tongues', was not invented by the New Testament writers, but borrowed from ordinary speech.[78]

In favour of this contention House presents the following considerations: Paul's mention of "gongs and cymbals", reminiscent of the Mysteries, the Corinthian use of the term πνευματικός, Paul's use of the term μυστήριον in 1 Corinthians 14.2 (which he takes to be an allusion to pagan mysteries), the self-centered attitude to worship he believes to be common to both the Mysteries and the Corinthians, the problem over the vocal role of women, and the interest in spirits and in ecstasy.[79] He also cites F.F. Bruce and R. and C.C. Kroeger in support of various of his points.

It is important to point out that there are a number of very doubtful statements in all this, even if the consensus view here propounded is correct. First, there is no evidence at all that "spirits of Python" were identified with Apollo. Python, the ancient serpent of Delphi, was slain and replaced by Apollo, and nothing in our evidence about "pythons" in the Hellenistic period suggests that anybody thought they were inspired by Apollo. Second, there is no suggestion of which I am aware that anything resembling glossolalia was to be found in the cult of Apollo *anywhere else but at*

---

[77] J. Painter, "Paul and the Pneumatikoi at Corinth", in *Paul and Paulinism*, ed. M.D. Hooker and S.G. Wilson, London, 1982, pp. 237-250, esp. p. 240, p. 247 note 22, p. 243.

[78] H.W. House, "Tongues and the Mystery Religions of Corinth", *Bib. Sac.*, vol. 140, part 558, pp. 134-150, esp. pp. 135, 138 and 139.

[79] H.W. House, *art.cit.*, pp. 140-142.

Delphi, as part of the cult of *Delphic* Apollo (and just possibly at Delos: but House does not suggest this). There is certainly no evidence that it was widespread in the cult of Apollo more generally. We also see here again the straightforward link between ecstaticism and glossolalia that characterises so many of the arguments brought forward in support of the "consensus".

The one major recent exception, at the exegetical level, to this consensus, is the article of A. Méhat, "L'enseignement sur «les choses de l'esprit»".[80] Méhat argues that under the almost universal effect of the view that phenomena influenced by paganism are under consideration in 1 Corinthians 12, verses 1-3 have been badly misunderstood. He points out that it is very odd that, having suggested that the problem in Corinth may be due to Corinthian *ignorance* about spiritual gifts, he should then suggest that the problem is due to *prior knowledge* of pagan ecstasy. He argues that the term μαίνεσθε in 14.23 need have no reference to religious frenzy at all, that the "gongs and cymbals" of 13.1 are simply metaphors of noise, and that ἀπαγόμενοι in 12.2 can have several meanings other than a reference to ecstatic experiences in the Mysteries. He also asks whether there could have been sufficient initiates in the Mysteries in Corinth to force us to assume that some must have been present among the converts of Paul.[81] All of this is, it seems to me, a timely reminder that what looks to one scholar like exegetical evidence supported by cross-cultural parallels may look to another like a circular argument. Whether Méhat's argument is convincing or not, his article sharply raises an issue which, as we have seen, has been increasingly taken for granted. Méhat's view has recently been accepted by D.A. Carson.[82]

In 1985 T. Callan published an important review of the nature of prophecy in both early Christianity and its environment.[83] His article is significant, because it takes account of the work of Bacht, Crone, Engelsen, Hill and others. He, however, is not concerned with glossolalia, but with prophecy. In brief, he argues that the term προφήτης is most commonly used in our period, in relation to oracles, to designate the person more accurately called the μάντις, the inspired person who, in a trance or ecstasy, receives an oracle. It is, in Callan's view, less commonly used of

---

[80] *Revue d'histoire et de philosophie religieuses*, vol. 63, no. 4, 1983, pp. 395-415.
[81] A. Méhat, *art.cit.*, pp. 398, 402.
[82] D.A. Carson, *Showing the Spirit*, p. 26.
[83] T. Callan, "Prophecy and Ecstasy in Greco-Roman Religion and in 1 Corinthians", *Nov.T.*, vol. 27, part 2, 1985, pp. 125-140.

non-inspired persons who act as spokesmen in other capacities. Against this background Hellenistic Judaism developed theories about kinds of prophecy which did, and which did not, involve trance. In this context Callan suggests that Paul, faced with a view that did not differentiate glossolalia from prophecy, made use of this pre-existing distinction to focus the Corinthians' attention on what he saw as the more productive forms of inspired speech. Callan's case is dealt with in detail in Chapter 8, but here I must simply say briefly that his main case seems to me to be mistaken.

In 1986, W. Richardson cited with approval the general conclusions of Nils Engelsen, arguing that

> He shows convincingly that similar phenomena occurred in various circles, Greco-Roman as well as Jewish, but they were referred to under the general category of 'prophecy' or 'divination'. It appears that Paul is the only one who narrows the meaning of the phrase (sc. speaking in tongues?) to unintelligible speech, and thus puts prophecy in a separate category.[84]

Two major works remain for us to complete our survey. The first of these, which I have held up a little in terms of strict chronological order, is G. Dautzenberg's major article on glossolalia in the *Reallexikon für Antike und Christentum*.[85] This is the best and most detailed recent survey of the subject, and summarises the modern debate very well. He prefers the parallels with prophetic mania to those with Dionysiac ecstasy, citing Plato's discussion of prophecy and its interpretation in the Timaeus, though he, like James Dunn, notes that the parallel between Paul and Plato on this point is not perfect. He thinks there is a distant link only between glossolalia and the Magical Papyri, but cites Tschiedel for the concept of miraculous languages related to heavenly languages. He is cautious of the evidence of Celsus reported by Origen, rightly arguing that we cannot know to what extent this report has been coloured by Christian elements, but more confident of parallels within Gnosticism. He believes that the Testament of Job and the Apocalypse of Zephaniah provide the closest substantial parallel to early Christian glossolalia, and argues that the concept of divine or angelic languages is again the important link that unites the various phenomena. Thus, while Jewish parallels help us to understand the origins of glossolalia, the Hellenistic parallels explain how it so easily took root in the Hellenistic churches such as that in Corinth. Ecstatic speech, according to Dautzenberg,

---

[84] W. Richardson, "Liturgical Order and Glossolalia in 1 Corinthians 14.26c-33a", *N.T.S.*, vol. 32, 1986, pp. 144-153, esp. p. 149.

[85] G. Dautzenberg, "Glossolalie", cols. 225-246.

is a universal human phenomenon. Glossolalia is the particular form that it took on within early Christianity, with its own characteristic terminology and conceptual framework.[86]

This is clearly a nuanced piece of argument, but the claim remains that substantial parallels exist at the phenomenological level between glossolalia and "ecstatic speech" in the Hellenistic world. Dautzenberg doubts, however, that these parallels explain the dispute in Corinth.

The final work which must be taken into consideration here is the massive contribution of D.E. Aune, *Prophecy in Early Christianity and the Ancient Mediterranean World.*[87] It would be folly to pretend that what follows is anything more than the briefest of comments on the five hundred and some pages of Aune's masterly survey, but none the less some comments must be made.

Aune's primary concern is not with the phenomena of early Christian prophecy, but with the detection of the fossilized remnants of prophecy embedded in the New Testament and other early Christian literature. Naturally, however, this leads him to an extensive consideration of the phenomena themselves. He accepts the suggestion of Engelsen that Paul was probably the first to differentiate between glossolalia and other forms of inspired speech, and that of Gillespie, that glossolalia was often viewed as divine legitimation of prophecy. He also argues that in 1 Corinthians 12.2 Paul "was in all probability referring to pagan religious experiences of possession trance".[88] He is one of the few, however, to point out that there is very little evidence to support the view that the Pythia's words were "ecstatic gibberish", thus implicitly raising doubts about the parallel between Delphi and glossolalia[89] He makes no comment of which I am aware on the postulated Dionysiac parallels, but (unlike House, for example) distinguishes correctly between Delphic and Dionysiac ἐνθουσιασμός.[90]

Aune is highly critical of the kinds of distinction between Christian and Hellenistic prophecy suggested by Bacht and L.T. Johnson, arguing (rightly, in my view) that they are, by and large, theologically motivated, and not

---

[86] G. Dautzenberg, "Glossolalie", cols. 234-236.

[87] Grand Rapids, 1983.

[88] Aune, *Prophecy*, p. 195, pp. 42 and note 221, 72 and note 133, p. 257.

[89] Aune, *Prophecy*, p. 31, note 103, pp. 39 (discussing Plato, Timaeus 71-2), 50-52.

[90] Aune, *Prophecy*, pp. 21, 42

very useful historically.[91] His own view is more difficult to summarise. He does believe, however, that

Although Israelite-Jewish and Greco-Roman revelatory traditions have many mutually distinct features, the interpenetration of east and west during the Hellenistic and Roman period makes it very difficult if not impossible to untangle the blended elements (even if such an untangling were desirable). Christian prophecy is most adequately treated if it is regarded as a distinctively Christian institution; if so, any typology of Christian prophetism should be based primarily on internal rather than external criteria.[92]

Beyond this Aune does not summarise his own views as to the relationship between Christian prophecy and prophecy in its environment, though a large number of issues in that relationship are treated individually. He sees clearly, for example, that Graeco-Roman prophecy is far more strongly institutionalised than Christian prophecy, and far more closely related to particular places: early Christianity knows of no oracular shrines, but only of oracular people.[93] He also argues for the well-known distinction between technical divination and inspired prophecy, but surprisingly does not point out that early Christianity totally eschewed all forms of technical divination.[94] But Aune is far more interested in the literary forms taken by prophecy than in such matters. His work ought not to be judged by what it does not do, when it does so much. Other matters related to his view of "congregational prophecy" and the spontaneity of Christian prophecy will be discussed in detail in Chapters Ten and Eleven.

We have seen that the hypothesis that Paul's dispute with his Corinthian converts has to do with a view of inspired speech they have inherited from their pre-Christian religious experience has much to commend it. Several features of Paul's argument - his mention of their experience of being "carried away to dumb idols", his negative use of the images of gongs and cymbals, his disparaging of glossolalia in favour of prophecy, and his view of the "sign" value of glossolalia - can be plausibly interpreted in the light of such an hypothesis. Likewise, a quantity of external evidence has been amassed which would seem to suggest strongly that glossolalia or something very similar was widely known in Hellenistic religion. We have seen that scholars have generally argued that Christian prophecy is less closely related to Hellenistic phenomena than is glossolalia, and that again this helps us to

---

[91]   Aune, *Prophecy*, p. 21.
[92]   Aune, *Prophecy*, p. 230.
[93]   Aune, *Prophecy*, pp. 230-231, cf. pp. 37-8.
[94]   Aune, *Prophecy*, pp. 35-6. On this matter see also chapter 11.

understand Paul's preference for prophecy over glossolalia. But in each case dissenting voices have been raised. A. Méhat has strongly criticised the exegetical consensus, while R.H. Gundry, T.M. Crone and D.E. Aune have raised doubts about certain features of the Hellenistic evidence.

Yet at the same time the general hypothesis has become so firmly entrenched that scholars as diverse as F.F. Bruce and U.B. Müller can take it for granted or make it the basis of further work, and others, such as Morton Smith and H.W. House, can argue it with little regard for the niceties of the evidence. What is needed is a thorough-going investigation of this evidence: not merely the exegetical evidence, but more importantly the direct evidence for inspired speech phenomena in the immediate environment of the New Testament. If this evidence proves adequate to sustain the hypothesis, then the exegesis of 1 Corinthians 12-14 can be developed in detail. If, however, as I contend, the evidence will not support the hypothesis, then exegetical alternatives can be considered.

We turn, then, to the main section of this thesis. In the next two chapters, numbers Three and Four, the New Testament evidence on glossolalia will be examined in detail. The following three chapters, numbers Five, Six and Seven, will cover the proposed Hellenistic parallel phenomena, and consider some of the exegetical consequences if (as I argue) the "consensus" hypothesis is to be abandoned. The next three chapters will examine prophecy, chapter Eight generally, and chapters Nine and Ten as we find it in Acts and the letters of Paul. The focus will be on 1 Corinthians chapters 12-14. Chapter Eleven will survey the relationship between early Christian prophecy (as described in the previous chapters) and prophecy in the wider Hellenistic world.

Chapter 3

Glossolalia in Early Christianity: Terminology and Phenomena.

The secondary "long ending" of Mark's gospel, the book of Acts, and Paul's first letter to the Corinthians all testify to the existence within early Christianity of the phenomenon known variously as "speaking in new tongues", "speaking in other tongues", or, simply, "speaking in tongues".[1] It is obvious that these phrases constitute technical terminology. Yet the origins of the terminology are obscure, and scholars are divided as to what the "original form" of the term, from which the other usages developed, may have been. The problem is complicated by the fact that there appear to be major differences between our two substantial sources, Luke and Paul, as to the nature of the phenomenon so designated. In nearly all cases scholars either propose a diversity of phenomena, or suggest that Luke's account ought to be treated as secondary. Further, there is considerable disagreement among scholars as to the nature of even the phenomenon described at first hand by Paul. Some scholars also urge that other less explicitly relevant passages must be included in any discussion of glossolalia.[2] In brief, our evidence as to the nature of early Christian glossolalia is limited, situationally conditioned (or even polemical), and controversial. The claim that the phenomenon is widely paralleled in the history of religions, including those in the modern world, is of no assistance to us in understanding the phenomenon until its description within early Christianity

---

[1] Mark ch. 16.17, γλώσσαις λαλήσουσιν καιναῖς; some manuscripts in this tradition omit "καιναῖς". Acts chs. 2.4, λαλεῖν ἐτέραις γλώσσαις, 10.46, λαλούντων γλώσσαις, 19.6, ἐλάλουν τε γλώσσαις; 1 Corinthians 12-14, variously. One can also "pray in a tongue", 1 Corinthians 14.14, which is more generally described as "praying with (my) spirit" only - i.e. without the benefit of the other faculties.
[2] See, most importantly, E. Käsemann, "The Cry for Liberty in the Worship of the Church", in *Perspectives on Paul*, London, 1969, and *Commentary on Romans*, trans. G.W. Bromiley, Grand Rapids, 1980, pp. 239ff, arguing that Romans 8.26 refers to glossolalia. K. Stendahl and G. Dautzenberg briefly argue similar cases in "Glossolalia and the Charismatic Movement", in *God's Christ and His People*, ed. J. Jervell and W. Meeks, Oslo, 1977, p. 126, and "Glossolalie", col. 239-40, respectively. For the opposite point of view see J.P.M. Sweet, "A Sign for Unbelievers: Paul's attitude to glossolalia", *N.T.S.*, vol. 13, 1966-7, pp. 247-8, and A.J.M. Wedderburn, "Romans 8.26 - Towards a Theology of Glossolalia?", *S.J.Th.*, vol. 28, 1975, pp. 369-377, and the references cited there. The criticisms made by these two scholars seem to me to be thoroughly justified.

is clarified, for only when this has been done can the postulated parallels be examined. However, even with all these cautions stated, a good deal can be said about glossolalia, provided the limitations of our evidence are kept in mind.

1. Terminology

The most recent thorough discussion of the terminology of glossolalia is that of R.A. Harrisville.[3] He suggests that there are two major issues to be resolved: the question as to which of the three main forms of the terminology - the Markan, Lukan or Pauline - is the earliest, and the question as to the origins of these phrases as technical terms within early Christianity for the phenomenon now known as glossolalia. His treatment of the two issues is, however, combined. From a careful survey of the Septuagintal, secular Greek, Qumran, New Testament and post-apostolic usage of the term γλῶσσα, etc., he concludes that

the Septuagint translator appears to have known nothing of a technical term for speaking in tongues . . . profane or non-ecclesiastical Greek knew of no technical term for speaking in tongues . . .[4]

However, on the basis of the striking similarity between the translations of Isaiah given by the Septuagint, Aquila, and the Qumran community, he argues that

if something akin to glossolalia was practised in Jewish circles, particularly among those who nourished apocalyptic hopes, the community at Qumran furnished an atmosphere congenial to the emergence of the technical terms under discussion . . . Thus, by the time Paul and the author of Acts had put pen to paper the terms had become more or less fixed, a possibility which would also explain the combination of γλῶσσα with λαλεῖν but never with λέγειν . . . If this is true, then those scholars who elect for ἑτέραις γλώσσαις λαλεῖν or ἑτερογλώσσαις λαλεῖν as the more original, and the simpler γλῶσσα λαλεῖν as an ellipse, have the probabilities in their favour. The only other

---

[3] R.A. Harrisville, "Speaking in Tongues: a Lexicographical Study", *C.B.Q.*, vol. 38, 1976, pp. 35-48.

[4] R.A. Harrisville, *art.cit.*, pp. 39, 41. The extraordinary suggestion of F.C. Conybeare, cited with approval by H.W. House, "Tongues and the Mystery Religions of Corinth", *Bibliotheca Sacra*, vol. 140, part 558, 1983, p. 139 that "The very phrase γλώσσαις λαλεῖν, 'to speak with tongues' was not invented by the New Testament writers, but borrowed from ordinary speech" is not supported by any evidence at all, so far as I am aware. Certainly Conybeare only discusses Vergil's account of the Cumaean Sibyl in this context, and the terminology is manifestly not used there. A computerised search of the Thesaurus Linguae Graecae failed to produce a single case of the use of the terms in question to describe such a phenomenon as glossolalia outside early Christianity.

alternative to this hypothesis is to fix the origins of the term with Jewish Christianity or with Paul, and regard its occurrence elsewhere as merely coincidental.[5]

Thus it proves impossible to divorce the question of terminology from that of the occurrence of the phenomenon of glossolalia itself. If there existed at Qumran phenomena sufficiently similar to glossolalia, then Harrisville can suggest that it was there, or, in similar circumstances, that the Septuagint reading of Isaiah 28 or its prototype gave rise to a technical term later taken up by early Christianity. But that "if" is a very large one indeed. I know of no suggestion that glossolalia was practised at Qumran, nor any evidence that might suggest it; indeed, the Qumran interpretation of Isaiah 28 (as well as several passages in the LXX) suggests that if anyone speaks foreign languages to God's people, it will be false prophets.[6] The evidence presented by Harrisville to suggest that glossolalia was practised "among those who nourished apocalyptic hopes" is singularly unconvincing.[7] In his view, this

---

[5] R.A. Harrisville, *art.cit.*, pp. 45-46. Nils Engelsen, *Glossolalia*, p. ii, argues that "The most reasonable background for the technical term seems to be the poetic, half-metaphorical use of γλῶσσα in Old Testament sources." and that "The shorter form is probably an ellipsis." (p. 83.)

[6] See, for example, the interpretation put on Isaiah 28.11 in the Qumran hymns, nos. 1 and 7, G. Vermes, *The Dead Sea Scrolls in English*, Harmondsworth, 1968, pp. 154 and 161-2, cited by Harrisville, *art.cit.*. See also the similar interpretation implied by the LXX translation of Isaiah 28, Jeremiah 5.15, 9.4 and 23.31, Ezekiel 36.3, Psalm 11(12).4, Psalm 80(81).6(5)(?) Sirach 17.6 and Psalms of Solomon 12.1-2. In all these cases it is the enemies of Israel or of the writer, or the "false prophets", who have a "tongue" with which to speak. I am not implying that the LXX is here describing the phenomenon later described as "speaking in tongues": I am suggesting that, given the phenomenon, these passages might suggest the terminology, despite the negative connotations. This is Harrisville's alternative, less preferred view, *art.cit.*, p. 46. Passages which might provide a more positive background include Psalm 36.30, Psalm 118/9 v.172, Zephaniah 3.9, and most importantly, Sirach 51.22, and Testament of Job 48ff, for which see below. The predominance of the pejorative sense seems to tell against the suggestion of J.P.M. Sweet ("A Sign for Unbelievers: Paul's attitude to Glossolalia", *N.T.S.*, vol. 13, 1966-67, pp. 240-257) that Paul could have been modifying an early Christian apologetic in favour of glossolalia when he quoted Isaiah 28.11 in 1 Corinthians 14.20-25. Such an apologetic would have been very risky.

[7] R.A. Harrisville, *art.cit.*, pp. 45, 47. The only parallel of any substance is that in the Testament of Job, 48-52, the date of which is highly problematical. For a detailed treatment of this and the other postulated Jewish evidence see the Appendix. Harrisville is here dependent on N.I.J. Engelsen, *Glossolalia*, and argues that "these parallels appear to support the contention that for the O.T. and inter-Testamental community, glossolalic utterance was not regarded as a category separate from the ecstatic per se." Harrisville argues that the intertestamental references yield "soil for the development of a term exclusively applied to ecstatic speech." (p. 47) This whole case is of course dependent on

would leave us with only one alternative. If the terms did not originate (with the phenomena) in pre-Christian Judaism, then they must have originated (with the distinctive conception of the phenomena) within early Christianity.

However, before this problem can be properly resolved we will have to turn to a consideration of the evidence for the nature of early Christian glossolalia, especially in terms of the differing perspectives of Luke and Paul. Once some conclusions have been reached in this area, we will be in a better position to solve the problem of the origins of the terminology.

2. Luke and Paul.

That there are substantial differences between the accounts of glossolalia in 1 Corinthians 12-14 and Acts 2 is clear from even a superficial reading. In Acts the "tongues" are widely intelligible; in 1 Corinthians they are unintelligible, and require "interpretation".[8] In Acts ch. 2 they are a sign of the first great outpouring of the Holy Spirit upon the church in his eschatological fullness. In the later references in Acts they are in every case closely associated with the experience of conversion and baptism.[9] In other words, tongues are an initial Christian experience. Yet in 1 Corinthians they are never noted as an initial experience; rather they are part of the ongoing life of the individual and the community. Finally, in Acts glossolalia is a communal experience, occurring always within Christian *groups*, and there is no mention of a complementary gift of interpretation. In 1 Corinthians, though it is clear that uninterpreted glossolalia had been characteristic of the Corinthian assembly, Paul limits its value to individual use, and insists on interpretation or silence within the assembly.

"ecstatic speech" of a glossolalic kind having previously existed, not clearly distinguished from other kinds of "ecstatic speech".

[8] It is extraordinary that Behm, *T.D.N.T.*, vol. 1, 1932, E.T. 1964, p. 724, can suggest that the phenomena have "essentially the same characteristics". Behm sees both sets of phenomena as being outbreaks of ecstatic gibberish, differently interpreted by Luke and Paul, but both explicable in terms of the postulated widespread belief in angelic or heavenly languages. The differences are minimised by R.H. Gundry, "'Ecstatic Utterance' (N.E.B.)?", *J.Th.S.*, vol. 17, part 2, 1966, p. 303, who says: "At Corinth interpretation was necessary because the audiences were local. On the Day of Pentecost interpretation was unnecessary because the audience was cosmopolitan." But Corinth, as a port city, is likely to have been just as cosmopolitan as Jerusalem, and Gundry's comment does not take into account the other differences which do exist between Luke and Paul.

[9] See D. M. Smith, "Glossolalia and other Spiritual Gifts in a New Testament Perspective", *Interpretation*, vol. 28, 1974, pp. 312-3: "in each case glossolalia is related to the initial onset and reception of the Spirit."

These differences, along with other problems in the passage, have led many to argue that Luke's interpretation of (at least) the Pentecostal glossolalia of ch. 2 as unlearned foreign languages is secondary and unhistorical, and determined by his theological interests.[10] Some have gone

---

[10] That this was Luke's interpretation can hardly be doubted, in view of the comments of the crowd and the parallel use of ἑτέραις γλώσσαις and διάλεκτος in vv. 4, 6, 8 and 11. The view of G.J. Sirks, cited with approval by C.S. Mann in Appendix 3 to J. Munck's *The Acts of the Apostles*, p. 295, that what the apostles and others were actually doing was quoting new interpretations of familiar Pentecost liturgies is not supported by any evidence, either in the passage or elsewhere, as far as I can see. In view of the widespread opinion that what Luke was reporting was in fact an outbreak of "ecstatic speech", it is ironic that in Luke's view it is the crowd who are "ecstatic": "And they were amazed (ἐξίσταντο) and marvelled . . .", Acts 2.7. (W.G. MacDonald, "Glossolalia in the New Testament", *B.Ev.Th.S.*, vol. 7, Spring 1964, p. 60.) Compare similarly Luke 5.26, 24.22, and Acts 2.12, 3.10, 9.21 and 10.45. Ecstasy here is more a response to the extraordinary or paranormal than a cause of it. The term is used of Peter's trance in Acts 10.10 and 11.5, and of Paul's in 22.17, but *never* of the state of an inspired speaker. For the consensus view see Behm, *art.cit.*, p. 725, E. Lohse, "Pentecost", in G. Friedrich, ed., *T.D.N.T.*, vol. 6, 1959, E.T. 1968, pp. 50-52, E. Haenchen, *The Acts of the Apostles, A Commentary*, Oxford, 1971, pp. 172-175, D.M. Smith, *art.cit.*, p. 314. It is variously suggested that Luke is picturing the event as a reversal of the curse of Babel (E. Trocmé, *Le 'Livre des Actes' et l'histoire*, Paris, 1957, pp. 202-206, C.S.C. Williams, *A Commentary on the Acts of the Apostles*, London, 1964, pp. 62-3, K. Stendahl, *art.cit.*), as a parallel to the Rabbinic and Philonic traditions about the multi-lingual giving of the Law at Sinai (E. Haenchen, *op.cit.*, p. 174, though he admits that Luke's knowledge of such traditions is only an assumption, James Dunn, *Jesus and the Spirit*, London, 1975, pp. 139, 147-8, and W.E. Mills, *A Theological / Exegetical Approach to Glossolalia*, Lanham, 1985, pp. 47-51), and as an indication of the universality of the coming Christian mission (F.W. Beare, "Speaking with Tongues: a Critical Survey of the New Testament Evidence", *J.B.L.*, vol. 83, part 3, 1964, p. 237, K. Stendahl, *loc.cit.*, D. Hill, *Prophecy*, p. 95), or perhaps simply as a "convincing miracle" (R.H. Gundry, *art.cit.*, pp. 303-4). It is perhaps a little surprising that this "reinterpretation" of the events is almost always ascribed to Luke, and the possibility that it may have come to him in his sources scarcely rates a mention. The most detailed survey of interpretations is probably that of Dunn *op.cit.*, pp. 148ff., (who, with M.E. Hart, *Tongues And Prophecy*, p. 63, is among the few to suggest that the interpretation of what he believes likely to have been ecstatic glossolalia as languages probably goes back to the disciples themselves). The most recent, and to me the most sensible, is that of I.H. Marshall, "The Significance of Pentecost", *S.J.Th.*, vol. 30, 1977, pp. 347-369, who comments that "if the description of Pentecost is meant to foreshadow the world-wide expansion of the church, it is an expansion among *Jews* scattered throughout the world that is used to provide the picture" (p. 357). The view that the miracle at Pentecost was one of hearing rather than one of speech (recently argued with reference to a claimed parallel in the Delian Festival of Apollo by H.J. Tschiedel, "Ein Pfingstwunder im Apollonhymnus", *Zeitschrift für Religions- und Geistesgeschichte*, vol. 27, 1975, pp. 22-39) seems to me to have very little to recommend it, in either the case of the Festival

so far as to argue that in all probability "Luke" (who on this view is unlikely to be the companion of Paul) had had no first-hand experience of glossolalia, and misunderstood it quite badly.[11] In the first category, T.M. Crone suggests that the account in Acts can have had only two sources: either the story of a language miracle (subsequently interpreted by Luke as glossolalia), or the story of an outbreak of glossolalia, in the sense of unintelligible inspired speech, which Luke has understood as a miracle of languages.[12]

---

of Apollo, or in that of Pentecost. See, for example, the critique and references in Mills, *op.cit.*, pp. 60-62. Tschiedel's view will be dealt with in more detail below, in Chapter 5.

[11] See, for example, H. Conzelmann, *Die Apostelgeschichte*, 2nd edition, Tübingen, 1972, pp. 32-3: "Es ist zu beachten, dass Lukas selbst von der ursprünglichen Glossolalie keine eigene Vorstellung mehr hat. Er identifiziert sie mit der Prophetie, wodurch die Synthese mit dem Sprachenwunder erleichtert wird." Cf. T.W. Gillespie, *Prophecy and Tongues*, 1971, pp. 111-112, who argues that it is probable that Luke had no knowledge of the phenomenon. Naturally, this view is more prevalent among those who suggest a later date for Acts, and doubt that its author was a companion of Paul. More conservatively, D.M. Smith, *loc.cit.*, points out that glossolalia is never mentioned in the "we" passages in Acts, and though he doubts Luke's first-hand knowledge of the phenomenon, he is willing to admit its possibility.

[12] T.M. Crone, *Prophecy*, pp. 190-195. Crone argues that the charge of drunkenness levelled at the disciples by the crowd does not sit well with the "languages" interpretation, and therefore suggests glossolalia. Likewise F.W. Beare, *art.cit.*, p. 237, who believes that the "Jews from every nation" were residents rather than pilgrims, asks: "if we are to be literal-minded, how could such a multitude distinguish one language from another if so many were speaking different languages at the same time?" I.H. Marshall argues that this is not necessarily so, as "the same verb is used in 2.9 of one section of this people and describes them as residents in Mesopotamia . . . Luke says nothing about the proportion of visitors and residents" (*art.cit.*, p. 357). C.G. Williams argues, *Tongues of the Spirit*, Cardiff, 1981 p. 36, that since even pilgrims would all be able to speak Greek or Aramaic, no miracle of languages is necessary for communication. Luke, however, does not suggest that it was necessary: merely that it happened. Marshall elsewhere points out that "this (the charge of drunkenness) would be a very natural interpretation to offer if one heard people making unintelligible noises, as some of the sounds must have seemed to those of the hearers who did not recognise the particular language being used." (*The Acts of the Apostles*, Leicester, 1980, p. 71.) Cf. Marshall, *art.cit.*, p. 361: "There is no basis for tracing two sources or an edited narrative here." Alternatively, Gundry (*art.cit.*, p. 304) points out that according to Luke, it was "Jews from every nation" (whom he also convincingly argues, p. 300, to have been pilgrims, contra Beare) who heard "the wonders of God" in their own languages, whereas it was "others", presumably native Palestinians, who would not understand those languages, who raised the charge of drunkenness. Such a view would confirm rather than deny the linguistic nature of the Pentecostal glossolalia.

If the original referred to some type of language miracle by which the disciples spoke foreign languages, it is difficult to understand why Lk. would have added the allusions to glossolalia . . . On the other hand, the entire account can be explained if we accept an original tradition of glossolalia or unintelligible speech. We know from Paul that such a phenomenon existed in the early Church.

But Crone takes far too little account of the fact that, as we shall see, Paul, just as much as Luke, understood glossolalia as the miraculous ability to speak foreign languages. The difference between them is only that Luke postulates hearers who know the languages, and Paul requires a specific charisma of interpretation. Luke's account is not as internally inconsistent as Crone, and others, suggest.[13] It is entirely likely that in viewing glossolalia as the miraculous ability to speak otherwise unknown human languages, Luke is quite simply accepting the uniform view of the early church, as he found it in his sources and as he knew it from the churches of his own day.[14]

---

[13] For criticisms of the account suggesting Lukan redaction see F.W. Beare, *art.cit.*, pp. 237-8, D.M. Smith, *art.cit.*, p. 313, K. Stendahl, *loc.cit.* The criticisms are conveniently summarised in Marshall, *art.cit.*, p. 360. E. Haenchen argues, for example, that "Joel does not mention speech in foreign languages, which is reason enough why Peter's discourse cannot refer to the miracle of languages. Ecstatic utterance, on the other hand, is covered by the προφητεύειν of the quotation." (*op.cit.*, p. 178, n.11.) This statement seems to me to miss completely Luke's special perspective on glossolalia, outlined below. Haenchen's comment on the perceived historical and internal inconsistencies of the account is simple: "But these are not considerations which are likely to have troubled Luke . . ." (*op.cit.*, p. 172 n.1).

[14] The suggestion that Luke could not have known of glossolalia as a common experience in the church of his day seems to me to be incredible. While glossolalia is not mentioned in the Epistles outside of 1 Corinthians, it is still known as late as Irenaeus (see the next chapter), and I am not aware of any suggestion that Acts should be dated as late as that. While it may not have been a common experience, it was known. If Luke was, as I would argue, a companion of Paul, the suggestion becomes unthinkable. (Compare C.G. Williams, *op.cit.*, p. 33: "it is as hard to believe that Luke was insufficiently informed of a phenomenon acknowledged as the work of the Spirit as it is to believe that glossolalia was an uncommon experience in the early Apostolic church.") It remains possible, however, that Luke may have conceived of it and categorised it in an independent fashion, as I am suggesting. The reverse side of this argument is worth noting, and has not figured in the modern debate, as far as I am aware: if Paul knew of Pentecost, it is highly unlikely that he would have used the common term for the Pentecostal speech miracle to describe a phenomenon which he understood to be fundamentally different. (For this suggestion I am indebted to Dr Peter O'Brien.) Paul is very particular about the distinctions between varying gifts of inspired speech, as his discussion of prophecy, tongues, words of wisdom and words of knowledge in 1 Corinthians 12 demonstrates.

One factor, however, that has led to some confusion is that, unlike Paul, Luke conceives of glossolalia as a subspecies within the broader category of "prophecy", rather than as a separate, though related, phenomenon. That this is so is clear from the following observations. The Pentecostal glossolalia is argued by Peter to fulfil the prophecy of Joel that "your sons and your daughters will prophesy" (v.17); "and they will prophesy" (v.18).[15] Secondly, the content of the speech of the disciples, as understood by the crowd, is described as "the wonders of God" (Acts 2.11.). In Acts 4.31 being filled with the Holy Spirit means that the disciples speak the word of God more boldly. In Acts 10.46 the household of Cornelius is described as "speaking in tongues and praising God". In Acts 19.6, when Paul laid hands on the disciples of John at Ephesus, "they spoke in tongues and prophesied". "Praising God", "speaking the word of God", "telling of the wonders of God", "prophesying" and "speaking in (other) tongues" all result from being baptised or filled with the Holy Spirit.[16]

To supplement this material we may turn to the opening chapters of Luke's Gospel. In Luke 1.41-2 Elizabeth's response to being "filled with the Holy Spirit" was her outburst of blessing and praise. In v. 67 Zechariah's psalm of praise, full of Old Testament allusions to the great works of God in the past, is described as being the result of his being filled with the Holy Spirit, and is also called prophecy. In Luke 2.25-32 Simeon, a man upon whom was the Holy Spirit, "moved by the Spirit" came to the Temple, and,

---

[15] Luke's (or Peter's) addition of the second "and they will prophesy" to the text of Joel underlines the close relationship between the giving of the Spirit and prophecy in his mind, as in the minds of many in this period; cf. T.M. Crone, *Prophecy*, p. 194, J. Blenkinsopp, "Prophecy and Priesthood in Josephus", *J.J.S.*, vol. 25, 1974, pp. 239-262, esp. pp. 261-2, Meyer in G. Friedrich, ed., *T.D.N.T.*, vol. 6, 1959, E.T. 1968, pp. 816-828, and M.E. Isaacs, *The Concept of Spirit: A Study of Pneuma in Hellenistic Judaism and its Bearing on the New Testament*, London, 1976, pp. 47-51. It also emphasises the close association of prophecy and glossolalia in Luke's mind. See T.W. Gillespie, *Prophecy and Tongues*, p. 116 and M.E. Hart, *Tongues And Prophecy*, p. 71.

[16] Thus M. Turner, "Spiritual Gifts Then and Now", *Vox Evangelica*, vol. XV, 1985, p. 11, suggests that for Luke "to prophesy" means "to speak while under the external influence of the Spirit". The suggestion of M.E. Hart (*Tongues And Prophecy*, p. 60) that since Luke only uses ἕτερος in chapter 2 of Acts, he may have had what he considered a different phenomenon in view in chapters 10 and 19, seems to me to be highly unlikely. It ignores Peter's comment in 10.47 that Cornelius and his family had received the Holy Spirit "just as we have" (though see pp. 31-2 below), as well as Luke's clear intention to describe all three instances in parallel terms as major stages in the extension of the Gospel.

seeing Jesus, foretold his role in the eschatological future. In Luke 2.36-38, Anna, "the prophetess", "gave thanks to God and spoke about the child to all who were looking forward to the redemption of Jerusalem".

A community of ideas is revealed here. For Luke, inspired speech generally is the work of the Holy Spirit. Praising God under his inspiration, giving thanks to God, telling of the great works of God, prophesying, and telling of the great works of God in other tongues (glossolalia) are all part of the one essentially undifferentiated view of inspiration. It would seem, in the light of Acts chapter 2, that "prophecy" is the general term under which Luke grouped inspired speech phenomena. For him glossolalia is simply one form of prophetic speech.[17] Luke's identification of glossolalia as prophecy is thus not an isolated example, and proof of his redactional work, but of a piece with his view of inspiration generally. If the interpretation is his, rather than being that of his sources, it is not one that he adopts purely for the purposes of the Pentecost narrative.

In another area as well the incompatibility of Luke's and Paul's conceptions of glossolalia has been somewhat exaggerated. It is true, as we noted above, that Luke views glossolalia as an initial and usually communal experience of the Holy Spirit, whereas Paul conceives of it as being valuable

---

[17] Engelsen thus has matters precisely the wrong way round when he says that "In Acts the term (sc. γλώσσαις λαλεῖν) covers a wide spectrum of speech." (*Glossolalia*, p. 95, but cf. p. 97.) The term "prophecy" covers a wide spectrum, and γλώσσαις λαλεῖν is one element within it. Compare Tugwell's comment ("The Gift of Tongues in the New Testament", *The Expository Times*, vol. 84, no. 5, 1973, p. 137.) "In Acts 2 the disciples are *overheard* speaking the wonderful works of God in other tongues, and the crowd is amazed to recognise all kinds of languages; but so far as the disciples themselves are concerned, they are not engaged in preaching, but in praying." This is also the view of M. Turner, *art.cit.*, p. 17.

It might be further argued that for Luke glossolalia is that form of inspired speech characteristic of an individual's initial experience of the Holy Spirit: see W.G. MacDonald, *art.cit.*, p. 61. But this would mean ignoring the communal nature of the experiences recorded in Acts, as well as the fact that in Acts 8.9-17, 36-38, 9.1-6 and many less specific passages where initial experiences of the Spirit are recounted, they are not noted as being accompanied by glossolalia. It would also put too much weight on Luke's highly compressed and selective narrative. MacDonald's argument that glossolalia ought to be inferred in Acts 8 and 9 is far from satisfactory.

Whether Luke would have allowed glossolalia as part of the individual's ongoing experience of the Spirit must remain a matter for speculation, but it is a possibility which may not be ruled out. His omission of glossolalia in other contexts might then be explained in terms of his overwhelming concern with origins, where Paul, by contrast, is concerned with situations in the ongoing life of the church. But I am not certain how far such an argument could be extended.

in the ongoing Christian life of the individual believer. But there is no *necessary* contradiction between these views. Paul says nothing at all to contradict the Lukan view of glossolalia as an initial and communal experience, because he simply never addresses such a topic. He is only concerned with the ongoing experience of his churches. Here, he insists, glossolalia that is not interpreted ought to be discontinued.

Third, we note that while it is widely granted that Luke conceived of at least the Pentecostal glossolalia as the miraculous ability to speak unlearned human languages, scholars have often doubted that this is what Paul was discussing in 1 Corinthians 12-14. They have suggested either that Paul views glossolalia as unintelligible noise, not language, and needing a specific charisma of interpretation to make any sense of it at all, or that he views it as being some sort of heavenly language.[18] The issue of the nature and understanding of glossolalia within early Christianity must now be treated in detail.

3. The Nature of Glossolalia

The Question of Ecstasy

"Ecstasy" is one of the most misused terms in the vocabulary of New Testament scholarship in our area. The question of whether glossolalia was, within early Christianity, a characteristically ecstatic phenomenon is simply not worth asking unless the term is carefully defined. Even when it has been decided what the question means, it is not easy to answer. As has been pointed out many times, our only really strong evidence on the matter comes from 1 Corinthians 12-14, where Paul is engaged in a polemic against what he sees as a misuse of glossolalia. In other words, his evidence itself proves that his view was not the only one possible, and yet we can know very little for certain about the Corinthian view. However, the question must be attempted, and therefore it must be defined. The modern term "ecstatic" is not at all identical in meaning with the Greek term ἐκστατικός. Most scholars use the term in its modern sense, loosely defining it as "having to do with an abnormal state of mind, a religious frenzy", or similar. Most seem to imply by the term "ecstatic" that the person so affected is only partially

---

[18] Thus, for example, C.K. Barrett, *The First Epistle to the Corinthians*, London, 1968, p. 300, J.D.G. Dunn, *Jesus and the Spirit*, London, 1975, pp. 243-4, and H. Güntert, *Von der Sprache der Götter und Geister: Bedeutungsgeschichtliche Untersuchungen zur homerischen und eddischen Göttersprache*, Halle, 1921, pp. 23-25.

responsible for his or her own actions, and may even be in a kind of trance, unaware of their own actions and the actions of those around them.[19] Others use the term more loosely, seemingly as a synonym for "inspired";[20] it is doubtful whether this is in any sense a useful definition for the word.

W. Grudem has suggested four tests by which we might judge whether a given case of inspired utterance should be described as "ecstatic".[21] They are as follows: (a) was the utterance forced on the speaker "against his will"? (b) Did it involve loss of self control, or violent raving? (c) Did it take a form incomprehensible to the speaker? Finally, (d) did it involve a mental state in which the speaker lost awareness of his surroundings? If the answer to any of these questions is yes, Grudem suggests, then the term "ecstatic" is appropriate. On this definition glossolalia would certainly have to be described as "ecstatic" under (c), but, according to Paul at least, ought not to

---

[19] Thus, for example, Behm, *art.cit.*, p. 722, F.W. Beare, *art.cit.*, p. 237, T.W. Gillespie, *Prophecy and Tongues*, pp. 103-119, and "A Pattern", p. 81, and M. Smith, "Pauline Worship as seen by Pagans", *H.Th.R.*, vol. 93, part 1-2, 1980, p. 246. Against the view that glossolalia should be seen as ecstatic in this sense see D.M. Smith, *art.cit.*, p. 317, S. Tugwell, *art.cit.*, p. 137, R.H. Gundry, *art.cit.*, p. 305-6 and Engelsen, *Glossolalia*, p. 204.

[20] In oracular contexts the term is sometimes simply used in opposition to the "technical" forms of divination. This seems to be the case in H.W. Parke, *The Oracles of Apollo in Asia Minor*, London, 1985, pp. 29-30. Likewise loose in their use of the term are T.M. Crone, *Prophecy*, p. 292, P. Roberts, "A Sign - Christian or Pagan?", *Exp. Times*, vol. 90, no. 7, April 1979, p. 201, G. Dautzenberg, "Glossolalie", col. 227, J.W. MacGorman, "Glossolalic Error and its Correction: 1 Corinthians 12-14", *Review and Expositor*, vol. 80, 1983, p. 390 (who believes glossolalia is ecstatic even though it is subject to conscious control), and W.E. Mills, *op.cit.* Cf. C.G. Williams, "Glossolalia as a Religious Phenomenon: Tongues at Corinth and Pentecost", *Religion*, 1975, vol. 5, part 1, p. 21: "Ecstasy is much too vague a term to employ . . . " D.E. Aune, *Prophecy*, pp. 20-21. He also notes in passing (pp. 21, 230) that it is often when glossolalia is understood as ecstatic that it is linked with (presumed) similar phenomena in Graeco-Roman religion. (See, i.e. J.D.G. Dunn, *op.cit.*, pp. 242-3.) In my view his criticism of the use of the term is thoroughly justified, and can be extended even further.

[21] W. Grudem, *Gift*, pp. 150-151. Also concerned with the question of definition are C.G. Williams, "Ecstaticism in Hebrew Prophecy and Christian Glossolalia", *Studies in Religion*, vol. 3, part 4, 1974, pp. 322-325, who is, however, mainly interested in O.T. phenomena in their relationship to glossolalia, R. Wilson, "Prophecy and Ecstasy: a Reexamination", *J.B.L.*, vol. 98, 1979, pp. 321-327, T. Callan, "Prophecy and Ecstasy in Greco-Roman Religion and in Corinthians", *Nov.T.*, vol. XXVII, part 2, 1985, pp. 125-140, who takes into account some helpful Hellenistic evidence, and D.A. Carson, *Showing the Spirit*, pp. 77-79.

fall under (a), (b) or (d).[22] For this reason I would prefer a definition which was less ambiguous.

D.E. Aune has suggested that we need a more refined set of terms for non-normal mental states than the simple alternatives of "ecstatic" and "non-ecstatic". He offers a typology of "altered states of consciousness" based on recent anthropological research, with its major categories being "possession trance" and "vision trance".[23] These are distinguished by their causes: the former is believed to be the result of the action of external "spiritual" beings on the subject of the trance, while the latter has to do with experiences of visions and "out of body" experiences believed to be brought about in other ways. These two categories are then sub-divided further, into controlled and uncontrolled states.[24]

While this terminology is a distinct improvement on the value-laden term "ecstasy", it has problems of its own. The experience reported by John in Revelation ch. 1 vv. 9-13, for example, would appear to fall neatly across the border between the two terms proposed: both possession trance (I was in the Spirit on the Lord's day) and vision trance (and I heard behind me . . . and when I turned I saw seven golden lampstands). Now it may be that this overlap of categories is no major problem, but the term "possession" has problems all of its own. It may be a valuable term for the understanding of many kinds of mediumship and shamanism, but it has very questionable value as a category to explain the religious experience of pre-Christian Greek and Hellenistic culture.[25] It may still be appropriate to a discussion of early Christianity, but not, I think, for one that attempts to draw parallels between early Christianity and its environment. Here we need some alternative typology. However, Aune's point that both "possession" and vision can be controlled, uncontrolled, or partially controlled is well taken, and goes far towards clarifying an issue that the term "ecstasy" had

---

[22] Clearly the whole force of 1 Corinthians 14.13-15 is that the speaker in a tongue is, like the listeners, unaware of the sense of his or her own utterance. Equally clearly, in Paul's view such utterance is and ought to be under conscious control.

[23] D.E. Aune, *Prophecy*, p. 19ff, p. 33. J.D.G. Dunn attempts such a terminology when he distinguishes between "glossolalia . . . which was ecstatic only in the technical sense of being automatic speech in which the conscious mind played no part, but not ecstatic in the more common sense of 'produced or accompanied by exalted states of feeling, rapture, frenzy'." (*op.cit.*, p. 243.)

[24] D.E. Aune, *Prophecy*, p. 34, and the literature cited at note 133.

[25] This point has been argued with reference to the terms κάτοχος and ἐνθουσιασμός by W.D. Smith, in the paper cited in chapter 2, and footnotes 22-24.

confused. But whatever view one takes, it is not possible to argue any simple opposition between, say, "ecstatic" glossolalia and "non-ecstatic" prophecy, or teaching, at least in Paul's theology.[26] According to 1 Cor. 14, prophecy and glossolalia are subject to virtually identical controls. Engelsen is quite correct when he says: "One is not more ecstatic than the other".[27]

The Question of Languages

I suggested above that those who attempt to drive a wedge between what they see as Luke's secondary interpretation of glossolalia as the miraculous ability to speak unlearned human languages, and the view adopted by Paul, are mistaken on two counts. First, they treat the Acts chapter 2 passage in isolation from other Lukan passages concerned with inspired speech. Secondly, they suggest that Paul does not believe that glossolalia is to be understood as unlearned human languages, but rather either as heavenly languages of some kind, or as mere "ecstatic" gibberish, the babbling of those in a state of religious frenzy. This point must now be considered.

The question as to what early Christian glossolalia "actually was" is not one that can be approached directly. We have no recorded examples of it in any form, and it is thus simply not available for analysis. What we do have is a body of evidence about how it was described and understood by Paul, and, where we can infer this from Paul, by his correspondents. From this evidence inferences can be drawn. We may end up disagreeing with Paul's description, but it is none the less our best evidence. What glossolalia *was* can only be approached via the way it was understood.[28]

---

[26] As do, for example, B.A. Pearson, *The Pneumatikos-Psychikos Terminology in 1 Corinthians*, Missoula, 1973, pp. 44-45, J. Héring, *The First Epistle of St. Paul to the Corinthians*, trans. A.W. Heathcote and P.J. Allcock, London, 1962, p. 148, and L.T. Johnson, "Norms for True and False Prophecy in First Corinthians", *American Benedictine Review*, vol. 22, 1971, p. 31, T.M. Crone, *Prophecy*, p. 292 (with reservations), M.E. Hart, *Tongues And Prophecy*, G. Dautzenberg, "Glossolalie", col. 227, and T. Callan, *art.cit.*, p. 140. Hart is aware that the principles Paul lays down for regulating glossolalia apply to the other charismata (and especially prophecy) as well (p. 253), but mistakenly argues for a distinction between ecstatic glossolalia and non-ecstatic prophecy none the less (p. 62). This is incorrect even on her own definition of ecstasy (p. 4), based on the inactivity of the mind of the glossolalist, as the human mind likewise plays no active part in the formulation of prophecy. G. Dautzenberg argues a similar case to Pearson et.al. above, "Glossolalie", cols 227 and 229, but argues with greater caution; T. Callan, *art.cit.*, pp. 137-140, argues the distinction with reference to Greek oracular practice, for which see Chapter 5.

[27] N.I.J. Engelsen, *Glossolalia*, p. 204.

[28] The best survey of options it that of V. Poythress, "The Nature of Corinthian

In what follows I will first summarise the state of the argument up until recent times and present my own conclusion, and then deal separately with the recent major contribution of A. Thiselton.

The established views.

Four basic options and one minority view present themselves. (a) Paul, like Luke, thought of glossolalia as the miraculous ability to speak unlearned human languages.[29] (b) Paul thought of glossolalia as the miraculous ability to speak heavenly or angelic languages. (c) Paul thought of glossolalia as some combination of (a) and (b). (d) Paul thought of glossolalia as a kind of sub- or pre-linguistic form of speech, or possibly as a kind of coded utterance, analogous but not identical to speech. In the latter case it would be articulate, though in modern terms non-linguistic;[30] in the former it would be inarticulate, but none the less capable of conveying some meaning. (e)

Glossolalia: Possible Options", *Westminster Theological Journal*, vol. 40, 1977, pp. 130-135. I have not attempted to give references for all the various points of view here, as virtually all the articles cited in the surrounding discussion may readily be consulted for their positions on this issue as well. The failure to distinguish between what glossolalia actually *may have been* and the way it was *understood* is the major flaw in the otherwise excellent discussions of M.E. Hart (*Tongues And Prophecy*, p. 237ff.) and C.G. Williams (*op.cit.*, pp. 32-3) and, I would argue in the case of Hart, the reason she opts for an "ecstatic speech" view of glossolalia. The recent major contribution to this debate by D.A. Carson, *Showing the Spirit*, came to my attention when this chapter was substantially complete: he and I are in agreement on all but one point, noted below.

[29] We may safely ignore the suggestion of Klein, "The Church and its Prophets", *Anglican Theological Review*, vol. 44, no. 1, January 1962, p. 7, that for Paul "to speak in tongues" is merely a high-sounding description of his own learned ability to speak foreign languages. This kind of rationalisation does not sit well with Paul's statements about the nature of glossolalia as inspired prayer and a revelatory medium. Nor does it really explain why Paul would say that in glossolalia the mind is unfruitful, unless he was distinguishing sharply between his own "speaking in (natural) tongues" and the less prosaic charismatic gifts of the Corinthians - and of this there is no suggestion in the text.

[30] This is the view of Carson, *Showing the Spirit*, pp. 83-86, alluded to in note 28 above. This demands rather more linguistic sophistication of Paul than is reasonable. Carson's view is a very reasonable twentieth century speculation, but I doubt that Paul, without the benefit of a training in modern linguistics, can be expected to conceive of something analogous to language, possessing cognitive content, but of no recognisable linguistic structure. Such concepts were simply not available to him. If this is what glossolalia actually *was*, Paul would almost certainly simply have assumed that it was just a (real) language he did not know. Thus, for example, M. Turner, *art.cit.*, p. 46: "It would have been virtually impossible for Paul to distinguish xenolalic TS (*sc.* tongues speech) from non-xenolalic TS performing a similar function - so he could well simply have lumped together, phenomenologically, what *we* would regard as two distinct types of TS."

Paul thought of glossolalia as (or glossolalia actually was) an idiosyncratic form of language, a kind of dialect for prayer, in which archaic or foreign terms dominated. This suggestion would perhaps make glossolalia an extreme first century equivalent of praying in "King James English".

The following contentions are advanced in favour of (a): the parallel with Luke suggests *a priori* that a miraculous gift of language is intended, as does the closely related terminology. The Greek γλῶσσα, like the English "tongue", can mean little else in this context, and the related gift, "interpretation" (1 Corinthians 12.30, 14.5, 13, etc.), is most naturally understood in its primary sense of (inspired) "translation". Paul's explicit statement, "If I speak in the tongues of men and angels" (13.1) is clearly central here. Likewise important is his argument that "If I do not grasp the meaning of what someone is saying, I am a foreigner (βάρβαρος) to the speaker, and he is a foreigner to me" (14.11). It is further urged that the plain meaning of Paul's quotation from Isaiah 28. 11-12, in ch. 14.20ff., has to do with foreign languages.

Clearly the case in favour of angelic languages also appeals to several of these passages, though 1 Corinthians 13.1a, "the tongues of men", is something of a puzzle, unless it is understood only as a parallel to ch. 14 vv. 7-8, "even in the case of lifeless things that make sounds, such as the flute or harp", and the language metaphor is de-emphasised. This case is usually urged with reference to the belief in divine languages in the Hellenistic world (for which see Chapter 7), or the belief in angelic languages expressed in some Jewish intertestamental works (for which see the Appendix). Those who wish to argue that *only* angelic languages (not some unspecified mixture of angelic and human languages) are what Paul intends his readers to understand are compelled to ignore 1 Corinthians 13.1a, "the tongues of men", or avoid its force by arguing it means non-glossolalic speech. Those who wish to argue in favour of human languages *only* must argue that 13.1b, "and angels", is hyperbole, in parallel with understanding "all mysteries and all knowledge", and surrendering one's body to the flames, in vv. 2-3.

A different case in support of the "angelic language" interpretation is put forward by Earle Ellis. He argues that the repeated use of the term "spirit/s" in 14.12, 14.14, 14.15, 14.16 and 14.32 (and other references) strongly suggests that Paul and the Corinthians believed that spiritual beings mediated prophecy and tongues, which reinforces the case in favour of angelic languages.[31] Ellis correctly points to "a subtle distinction between 'the Spirit of God' and 'every spirit . . . from God'." (p. 32), and brings forward parallels from Qumran and elsewhere. He finds the origin of this "oscillating pattern of thought" (p. 41) in A.R. Johnson's work on *The One and the Many in the Israelite Conception of God*.[32] However, Paul's insistence that the various charismata are the gifts of the (singular) Spirit (1 Cor. 12.4) is hard to fit into this framework. Grudem and Fee suggest an alternative "oscillating pattern", between the human spirits (in the plural) of the various Corinthians and the Spirit (in the singular) at work in various ways in all of them.[33] There is only the finest of lines between these two interpretations. Grudem claims that Ellis cannot produce a single case in Paul where πνεῦμα unambiguously means a *good* spiritual being, and that the theory therefore fails.[34] Ellis might well point to the gift of διακρίσεις πνευμάτων (will *every* spirit fail the test?) and 1 Cor. 14.12, the Corinthian zeal for "spirits". I would tentatively propose that Paul's comment that the Corinthians are ζηλωταί . . . πνευμάτων ought to be taken as an implied critique of their concept of inspiration, and that Paul's own view is probably more clearly described by Grudem and Fee than by Ellis. But the balance is a fine one, and if Ellis is correct, the case in favour of glossolalia being conceived of as including (without being limited to) angelic languages is somewhat strengthened.

The fourth case, sub-linguistic noise, is advanced with reference to 1 Corinthians 13.1c: loveless glossolalia is simply meaningless sound; it is talking "like a child", mere babble (1 Corinthians 13.11); it is spoken to God, not men (14.2) and cannot be understood. It is like the sounds of musical instruments played indistinctly, and is thus inarticulate; it is contrasted with speech "with the mind", for in glossolalia the mind is "unfruitful". It is thus the product of an abnormal mental state. It is argued that Paul's language metaphors ought not to be pressed beyond the sense of

---

[31] E.E. Ellis, *Prophecy and Hermeneutic in Early Christianity*, Grand Rapids, 1978, pp. 29ff.

[32] Cardiff, 1942.

[33] Grudem, *Gift*, p. 128 proposes that the oscillation suggests "manifestations of the Holy Spirit at work in prophets", and argues that "There is a similar willingness to talk about both the one Spirit of God and his plural manifestations in 1 Jn. 4.2 . . ." The 1 John passage is used to the opposite effect by Ellis. G.D. Fee, *The First Epistle to the Corinthians*, Grand Rapids, 1987, pp. 204-5, p. 666, p. 670, p. 696, argues very similarly to Grudem.

[34] W. Grudem, *Gift*, p. 120-122.

verses 7 and 8, "lifeless things that make sounds, such as flutes and harps . . . if the trumpet does not sound a clear call, who will get ready for battle?" Paul's consistent omission of ἕτερος and διάλεκτος from his discussion is taken to indicate that he does not think of glossolalia as linguistic. The gift of "interpretation" must be understood more broadly than in the literal sense of "translation": "explanation" or "interpretation" are suggested as better matching the sense intended by Paul.[35]

The fifth alternative, archaic or idiosyncratic language, though held by few, has its basis in the use of the term γλῶσσα by some ancient authors as "a technical term to designate an archaic language, often used in a cult, and sometimes speech that was incomprehensible like that of the Pythia of Delphi".[36] This suggestion is based on extremely scant evidence. Héring himself cites only three references: Plutarch, *Mor.* 375f, 406e and Quintilian 1.1.35.[37] While it is true that these references suggest that γλῶσσα could be used as a technical term for archaic words or phrases (*not* languages), the suggestion that these were "often used in a cult" is unsupported by any citation of evidence, and I know of no evidence whatever that the term was used of the "unintelligibility" of Delphic utterances. Plutarch clearly states that the oracle no longer uses γλῶσσαι, in the sense of archaic and poetic

---

[35] See S.D. Currie, "Early Evidence", pp. 274-294, and T.W. Gillespie, "A Pattern", p. 81, who argues that "For the analogy (sc. with unclear bugle calls) to hold up in relation to the ecstatic speech of "tongues", the latter must also have an inarticulate character." Cf. pp. 67, 103, 106. A similar suggestion is made by C.G. Williams, *art.cit.*, n.68. For Paul's omission of διάλεκτος and the adjective ἕτερος see M.E. Hart, *Tongues And Prophecy*, p. 237-8. She does not note, however, that Paul *does* use ἑτερογλώσσοις in his quotation of Isaiah in 1 Cor. 14.21.

[36] J. Héring, *op.cit.*, p. 128; the issue is discussed by F.W. Beare, *art.cit.*, p. 243, S.D. Currie, "Early Evidence", pp. 280ff, M.E. Hart, *Tongues And Prophecy*, p. 11, G. Dautzenberg, "Glossolalie", cols 230-231, with varying degrees of support. N. Turner, *op.cit.*, pp. 460-461, makes this usage one of his interpretative keys for understanding the phenomenon. He argues that glossolalia was "a dialect or variety of the Hellenistic Greek language . . . a new dialect which we have called 'Christian Greek', a dialect heavily impregnated with Semitic constructions and vocabulary and not as yet generally understood . . . " (p. 461) Dautzenberg inexplicably argues that this technical grammatical usage, if linked to the concept of heavenly languages in Homer, the "Homeric" Hymn to Apollo, and some Gnostic references, helps us to understand the early Christian terminology. I can see no reasonable link between these very different phenomena at all: see below, Chapters 5 and 7.

[37] It ought to be noted in passing here that the Loeb translation of the Quintilian passage is very inaccurate, confusing the ancient sense of the term "gloss", meaning "archaic term requiring explanation" with the modern sense, "marginal explanation of such a term".

terms, though she once did. But incomprehensibility, in the sense in which glossolalia is incomprehensible, is not under discussion in these passages at all. The Pythia's language may have been archaic and poetic, but it was Greek. For the evidence on this point, and the distinction between oracular ambiguity and glossolalic unintelligibility see, in detail, Chapter 5. Various scholars have found additional uses of the term γλῶσσα with this sense, [38] but the case must be judged to be insufficiently supported to really help us to explain early Christian terminology or ideas. R.H. Gundry is far more correct when he says that "Although γλῶσσα could mean archaic or mysterious (e.g., oracular) expressions, to say that the word became a technical term for such expressions is an overstatement."[39] If the words "(e.g., oracular)" were removed his statement would be unimpeachable. Rather than make the Christian use of the term technical, it is better to argue that both the Hellenistic grammarians and the early Christian writers are drawing on the general sense of the term γλῶσσα, meaning "language", and giving it special connotations. At an exegetical level we ought to note that such "tongues" would need "interpreting" every bit as much as would foreign or angelic languages. However, while glossolalia may have been in fact merely a linguistic oddity on a par with archaism, it would be hard to argue that this is what it was *thought* to be. In what sense would such a gift be thought of as prayer? This proposed explanation does not flow naturally from Paul's discussion of "being a foreigner" in 1 Corinthians 14.10-11, nor from the remainder of his discussion. We will therefore leave this fifth alternative out of contention, and return to the four most widely held views.

Faced with the four conflicting arrays of argument above, we must ask whether one case might be argued so as to subsume the evidence of the others. It would seem to me that the widely held view that Paul must *primarily* mean heavenly languages is implausible, being as it is based heavily on the phrase "and angels" in 1 Corinthians 13.1, which does look like a rhetorical flourish. "Or even those of angels" may well be the sense Paul intended here: clearly his is not really claiming "all mysteries and all

---

[38] H. Conzelmann, *A Commentary on the First Epistle to the Corinthians*, trans. J.W. Leitch, Philadelphia, 1975, p. 234 note 14, adds to this scant evidence Diodorus Siculus 4.66.6, but γλῶσσα in this passage simply means "the organ of speech". Héring and Conzelmann are correct in not placing any interpretative weight on the suggestion. F.W. Beare, *art.cit.*, p. 243 adds to this list Aristotle's Poetics 22a, and M.E. Hart, *Tongues And Prophecy*, p. 11, adds Aristotle, Rhetorica 1410 b 12.

[39] *Art.cit.*, p. 299.

knowledge", or to have sold all that he has. The Jewish parallels for the concept of angelic languages are interesting but not finally convincing (see the Appendix for further discussion), and the theory puts altogether too much weight on one flimsy exegetical peg.[40] Dunn's supporting argument, that "the analogy Paul uses in 14.10f. between glossolalia and foreign

---

[40] Thus, for example, R.H. Gundry, *art.cit.*, p. 301, T.L. Wilkinson, "Tongues and Prophecy in Acts and 1st Corinthians", *Vox Reformata*, No. 31, Nov. 1978, p. 4. This is so, I believe, despite the argument of Dunn that "the subject matter (*sc.* of glossolalia) is the eschatological secrets known only in heaven; so presumably the language used is the language of heaven." (*op.cit.*, p. 244. Dautzenberg argues a similar case, "Glossolalie", cols 227, 234-5.) His logic would, of course, apply equally well to prophecy, but in that case would produce the absurd result that prophets would also have to speak in heavenly languages. As Carson (*Showing the Spirit*, p. 82) points out, Paul several times expresses "mysteries" in straightforward Greek (see Romans 11.25ff, 16.25-26, 1 Corinthians 2.7, 15.51ff, (which, as M. Turner, *art.cit.*, p. 19, correctly notes, is in the chapter which follows this discussion of glossolalia) Ephesians 3.3-9, 5.32, 6.19, Colossians 1.26-27, 2.2, 4.3, 1 Timothy 3.16; whether Paul's usage of the term in this instance must mean "eschatological secrets known only in heaven" will be considered in the next chapter. "Mysteries" (in whatever sense) is not a term that requires us to posit heavenly languages. The suggestion of Barrett, *loc.cit.*, Hart, *Tongues And Prophecy*, p. 243, and D. Hill, *Prophecy*, p. 136, that "the tongues of men and angels" means "in normal human speech and in glossolalia" is more plausible, but still relies far too heavily on the one occurrence of the phrase "and of angels". For the Rabbinic and intertestamental parallels see the Appendix, and the very concise summary of Dautzenberg, "Glossolalie", cols 233-5, who believes angelic languages to be the earliest concept of glossolalia. 2 Corinthians 12.4 and Paul's "unspeakable revelation" are not relevant here, as nothing suggests a special angelic language. The words are ἄρρητα because they are forbidden, not because they are in a secret language. See C.K. Barrett, *A Commentary on the Second Epistle to the Corinthians*, 2nd Edition, London, 1973, p. 311. At least one other early Christian source took up the idea of angelic languages. In the apocryphal "Acts of Paul" (E. Hennecke, *New Testament Apocrypha*, ed. W. Schneemelcher, 1964, E.T. London, 1965, vol. 2, pp. 387-8) a discussion Paul has with an angel while in Ephesus is incomprehensible to those around them, and is later said to be "in tongues". Currie notes, however ("Early Evidence", p. 284), that Chrysostom, who believed angels to be incorporeal, could not have thought that glossolalia would be angelic languages, as these would have been beyond the ability of corporeal humanity to reproduce. Chrysostom's comment (Homilies on 1 Corinthians 32.6-7) that "should I even so speak as angels are wont to discourse unto each other . . ." is made to the effect that even if it were possible to speak to each other in the way angels do, i.e. about the kinds of subjects and in the style which they use, without love it would be useless. His statement seems to me to leave open the possibility that he considered the "or of angels" an hyperbole, though this is not required by his words. Finally, as noted in Chapter 2, R.P. Martin, *The Spirit and the Congregation*, Grand Rapids, 1984, p. 88, suggests that the Corinthian πνευματικοί may have believed themselves to be already some form of angelic beings, and hence viewed their glossolalia as angelic languages. This hypothesis must remain purely speculative, however, as Martin provides no evidence or argument to support it.

language cannot be taken as evidence that Paul thought of glossolalia as foreign language" (a very similar suggestion is made by C.G. Williams, *Tongues of the Spirit*, Cardiff, 1981, p. 31) seems to me entirely false. Foreign languages, or, more precisely, the *miraculous ability* to speak foreign languages otherwise unknown to the speaker (the analogy, *pace* Williams, is not mere redundancy) is *precisely* what it suggests. It is true that one does not draw analogies between like phenomena, but between unlike; Paul is comparing naturally known languages with what he sees as special gifts of languages. Our two main contenders are unlearned human languages, as in Luke (and *perhaps* angelic languages *as well*), and inarticulate speech.

Here I think the weight of argument inclines to the side of the "languages" interpretation. The common "inarticulate speech" view may be able to explain Paul's reference to speakers in different languages as being foreigners one to another as mere metaphor, like the reference to musical instruments. But the reference to "tongues of men" in 1 Corinthians 13.1 can hardly be so explained, and if it is allowed to remain, the presumption must be strong that Paul's reference to speakers of mutually foreign languages implies that foreign languages were what he thought glossolalists spoke. The point of the comparison with unclear bugle calls then becomes their failure to communicate, rather than simply their lack of clarity. Further, this interpretation is quite capable of taking up the positive points made in favour of the "inarticulate speech" view. Glossolalic languages spoken without love - that is, in an inconsiderate and arrogant fashion, as proof of spiritual achievement - might as well be just noise for all the good they do to the community.[41] The reference to speaking "like a child" (ch. 13.11) need not

---

[41] This point disposes of the objection of A.C. Thiselton, "Interpretation", pp. 30-31, that Paul would hardly have criticised the use of the miraculous ability to speak foreign languages. If this was done for show, or to prove a certain level of maturity, Paul would in all likelihood treat it exactly like even the greatest prophetic powers exercised without love. Perhaps there is a polemical reference here to the din of the Mystery cults, for which see Chapter 6, but the alternative view which suggests that the metaphor of gongs and cymbals is one used of popular (but vacuous) rhetorical teachers has much in its favour. It is probably significant, for example, that Paul says that if his tongue is uttered without love, *he* becomes nothing more than the equivalent of a gong or cymbal. This suggests the rhetorical metaphor ("I am just making a lot of noise") rather than that derived from the Mysteries ("my speech becomes the equivalent of pagan ceremonial instruments, it is meaningless"). See K.L. Schmidt, in *T.D.N.T.*, vol. 3, E.T. 1965, pp. 1037-1039, footnote 10, and the literature there cited; for the use to describe teachers

refer to glossolalia, and the view that glossolalic prayer is unintelligible, and directed towards God, not men, could accord well enough with either view.

Likewise, the fact that in glossolalia "my mind is unfruitful" (14.14) makes perfect sense either way, for it is quite clear that Paul does not think that the glossolalist normally understands his own utterance. Otherwise there would be no need for him to pray for such understanding (14.13). Nor is this verse clear evidence for a trance-like state: that the mind is unfruitful does not necessarily mean that it is unconscious. The fact that "The contrast to γλώσσαις λαλεῖν is not speech ἰδίᾳ διαλέκτῳ but rather speech ἐν τῷ νοΐ" (14.15) is likewise ambiguous: the emphasis in Paul's argument is on intelligibility and the participation of the human mind in the process of glossolalia, and this concern can be equally accommodated by either the "languages" or the "ecstatic speech" view.[42] Finally, the argument that the verse "where there are tongues, they will be stilled" rules out the "languages" interpretation cannot be sustained. Paul is not claiming that languages as such will cease at the consummation, any more than he is claiming that knowledge will cease. He is arguing that specific charismatic *gifts* of languages, like specific endowments of prophecy and knowledge, will cease as perfection comes and the imperfect is swallowed up.[43]

On the basis of these arguments I am confident that Paul, like Luke, understands glossolalia as the miraculous ability to speak unlearned human and (possibly) divine or angelic languages. There is little in the argument that is new. Very recently, however, a profound challenge to this view of

---

see, for example, Plato, Protagoras 329 a, and Pliny, N.H. Preface 25, where Pliny cites Tiberius Caesar's description of Apion as the "cymbalum mundi"; Pliny adds his own comment to the effect that the man might have been better described as a drum. Presumably he means that drums are hollow. "Dodonite" gongs provided excellent material for the metaphor: they rang for several minutes after being struck, Strabo 7, fragment 3. The two senses of the "gongs and cymbals" metaphor are sometimes combined. See also the recent and intriguing suggestion of W.W. Klein, "Noisy Gong or Acoustic Vase? A Note on 1 Corinthians 13.1", *N.T.S.*, vol. 32, 1986, pp. 286-289.

[42] For the contrast between glossolalia and speech "with the mind" see M.E. Hart, *Tongues And Prophecy*, p. 231. The question as to for whom the mind is unfruitful (the glossolalist or his/her fellow-Christians) is discussed by T.L. Wilkinson, *art.cit.*, p. 4-5, and Hart, p. 230, where the contrast between unfruitfulness and unconsciousness is also noted.

[43] The suggestion is that of N.I.J. Engelsen, *Glossolalia*, p. 203. W.G. MacDonald, *art.cit.*, p. 67 adds the point that Paul uses the same Greek word for the five intelligible words he might speak for edification and the ten thousand words he might speak in a tongue.

glossolalia has been thrown down by A. Thiselton. His argument does offer a new approach to the question, and deserves careful and detailed treatment.

Thiselton's challenge

What Thiselton attempts to show is that one of the main supports of the "languages" interpretation, the relationship between glossolalia and the complementary gift of "interpretation", may have been seriously misconceived by modern authors.[44] Whereas scholars such as Dunn have argued that "we have to consider the basic meaning of the word (ἑρμηνεύειν) in wider Greek thought -viz., 'to interpret, expound, explain' ",[45] Thiselton contends that the words used could well mean "to articulate" or "to put into words" something that was previously inarticulate: to take inchoate or unexpressed feelings or ideas, and to give them articulate linguistic form.

This conclusion is based on a detailed analysis of the use of the various ἑρμηνεύω terms in Philo and Josephus. It must be admitted immediately that there are a reasonable number of cases in which Thiselton is correct: ἑρμηνεύω, διερμηνεύω etc. clearly can take the meaning he suggests. But as Thiselton will also admit, there are a large number of cases where "to translate" or "to interpret or expound" is the translation required. In the case of 1 Corinthians 12-14 only contextual considerations can decide for us. Thiselton's argument, then, must be discussed at two levels: the philological and the contextual/exegetical. The philological must be dealt with first.

Thiselton's philological argument

Thiselton suggests that "no less than three-quarters of the uses (sc. of the term διερμηνεύω and διερμήνευσις in Philo) refer to the articulation of thoughts or feelings in intelligible speech" and that, by contrast, "the passages in Philo in which διερμηνεύω means 'to translate' do so in a thoroughly obvious and straightforward way".[46] What Thiselton does not say is that if one includes all the various ἑρμηνεύω terms *without* the διά prefix as well, the statistics are turned round fairly radically. Thiselton's narrowing of the case in his emphasis on the terms with the διά prefix is unsound. Philo's terminology may permit a differentiation between the two groups of terms in his writings, but there is certainly insufficient evidence for us to

---

[44] A.C. Thiselton, "Interpretation", pp. 15-36.
[45] J.D.G. Dunn, *op.cit.*, p. 247.
[46] A.C. Thiselton, "Interpretation", p. 18, p. 20.

argue that Paul makes any such distinction. (Compare, for example, 1 Cor. 12.10 and 30.) To develop a case for a Pauline parallel we really must include ἑρμηνεύω, etc. in our discussion as well. When we do so, we find that of some 240 uses of the terminology in Philo, 144 obviously and straightforwardly mean "to translate" or "to interpret / explain / expound". Most of these cases are of the form "Such and such (usually the name of a Biblical character or place), being interpreted, means . . ." Thirteen of these cases include the use of the verb μεταλαμβάνω, Philo's other regular term for linguistic translation, and several include phrases such as "in our language" or "in the Greek language". The word is used thirty times in similar contexts, and its meaning in these cases is not in doubt.[47] Clearly, by ἑρμηνεύω Philo must mean something in the range between "to translate" and "to interpret, expound". This usage is far and away the most common in Philo. In eight other cases the straightforward use of a translator between speakers of different languages is indicated by the terms.[48]

In other words, some 60% of Philo's usage of the terms does not support Thiselton's case. Further, not even all the cases claimed by Thiselton can be shown to support his contention. De Sobrietate 33, "Let us . . . expound in full the inward interpretation" (διερμηνεύσωμεν) can only mean "expound", de Vita Mosis 2.34 appears to mean "to translate", and Quis Rerum 63 means "to explain/expound".[49] There is even one particularly striking case (not quoted by Thiselton) in which ἑρμηνεύω cannot by any stretch of the imagination mean "to articulate": de Vita Mosis 84 has the verb ἀρθρωθήσεται for "to become articulate" - God says to Moses that "at a sign from me all will become articulate . . . and if thou shouldst have need of an interpreter (ἑρμενεύς) . . . " then one will be provided. It is apparent that

---

[47] References: In parallel with ἑρμηνεύω or similar: Leg. Alleg. 3.93, de Plantatione 134, de Ebrietate 145, de Migratione 165, de Fuga 44, 45, 208, de Mutatione 98, de Somniis 2.36, 2.192.

    With reference to translation into or out of particular languages: de Sobrietate 28, de Somniis 2.250, de Abrahamo 201, de Praemiis 14.

    On its own: de Posteritate 69, de Migratione 205, 221, Quis Rerum 54, 97, de Congressu 2, 30, 55, 60, de Fuga 50, de Mutatione 92, 103, 106, 126, 193, de Somniis 1.254.

[48] de Iosepho 175, de Vita Mosis 27, 31, 34, 40 (twice), 41, and Legatione ad Gaium 4.

[49] These references are among those listed without citation by Thiselton, "Interpretation", p. 19. There remain a number of cases, some 25 by my count, in which the sense suggested by Thiselton is possible, but not positively required by the context.

even once things have *become* articulate, one might still need a ἑρμενεύς! Clearly the sense that is required here is "mediator".[50]

When we turn to Josephus the picture is less complex. For a start, Josephus does not use the terms with the διά prefix at all. Secondly, he only uses the ἑρμηνεύω terms twenty-four times in all, and in virtually all cases his meaning is clear. In fifteen cases the terms mean to translate, translator or translation.[51] In three others it means to expound or explain.[52] In one it means mediator in the most general sense,[53] and in three it means to express or to put into words.[54] In one case the meaning is uncertain: in Jewish War 7.455 it may mean "express" or "render into Greek".[55] But this one case does not really make much of a difference. Clearly the overwhelming sense of the terminology in Josephus is the linguistic sense.

---

[50] Josephus, Antiquities 12.11, 12.39, 12.49, 12.87, 12.104 (twice), 12.106, 12.107 (twice), 12.108 (twice), 12.114, 18.197, Jewish War 6.327, Against Apion 2.46. Though Thiselton is correct to say that the great majority of these references do come from Book 12, and the account of the translation of the O.T. Scriptures ("Interpretation", p. 25), it is not clear to me how this lessens their importance as counter-examples to his case. They still constitute the majority usage of the terminology.

[51] We should also note a number of other cases in which the terminology of articulation is used in Philo: de Fuga 22 describes the noise of drums as ἀνάρθρων and meaningless (ἀλόγων). says: "In articulate sound (ἐνάρθρου φωνῆς), moreover, an advantage possessed by man alone of all living creatures, there are particulars of which we are aware; as, for example, that it is sent up from the understanding, that it is in the mouth that it acquires articulation (ἀρθροῦται), that it is the beat or stroke of the tongue that imparts articulation (τὸ ἔναρθρον . . . ἐνσφραγίζεται) and speech to the tension of the voice, but does not produce simply just an idle sound and unshapen (ἀδιατύπωτον) noise since it holds to the suggesting mind the office of its herald and interpreter (κήρυκος ἢ ἑρμηνέως: mediator) . . ." de Vita Mosis 2.164 describes the φωνῆς ἀνάρθρου καὶ ἀσήμου of the crowds around Sinai. Significantly, in de Praem. 2 "the Ten Commandments were not delivered through a ἑρμενεύς but were (none the less, C.F.) shaped high in the air into the form of articulate speech (σχηματιζόμενα καὶ ἄρθρωσιν ἔχοντα λογικήν)". Note that in each case it is sound, not thoughts, that are inarticulate and must be given meaningful form. For Paul, glossolalia is neither thoughts nor noise that must be articulated, but language that must be interpreted. Whereas some noises are meaningless, like the noise of drums, above, no language is meaningless (1 Cor. 14.10), even if it is not currently understood.

[52] Josephus, Antiquities 1.29, 2.72, 6.156, 20.264.

[53] Josephus, Antiquities 3.87: this is the one case where I find myself disagreeing with Thiselton's interpretation. He argues that Moses must be understood as putting into words the revelation of God, but I see no necessity for this. The passage can quite readily be understood in terms of simple mediation.

[54] Josephus, Antiquities 6.230, Jewish War 5.182, 5.393.

[55] Thiselton, "Interpretation", p. 26.

Thiselton's philological case concludes with a brief collection of citations from classical and Hellenistic authors, cases where the terms can mean "to put into words". That the terms can mean this is not in dispute, and Thiselton is to be thanked for pointing it out so clearly. The real question here is whether he is correct when he says that "the thought of 1 Cor. XIV is far closer to the contexts in Josephus [and Philo, C.F.] which concern communication as such, rather than those which relate to routine matters about translation . . ."[56] To that question of contextual exegesis we now turn.

Thiselton's exegesis

We must now ask whether Thiselton has anything new to add to the well-trodden ways of the debate on the exegesis of 1 Corinthians 12-14. The exegetical arguments he uses to support his philological point are as follows. First, Thiselton is quite correct to argue, with Stendahl, that the Pentecostal tongues of Acts 2 cannot be allowed to dominate our interpretation totally.[57] They are unique in that they are the only known case in which glossolalia was recognised as foreign languages by native speakers of those languages. The situation in Corinth is obviously different. But his second point, that it would be quite astonishing if the early church possessed a gift of miraculously speaking foreign languages and showed so little interest in the fact as not to discuss it beyond our one or two references, is not nearly so strong. It holds only if glossolalia *actually was* the gift of foreign languages, *and* was commonly noted to be so by native speakers of those languages. If it was rather, as Dunn has suggested, some form of "sub-linguistic" behaviour of the sort commonly (but erroneously) described as "ecstatic speech", which was mistakenly understood by the early Christians to be foreign languages, *or* was actually a gift of foreign languages, but not generally ones known by those present, then the point loses all its force. Naturally, though glossolalists would believe they spoke unlearned human languages, they would never be able either to verify or disprove their belief, and the point would not become a major one in the church's apologetic.[58] It

---

[56] *Ibid.* It ought to be noted in passing that there is no objection in principle to Thiselton's conception of prophetic or glossolalic inspiration as the articulation of non-verbal revelation: a very similar concept is to be found Plutarch, Mor. 589c, in his discussion of Socrates' δαίμων.

[57] Thiselton, "Interpretation", p. 28, citing K. Stendahl, *art.cit.*, p. 117.

[58] J.D.G. Dunn, *Jesus and the Spirit*, London, 1975, pp. 148-152. Dunn is here discussing the events of Acts 2, but the point is equally applicable to our question. The suggestion that Paul would never have criticised an actual gift of foreign languages, due

should also be noted that Thiselton's point is weak from another perspective: it is quite clear that Irenaeus (and Chrysostom) *did* believe that glossolalia, which was still common occurrence in churches known to him, was the miraculous gift of foreign languages.[59]

Thiselton's next point, that if glossolalia is the speaking of foreign languages unknown (in human terms) to the speaker, it is hard to tell in what sense he "edifies himself", is an important one. It raises the question of the function of glossolalia within the individual devotional life of the Christian,

---

to their evangelistic value, is also made by E. Best, "The Interpretation of Tongues", *S.J.Th.*, vol. 28, no. 1, 1975, p. 47. Best goes on to argue that such a gift could hardly have been described as speaking "to God alone" (1 Corinthians 14.2). But the same point applies. If it was normal that the "tongue" in question was not recognised, Paul's comment is perfectly comprehensible. Thus also M. Turner, *art.cit.*, p. 18.

[59] Irenaeus, Adversus Haereses 5.6.1, Chrysostom, Homily 29. Currie makes a similar error when he presumes that the fact that Peter needs an interpreter (Mark) proves he could not commonly have spoken in tongues. For a more detailed discussion of the question of the persistence of glossolalia within early Christianity see below. Thiselton's second point in this argument, citing Origen's debate with Celsus about prophecy in late second-century Palestine, suggesting that early Christian sources understood glossolalia as some form of pre-linguistic babble, is also weak. It is not at all certain that these "prophets" were either Christian, or glossolalic. For a fuller discussion of this matter see Chapter 7. If "the most that can be offered" to support the 'languages' interpretation is "Irenaeus, Chrysostom, and perhaps the longer ending of Mark" (Thiselton, "Interpretation", p. 29), then we must simply note that this is the great bulk of the patristic evidence about the nature of speaking in tongues anyway, and that no other theory is offered by our sources. To Thiselton's list ought to be added Origen, who, in his Commentary on Romans 1.13, argued that Paul felt under an obligation to all nations because he had received the gift to speak all their languages. That he is referring to glossolalia cannot be doubted, as he cites Paul's "I thank God that I speak in tongues more than you all" in support of his view. So far as I am aware, *no* ancient writer drove a wedge between Acts 2 and 1 Corinthians 12-14; they presumed the phenomena were the same. Again citing Currie ("Early Evidence", pp. 290-291), Thiselton suggests that in his description of Marcus Gnosticus Irenaeus may be reflecting on glossolalia, suggesting it to be "a meaningless babble of sounds, a random vocalisation, or 'lalling' " (Thiselton, "Interpretation" p. 29). Currie says: "it could easily be confused with the sort of charlatanry which Irenaeus describes or with the practice of sorcery and magic." ("Early Evidence" p. 292.) It is therefore to be noted that *Irenaeus* does not confuse the two: it is not he who introduces glossolalia into the discussion of Marcus, but Currie and Thiselton. I repeat, our sources do not suggest any understanding of glossolalia other than that they are unknown, but real, languages. The suggestion of M.E. Hart (*Tongues And Prophecy*, p. 234), that Tertullian did not believe glossolalia to be human languages, but rather a form of "ecstatic speech", is not supported by any citation of evidence, and seems to be a presumption based on his Montanist position. As we shall see in the next chapter, Tertullian had things to say about glossolalia before he turned to Montanism.

and within the congregation more generally. Paul does seem to think of the phenomenon separately in these two differing contexts, and ascribe to it two differing functions. For the individual it is described as a form of prayer; for the group it is a revelatory medium. But this point requires detailed elaboration, which must be postponed to the next chapter.

Thiselton's final point, citing J.C. Hurd, is that Paul would hardly describe a gift of speaking foreign languages as one of the "childish ways" which were to be given up with maturity (1 Cor. 13.11). But it seems to me most unlikely that glossolalia is the point of this statement. Paul has not given it up; he is willing to argue that he speaks in tongues more than all the Corinthians put together! (14.18) What is described as childish, and contrasted with maturity, here, is not glossolalia but the whole state of Christian existence before "the perfect comes". Nor is it useful to refer here to 14.20 ("Brothers, stop thinking like children"), as it is precisely the *thinking* of the Corinthians about glossolalia's value, rather than the phenomenon itself, which is under discussion.[60]

Thiselton's contextual arguments, then, are finally no more persuasive than his lexicographical ones. While he has shown that it is possible that the ἑρμηνεύω terminology in Paul *might* be understood as meaning "to articulate", he has not shown that this is the most common meaning of the terms in Philo and Josephus. Nor has he been able to show that contextual considerations force us to adopt this meaning.

The use of the terms in Philo and Josephus is also different from Paul's in other important ways. In Philo and Josephus the ἑρμηνεύω terminology is independent: the object of the verb may be a text such as a Biblical passage, or an inarticulate thought; the noun may designate a linguist, an intermediary more generally, or simply someone explaining something. In Paul it is always the interpretation *of tongues* that is discussed. Thus in Paul the meaning of "interpretation" cannot be separated from the meaning of the γλῶσσαι to be interpreted.[61] Thiselton has the cart before the horse here: general lexicographical considerations ought not to be allowed to dominate immediate, contextual exegesis - especially when lexicography itself provides an alternative, and more exegetically suitable, meaning for ἑρμηνεύω anyway. Naturally, this leads us back to the question of the

---

[60] Thus, correctly, J.P.M. Sweet, "A Sign for Unbelievers", *N.T.S.*, vol. 13, 1966, p. 256, and W.E. Mills, *op.cit.*, p. 100.

[61] This point is also made by M. Turner, *art.cit.*, p. 19.

nature of glossolalia itself. We have seen that there are no insuperable objections against the view that glossolalia was uniformly understood within early Christianity to be the miraculous ability to use a language which one did not know. The terms used for the gift of interpretation are quite consistent with this, as their normal range of meaning includes "to translate", "to explain" and "to expound".

Finally we may return briefly to the question of the differences of outlook between Luke and Paul with respect to the phenomena of glossolalia. These do not show that Luke's view is secondary, a misunderstanding of phenomena similar to those described by Paul. But what do they show?

First, we know very little about Luke's view of glossolalia outside of Pentecost, which all agree was a special case. That Peter said that Cornelius' household received the Holy Spirit "just as we did" is fairly limited as an argument - there were substantial differences (the lack of sounds like mighty winds, the lack of tongues of fire, the absence of multi-lingual communication) between the accounts along with the similarities noted above, and it is not clear what similarities Luke may have wanted us to see between the experiences, beyond the basic fact of the common reception of the Spirit.

Secondly, that Luke and Paul chose to use essentially the same terminology to describe the phenomena must mean either that they none the less perceived an underlying unity, or that they were willing to include a variety of phenomena within the one terminological category. Paul's tantalising mention of "different kinds of tongues" (1 Cor. 12.10) suggests as much, but gives us nothing on which to build further.

One final question must be answered. As years went by, and, as far as we know, no-one after Pentecost ever "naturally" understood glossolalia, is it not likely that it would come to be seen as a separate category - not really human languages, but some special category of (perhaps heavenly) language, or as language only in some metaphorical sense? And might this not be behind the mixture of metaphors, susceptible (so it might be argued) to more than one interpretation, that Paul uses in 1 Cor. 12-14?[62]

---

[62] Such a suggestion is advanced by C.G. Williams, *op.cit.*, p. 27, where he argues that "St. Paul could employ the terms γλῶσσα and ἑρμηνεύω to indicate a new kind of 'tongue' and a new kind of 'translating' . . . " This suggestion might provide an exegetical basis for the case of D.A. Carson, referred to in note 30, above.

While *a priori* this suggestion is very attractive, and it is clear that glossolalia *was* seen in some sense as a separate category of speech, none the less the theory founders on the near-total lack of evidence that anybody did take such a step. Within early Christianity only the "Acts of Paul" cited in note 40 above (and the Testament of Job, if it has undergone a Christian redaction) even takes up the "angelic languages" interpretation, and they may well be dependent on 1 Corinthians for this concept. As we shall see in the next chapter, there is little or no evidence that anyone within early Christianity doubted that glossolalia was unlearned human languages, despite the apparent lack of corroborative evidence.

4. The Original Form of the Terminology

With this issue of the nature of the phenomena settled, we may return to the question of the terminology of "speaking in tongues". Our original question was: which of the three forms of the terminology is likely to have given rise to the other two? Is the Pauline "to speak in tongues" original, or is it a shortened form of the Lukan "to speak in other tongues"?[63] Or is it possible that we must treat all of them as equally "original", and thus simply as alternatives? Opinion on this matter has been long divided, as the survey of Harrisville demonstrates.

In my view the most important point to be made here is that the Lukan form of the terminology used in the Pentecost account is immediately understandable, whereas the Pauline and Markan forms are not. Ἑτερόγλωσσαις λαλεῖν means simply "to speak in other languages", and though it is technical terminology its meaning is plain, and in full agreement with the general sense of the passage, and with the uniform understanding of glossolalia throughout the early church. We must therefore consider whether there are any factors which, along with the simple familiarity of long usage,

---

[63] Insofar as I am aware, no-one is suggesting that the Markan form of the terminology is in any sense original. S. Tugwell (*art.cit.*, p. 138), citing Cranfield, is quite correct to point to the theological motive behind the addition of "new": the eschatological newness of salvation leads to the call to "sing a new song" in Revelation 14.3, and the same idea seems to be present in Mark 16. M.E. Hart takes the suggestion further by pointing out that καινός can mean "new" or "strange": "If understood as 'strange', the reference may be to unlearned human languages; if 'new', one may think either of ecstatic utterances or of language representative of a new age." (*Tongues And Prophecy*, pp. 40-1.) See also C.E.B. Cranfield, *The Gospel according to St. Mark*, Cambridge, 1963, p. 474, and V. Taylor, *The Gospel according to St. Mark*, 2nd edition, London, 1966, p. 612.

might facilitate the shortening and formalising of the terminology into the Pauline form.

I noted above, in Footnote 6 of this chapter, that several passages of the Septuagint may have suggested themselves to the early Christians as reminiscent of their experience of glossolalia. As was also noted, Nils Engelsen has argued that "the most reasonable background for the technical term seems to be the poetic, half-metaphorical use of γλῶσσα in Old Testament sources."[64] The examples of this which are most suggestive for our purposes are as follows: Psalm 118/9, v.172, "Let my tongue utter your oracles . . ."; Zephaniah 3.9, "For then I will turn to the peoples a tongue for her generation, that all may call on the name of the Lord, to serve him under one yoke", a passage which might easily have been linked with the Pentecost account; Psalm 36.30, "The mouth of the righteous will meditate on wisdom, and his tongue will speak of judgement"; and most importantly, Sirach 51.22, "The Lord has given me a tongue with which I shall sing his praises." (Jerusalem Bible.) These two last passages seem to have some affinity with Luke's concept that glossolalia involved "telling of the marvellous works of God".

It must be admitted immediately that there is no proof that these passages did occur to the earliest Christians as they gave a name to their shared experience of glossolalia, but they may have served to ease the path of the shorter, more compressed form of the terminology to which Paul witnesses.

While these passages may or may not strengthen the presumption that the Pauline terminology is an ellipsis, it is not easy to see how that shorter Pauline form could qualify as original. Its meaning is not clear, and it is not at all easy to see what would suggest it, other than the Lukan form. Of course, if the Pauline "to speak in tongues" were once established, it is relatively easy to see how the Lukan form, "to speak in other tongues", might develop as an explanation of the more cryptic Pauline form. But given that our evidence shows that the early church had no other explanation of glossolalia than that it was the miraculous ability to speak unlearned languages, it is far easier to see how the form of the terminology to which Luke witnesses might have originated, and then been shortened by common usage, than it is to see what would have suggested the shorter Pauline form "ex nihilo", whether this is conceived of as happening alongside the

---

[64] N.I.J. Engelsen, *Glossolalia*, p. ii.

development of the Lukan form, or in its absence. Given also that (as we shall see in the following chapters), no origin for either the terminology or the phenomena of glossolalia outside of early Christianity can be substantiated, we must argue that the form of the terminology used by Luke has the greatest claim to represent truly primitive Christian usage.

Chapter 4

Glossolalia in Early Christianity: History and Theology

Having disposed of the main issues of terminology and of the question of the linguistic nature of glossolalia as it was understood and practised within the early Christian churches, we are now in a position to consider other related questions. We must ask about the extent of the phenomenon in both space and time. In order to understand the functions and status of glossolalia within early Christian experience we must inquire further about the complementary "gift" of interpretation, and about the link between these two related phenomena and early Christian prophecy. This will finally lead to the related question of the controversy between Paul and the Corinthian congregation on the subject of glossolalia.

1. The extent of glossolalia within the early churches

The question of how widespread glossolalia was within the churches of the first century has been given very different answers by different scholars. Those who, like J.P.M. Sweet, believe it to have been a Palestinian phenomenon characteristic of the early Jewish churches, often suggest that its spread was extremely limited.[1] Those who see its origins as being in the Hellenistic world,

---

[1] J.P.M. Sweet, "A Sign for Unbelievers: Paul's Attitude to Glossolalia", *N.T.S.*, vol. 13, 1966-7, pp. 240-57, argues that "this and similar phenomena are Asiatic in origin, not Greek . . . Paul treats them as something *new* - the fact that he (Paul) can thank God he outdoes them all suggests that the practice had not yet reached imposing proportions" (in Corinth, p. 246). Though Sweet's argument is confined to Corinth it seems to me to be mistaken. Paul's "more than all of you" in 1 Cor. 14.18 proves little about the incidence of glossolalia in Corinth. It is a typically Pauline flamboyance - see K. Stendahl, "Glossolalia and the Charismatic Movement", *God's Christ and His People*, ed. J. Jervell and W. Meeks, Oslo, 1977, pp. 122-3 - and tells us more about Paul than about the Corinthians.

on the other hand, often suggest that it was widespread both within the early churches and beyond them.[2]

Those who believe Luke's account of Pentecost to be basically unhistorical also commonly argue that this means that Paul's comments in 1 Corinthians are the only reliable evidence for the phenomenon in first-century Christianity,[3] and that its spread may have been very limited indeed. Between these basic points of view are a variety of intermediate views.

For reasons related to modern theological concerns, the two related issues of the geographical and chronological extent of glossolalia have too often been separated. Some scholars have only been concerned with "Biblical" evidence, and have ruled out of court the "secondary" longer ending of Mark. It has not often been pointed out that if the "longer ending" is secondary, then it is clear evidence for the survival of glossolalia into the second century. The point to be made is this: our attitude to the evidence for the chronological distribution of glossolalia will determine how widely we believe it to have been distributed geographically. If the Patristic evidence for glossolalia is to be minimised, that will also minimise the geographical area involved.

I have already indicated, in the previous chapter, that I do not believe that Luke's view of the phenomena of glossolalia ought to be dismissed as secondary. Rather it should be treated as a legitimate and, in some ways, complementary view to that of Paul. There seems no good reason to deny that glossolalia was associated with the very earliest days of the churches' existence. There is, however, no other incontrovertible New Testament evidence for glossolalia outside 1 Corinthians. To argue that this shows that the practice was either unknown or very rare, except in Corinth, is not justified. There is likewise no Pauline evidence outside 1 Corinthians for the practice of the Lord's Supper, but no-one suggests that it was not practised in the other Pauline churches. The post-Apostolic evidence which we are about to examine

---

[2] Typical of this point of view is Engelsen, *Glossolalia*, p. 23, where he argues that glossolalia and similar phenomena are "pan-human", and can be detected across a multitude of human cultures. G. Dautzenberg, "Glossolalie", cols 229-235, believes analogies may be traced in both Jewish and Hellenistic culture, but does not particularise further.

[3] Thus, for example, R.H. Fuller, "Tongues in the New Testament", *American Church Quarterly*, no. 3, 1963, pp. 162-8, F.W. Beare, "Speaking with Tongues: a Critical Survey of the New Testament Evidence", *J.B.L.*, vol. 83, part 3, 1964, pp. 229-246.

makes it quite clear that the practice was indeed fairly widespread. We must therefore assume that, like the Lord's Supper, it only became a matter for Paul to treat when, in Corinth, it became a contentious issue for the congregation.

The origin of the "longer ending" of Mark's gospel is a matter of some dispute among scholars.[4] The one clear datum is that it was an accepted part of the text by the time it was quoted by Irenaeus in his Adversus Haereses, 3.10.6. Whether it originates in the 50's or 60's of the first century, with the Gospel itself, or nearly a century later, must be left uncertain.[5] What it is, however, is a clear and independent witness to a belief within at least some of the early Christian churches that something akin to glossolalia ought to characterise the missionary movement of the Church, as one of the "signs" of those who believe. *Pace* D.M. Smith, the passage is too different in style and content to be likely to be dependent on 1 Corinthians 12-14 or Acts 2, but beyond that it provides us with insufficient evidence to say much that is constructive. The eschatological tone of the adjective καινός has been commented on in footnote 1 of Chapter 3.

Some scholars have laid much weight on the silence of Clement, Polycarp, Justin Martyr, Ignatius of Antioch, "Barnabas", Hermas, the writers to Diognetus and of the Didache, and have argued that any phenomenon which is never mentioned by any of these writers cannot have been significant in immediate post-Apostolic Christianity. Particular weight is given to the failure of Justin Martyr to discuss glossolalia by C.L. Rogers and G.W. Dollar. They argue that since in Dialogue with Trypho 39 Justin's subject is the transfer of all the gifts of the Holy Spirit once held by the Jewish people to the new "People

---

[4] The discussion of Hart, *Tongues And Prophecy*, pp. 39-41, surveys some recent debate on the matter. See also the commentaries of C.E.B. Cranfield, V. Taylor and W. Lane, D.M. Smith, "Glossolalia and Other Spiritual Gifts in New Testament Perspective", *Interpretation*, vol. 28, 1974, pp. 307-320, argues that the passage "probably indicates that glossolalia continued into the second century" (p. 315). S.D. Currie, "Speaking in Tongues: Early Evidence Outside the New Testament Bearing on *Glōssais Lalein*", *Interpretation*, vol. 19, 1965, p. 277) argues briefly that it may have been known to Justin Martyr, c. A.D. 150. The Markan "καιναῖς" is discussed by Cranfield, p. 474, and Taylor, p. 612.

[5] The suggestion that the passage may have been written by one Aristion around A.D. 100 is based only on the evidence of one tenth-century manuscript, and must be treated as very doubtful. It may have been known as early as Justin Martyr's First Apology, where, in 45.5, v.9 of Mark 16 seems to be alluded to.

of God", it is particularly significant that glossolalia is completely omitted from the discussion. But this argument from silence is distinctly vulnerable. As H. Hunter points out, it presupposes that Justin is working with the list of 1 Corinthians 12 in mind. Hunter argues persuasively that Justin's case is based around an exposition of Isaiah 11.1-3, where (naturally) glossolalia is not mentioned. Not only so, but Rogers himself explicitly notes that Justin's discussion is limited to "the gifts formerly among your nation" (p. 137). Since the Old Testament mentions no glossolalic gift in ancient Israel, the topic naturally falls outside Justin's brief, and the case of Rogers and Dollar loses much of its force.[6] The further argument that glossolalia is a perfect apologetic argument for Christianity despite the lack of Old Testament precedent is also weak. Neither Luke nor Paul describes glossolalia as having any apologetic value, either to Jews or Gentiles, and Paul is quite explicit in 1 Corinthians 14 that it ought not to be practised (uninterpreted?) in situations where unbelievers are likely to be present. With such considerations before him, it is hardly likely that Justin would make apologetic use of the phenomenon.

The more general arguments of Rogers and Dollar about the silence of the Patristic writers may only be maintained if that silence is maintained. Hence the evidence of Irenaeus, to which we now turn, is particularly critical.

Commenting on the phenomenon in question, Irenaeus writes as follows:

> Therefore the Apostle says, "We speak wisdom among the perfect", calling "perfect" those who have received the Spirit of God and speak in all tongues (omnibus linguis loquuntur) through the Spirit just as he himself spoke. In the same way we also hear [or: have also heard] many brethren in the church having prophetic gifts and speaking through the Spirit in all tongues (universis linguis loquentes, παντοδαπαῖς λαλούντων διὰ τοῦ πνεύματος γλώσσαις) and bringing to light men's secrets for the common good and explaining mysteries of God. Such persons the Apostle calls "spiritual".[7]

[6] G.W. Dollar, "Church History and the Tongues Movement", *Bib. Sac.*, vol. 120, October 1963, pp. 316-321, C.L. Rogers, "The Gift of Tongues in the Post-Apostolic Church", *Bib. Sac.*, vol. 122, part 486, 1965, pp. 134-43. See also S.D. Currie, *art.cit.* p. 281. Better in terms of the breadth of material cited is H.H. Hunter, "Tongues-Speech: a Patristic Analysis", *J.E.Th.S.*, vol. 23, part 2, 1980, pp. 125-137, esp. pp. 127-8.

[7] The first half of the passage exists only in Latin: the second half, from "in the same way" exists both in Greek, in Eusebius, H.E. 5.7.6., and in Latin, in Adversus Haereses 5.6.1. The only significant difference between the two versions is that where the Greek has the present tense ἀκούομεν, "we hear", that Latin has the perfect audivimus, "we have heard". Any attempt to use this distinction to argue that Irenaeus does not regard the phenomenon as current in his own time must be regarded as special pleading. The Latin version is of

The suggestion of Rogers, that Irenaeus meant us to understand that "Montanism was one of the bad elements at Lyons . . . he had evidently heard of the spiritual excesses of those who were influenced by Montanus"[8] is highly unlikely. Irenaeus does not mention Montanism in this passage, and, as we shall see in Chapter 7, there is no evidence that Montanists spoke in tongues at all, let alone anything to suggest that glossolalia was characteristic of Montanism. There seems to be no good reason not to accept the passage at face value, and argue that Irenaeus knew of glossolalia (as well as prophecy) in his churches, and accepted what he believed to be Paul's high estimate of those gifts. In the late second century, then, glossolalia was still a feature of Christian life, far from either Jerusalem or Corinth.

The confusion of the modern argument about the continuing presence of the charismata in the church is well illustrated by the case of Tertullian. While it is the consensus that he never mentions glossolalia as a continuing phenomenon, many argue both that Tertullian (in his Montanist period) believed that "the new prophecy" continued in the church of his day, and that Montanist prophecy took some form analogous to glossolalia. Yet it is quite clear from at least one piece of evidence that Tertullian, even in his pre-Montanist days, does claim that glossolalia continues. In Contra Marcionem 5.8 he argues as follows:

Let Marcion then exhibit, as gifts of his god, some prophets, such as have not spoken by human sense, but with the Spirit of God, such as have both predicted things to come, and have made manifest the secrets of the heart; let him produce a psalm, a vision, a prayer - only let it be by the Spirit, in an ecstasy, that is, in a rapture, whenever an interpretation of tongues has occurred to him (si qua linguae interpretatio accessit); let him show to me also, that any woman of boastful tongue in his community has ever prophesied from amongst those specially holy sisters of his. Now all these signs are forthcoming from my side without any difficulty, and they agree too with the rules, and the dispensations, and the instructions of the Creator . . .[9]

---

indeterminate date, and the perfect tense used is simply not decisive enough to restrict the phenomenon to the distant past, even if it does reflect Irenaeus' original thought. Eusebius makes his own view perfectly clear when he says of Irenaeus that "he proves in the following words that manifestations of the divine and marvellous power had remained in some churches even as far as his time" (5.7.1), and follows the passage with "So much on the point that variety of gifts remained among the worthy (*not* Montanist heretics, C.F.) up till the time spoken of." (5.7.6.) See also C.M. Robeck, "Irenaeus and 'Prophetic Gifts'", in P. Elbert, ed., *Essays on Apostolic Themes*, Mass., 1985, pp. 104-114, esp. p. 110.
[8]   Rogers, *art.cit.*, p. 139.
[9]   Tertullian, Against Marcion, 5.8, from *The Ante-Nicene Fathers* vol. 3, Grand Rapids,

Clearly, "all these signs" which Tertullian claims he can produce with ease from the assemblies of "his side" include the "interpretation of tongues"; it is hard to see how this could be the case if glossolalia itself were not also present. The addition of Tertullian's evidence means that we now have evidence of glossolalia from the eastern Mediterranean coast (Jerusalem), western Europe (Lyons) and early third-century North Africa.

From a period more than a generation later, but in the same geographical area, comes the following evidence from Novatian. In his *de Trinitate*, 29, he deals with the trinitarian origins of the charismata:

This is He who strengthened (firmavit) their (sc. the Apostles') hearts and minds, who marked out (distinxit) the Gospel sacraments, who was in them the enlightener of divine things; and they being strengthened, feared (timuerunt), for the sake of the Lord's name, neither dungeons nor chains, nay, even trod under foot the very powers of the world and its tortures, since they were henceforth armed and strengthened by the same Spirit, having in themselves the gifts which the same Spirit distributes, and directs (distribuit et dirigit) to the Church, the Spouse of Christ, as her ornaments.

This is He who places (constituit) prophets in the Church, instructs (erudit) teachers, directs (dirigit) tongues, gives (facit) powers and healings, does (gerit) wonderful works, offers (porrigit) discrimination of spirits, affords powers of government, suggests counsels, and orders and arranges (componit et digerit) whatever other gifts there are of charismata; and thus makes the Lord's Church everywhere, and in all, perfected and complete.

This is He who, after the manner of a dove, when our Lord was baptised, came and abode (venit et mansit) upon Him . . . [10]

---

reprint of 1973, p. 447, trans. P. Holmes. That Tertullian never mentioned glossolalia as a present reality is explicitly argued by Dollar, *art.cit.*, p. 317, and Rogers, *art.cit.*, p. 140, who even cites the passage quoted above! In the context of the arguments about the relationship between Montanism and glossolalia, it is important to remember that Against Marcion was written before Tertullian's conversion to Montanism. See E. Evans, *Tertullian, Adversus Marcionem*, Oxford, 1972, p. xviii. Evans notes that the work was produced in several editions between 198 and 208, whereas it was not till approximately 212 that Tertullian broke with orthodoxy. Evans comments that "We do perceive however in these five books indications of his interest in that movement", but he does not cite this passage, nor would it make sense to do so. Tertullian is describing the assemblies of the orthodox, not Montanist groups.

[10] Novatian, de Trinitate, 29. The translation used here is that of R.E. Wallis, from *The Ante-Nicene Fathers*, Vol. 5, eds. A. Roberts and J. Donaldson, Grand Rapids, reprinted 1975, pp. 640-1. For the text see the Corpus Christianorum edition (Series Latinae, vol. 4) of G.F. Diercks, Turnhout, 1972 (cf. Migne, *Patrologiae Cursus Completus Latinae*, vol. 3, cols. 943-946, esp. 944 A-B).

It has recently been argued, on the basis of this evidence, that it is entirely possible that glossolalia was still practised in the church of approximately A.D. 240.[11] The suggestion was advanced as follows: though clearly dependent on 1 Corinthians 12-14, this passage also shows us that Novatian himself believed the charismata were an important theological phenomenon.

Novatian, in De Trinitate, 29, points to various areas in which he believes the Holy Spirit is working. Reference is made to doctrinal unity, holiness, prayer, baptism, and spiritual gifts. There is no discernible difference in the manner in which he talks about the Spirit's activity in these areas . . . If we assume that any of these occurrences were present in the Church of Novatian's time, we may also be able to assume that they were all there.

Although Kydd is willing to concede that the present tense in the passage of Novatian may be simply an "extended present", perhaps to underline the theological position he is taking, he does believe that it *may* indicate the presence of charismatic gifts in the Church of the 240's. I believe his argument is further strengthened by the observation that Novatian clearly differentiates between past and present in this passage, and none the less uses the present tense of the charismata. His description of the Holy Spirit's work in the Apostles, in terms of empowering and strengthening, is cast in the perfect tense, precisely up to that point at which the writer wishes to emphasise that the Holy Spirit is the same one who currently empowers the church. The apostles had "the gifts which the same Spirit distributes, and appropriates to the Church" - now! Those gifts are then enumerated in the present tense, before Novatian shifts back to the perfect tense to discuss the Spirit's work in the Baptism of Jesus. The suggestion that at least some of the charismata were present in Novatian's churches (and his list does include glossolalia) is therefore quite strong.

Even as late as the fourth century the evidence continues. There is even one suggestion that glossolalia was believed to occur within the early Monastic movement. The following story is told of Pachomius, the founder of eleven monasteries in the Theban district of Egypt, and one of the most formative figures in early Monasticism. He was visited by a Roman who wished to confess himself to Pachomius. Pachomius, however, spoke no Latin or Greek, and the Roman spoke no Coptic.

---

[11] R. Kydd, "Novatian's *De Trinitate*, 29: Evidence of the Charismatic?", *S.J.Th.* vol. 30, 1977, pp. 317-8.

The Blessed Man left him and went to pray by himself. Stretching out his hands to heaven, he prayed to God, saying, 'Lord Almighty, if I cannot profit the men whom you send to me from the ends of the earth because I do not know the languages of men, what need is there for men to come? If you want to save them here through me, grant, O Master, that I may know their languages for the correction of their souls.'

He prayed for three hours, entreating God earnestly for this. Suddenly something like a letter written on a piece of papyrus was sent from heaven to his right hand. Reading it, he learned the speech of all the languages (καὶ ἀναγνοὺς αὐτὸ ἔμαθεν πασῶν τῶν γλωσσῶν τὰς λαλιάς). Having sent up praise to the Father, the Son, and the Holy Spirit, he went back to that brother with great joy, and began to converse with him faultlessly in Greek and Latin . . . [12]

This evidence is a little harder to assess than that of Novatian. Firstly, it occurs only in the Paralipomena that the pastoral problem described is solved with the gift of languages. In the Bohairic Life of Pachomius, chapter 89, the same story is told, but the problem is solved with an interpreter of an entirely natural kind. The same source tells us that Pachomius in fact struggled to learn Greek, but never became fluent. Secondly the language used is not precise. It may be hagiographic hyperbole to say that Pachomius received "the speech of *all* languages", or it may simply mean "all the relevant ones"; i.e. Latin and Greek. Alternatively we may see a link here to Irenaeus' description of glossolalia above: he also describes it as the ability to speak "all languages". The overall colour of the story does not encourage confidence in its historicity, however. It is clearly folklore. But regardless of whether it reflects (in however distorted a fashion) an actual occurrence in the life of Pachomius, it is quite clear that its author, at least, had no problems in believing that a miraculous gift of languages could occur in his own time, even though it might be limited to a great saint, and taught to him by way of an intermediate literary process instead of by direct inspiration. The evidence does not, however, encourage us to believe that such gifts were common.

A distinction between the past and present tense in the discussion of the work of the Holy Spirit very similar to Novatian's is to be found in Ambrose's "On the Holy Spirit". In Book 2.150 he writes as follows:

Behold, God established apostles, established prophets and teachers, gave (dedit) the grace of healings, . . . gave divers kinds of tongues (dedit genera linguarum). But yet not all are apostles, not all prophets, not all teachers. Not all, he says, have the grace of healings, and

---

[12] Pachomius, Paralipomena 27, from *Pachomian Koinonia* vol. 2, trans. A. Vieilleux, Michigan, 1981, p. 52. Pachomius' dates are 290-346.

not all speak with tongues. For not all divine gifts can be in each man individually; each one receives according to his capacity that which he either desires or deserves. But the power of the Trinity which is bountiful with all graces is not like this weakness.

Finally, God established (posuit) apostles. Those whom God established in the Church, Christ chose and ordained as apostles, and he ordered them into the world . . . Behold, the Father established the teachers; Christ also established them in the churches; and just as the Father gives (dat) the grace of healings, so the Son also gives (dat) it; just as the Father gives the gift of tongues, so the Son also has bestowed it (sicut Pater dat dona linguarum, ita largitus est et Filius).[13]

Once again a clear distinction is made between the past, in which God established apostles and instituted various gifts, and the present, in which he gives the graces or gifts of healings and tongues. One might suggest that this is also a form of the "extended present", dealing with theological principle rather than with contemporary fact, but the passage does not read that way, and since there is little doubt that miraculous healings were still believed to occur in the church of Ambrose' time, the possibility of glossolalia still occurring in the late fourth century cannot be ruled out.[14]

This conclusion raises a difficult problem. The one definite negative piece of evidence on the continuity of glossolalia within the church is the clear statement of John Chrysostom, in his Homilies on 1 Corinthians, specifically ch. 12, that "the whole passage is very obscure, but the obscurity is produced by our ignorance of the things referred to, and by the fact that they have ceased, since they are things that used to occur, but do so no longer."[15] The passage is itself something of a problem. I do not doubt that Chrysostom is telling us the truth as he sees it when he says that glossolalia no longer occurs. This passage may be

---

[13] Ambrose, On the Holy Spirit 2. 150-152, from *St. Ambrose, Theological and Dogmatic Works*, trans. R.J. Deferrari, Washington, 1963, pp. 149-50. The suggestion of Hunter, *art.cit.*, pp. 132-3, that the Ambrosiaster commentary's use of the present tense evacuari for the Greek παύσονται of 1 Corinthians 13.8, "tongues will cease", means that "the cessation of tongues-speech has not been completed but is in the process of ceasing" (*sic*) is not convincing: in later Latin the present infinitive often does duty for the future, and the Ambrosiaster is quite explicit. The statement "Omnia charismatum dona evacuari *dixit*" can only mean "As Paul says", and therefore we must argue that the present infinitive is here being used with a future sense.

[14] For examples, drawn in this case from the writings of Augustine, see City of God 22.28 (in the edition of Deferrari, 24.433-445): eighteen miracles are recorded, and Augustine comments that there are too many more to list them all.

[15] John Chrysostom, Homilies on 1 Corinthians, No. 29.

taken as proof that it did not occur in the region around Antioch (or possibly Constantinople: the Homilies on 1 Corinthians cannot easily be dated) in the late fourth century. One may doubt, however, whether Chrysostom's statement ought to be generalised, in the light of the evidence of Ambrose.[187] But the real problem here is Chrysostom's claim that the passage's meaning is obscured by the lack of contemporary glossolalia with which to compare it. Having made the claim that the passage is obscure, Chrysostom goes on to give what must be regarded, by any standards, as an exemplary exposition of it. One can only conclude, it seems to me, that Chrysostom exaggerated his bafflement at the passage in order to throw the detail of his exposition into high relief. He is very well informed about glossolalia, whatever the source of his knowledge.

From the end of the fourth century onwards I have been able to find no clear suggestion of the continued practice of glossolalia within the church. Chrysostom's view, which is also Augustine's, becomes the standard, and little more can be said. What we have seen, however, is that glossolalia appears to have been known in three widely separated areas over a period of more than three hundred and fifty years of the church's life. In the light of this evidence, it becomes impossible to argue that glossolalia was a limited, anomalous phenomenon within the Apostolic generation. It was, on the contrary, a widespread and lasting (though far from universal) spiritual experience in the early formative centuries of Christianity.

---

[187] The suggestion of Hunter, *art.cit.*, p. 134 n. 41, that "Chrysostom seems to have waged an all-out war on tongues-speech", and that therefore his evidence must be regarded as polemical, seems to me to be untenable. Chrysostom's exposition in Homilies 29, 32 and 35 is extremely careful, and cannot be dismissed as unreasonably biased against glossolalia. He is very hard on the misuse of uninterpreted tongues, and does emphasise the low value of the gift, in that it can at best edify the speaker, but he does not on that basis dismiss it from consideration. His exposition seems to me to be very closely based on the Pauline text. Perhaps here we may fall back on the argument of Origen, de Oratione, cited in *Alexandrian Christianity*, vol. 2, J.E.L. Oulton and H. Chadwick, London 1954, p. 273, in order to explain Chrysostom's ignorance of the phenomenon. Origen suggests that the various gifts are differently distributed by God at various times and places, and we might simply say that Chrysostom's ignorance of glossolalia means that it was not widely practised in late fourth-century Syria and the region around Constantinople.

2. "If there are tongues, they will cease"

Having dealt with the question of the historical and geographical extent of glossolalia within early Christianity, we are now in a position to deal with 1 Corinthians 13.8-12. Here Paul argues that there will come a time when "tongues will cease", along with others of the charismata.[17] The two logically distinct, though related, issues, (a) when Paul expected tongues to cease, and (b) when/whether they actually did so, have far too often been confused.

When did Paul expect glossolalia to cease to be part of Christian experience? He suggests that this will occur "when the perfect comes (ὅταν δὲ ἔλθη τὸ τέλειον)". But when is that? Only three views require consideration. The older view, widely held by those who argued that glossolalia in fact ceased "at the close of the apostolic period" or "when the canon of Scripture was complete", is that "the perfect", or "completion", is to be identified with one or both of those events. Some of those who hold this view also argue for a distinction between the cessation of prophecy, knowledge, and other gifts, and that of glossolalia, pointing to the change from passive to middle voice in verse 8. Tongues, they argue, will in some sense "cease of themselves", while prophecy and knowledge will be abolished.[18] These two points will be dealt with separately in what follows. More recently, various scholars have suggested that due to the function of glossolalia (as defined by Paul) he would have expected it to die out within a fairly brief historical period. Naturally, this view must also separate glossolalia from the other charismata.[19]

---

[17] The attempt to divide the unity of the passage by arguing that Paul believes that glossolalia's cessation is a different matter to that of the other gifts is sometimes based on the distinction between the verbs used. It is argued that whereas prophecy and knowledge "will be abolished" (καταργηθήσονται, passive) tongues "will cease" (παύσονται, middle; in some sense "cease of themselves"). Such a case is argued by R.L. Thomas, "Tongues . . . Will Cease", *J.E.Th.S.* vol. 17, 1974, p. 81, who suggests that "revelational" gifts cease, and gifts for the purpose of "verification" cease of themselves. Another who makes this distinction is S.D. Toussaint, "First Corinthians Thirteen and the Tongues Question", *Bib.Sac.* vol. 120, October 1963, pp. 314-5. He argues that tongues cease before the other gifts mentioned. On this matter see below.

[18] Thus, for example, S.D. Toussaint, *art.cit.*, pp. 314-5, and R.L. Thomas, *art.cit.*, p. 81.

[19] Thus, for example, O.P. Robertson, "Tongues: Sign of Covenantal Curse and Blessing", *W.Th.J.* vol. 38, No. 1, 1975, pp. 43-53, esp. p. 53. The question of the function or functions of glossolalia will be discussed below.

Second is the consensus view, that "the perfect" must refer to the return of Christ, when all charismatic gifts will be superseded by the immediate presence of God, when childhood will be replaced with adulthood, dim reflections by face to face reality, partial knowledge by total knowledge. This view normally sees no distinction between the passive and middle forms in verse 8, referred to above. It has the advantage of making good sense of the context of the passage, and of not forcing Paul to identify as "the perfect" an event (the formation of the N.T. Canon) of which he can have had no inkling. It has therefore commanded majority support in discussion of the passage.[20]

Some weaknesses in the interpretation have, however, been identified (see below), and a third view proposed. Here, some condition of "perfection" or "maturity" is identified that Paul might be considering, short of the parousia. Thus glossolalia might be expected to cease "when the body comes to maturity",[21] or "when love rules".[22]

It goes virtually without saying in recent scholarship that the first view cannot be defended on exegetical grounds, but can only be maintained on a dogmatic, *a priori* basis. Maintaining a "canon" view of τò ν requires us to totally isolate v.8 from its immediate context, most especially the logically related comparisons that follow.[23] We must choose between the "parousia"

---

[20] It was also the view held by the Patristic writers who discuss the passage, despite the fact that some of them appear to have believed that glossolalia *had*, in fact, ceased. See, for example, the anonymous writer against Montanism quoted with approval in Eusebius, H.E. 5.17.4: "the apostle grants that the prophetic gift shall be in all the church until the final coming." See also Irenaeus, AH 2.28.7, 5.7.2 - 5.8.1, Clement of Alexandria, Quis dives salvetur 38, Origen, Contra Celsum 6.20, de Oratione 25.2, and Tertullian, de Patientia 12.10 and Adversus Marcionem 5.15.6, all of which are cited by C.M. Robeck, Jr., *art.cit.*, p. 111 and note 56. Compare John Chrysostom, Homily on 1 Corinthians No. 34, where the same view of the charisma is implicit, despite Chrysostom's view that glossolalia had in fact ceased. Grudem (*Gift*, pp. 214ff.) also notes Paul's use of the term καταργέω in other contexts of things that will come to an end at the Parousia.

[21] Thus R.L. Thomas, *art.cit.*, whose survey of interpretations is one of the best available.

[22] Thus B.C. Johanson, "Tongues", p. 197 and footnote 3, who argues that the use of πίπτω in the phrase "love never fails" in 13.8 indicates that love is "the perfect", *whenever* it might be that it occurs. He argues that πίπτω only has one other usage in a temporal sense in the N.T., Luke 14.17, and even that is uncertain, whereas it usually means "to fail" in the sense of "come to grief".

[23] Thus Thomas, *art.cit.*, M. Turner, "Spiritual Gifts Then and Now", *Vox Evangelica*, vol. 15, 1985, pp. 38-9 (who notes that this was also Calvin's view), and D.A. Carson, *Showing*

view and some variety of "pre-parousia maturity" interpretation. Major arguments raised against the consensus "parousia" view are as follows. (1) The term "perfect" (ν) is not otherwise used in this sense in Paul.[24] (2) In this view a quantitative term ("the partial", ἐκ μέρους) is contrasted with a qualitative ("the perfect"): "the two are not compatible antitheses."[25] (3) The entire thrust of verses 8-12 is one of progression over time; but on the "parousia" view v. 13 "And now these three remain" cannot have the same thrust without raising insuperable problems about how faith and hope can remain, with love, beyond the parousia.[26]

Of these three objections the first, though important, is not decisive, and the second may be asking a little too much precision of Paul. Further, Thomas' own solution, as he admits, does not help here at all.[27] The third objection is the most substantial. The problem is, however, a little more complex than Thomas allows. Two terms and a group of contextual problems have to be considered: the νυνὶ, "And now", of v. 13, and the μένει, "remains", and the question of the survival into the eschatological future of faith and hope.[28] First, is νυνὶ intended in the temporal sense, "so now, and in the eschatological state", or in

the Spirit, pp. 69-72.

[24] Thus Thomas, *art.cit.*, p. 83.

[25] *Ibid.*, though it should be noted that Thomas' solution does not solve this problem. Cf. p. 87, where he argues that v. 11, "when I was a child", refers to "dynamic and changing maturity", and v. 12, "we shall see face to face . . . I shall know fully" to "ultimate and fixed maturity". But this is highly artificial. Childhood can hardly be seen as a metaphor for any sort of maturity, no matter how "dynamic and changing". The solution to this problem, it seems to me, is most probably to be found along the lines of R.A. Horsley's analysis of the "perfect / child" distinction in Philo. The terminology is not so much Paul's as his opponents', who claimed that a perfection was possible in this life. Paul replied that when the perfect truly came, the gifts they most valued would be done away with. See, most recently, R.A. Horsley, "Spiritual Elitism". On the ἐκ μέρους terminology otherwise see Grudem, *Gift*, p. 148, note 59.

[26] R.L. Thomas, *art. cit.*, pp. 83-4, E. Miguens, "1 Cor 13:8-13 Reconsidered", *C.B.Q.* vol. 37, 1975, pp. 76-97. Carson tries to take the sting out of these objections by defining ways in which faith and love might be seen as continuing in the eschatological state, *Showing the Spirit*, pp. 74-5, referring (note 73) to various articles and Barrett's Commentary.

[27] *Op.cit.*, p. 87.

[28] See C.K. Barrett, *A Commentary on the First Epistle to the Corinthians*, London, 1971, pp. 308-311, who argues in detail for a sense in which faith and hope may continue in the eschatological state as do Carson, as noted above, and H. Conzelmann, *1 Corinthians*, trans. J.W. Leitch, Philadelphia, 1975, pp. 230-231, whose general analysis I am following here.

the logical sense, "so, now, on the basis of what has gone before"? Secondly, in which of these senses is μένει meant? "These three remain (for ever?)" or "these three are left, out of all we have discussed"? If we take the more common view that νυνὶ (and consequently μένει) ought to be read in the chronological sense, in line with the rest of the section, we are left with the puzzle of the "remaining" of faith and hope. If we opt for the logical sense of νυνὶ we may still take μένει either way, but are left with v. 13 patently not following from its context. For this reason the chronological or temporal sense is still to be preferred.

Thomas and Miguens have quite correctly pointed out problems with the "parousia" interpretation, as we have seen.[29] These problems are, however, minor, compared to those their suggested solutions would generate. These are as follows: according to Paul the "perfection" which will render all charismatic endowments unnecessary is a stage of maturity in the growth of the body of Christ, which is conceived of as

the Christian church collectively, growing up as one body, beginning with its birth, progressing through different stages of development during the present and reaching complete maturity at the parousia . . . he conceived of a constant growth process in the body of Christ and a gradual attainment of new degrees of maturity . . . it conceivably to Paul might reach a point before the parousia where continuing revelation was no longer necessary . . . To Paul it was not revealed which of these two states would come first . . . [30]

While this view makes very good sense of the child/adult metaphor in verse 11, the same cannot be said of 12b, "face to face", and "as fully as I have been known". There is also a problem with identifying "the perfect" with an earthly stage in which prophecy will cease to be necessary in 14.20, where the Corinthians are urged to be τέλεος in their thinking, and thus to prefer prophecy to glossolalia. Ought they not rather to do without either, on Thomas'

---

[29] Thomas also makes the point that the difference between childhood and adulthood is not a normal metaphor for this world and the parousia in Paul, *art.cit.*, p. 85. Miguens develops the point in detail, *art.cit.* pp. 88ff. Similar considerations lead B.A. Pearson, *The Pneumatikos-Psychikos Terminology*, Missoula, 1973, pp. 27-30, to suggest that this passage is Paul's reshaping of the Corinthians' own terminology, which was heavily influenced, he suggests, by Hellenistic Judaism. A very similar metaphor is, however, used in Ephesians 4.13, where ἄνδρα τέλειον is used in contrast to the state of being νήπιοι in v. 14. Yet the language is again so strong as to virtually preclude any non-eschatological interpretation.

[30] *Art.cit.*, pp. 86-88.

view? Not only so, but such a view as Thomas' assumes a "church universal" view of the body of Christ on earth which is entirely alien to Paul's thought. Does every one of the scattered churches come to maturity at the same rate? Or does revelation (and knowledge, it should be noted) end in some places and not others, revive due to a lapse back into immaturity (if such is possible once τὸ τέλειον is achieved), and then cease again as the requisite degree of "perfection" is again attained? That would surely strain the sense of καταργηθήσονται in 13.8, and still the qualitative "perfect" clashes with the quantitative "in part". Any suggestion Thomas makes to mitigate the clash weakens his own case against the "parousia" view. As for the suggestion that there was, for Paul, the possibility of some pre-parousia perfection, and that he was not sure "which of the two states would come first" and deliberately chose ambiguous language accordingly, the simple logical alternative is that Paul assumed that the two would coincide.[31]

And this remains the major objection against his "body maturity" view. I doubt whether Thomas' and Miguens' (differing) suggestions of a τέλειον before the parousia can be sustained in the face of v.12. Grudem has shown that the mirror/reality and knowledge metaphors used here belong to theophanic language; Carson's statement that "*any* pre-parousia maturity simply trivialises the language of v.12" is thoroughly justified.[32] Further points in favour of the

---

[31] Johanson's case in favour of the "when love rules" interpretation, on the other hand, ignores both the strength of v. 12 and the parallelism with the other gifts, for I doubt that the verbs used of *their* ending can be explained as meaning "to fail, come to grief". They seem to mean "to be abolished". Further, it would normally be argued that the "in part" is not due to lack of love, but to the incompleteness of all Christian experience until "the perfect" comes. Not only so, but Thomas is almost certainly correct to argue that "In v. 8 the adverb οὐδέποτε contrasts with the future tenses of verbs indicating cessation. In vv. 9-10 the future arrival of τὸ τέλειον necessitates a consequent doing away with the partial, which belongs to the present. In v.11, in the illustration of growth, a replacement of childhood habits by those of the adult transpires as time elapses. In v. 12 there is the dual occurrence of ἄρτι and τότε, representing contrasts between the present and the future. Time is clearly the uppermost consideration in this closing part of the great love chapter." ("Tongues", p. 81)

[32] W. Grudem, *Gift*, p. 213 and note 57, D.A. Carson, *Showing the Spirit*, p. 71, and compare M. Turner, *art.cit.*, pp. 38-9, who notes that Paul's high view of prophecy makes it unlikely that he would have envisaged a "mature" church without it, and that 1 Corinthians 1.7 seems to confirm the eschatological view of τὸ τέλειον. I agree, and would add Ephesians 4.13 as further confirmation, arguing that its language is again so strong as to rule

"parousia" view can be added: the Spirit (and his gifts) are "first-fruits" and as such of course only last until τὸ τέλειον comes (2 Cor. 1.22, 5.5, Rom. 8.23); likewise the content of glossolalia is the sort of mysteries which will then (and only then) be known in full.[33]

One of the most important points Thomas has made, however, still stands. This is his criticism that τὸ τέλειον in Paul does not normally refer to the parousia. In this he is correct, and it is the great strength of his suggestion that it does attempt to take Paul's usage seriously (with the exception of 14.20, noted above). But a more thorough examination of Paul's usage brings to light material quite consistent with the parousia interpretation.

The well known "eschatological tensions" in Pauline theology between the present realisation of salvation and its future completion, and between the indicative and the imperative, are to be found in Paul's usage of the τέλειος / τελειόω word group. Paul can, without a hint of irony, describe certain members of his churches as being τέλειοι (1 Cor. 2.6), urge certain courses of action on "those who are τέλειοι" (Philippians 3.15), urge the perfecting (ἐπιτελοῦντες) of holiness on his charges (2 Cor. 7.1), and assure the Colossians that Epaphras is praying for them to become τέλειοι (Col. 4.12).[34] Passages that look forward to a future "perfection" or maturity are Colossians 1.28, where the aim of Paul's preaching is to "present everyone perfect in Christ" (compare Ephesians 5.27), and Ephesians 4.13, where the orders of apostles, prophets, evangelists, pastors and teachers all work towards the church reaching "a perfect man" and growing up into "the Head". Finally, in Philippians 3.12 Paul disclaims perfection ("not that I have already achieved this, or have already been made perfect"): in conjunction with 3.15, "all of us

---

out anything less than an eschatological interpretation. Similar points are made by W.G. MacDonald, "Glossolalia in the New Testament", *B.E.Th.S.*, Spring, 1964, p. 66. Miguens' view that "Prophecy, as well as gnosis, will come to an end, not because the gift of prophecy will not exist - on the contrary, it will be the abundance of this gift that will render the present ("now") prophecy inoperative and meaningless" (*art.cit.* p. 91) seems to me to run counter to the plain sense of the words. The solution he proposes is worse than the problem he (correctly) perceives.

[33] See M.E. Hart, *Tongues And Prophecy*, pp. 247-8.

[34] Naturally, this is only relevant if the Pauline authorship of Colossians is presumed. The same holds for the Ephesians passages cited below. 2 Cor. 12.9 and Galatians 3.3 also make use of the present sense.

who are τέλειοι should take such a view of things", the range of meanings the term can take becomes clear.[35] There are those who are perfect, there is the general call to be perfect, and there is a time when all will be perfect. Only the context can tell us which meaning Paul intends: in 1 Cor. 13 the context is particularly clear. Nothing short of the Parousia and its results for the church can be in view.[36]

Finally, we must ask whether Paul's choice of verbs and voices in 13.8 is intended to make a distinction between the fate of prophecy and knowledge, and that of glossolalia. Attention has focussed on the middle form παύσονται used of glossolalia. But what precisely would the distinction Paul is making be? This question cannot be answered from this passage alone, but would have to make sense of Paul's wider discussion of the functions of glossolalia, for, at the level of grammar alone, there is no good reason not to take the verb itself as a deponent, and the change of verb as a stylistic variation.[37] Unless, for example, Paul's view is that tongues are purely a sign for the verification of the apostolic message (as Thomas, for example, seems to imply, p. 88), then the reliance on the middle form of the verb to suggest that Paul thinks glossolalia has a strictly limited life in the history of the church simply will not do.

3. The functions of glossolalia within early Christianity

When we come to consider what functions early Christianity believed were fulfilled by glossolalia, the very multiplicity of points of view must warn us that the evidence is multi-faceted and complex. These points of view may be divided up into several broad, overlapping classes. The most basic division is between those that treat glossolalia *per se*, and those that include consideration

---

[35] Romans 12.2, "the good, acceptable and perfect will of God", is irrelevant here. For a thorough treatment of the tensions in Paul's usage of these terms see H.N. Ridderbos, *Paul: an Outline of his Theology*, Grand Rapids, 1975, pp. 265-272.

[36] As noted above, Thomas' suggestion that the variation in Paul's usage allows us to posit that he believed in the possibility of some pre-Parousia perfection does not follow. Final perfection, in the sense of 1 Cor. 13.10, cannot come before this. But that the word can have other senses is not in doubt.

[37] See most recently D.A. Carson, *Showing the Spirit*, p. 67, who supports the suggestion that the verb is deponent with a reference to Luke 8.24 as a parallel. After detailed consideration, he observes: "In short, I do not think that much can be made of παύσονται in v.8 . . ."

of the complementary gift of "interpretation". If we consider the matter another way, there are those whose interpretation is dominated by Luke's Pentecost account (often in combination with 1 Corinthians 14.20-25) and those who give priority to the Pauline evidence more generally. Scholars seem to be loth to attempt to bring these two approaches together, and many recent writers are unwilling to allow glossolalia to have more than one "function". This is so despite Paul's explicit statement that there are "kinds of tongues" (γένη γλωσσῶν, 1 Cor. 12.10, 28). The statement is, to be sure, open to over-interpretation, but it is not to be ignored.[38] There is likewise the problem that very few scholars do more than attempt to synthesize the point (or points) of view of the New Testament. The question of the "social" or "communal" functions of glossolalia in the New Testament period, or even the question of its general psychological function, is rarely taken up. Beyond even this, modern scholarship has been dominated by a concern to understand the point of view of, for example, Paul, over against that of those to whom he wrote on the subject.[39] This tendency is understandable, given the nature of our evidence (and I will not often go beyond the evidence for the views of Luke and Paul myself), but it ought to be noted from the outset that this question is not the only one worthy of discussion.

Examined in more detail, modern interpretations of the function of glossolalia may be grouped as follows. One major view describes it as a form of inspired prayer and praise, to be identified (at least in 1 Corinthians) with praying or singing "in the Spirit" (14.15), and "blessing in the Spirit" (14.16). It

---

[38] G. Dautzenberg, for example, in "Glossolalie", speaks of the "structured multiplicity" of the gift ("eine strukturierte Vielfalt", col. 227), and suggests that the gift has two main uses: for the conveying of prophetic information or mysteries, and for private prayer. Hart, *Tongues And Prophecy*, p. 241, speaks of the "wealth and variety of γλῶσσαι". This seems to me to go beyond the evidence, as only two "kinds" are ever explicitly discussed by Paul.

[39] See the strictures of D.E. Aune on the similar problem of the interpretation of the function of New Testament prophecy, *Prophecy*, pp. 10-19. A notable exception to this problem is the work of T.W. Gillespie, who in his *Prophecy and Tongues*, and in his subsequent article, "A Pattern", makes a thorough attempt to analyse the understanding of glossolalia likely to have confronted Paul in Corinth. In my view, however, Gillespie's conclusions are in error on many points. Others undertaking the same task include J.P.M. Sweet, *art.cit.*, pp. 240-257, and B.A. Pearson, *op.cit.* The problems associated with this task are many, not the least being the lack of certainty with which statements in Paul's letters may be treated as citations of or reactions to the views of his opponents.

is thus a form of devotional practice, a form of praise and thanks directed to God (14.2) (not invocation), sometimes corporate, which Paul wishes to restrict to private use.[40] Some suggest that even this is a concession he would prefer not to have made, and that his real view is that all glossolalia is self-indulgent and to be restricted to a minimum. Those who argue such a case must maintain that Paul's statement "he who speaks in a tongue edifies himself" is either a minimal concession or a negative comment.[41]

A second major view sees glossolalia primarily as a "sign", which appears to mean (the term is often left undefined) a miracle designed to draw attention to something else. This view takes many forms. In some it takes its cue from the citation of Joel in Acts 2, describing "wonders in the heaven above, and signs on the earth below", and argues that the Pentecost glossolalia were understood by Luke as a sign of the fulfilment of prophecy.[42] In others it is based on the much-disputed 1 Corinthians 14.20-25. Here, tongues are seen variously as a

---

[40] Thus, in detail, T.M. Crone, *Prophecy*, p. 219, M.E. Hart, *Tongues And Prophecy*, pp. 224-6, G. Dautzenberg, "Glossolalie", col. 227, K. Stendahl, *op.cit.*, pp. 124-5, who describes it as "communication between the believer and God" which "has no function as a means towards impressing the outsiders, (but) belongs to the warmth of individual thanksgiving, not to the public realm". A similar point of view is taken by J.W. MacGorman, "Glossolalic Error and its Correction: 1 Corinthians 12-14", *Review and Expositor* vol. 80, 1983, p. 390; Behm, *art.cit.*, p. 722; S. Tugwell, *Expository Times*, vol. 84, no. 5, 1973, p. 138. Those who propound this view are not generally as guilty of excluding other aspects of glossolalia as some who maintain the view that glossolalia is primarily a "sign" of one sort or another.

[41] Thus, for example, H.W. House, "Tongues and the Mystery Religions of Corinth", *Bib. Sac.*, vol. 140, 1983, pp. 134-150, who argues that "The statement 'One who speaks in a tongue edifies himself' (1 Cor 14:4) is not commendatory. Paul merely conceded a point here for argument; he did not affirm the legitimacy of that believer's experience as from the Holy Spirit. One might even say that irony is to be found in Paul's statement . . . In addition, if Paul's statement is one of truth, not irony, then it contradicts 1 Corinthians 12:7, that grace-gifts (*charismata*) are 'for the common good', and also 13:1-3, that gifts are not to be self-centred". (pp. 143-4). This case, however, has been overstated: there is no necessary contradiction. Paul is not condemning glossolalia here, but revaluing it. Why should the statement not be commendatory? Paul himself admits, if that is not too weak a word, that he himself speaks in tongues. M.E. Thrall, *The First and Second Letters of St. Paul to the Corinthians*, Cambridge, 1965, p. 99, also thinks that "builds himself up" is a negative statement, but against this see D.A. Carson, *Showing the Spirit*, p. 102, note 89, whose treatment is very persuasive.

[42] Thus R.H. Gundry, " 'Ecstatic Utterance' (N.E.B.)?", *J.Th.S.* vol. 17 part 2, 1966, pp. 299-307, who describes it as a "convincing miracle" (p. 303).

sign of God's judgement on unbelieving Jews,[43] on unbelievers in general,[44] a sign of the covenantal rejection of national Israel,[45] or as a sign of divine activity or attitude, its nature unspecified by the terminology.[46] Other scholars, however, argue that the attempt to say in what sense Paul saw glossolalia as "a sign" is futile, as in using this terminology Paul was echoing and responding to that of his opponents.[47]

A third major group of interpretations, surprisingly the least popular, focuses around the evidence that glossolalia was seen by both Luke and Paul as being revelatory, most especially, though not exclusively, when interpreted. This view is often held alongside one of the others outlined above: some scholars suggest that Paul saw glossolalia as having one set of functions when uninterpreted, and another when interpreted.[48] That Luke saw glossolalia as either itself revelatory

---

[43] A sign of judgement on unbelieving Jews: thus S.L. Johnson, "The Gift of Tongues and the Book of Acts", *Bib. Sac.*, vol. 120, 1963, pp. 309-311; O.P. Robertson, *art.cit.*, pp. 43-53 (where the case is based on the quotation from Isaiah being an anti-Jewish testimonium).

[44] A sign of God's judgement on unbelief generally: thus J.W MacGorman, *art.cit.*, p. 398; Behm, *art.cit.*, pp. 726-7.

[45] A sign of the covenantal rejection of national Israel: thus O.P. Robertson, *art.cit.* This case is best seen as a more refined version of the two above.

[46] A sign of divine attitude or activity more generally: thus, very differently, W. Grudem, "1 Corinthians 14.20-25: Prophecy and Tongues as Signs of God's Attitude", *W.Th.J.*, vol. 41 No. 2, Spring 1979, pp. 381-396, who argues that *uninterpreted* glossolalia is held to be a sign of divine disapproval; and "a sign of divine or spiritual activity" - P. Roberts, "A Sign - Christian or Pagan?", *Expository Times*, vol. 90 no. 7, April 1979, p. 200. Arguing from the "consensus" position that glossolalia or similar phenomena were widely known in antiquity, Roberts says that "Tongues are the proof of divine activity for which non-Christians look" (p. 201). In this he is in partial agreement with the case of Gillespie, discussed below.

[47] Thus variously Sweet, *art.cit.*, p. 241; T.W. Gillespie, *Prophecy and Tongues*, p. 127; M.E. Hart, *Tongues And Prophecy.*, p. 252. The case of Johanson, "Tongues", p. 193, might be classified as an extreme version of this view, in which Paul puts forward the statement 'are tongues, then, a sign . . .' as a rhetorical question. This will be dealt with below.

[48] Thus, for example, M.E. Hart, *Tongues And Prophecy*, pp. 249-253, though she argues that these functions are likely to have been closely related. Those arguing that glossolalia has a revelatory function include O.P. Robertson, *art.cit.*, p. 50, who argues, however, that this was very much subsidiary to their "sign" function (p. 49). T.L. Wilkinson, however, in "Tongues and Prophecy in Acts and 1 Corinthians", *Vox Reformata*, No. 31, 1978, pp. 1-20, esp. p. 8, and Boring, *Sayings*, p. 108, point out the significance of Paul's use of the term μυστήριον in connection with glossolalia (which will be discussed in detail below), and

or very closely related to revelation is evident not only from Acts 2 (the Pentecost account), but also from the close relationship he assumes between glossolalia and other forms of inspired speech generally (as argued in the previous chapter). The case that Paul also believed it to be revelatory requires detailed argumentation.

The case is made up of two points. The first is that Paul does suggest that glossolalia, when interpreted, functions to edify the gathered congregation in the same way as prophecy. This, of course, does not prove that it is therefore equivalent to prophecy in any other way. It does, however, suggest that there is some parallel between the two in Paul's thought, rather than simply a contrast between the Corinthian preference for glossolalia and Paul's for prophecy. It would appear to be Paul who is stressing interpretation of tongues, not the Corinthians.[49] Several scholars, however, have been at pains to deny the inference that he therefore believes glossolalia to be revelatory.[50]

W.G. MacDonald, *art.cit.*, p. 65, makes the distinction between "personal, "devotional" and evidential γλῶσσαι" and "the gift of γένη γλωσσῶν to the church for a ministry of edification" (*sic*). Though the distinction between "devotional" or private tongues and tongues for interpretation in the assembly seems to me important, and has not been sufficiently noted, I doubt that MacDonald has the terminology right here. Surely γένη γλωσσῶν is the broader category encompassing both types. R.L. Thomas, *art.cit.*, p. 81 also draws a distinction between "revelational-type gifts (prophecy and knowledge)" and tongues, which he sees as being "evidential in nature" or "for the purpose of verification" (of the truth of the Gospel?). On glossolalia as revelation see also Dunn, *Jesus and the Spirit*, London, 1975, p. 244, and E.E. Ellis, "Prophecy in the New Testament Church - and Today", in Panagopoulos, *Vocation*, p. 53.

[49] For the parallel see 1 Cor. 14. 5b, 27-8 and 29-30. T.L. Wilkinson's statement of the inference to be drawn from Paul's parallel between interpreted tongues and prophecy is the most precise: "The exception apparently means that when tongues are interpreted they serve to edify the church as a whole in the way prophecy does" (*art.cit.*, p. 7). D. Hill, *Prophecy*, pp. 97-8, correctly notes that Luke is very concerned with the Spirit's role in communicating the Gospel, and therefore doubts that Luke can have uncommunicative "Pauline" glossolalia in mind. But Paul's insistence on interpretation shows that his concern for communication is just as strong as Luke's. The gap between the two phenomena is again not as great as has been claimed.

[50] MacGorman, for example, says (*art.cit.*, p. 397) "But this (v. 5b, C.F.) still does not indicate that glossolalia, when interpreted, becomes the equivalent of prophecy." That is "a mere exceptive clause". But "mere" may be inappropriate. The exceptive clause is there! Similarly Hart says that "There is a possibility that Paul accepted some of the interpretations of tongues as prophecy, although not very probably (*sic*)" (*Tongues And Prophecy*, p. 126, note 129). This suggestion is made without supporting argument. Hart's later comment that

The second point is that Paul explicitly argues that "anyone who speaks in a tongue . . . utters mysteries with his spirit / by the Spirit" (1 Cor. 14.2) With the two exceptions of 2 Thessalonians 2.7 and Ephesians 5.32, the term μυστήριον is uniformly a term of revelation in Paul. It would take considerable evidence to show that a revelatory sense is not applicable here, yet again scholars have tried to avoid the force of the term. Nils Engelsen suggests, for example, that the sense ought be reduced to "speaks mysteriously",[51] while L.T. Johnson suggests it must mean to "speak mysterious things". Revelation is ruled out (they argue) because no one understands.[52] More carefully, D.A. Carson cites C.K. Barrett to the effect that "The word (*sc.* mysteries) may be used here in a non-technical sense to suggest that 'the speaker and God are sharing hidden truths which others are not permitted to share.'"[53] But the use of

---

"interpreted utterances have something of the same value for the church that prophecy has is no indication that the content of the two charismata is similar in the least" (p. 242) is nearer the mark, but still in error. Her later statement "that the utterance is addressed to God (14:2) and is basically praise tells us that the content differs decidedly from prophecy" (p. 261) is partly true, but ignores the question of the differing functions of glossolalia. *Uninterpreted* tongues (by default?) are viewed as prayer. But tongues that *are* interpreted must, by definition, have some content to be interpreted. Barrett, for example, disagrees, arguing (*op.cit.*, p. 316) that "it (sc. interpretation) had the effect of turning tongues into prophecy." Likewise W.G. MacDonald, *art.cit.*, p. 65. G. Dautzenberg, "Glossolalie", cols. 228-9, argues that glossolalia is closely linked to prophecy, whether interpreted or not. In favour of this contention he offers the following considerations: the position of the two gifts in the list in 1 Cor. 12.10, their shared (though differing) ecstatic character, their common link with "Mysteries", and the pairing of gifts (glossolalia and interpretation, prophecy and discernment). See also his *Urchristliche Prophetie*, Stuttgart, 1975, pp. 146, 234-8.

[51] N.I.J. Engelsen, *Glossolalia*, pp. 143 and 148, though he admits, p. 148, that Paul's view of the interpretation of tongues being equivalent to prophecy, which reveals μυστήρια, suggests that revelations are to be found in glossolalia.

[52] L.T. Johnson, "Norms for True and False Prophecy in First Corinthians", *American Benedictine Review*, vol. 22, 1971, p. 37. Likewise M.E. Hart, *Tongues And Prophecy*, p. 238, who says that μυστήρια cannot have its normal meaning here because "the uninterpreted utterances of the tongue speaker are never revealed." That does not rule out that in Paul's mind they may have been known to God to be identical to μυστήρια which had been explained. Hart may be correct to sever the direct link between μυστήρια and prophecy (pp. 306-7), but not between μυστήρια and revelation. They are surely also closely allied to Luke's "the wonders of God" in Acts 2.

[53] D.A. Carson, *Showing the Spirit*, p. 102. G. Bornkamm, *T.D.N.T.* vol. 4, pp. 820-822, and G. Dautzenberg, *Urchristliche Prophetie*, Stuttgart, 1975, pp. 234-238, on the other hand, take the terminology at face value, and argue for a revelatory sense.

the term in this sense is still unparalleled in Paul. Far more extreme is the suggestion of H.W. House that in this context Paul's use of the term is an allusion to the Mystery cults of Corinth, and is hence totally negative: glossolalists speak pagan mysteries.[54]

If this use of the term μυστήριον were the only evidence for glossolalia's revelatory character, one might perhaps be justified in searching for an alternative sense. As we have seen, it is not. If we grant that Paul views glossolalia as inspired, it is hard to make any sense of the gift of interpretation of tongues unless tongues contain matter to be communicated. If they do, and edify in the same way as prophecy, on what basis are we to rule out (contrary to the normal meaning of the term μυστήρια in Paul) the concept of divine revelation?

Having established, then, that revelation ought not to be ruled out as one of the functions of glossolalia, we are in a position to review the question.[55] How may the whole range of conflicting views be resolved?

First, in my view any solution which ignores the existence of the gift of the interpretation of tongues as a factor for the Pauline evidence must be ruled out of court.[56] The work of W. Grudem has made it clear that for Paul, at least, it is

---

[54] H.W. House, "Tongues and the Mystery Religions of Corinth", *Bib. Sac.* vol. 140, part 558, 1983, pp. 134-150 esp. p. 141: he argues that "Possibly Paul spoke of these mysteries when he wrote that 'one who speaks in a tongue . . . speaks mysteries' (1 Cor. 14:2). If this is not an allusion to mystery terminology, it is certainly not a commendation from the apostle." But that is to ignore the Pauline usage of the term μυστήριον completely, including the usage in the immediate context in 1 Cor. 13.2, not to mention 2.7, 4.1, and 15.51. On the use of the terminology see A.E. Harvey, "The Use of Mystery Language in the Bible", *J.Th.S.*, vol. 31, 1980, pp. 320-336, esp. p. 326, 329, and, for his view of 1 Corinthians 14.2, p. 332. He suggests a revelatory sense with a vague allusion only to Hellenistic mysteries.

[55] The only major view excluded from this review (so far as I am aware) is that of T.W. Gillespie, in both *Prophecy and Tongues* and "A Pattern", that glossolalia was seen in Corinth as "a confirmation of prophetic utterance", "A Pattern" p. 82-3. Exegetical reasons for doubting this very original hypothesis have been given in the literature review chapter, above, while reasons for doubting Gillespie's view of the Hellenistic background will be given in Chapters 5, 6 and 7.

[56] A good example of those that exclude interpretation is the otherwise excellent treatment of M. Turner, *art.cit.*, p. 20, where the topic is dismissed with one brief paragraph, and p. 46. A similar error dominates the treatment of W.E. Mills, *A Theological / Exegetical Approach to Glossolalia*, Lanham, 1985, and K. Stendahl, *op.cit.*, who argues that private

uninterpreted tongues that are "a sign for unbelievers", not tongues per se.[57] Second, certain versions of the "sign" interpretation do not account for even the whole of the evidence on uninterpreted tongues. To argue that tongues are *exclusively* a sign (in one sense or another) *for unbelievers* is to ignore Paul's dismay over its effects on the hypothetical unbeliever of 1 Cor. 14.23 (this point will be treated in detail in Chapter 7), as well as and the question of interpretation, and those passages in Acts where glossolalia is practised with no unbelievers present (Acts 10.44-46, and 19.4-6). On such a view, *all* of the evidence of Acts (with the exception of Chapter 2, admitted on all sides to be anomalous), must be ignored. These points apply whether the "sign" is seen as given to Jewish unbelievers or unbelievers in general.[58] In my view we are forced to recognise that Paul viewed glossolalia as being capable of supporting a variety of functions, differing primarily according to the context within which it was exercised. He believed glossolalia could function as inspired prayer and praise to God, in which God placed into the believer's mouth praise related to revelations of God's secret purposes, now coming to light: in a word, mysteries. He believed that when the gift was used in this fashion, it ought to be exercised privately. He also believed that the gift was capable of interpretation, so that the revelatory content of the glossolalia could be made known, not only to the believer speaking (who in private glossolalic prayer did not understand his own

---

devotional glossolalia can unfortunately become a (negative or mere) sign for unbelievers which leads to alienation, à la Isaiah 11. We should note, however, that this ignores 1 Cor. 14.25ff and "when you come together . . . one has a tongue, one has an interpretation." *That* is clearly not private devotional practice. Similarly the views of Toussaint, Johnson, Robertson and MacGorman cited above virtually ignore the issue.

[57] W. Grudem, "1 Corinthians 14.20-25: Prophecy and Tongues as Signs of God's Attitude", *W.Th.J.*, vol. 41, No. 2, Spring 1979, pp. 381-396. Grudem argues that "Paul is not talking about the function of tongues in general but only about the negative result of one particular abuse of tongues, namely, the abuse of speaking in tongues in public without an interpreter . . ." (p. 393). We might add: when there are unbelievers present.

[58] Naturally, the hypothesis that it is Jewish unbelief that receives this "sign" is further weakened by the fact that Paul makes no such suggestion in 1 Corinthians 14.20-25, where "the unbeliever or person who does not understand" might equally be a native Greek. H.W. Hoehner is quite correct to say (*Walvoord, a Tribute*, Chicago 1982, p. 59) that "When tongues are used in the book of Acts they are employed as an aid to faith rather than as a sign of judgement." He goes on to suggest that "(interpreted?) tongues were used to serve as a sign to authenticate God's activity among unbelievers in an evangelistic setting" (p. 60).

words), but also to the wider Christian assembly. Finally, he believed that in certain contexts, glossolalia functioned as a "sign" to unbelievers. Knowing in what sense he intended this statement will require a detailed analysis of 1 Corinthians 14.20-25, to which we will turn at the end of chapter 7.[59]

The question of whether Paul identified these three broad categories of function with what he calls "kinds of tongues" is not one, I believe, that we are ever likely to be able to answer with any certainty. He may have believed that there were two or more different gifts, one for private use, and the other for interpretation in the assembly, and one to be used as a sign. The existence in *his* mind of this third possible "type" seems to me to be very unlikely, due to his negative comments on tongues as a sign. Alternatively he may simply have thought that there was one gift of "tongues", which was capable of different functions depending on its context. The first view is suggested by the phrase "kinds of tongues", while the second is suggested by Paul's use of the same terminology for each "kind" of tongue.[60]

In my view, a position such as that outlined above overcomes the objections of Thiselton, mentioned in the previous chapter. Thiselton argued that

if he himself (sc. the glossolalist) does not in fact know what he is saying whilst speaking a foreign language, we have a very curious kind of miracle indeed. We cannot even see in what sense it can be true that 'he who speaks in a tongue edifies himself' (xiv.4); nor in what sense tongues can be used for private devotion. [61]

Paul admits, however, that when one speaks in a tongue one's mind is not what benefits; he locates the benefit in the spirit (τὸ πνεῦμά μου, 1 Cor. 14.14). In this context we must presume that the edification is of a non-cognitive kind, (inferior, certainly, to the cognitive edification provided by prophecy), but real none the less. The contrast between the two major roles of glossolalia to which Thiselton points is certainly there; glossolalia *was* a very curious kind of gift - one with a double (or multiple) role - even in Paul's view.

---

[59] M.E. Hart, *Tongues And Prophecy*, pp. 249-253, takes a similar view, arguing that it has three functions: individual edification, sign value (the Corinthian view, she suggests, which Paul is at pains to deny), and revelation, though Hart is not confident of this third.

[60] The idea that Paul may perhaps think of glossolalia as one gift with varying functions is likewise strengthened by the fact that there is no evidence that he believes in a *false* gift of tongues - merely in a real one that is being used in an inappropriate way. In the same fashion he may well think of one gift having varying valid functions.

[61] Thus A.C. Thiselton, "Interpretation", p. 30.

4. The gift of interpretation

In the previous chapter I argued that Paul's use of the terms ἑρμηνεύω, etc., can not be made the basis of a case against his understanding glossolalia as the inspired use of unknown human languages. If that is what Paul, consistent with the uniform tradition of the early Christian churches, believed glossolalia to be, we must now briefly discuss the related gift of "interpretation of tongues". I believe that the combination of two major points made above - that both Paul and Luke believed glossolalia to be unlearned human languages, and that they both likewise believed it to be revelatory in a sense even when it was not interpreted (though they expressed that belief in very different ways), makes the issue relatively straightforward.[62] The interpretation of tongues must have been understood to be the equally inspired ability to render the particular glossolalic speech into the vernacular, thus making its content (whether praise, as in Acts 2, or mysteries, as in 1 Corinthians 14) available to the congregation. Whether such διερμήνευσις was understood as a literal, word-for-word translation of what had been said, or was more what we would call an interpretation than a translation, is probably not a matter on which the early Christians spent much thought. The gift of interpretation made it possible for the assembly to assess

---

[62] The best survey of options is still that of S.D. Currie, *art.cit.*, pp. 274-294, esp. p. 275: "Is the gift of 'interpretation of tongues' a gift . . . to translate into the common language of the hearers what is being uttered by one who is 'speaking in tongues'? Or does 'interpretation' here mean, rather, exegesis or explanation? For instance, what is 'spoken in a tongue' might be enigmatic or oracular . . . the gift of interpretation would then be the gift of the ability to make plain the meaning of what was being uttered. Or, to consider a third possibility, does 'interpretation' here mean what an art critic does when he reports on the message of a piece of music? In this case the interpreter would . . . explain the aim and the mood (praise, lament, thanksgiving, exultation) of the utterance." But there is no need, in these circumstances, to argue, with Currie, that "If 'speaking in tongues' in Corinth was some kind of cadence of vocalizations (constituting no language, human or non-human, bearing no message, however darkly uttered) and if its interpretation required of the interpreter something like what a music critic undertakes to do, . . ." then problems like those in Corinth are quite explicable. (Currie, p. 292: he is not, however, certain that this was in fact the case.) M.E. Hart, *Tongues And Prophecy*, p. 261, suggests that in the normal case that glossolalia was "unintelligible ecstatic utterance, no translation in a literal sense is possible; there can be only a general exposition. It may be that the διερμηνευτής has an inner conviction or confirmation as to the nature of the speaker's utterance, whether it is praise, blessing, petition etc., and on that basis is able to give expression to the general purport of the message . . ."

what had been said, and say or withhold its "Amen". No evidence at all suggests that the gift was believed to be a coincidental natural knowledge of the particular language in use: like glossolalia itself, it was seen as a divine endowment.

One question only remains. Whom did Paul expect to interpret? Here Paul's statements are a little ambiguous. Two of his statements, chapter 14 verse 5b ("He who prophesies is greater than he who speaks in tongues, unless he interprets, so that the church may be edified") and chapter 14 verse 13 ("For this reason the man who speaks in a tongue should pray that he may interpret [what he says]") strongly that the speaker himself ought to interpret.[63] Not so his third statement on the matter, chapter 14 verse 27 ("If anyone speaks in a tongue, two - or at most three - should speak, one at a time, and someone must interpret. If there is no interpreter (or: if he is not an interpreter; the Greek is very ambiguous), he [the speaker] should keep quiet in the church and speak to himself and God".) This leaves the option very much open that another member of the congregation will act as interpreter. In my view the most that can be said from this is that Paul would prefer that the speaker himself prayed for the ability to interpret, but is quite open to the possibility that this would not be the case. We might speculate that Paul's preference lays greater responsibility on the speaker to justify his use of the community's time, rather than using his glossolalic gift and laying blame for the lack of interpretation on others (as does the second half of the verse), but there is no real evidence to allow us to go even this far.[64]

---

[63] Thus Barrett, *op.cit.*, p. 316, A.C. Thiselton, "Interpretation", pp. 32ff, H. Kleinknecht, "Pneuma", in G. Friedrich, ed., *T.D.N.T.*, vol. 6, 1959, E.T. 1965, p. 349.

[64] According to M.E. Hart, *Tongues And Prophecy*, p. 260, citing Conzelmann's commentary, this may mean "if *he* is not an interpreter". But this seems to be merely a harmonisation with the other two verses cited. J.D.G. Dunn finds the role of interpretation confusing, and argues that it may be merely Paul's concession to the Corinthians: his personal preference would be to ban tongues from the assembly altogether (14.18-19, *Jesus and the Spirit*, London, 1975, p. 248). But surely Paul would prefer five intelligible words to ten thousand *uninterpreted* glossolalic words. He does not concede interpretation simply in order to "manage" glossolalia. It is already a recognised gift (12.10b, 14.5c, 14.13) on whose *appropriate* use he is insisting.

5. The problem in Corinth

It is perfectly clear that in 1 Corinthians we are dealing with a case of conflict between Paul and the congregation he had founded over the role of inspired speech in congregational life. What is not so clear is the precise nature and background of this conflict. In Chapter 2 I surveyed the various interpretations that attempt to link this problem with the other issues in 1 Corinthians. I argued that neither of the two prevalent theories as to the root cause of Paul's disagreement with his Corinthian converts (over-realised eschatology, Hellenistic-Jewish Wisdom speculation) really explained why glossolalia and prophecy had become issues in that disagreement. The time has now come to examine in detail the third major theory proposed by scholars to explain how inspired speech and other related issues became contentious in Corinth. What external evidence actually exists to support the hypothesis (which is quite plausible on exegetical grounds) that the Corinthian Christians' views on inspiration generally, and glossolalia in particular, were influenced by the existence and high valuation of parallel phenomena in the religions of the Hellenistic world? The evidence will be examined in the next three chapters under the following headings: (1) evidence related to the cult of Apollo as practised first and foremost at the famed oracular centre of Delphi, and secondly at Delos; (2) evidence related to both the cult myths and cult practices of the "Mysteries", more specifically the cults of Dionysus and Cybele, and Philo; and (3) scattered fragments of evidence commonly argued to give us insight into the general religious milieu of the New Testament in relation to inspiration and inspired speech.

Chapter 5

Glossolalia and Hellenistic Inspiration:

Delphic and Delian Apollo

One of the linchpins of the suggestion that early Christian gifts of "pneumatic" speech, and notably glossolalia, can easily be paralleled from the world of Hellenistic popular religion has always been the understanding of Delphic "inspiration manticism". For example, James Dunn has argued that Paul's understanding of the close relationship between interpreted tongues and prophecy mirrors the understanding of the parallel phenomena found in the case of the Delphic oracle. Here, it is widely believed, the Pythian priestess (μάντις) ascended Apollo's tripod, and either went into a trance or pretended to do so. In this state she spoke her oracles, in a mixture of broken, incoherent Greek and unintelligible free vocalisation. Her utterances were "interpreted" by the προφήτης, who declared them to the inquirer, usually in oracular, ambiguous hexameters, and, if requested, provided a written copy to be taken home. Dunn writes:

The more we recognise Hellenistic influence on Corinthian glossolalia, the more seriously we have to consider the basic meaning of the word ἑρμηνεύειν in wider Greek thought -viz., 'to interpret, expound, explain'. In particular, the relation between 'glossolalia' and 'interpretation' so closely parallels that between what we distinguished above as the 'prophecy of inspiration' and the 'prophecy of interpretation' that it becomes difficult to deny a close equivalence of function between, for example, the prophet who interpreted the utterances of the Pythia at Delphi and the interpreter of tongues at Corinth.[1]

---

[1] J.D.G. Dunn, *Jesus and the Spirit*, London, 1975, p. 247. A point of view very similar to Dunn's is developed by T.W. Gillespie, *Prophecy and Tongues*, p. 77 (as was noted in Chapter 2). The idea has highly respectable roots: it is briefly mentioned, with approval, by A.E. Taylor in his *A Commentary on Plato's Timaeus*, Oxford, 1927, p. 513. Dunn's view is echoed almost word for word by C.H. Peisker, *New International Dictionary of New Testament Theology*, Grand Rapids, 1978, vol. 3, p. 75. See also Kleinknecht, Πνεῦμα, πνευματικός, in G. Friedrich, ed., *T.D.N.T.*, vol. 6, p. 348, W. Keilbach, "Zungenreden", in *Religion in Geschichte und Gegenwart*, 3rd edition, vol. 6, 1962, col. 1941, M.E. Hart, *Tongues And Prophecy*, pp. 6-9, 12, and, more recently, F.F. Bruce, *Paul: Apostle of the Free Spirit*, Paternoster, 1977, p. 260, G. Dautzenberg,

Such appears to be the current understanding of Pythian procedure and its supposed Christian counterpart. The problem is that, at precisely the point where a parallel is alleged, this understanding proves to be based on a mistaken view of the evidence.

1. Terminology

For Paul the interpreter of an unintelligible glossolalic utterance is a διερμηνευτής, while a προφήτης is an inspired person who speaks intelligibly. In the Delphic case the inspired person is normally the μάντις or πρόμαντις; she is also described as a προφῆτις, though rarely if ever by Herodotus, who normally calls her ἡ Πυθία: the Pythia. The person who (it is suggested) interprets is described as προφήτης, and there is no suggestion that he is inspired. Dunn is partly aware of this problem, but does not properly take it into account.

What was prophecy in Paul's view? Does he in fact think of it as an inspired utterance? The question arises because in the Greek world προφήτης did not necessarily denote someone who spoke under inspiration. In particular Plato clearly distinguished two kinds of prophecy. One was mantic prophecy, the prophecy of *inspiration*, where the prophet was possessed by the god and became only the mouthpiece for the divine utterance. The other was the prophecy of *interpretation*, the conscious art of the augur, where prophecy was an acquired skill, the ability to interpret signs and omens, and where the prophet remained quite self-possessed. Thus in the case of the most famous of the Greek oracles, at Delphi, there was a clear difference between the Pythia who spoke in a state of ecstasy, and the prophet whose task was to interpret the Pythia's saying to the inquirer, the one speaking under divine constraint, the other using rational discernment.[2]

But the analogy here is false. Plato did not set out to distinguish "two kinds of prophecy", with prophecy defined in the general English sense Dunn is using. Plato would not have called both "prophecy of inspiration" and "prophecy of interpretation" prophetic (or inspired) in this sense. This point is driven home in precisely the two passages cited by Dunn. In the

---

"Glossolalie", col. 230, and H.W. House, "Tongues and the Mystery Religions of Corinth", *Bibliotheca Sacra*, vol. 140, part 558, 1983, p. 138. The only protests against this view of which I am aware are those of T.M. Crone, *Prophecy*, p. 310, n. 65, though Crone is not certain on this point, D.E. Aune, *Prophecy*, p. 31, and "Magic in Early Christianity", in *Aufstieg und Niedergang der römischen Welt*, II. 23.2, 1980, p. 1551, and W.E. Mills, *A Theological / Exegetical Approach to Glossolalia*, Lanham, 1985, pp. 82-88, though Mills' distinctions between Pythian speech and glossolalia have to do only with its content: he still believes that "its form bore some semblance to these phenomena" (p. 88).

[2] J.D.G. Dunn, *op.cit.*, p. 228.

Timaeus Plato denied that the προφήτης is inspired in any sense. He uses his rational faculties. That is the point of such people: to

pronounce judgement on inspired divination (μαντείαις). These are themselves given the name of diviners by some who are quite unaware that they are expositors of riddling oracle or vision, and best deserve to be called, not diviners (μάντεις), but spokesmen (προφῆται) of those who practise divination (μαντευομένων).[3]

It would appear that Dunn has fallen into the very terminological trap that Plato is discussing. In the Phaedrus, however, he is making a totally different point.

The ancients, then, testify that in proportion as prophecy (μαντική) is superior to augury (οἰωνιστική), both in name and in fact, in the same proportion madness (μανία), which comes from god, is superior to sanity (σωφροσύνη), which is of human origin. Moreover, when diseases and the greatest troubles have been visited upon certain families through some ancient guilt, madness (μανία) has entered in and by oracular power (προφητεύσασα) has found a way of release for those in need . . .[4]

---

[3] Plato, Timaeus 71e-72b. Kleinknecht, *art.cit.*, and Dautzenberg, "Glossolalie", note the difference between Plato and Paul over this point, but it is blurred by Hart, *Tongues And Prophecy*, p. 256, (who inexplicably says that "Plato apparently understood the interpreter to be inspired in some sense, for this was his concept of the prophet . . .") and by Mills, *op.cit.*, p. 20. Both Kleinknecht and Dautzenberg none the less maintain the parallel. Most recently, R.M. Berchman, "Arcana Mundi: Prophecy and Divination in the *Vita Mosis of Philo of Alexandria*", *S.B.L. 1988 Seminar Papers*, Atlanta, 1978, p. 387, argues that "humans who receive such visions . . . are called a prophet (*prophetes*), wise man (*sophos, spoudaos*), or a divine man (*theios aner*)." On the contrary, they are rarely called prophet. They are usually called μάντις. See the full discussion of the terminology generally, and Plato's usage specifically, in Chapter 8, below. Likewise, on p. 392, Berchman argues that "For Plato the prophet becomes synonymous with diviner (*sic.*) and the art of divination. Furthermore the prophet as diviner can be a poet, a priest, a statesman, or a philosopher." This completely muddles the very distinction Plato is setting out to clarify.

[4] Phaedrus 244 a-d. Here Plato does, however, discuss prophecy and mania together. This is virtually coincidental: it is μαντική and μανία that he is linking. None the less the contradiction is not easy to resolve, except by supposing that he is here using the word προφῆτις and its cognate verb in a looser sense than usual. This would be understandable in the case of the Pythia, who is referred to as the προφῆτις in several authors (notably Plutarch, but not Herodotus; for the one possible exception see below), though μάντις or πρόμαντις is more usual. In any case, neither reference supports the hypothesis of Dunn. This reference to the προφῆτις will be taken up again within the larger context of the προφήτης terminology in Chapter 8. The one case in which Herodotus *might* refer to the Pythia as προφῆτις is in 9.93, where inquiries are made of τοὺς προφήτας of both Dodona and Delphi. Here the term may be used of the officials of both shrines because it is appropriate at Dodona; but see Chapter 8 for a full discussion.

Plato is not distinguishing between "two types of prophecy", but between something that we *would* call prophecy, and something we would *not*. He is distinguishing divinely inspired speech and other revelation from rational discernment and interpretation (*not* augury) applied to such revelation. That is not a very close parallel to glossolalia and its interpretation. The use of terminology is fundamentally different (for one thing, nothing suggests that someone called a προφήτης does the discerning and/or interpreting). Dunn is aware of this, but not of all the consequences. As he says:

> The parallel with Plato's distinction between prophecy of inspiration and prophecy of interpretation breaks down. Prophecy is not to glossolalia as interpretation is to inspired utterance. Glossolalia does require interpretation, but that is a separate charisma from prophecy ('interpretation of tongues' - see below 41.3), so that Pauline prophecy is, if anything, more analogous to prophecy of inspiration in Plato's distinction.[5]

Insofar as this goes, it is correct. For Paul, it is precisely the προφήτης who is inspired, and who needs no spokesman beyond himself. He combines in his person the functions of both μάντις and προφήτης in the Platonic sense. But even terminology is not the real problem here. In the Timaeus passage it is the point of the προφήτης that he is *not* inspired, but in full control of his rational faculties. Paul would, I think, deny the antithesis, though the Corinthians may not have. But for Paul inspired speech and its interpretation are both equally inspired. One is not the merely rational explication of the other. Indeed, Paul does not seem to contemplate the possibility that glossolalia could be interpreted by any purely rational process: if one prays in a tongue, then one's own mind is unfruitful, and no one else understands. In the Phaedrus passage, on the other hand, the προφῆτις - the Pythian priestess - is described as being both inspired (ἔνθεος), and "manic", and yet there is no suggestion in Phaedrus that her utterances required interpretation either by one similarly "gifted", or more "sane", than she. The contrast Dunn is drawing between ecstasy and rationality is one founded more on modern psychology than on a study of the ancient evidence.[6]

---

[5] J.D.G. Dunn, *op.cit.*, p. 228.

[6] The ancients used the terms "manic" and "ecstatic" in far less clearly defined senses than those with which we are familiar. Neither "mania" nor "ecstasy" necessarily mean loss of consciousness or self-control, in the ancient world. These connotations to the terms are the result of psychological over-interpretation. The study of early Christian glossolalia and prophecy would be better off if these terms were not used at all, as I have argued above in Chapter 3.

2. Phenomena

More fundamentally, there is no decisive evidence to indicate that the Pythian priestess ever spoke her oracles in a form analogous to glossolalia. On the contrary, all our evidence suggests that she spoke in perfectly intelligible, though sometimes ambiguous, Greek. This point is not at all clear in the standard treatment of the matter. Parke and Wormell speak of the Pythia in these terms:

Before the inquirer entered, the Pythia was already under the influence of Apollo, and was in some abnormal state of trance or ecstasy. The Prophet or chief priest asked the inquirer's question, which he had already received in verbal or written form, and the Pythia's answer would vary in its degree of coherence and intelligibility. When it had been given, the prophet would reduce it to some form, and dictate it to the inquirer who could, if he wished, have it recorded in writing.[7]

Joseph Fontenrose, on the other hand, argues that

there is no reliable evidence in ancient literature or art for a frenzied or raving Pythia: the conception of the Pythia's madness, found in a few late writers, has its origin in Plato's conception of prophetic mania . . . the Pythia no more takes leave of her senses or enters into violent emotional outbursts than, as a rule, do poets or lovers in the inspiration and emotion which they experience. The Greek word *mania* was translated into Latin as *insania* or *vecordia* in Plato's meaning as in others, so that Lucan and other poets described a mad and raving Pythia . . . If we dispose of the Pythia's frenzy, we dispose also of her incoherent babbling . . . All records and responses that speak of the Pythia represent her speaking directly and clearly to the inquirer . . .[8]

---

[7] H.W. Parke and D.E.W. Wormell, *The Delphic Oracle*, Oxford, 1956, p. 33.

[8] J. Fontenrose, *The Delphic Oracle*, University of California Press, Berkeley, 1978, pp. 204, 212. Fontenrose' general conclusions about the transmission and historicity of reports of Delphic utterances are highly contentious. His views on the nature of Delphic inspiration, however, which are logically independent, are far less open to criticism, and are in line with much other scholarly work on the subject. The almost universal practice of translating μανία as "madness" has naturally helped to obscure the fact that the Pythia is not pictured as raving. Both A.E. Taylor and J. Pieper paraphrase the term as "in a state of exaltation", which quite properly leaves open the question of whether the person concerned retains any self-control or self-consciousness; see A.E. Taylor, *Plato: the Man and His Work*, London, 1926, and J. Pieper, *Love and Inspiration*, trans. R. and C. Winston, London, 1964, p. 52. Aune is likewise critical of the "raving" of the Pythia, *Prophecy*, p. 33. We note in passing that if Fontenrose' wider case, to the effect that historically genuine oracles are uniformly plain and banal, should be true, parallels with glossolalia would become even less likely. But regardless of this, what is clear is that the uniform popular view in the first century was that oracles were regularly ambiguous. This matter will be taken up further below.

The question of the mental state and verbal coherency of the Pythia, and the role of the προφήτης, therefore, will need systematic examination.

Was the Pythia frenzied?

Disposing of the Pythia's "frenzy" is not quite as straightforward as Fontenrose would like to think. His conclusion stands without contradiction for the classical period. For the Hellenistic and Roman period with which we are dealing here, the evidence is somewhat confusing. In favour of Fontenrose' interpretation is Plutarch's discussion of the effects of strong emotion on the Pythia, in Mor. 437 d. Here, as background to his discussion of a case where something went badly wrong at an oracular session, because of which the Pythia subsequently died, he says:

> you will at least all agree that the prophetic priestess herself is subjected to differing influences (πάθεσι), varying from time to time, which affect that part of her soul with which the spirit of inspiration (πνεῦμα, of inspiration implied) comes into association, and that she does not always keep one temperament (κρᾶσις), like a perfect concord, unchanged on every occasion. For many annoyances and disturbances of which she is conscious, and many more unperceived, lay hold upon her body and filter into her soul; and whenever she is replete with these, it is better that she should not go there and surrender herself to the god, when she is not completely unhampered (as if she were a musical instrument, well strung and well tuned), but is in a state of emotion and instability (ἐμπαθῆ καὶ ἀκατάστατον).[9]

In this passage, then, it is clear that the inspiration of the Pythia cannot be simply interpreted as hysterical frenzy, since any emotional disturbance of any importance means that the Pythia ought to take a couple of days' sick leave.

Some passages from Plutarch may be cited against this view, however, as well as for it: that

> in the same way (as Bacchants return to a normal frame of mind as the music becomes less frantic, C.F.) the Pythia regains calm and tranquillity (ἐν γαλήνῃ καὶ ἡσυχίᾳ διατελεῖ) once she has left her tripod and its exhalations (πνεύματα) . . .

clearly implies at least some degree of mental disturbance[10]. Likewise, while discussing three forms of enthusiasm, the Apolline, the Dionysiac and the Erotic, Plutarch says of a case of passionate erotic love:

---

[9]   Plutarch, "On the Obsolescence of Oracles", Mor. 437 d. The passage is cited by W.E. Mills, *op.cit.*, p. 84, as evidence for the symptoms of ἐνθουσιασμός recognised at Plutarch's time (change of voice, trance), without any recognition that Plutarch clearly sees the incident as completely atypical.

[10]   Plutarch, Mor. 759 b. Fontenrose' comment that the Pythia's state is "a return to calm after excitement, not a return to sanity after madness or frenzy or delirium" (*op.cit.*, p.

In Heaven's name . . . is not this a plain case of divine possession (θεοληψία)? Is it not a supernatural agitation of the soul (δαιμόνιος σάλος τῆς ψυχῆς)? Is the disturbance of the Pythia grasping her tripod so great? Do the flute, the tambourine (τύμπανον), the hymns to Cybele, cause so much ecstasy (ἐνθεαζομένων) in any of the devotees?[11]

There is some limited evidence, then, to support the "frenzy" interpretation of Delphic inspiration, since this inspiration did have some perceptible physical and mental symptoms. Whether these amounted to "violent emotional outbursts" is far more questionable. To that extent Fontenrose' case is still arguable. But he is most certainly correct to dispose of the Pythia's "incoherent babbling", for which there is no ancient evidence, as we shall see.

Oracular Obscurity

It is important here for us to distinguish clearly between the kind of "incoherent babbling" suggested above, a phenomenon which is unintelligible at a linguistic level, and the well known obscurity of Pythian oracular utterances. Unfortunately many modern writers have confused the discussion by using the term "unintelligible" indiscriminately for both phenomena.[12] The obscurity of Delphic utterances is not a matter of *linguistic* unintelligibility at all. It is simply that some such oracles were formulated, at the level of literary allusion and metaphor, in obscure, cryptic and enigmatic terms. They were, in a word, oracular. With this distinction in mind, then, we can say that Fontenrose' criticism of the popular picture of the Pythia's "incoherent babbling" is correct. The accounts of oracular consultations are quite clear on this point.

The role of the Προφήτης

The next question to be asked is: if Fontenrose' view is correct, precisely what is the role of the προφήτης? If the Pythia's inspired utterances are not

---

211) is weakened by his admission, paraphrasing Plutarch, that "It is the same kind of feeling . . . that a bacchant or corybant feels after the dance." Bacchic and Corybantic frenzy are more than just excitement. Thus also, correctly, T.M. Crone, *Prophecy*, pp. 31ff, though Euripides, Ion 533-4, which he cites, certainly does not prove it. This weakness of Fontenrose' case has also been noticed by F.E. Brenk, in his review of Fontenrose' book in *Gnomon*, vol. 52, 1980, pp. 700ff, esp. p. 705. See also Philo, de Vita Mosis 1.175, for a similar description of inspired behaviour.

[11] Plutarch, Mor. 763 a. The debate emanating from Rohde's work on the effects of the cults of Dionysus and Apollo on each other is too extensive to survey here.

[12] H. Krämer, in his portion of the article on "Προφήτης", in vol. 6 of *T.D.N.T.*, pp. 781ff, appears to be aware of the distinction, and to avoid the error as a result, but the point remains implicit rather than explicit.

incoherent but merely sometimes cryptic, what role does he play? For clearly the "official" versions of oracles, which have been through the hands of the προφήτης, are often cryptic and ambiguous too. Does he perhaps simply take a relatively straightforward prose utterance of the Pythia, and render it into a formal verse response?[13] Or does he simply write out the formal written reply?

The answer would appear to be, on both counts, no. In none of our sources is there any suggestion that the Pythia's originally prose oracle is versified by the προφήτης. In Herodotus there are more than forty cases where oracles are reported, and in none of these is the form or content of the oracle attributed to anybody other than the Pythia herself. Three times individuals conspire to pervert the oracle: in each case they conspire with the Pythia, not the προφήτης. In three cases it is explicitly said that the Pythia answered inquirers in particular verse forms. In a number of cases the inquirers write out the reply for themselves. In one notable case an oracle is so ambiguous that the inquirers return for an explanation: it is the Pythia who interprets her own words.[14] Further, Plutarch's whole discussion of why the Oracle of his own day no longer gave verse responses assumes that the verses of earlier days were the very words of the Pythia herself. He is discussing "the verses put forth by the Pythia" (Mor. 396 f) which specifically attributes the form to her. Again, he assumes that oracles in his own time were not normally written: "if it were necessary to write the oracles, instead of delivering them orally" (Mor. 397 b-c), then that could be done. There is, however, some evidence that oracles were versified after

---

[13] Thus T.M. Crone, *Prophecy*, p. 34, note 65 (p. 310): "It is best to assume that the prophets put the intelligible response of the unlearned Pythia into proper form." The case is made out in detail for the classical period by W.E. McLeod, "Oral Bards at Delphi", *T.A.Ph.A.* vol. 92, 1961, pp. 317-325 (cited by Aune, *Prophecy* p. 361, note 9, but misspelled McLeon), but it must be argued in the teeth of the evidence presented below. McLeod is forced to explain the lack of any positive evidence with the comment that "Naturally it would never do to advertise that there were men who could tamper with the words of the god's mouthpiece!" (p. 320.)

[14] Once or twice the oracles are credited to the shrine itself, as an institution, but in every case except 1.20 the Pythia is mentioned at some point as the actual speaker. For the conspiracies see Herodotus 5.63, cf. 5.90 and 6.123, 6.66 and 75, and Thucydides 5.16.2. In 1.47 and 7.220 the Pythia is said to deliver her oracles in hexameters, and in 1.174 in trimeters. In the majority of cases where oracles are reported in direct speech, rather than simply being mentioned, they are given in poetic form. In 1.47 Lydians, and in 7.141 Athenian envoys write out what they hear from the Pythia. In 1.91 she explains her own prophecy.

delivery, but it is not clear whether this was always regarded as proper. Plutarch, speaking of an era previous to his own, says:

Moreover, there was an oft-repeated tale that certain men with a gift for poetry were wont to sit about close to the shrine waiting to catch the words spoken, and then weaving about them a fabric of extempore hexameters or other verses or rhythms as "containers", so to speak, for the oracles. . .[15]

He cites this as one of the reasons that poetic oracles fell out of favour, and clearly does not treat the practice as a legitimate part of the oracle's activity. The men in question were working "free-lance". Strabo, on the other hand, thinks that such people were employed for the job:

They say that over the opening is set a high tripod on which the Pythia mounts, receives the πνεῦμα, and speaks oracles in both verse and prose; and these too are put into verse by certain poets who work for the sanctuary.[16]

In no case were the people in question the προφῆται.[17] In many other cases it seems to be presumed that the Pythia was responsible. It may be that the expedients mentioned above only arose as poetic oracles from the Pythia herself became less common, or the stories may be baseless. The question is, however, what was the task of the προφῆται? Does it have anything to do with the oracular function at all? Probably not. In Fontenrose' view,

in every account of a consultation we are told that the inquirer spoke directly to the Pythia (or to the god) and that the Pythia (or the god) responded directly to him. Nowhere are we told that the priest-prophet informed the inquirer of the god's response,

[15] Plutarch, "Why the Oracles at Delphi are no longer given in verse", Mor. 407 b. Many oracles were transmitted in verse form; see, e.g. Plutarch Mor. 399 c. Mor. 397 c is quite explicit as to the origin of the poetic form: "the voice is not that of a god, nor the utterance of it, nor the diction, nor the metre, but all these are the woman's . . . "

[16] Strabo 9.3.5. Plutarch, Mor. 403 e .also reports part of a scholarly debate between Theopompus and other, earlier writers about whether verse oracles occurred. Plutarch agrees with Theopompus' conclusion that they were more common in earlier days.

[17] R.M. Berchman, *art.cit.*, p. 387, suggests that "In rare cases, such as at Delphi, priests were called *prophetai* because they interpreted the obscure utterances of the mantis Pythia (*sic*) who was directly inspired by Apollo. Priests put her message into verse for those who consulted the oracle". In support of this contention he cites Sextus Empiricus Adv. Dog. 3.20, Aristotle, Problems 30, 945a 34ff., Cicero, de Divinatione 1.18, 1.64, 1.70, 1.113 and Plutarch, Mor. 431e-f. Though these passages discuss the nature of oracular inspiration, *not one* of them suggests that προφῆται interpret the obscure utterances of μάντεις, or that this was why they were called προφῆται. On the contrary: those called προφῆται were normally priests, and were called προφῆται because they were spokesmen. Our evidence will not support the claim that it was priests who versified, in the rare cases where it is suggested that anyone but the Pythia herself did so. Even Strabo, cited above, the only ancient writer who thinks the versifiers were officials of the sanctuary, does not say they were priests.

except when the actual inquirer was not himself present but had sent one or more envoys. Then the priest copied the response and sealed the copy within an envelope, which he delivered to the envoys . . .

. . . the title *prophetes*, then, is either an unofficial title that non-Delphians used after the analogy of usage at other oracular shrines, such as Didyma, or, more probably, was the designation of the *hiereus* who presided at an oracular session - it may be that two priests took turns in attendance. . . In most instances a *prophetes* is not himself a *mantis*; he is the god's representative, a man who oversees and administers an oracular session.[18]

Even this view, however, must be questioned. While it is very limited, there is some evidence that the προφήτης' role was that of intermediary between inquirers and the "inner staff" of the temple, and that he had no role in the "inner sanctum" at all. In Euripides' Ion, ll. 413-416, Xouthos, inquiring of the Oracle, asks Ion: "Now who is to speak for the god (προφητεύει)?" and Ion replies: "Outside it is me; inside others are in charge, Delphian nobles, who are appointed by lot to sit near the tripod." It may even be the case, then, that the προφήτης has no other role than that suggested by his title: to act as official spokesman.[19] The rest of our evidence, however, does suggest some formal supervisory role.

Insofar as this minimising argument is restricted to Delphi, it appears to be correct. When we cast our net more widely it must be qualified. We still find no evidence for frenzy as a regular part of Greek oracular practice, but we do find the term προφήτης being used of persons inspired by the gods or demigods, as in the Phaedrus passage. Plutarch in several places describes προφῆται as being inspired or as giving oracles directly, with no μάντις or other person mentioned. In Mor. 412 a. he describes the giving of an oracle to Mys, the Carian, by the προφήτης of Ptoan Apollo. In Mor.

---

[18] J. Fontenrose, *op.cit.*, pp. 217-8. Compare T.M. Crone's cautious assessment: "The exact function of the προφήτης at Delphi is never stated and is not so easy to determine." (*Prophecy*, p. 33.) The majority of scholars still assert, however, that the προφῆται played a mediating role of some sort: even the excellent article of S. Price, "Delphi and Divination", in *Greek Religion and Society*, ed. P. Easterling and J. Muir, Cambridge, 1985, which correctly criticises many aspects of the common view of Delphic practice, still suggests that the προφῆται were involved in the "ordering and writing down (in prose or verse) of the Pythia's responses" (p. 142).

[19] The reference and translation are from C.R. Whittaker, "The Delphic Oracle; Belief and Behaviour in Ancient Greece - and Africa", *H.Th.R.* vol. 58, no. 1, 1965, pp. 21-47, esp. pp. 24-5. The passage is, however, the only one that Whittaker can cite against the strong impression one gains from Herodotus and other sources that the public have a good deal to do with the Pythia herself, directly. It could well be argued that Ion's statement has more to do with the demands of his dramatic role than actual Delphic practice.

414 e Plutarch severely criticises a popular theory of the inspiration of prophecy, arguing that it would be foolish to suggest that the god himself actually enters the bodies of his προφῆται. The argument has no particular Delphic reference, but does suggest that people did believe that persons called προφῆται were inspired. In Mor. 431 b he discusses the causes of the inspiration of prophets and prophetesses in general. In Mor. 438 a he discusses the inspiration (ἐνθουσιασμός) of those who prophesy (προφητεύουσιν) generally. Finally, in Mor. 412 b, he mentions the oracle given to the Greeks while Echecrates was προφήτης of Tegyrae; the verb (προφητεύοντος) could be taken as meaning that he himself gave the oracle, or may (more likely) simply be a dating reference like the hundreds to be found in the inscriptions; for this see Chapter 8.

It would appear, then, that at Delphi the role of the προφήτης fell within the range defined above. At other cult centres, however, and in the popular mind, the term προφήτης was closely associated with the giving of oracles, and may have been used for the person inspired by the god in question.[20] The reason, as I will argue in detail in Chapter 8, is simple. In many cases μάντεις acted as their own προφῆται.

Oracular obscurity: terminology

The distinction between glossolalia and oracular speech in the Hellenistic world generally can be made even sharper. That world had available to it a well-recognised vocabulary to describe oracular vagueness. It included terms like ἀμφίβολος[21], ἀμφίλογος[22], ὑπόνοια[23], ἀσάφεια[24], and σκια[25].

---

[20] Cf. Aune, *Prophecy*, p. 31, who says "In all these cases there is not the slightest suggestion that the inspired utterances of the Pythia or any other *promantis* or *prophetes* of which we have knowledge was incomprehensible until "interpreted" by other cult officials." This is perfectly correct. In my own reading I have noted the term προφήτης as follows in reference to personnel at Delphi: the great majority of the references are from works of Plutarch.

Used of the Pythia: Mor. 397 b-c, and d, 414 b, twice. Plato, Phaedrus 244 a, the προφῆτις at Delphi. Diodorus Siculus 14.13.3, 16.26.2-6 (twice). See over.

Used of other Delphic officials: Plutarch, Mor. 407 d, ὑπηρέταις καὶ προφήταις (general reference only), 410 e, 438 b.

In nine cases the term was in the feminine, and referred to the Pythia herself. In the other three cases it referred to the προφήτης (male), but provided no evidence that this person had any oracular function. In one case a particular προφήτης was mentioned by name, and in the other the term was used in the plural of people who might be expected to offer a theological defence of oracles in general.

[21] e.g. Mor. 386 e, 408 e, f, 409 d, f., Diodorus Siculus 9.31.1; in a non-oracular context Polybius uses αἰνιγματώδεις, ἀμφιβόλους and ἐκφανεῖς (diminishing order of

These terms are *never*, so far as I am aware, used by Christian writers to describe inspired speech phenomena within their communities. The unintelligibility of glossolalia is never so described. Only the term αἴνιγμα seems to be common.[26] When early Christian writers wish to describe the unintelligibility of glossolalia, they describe it as an unknown language, or else as resembling the sounds of musical instruments, often when they are not played properly. This metaphor may have been suggested by the persistent tendency among non-Christian authors to describe inspiration with musical metaphors[27] but the description of it as unknown human or angelic language is far harder to parallel.

There do exist two passages, which, as far as I am aware, have not figured in the modern discussion of glossolalia and Hellenistic oracular practice, which suggest that the obscurity of oracular utterances was due to their having been translated not from human, but from divine languages. In his tenth Discourse, Dio Chrysostom has Diogenes the Cynic ask:

Do you think Apollo speaks Attic or Doric? Or that man and gods have the same language? Yet the difference is so great that . . . from this it naturally follows that the oracles are obscure (ἀσαφῆ) . . .[28]

---

obscurity!) in 15.25.31. Philo uses ἀμφίβολος for simple ambiguity in de Agricultura 16, and to describe soothsaying in de Spec Leg. 63.

[22] e.g. Plutarch, Mor. 407 e.

[23] e.g. Plutarch, Mor. 407 e.

[24] e.g. Plutarch, Mor. 407 c, 409 c, f.

[25] = obscurity, Plutarch, Mor. 407 a.

[26] For which, in an oracular context, see Mor. 347 d, and Diodorus Siculus 32.10.2. Paul uses the term once only, in 1 Cor. 13.12; it is not otherwise used in the N.T., though it later becomes a standard patristic term for the riddling quality of difficult Scripture passages. It need not have a more technical meaning than "dim" or "obscure": see note 21 above. For the patristic references see Lampe, *A Patristic Greek Lexicon*. Philo contrasts the αἰνιγματῶδες sense of Scripture with its literal sense in de Spec. Leg. 1.200. "Words in their plain sense are symbols of things latent and obscure (ἀδήλων καὶ ἀφανῶν). Kittel (*T.D.N.T.*, vol. 1 pp. 178-180) believes Paul's use of the term reflects the LXX usage.

[27] See, for example, Plutarch, Mor. 418 d, 431 a, 436 f, 437 d (cited above, n.9) and less directly, 404 f, Philo, Who is the Heir 266, and de Spec. Leg. 4.49.

[28] Dio Chrysostom, Discourse 10.23; cf. 11.22. Inexplicably, C.H. Talbert argues that we have in the sentences that follow, in 10.23-4, "hints at sham glossolalia in referring to 'persons who know two or three Persian, Median or Assyrian words and thus fool the ignorant' ", "Paul's Understanding of the Holy Spirit: the Evidence of 1 Corinthians 12-14", *Perspectives in Religious Studies*, Vol. 11, No. 4, 1984, p. 104. The statement has no connotations of inspiration at all: it describes people who fool the ignorant into believing they know foreign languages!

It should be noted, however, that there is no suggestion here that the divine language in question is what the Pythia speaks, or that anybody at all translates. Nor is there any suggestion that one ought to try to master such languages, in order, for example, to communicate with the gods in prayer. What Dio is suggesting is that oracles become obscure as they pass from the divine to the human realm, and are thus translated from the divine language into the normal human language of the Pythia, *not* as they pass from the unintelligible words of the Pythia to the normal language of the προφήτης.

Finally, the link is also made (though less explicitly) in the Stromata of Clement of Alexandria, where Clement cites a passage of Plato (either in error, or from some work which is no longer extant). Discussing the number of languages which exist, he says that

Plato attributes a dialect also to the gods, forming this conjecture mainly from dreams and oracles, and especially from demoniacs, who do not speak their own language or dialect, but that of the demons who have taken possession of them.[29]

It would seem likely that the same points apply here as applied to the Dio quotation. The Homeric concept of divine languages was still known in the second century A.D. But it ought to be noted that Clement *does not* make a link with the concept of glossolalia. This passage adds nothing to the information of Dio Chrysostom beyond the inclusion of demoniacs. Nothing here suggests oracles spoke in "other tongues", human, divine or angelic / daimonic. The question of "divine languages" in our Hellenistic sources will be taken up in detail in Chapter 7.

Oracular obscurity or unintelligible speech: a case study

The point about the distinction between oracular ambiguity and linguistic unintelligibility may be illustrated from Aeschylus' "Agamemnon". The prophetess Cassandra, doomed by Apollo never to be understood or believed until it is too late, foretells the woes to come upon Agamemnon's house. The Chorus several times say that they cannot understand her. At one point they say: "For now the riddling sayings leave me bewildered by their dim oracles" and at another point she is described as speaking "with inarticulate sound". Despite the fact that her prophecies are given in detail in the play, the suggestion has been made (on the basis of this description), that her speech is unintelligible. On the other hand, a little later in the play, when

---

[29] Clement of Alexandria, Stromata 1.21, *Ante-Nicene Fathers Library*, vol. 2, p. 332. The passage is cited by G. Dautzenberg, "Glossolalie", col. 231, but has not otherwise been given much prominence in the modern discussion.

she begins to make references in her prophecies to recent events, the Chorus respond: "What word is this that thou hast uttered all too plain? A little child that heard it might understand." When Cassandra later assures the Chorus: "And yet I know the speech of Hellas all too well", they respond: "Aye, so do the Pythian ordinances; but still they are hard to understand."[30] The point here is, I think, clear. It is not Cassandra's *language* that is the reason for her prophecies not being understood: it is the obscure allusions with which she expresses herself. According to the Chorus, this is also precisely the case with the Delphic oracle.

Only once does the pre-Christian Hellenistic world *ever*, so far as I am aware, describe the inspired speech of a prophet/mantis as resembling a foreign language. This is the case of Mys the Carian, who consulted many shrines in Greece during the time of the Persian Wars. His consultation of the oracle of Ptoan Apollo is described by Herodotus, Pausanias, and, twice, by Plutarch. Herodotus says that the πρόμαντις answered in a barbarian language, and notes that the accompanying Thebans were amazed not to hear Greek - clearly plain Greek was the norm - and that only the Carian realised that what the πρόμαντις (now described as a προφήτης) was saying was in Carian.[31] Plutarch, in Mor. 412 a., says that the person who

---

[30] In all cases the translation cited is that of E. Fraenkel, *Aeschylus' Agamemnon*, Oxford, 1962. The particular passages cited are as follows: Line 1112; "inarticulate sound", Line 1152 (the term is δύσφατος, which Fraenkel paraphrases as "hardly intelligible", *op.cit.*, p. 528. When used of oracular sayings, it normally indicates obscurity: cf. Euripides' Ion, line 782, and Plato, Timaeus, 50c); Lines 1162-3 and Lines 1254-5. For the suggestion that Cassandra's speech is a mixture of the linguistically intelligible and unintelligible see N.I.J. Engelsen, *Glossolalia*, pp. 14-16. Engelsen also argues that Cassandra's apparently meaningless cries, "Ityn", "Ototoi" etc., and the comparison of her speech to the twittering of swallows by the Chorus, reinforce the point: like all prophets she gives unintelligible cries, and χελιδονίζω is a functional equivalent of βαρβαρίζω (pp. 14-16). It is true that bird noises are occasionally used as a metaphor for barbarian speech, and this appears to be the case here. But neither βαρβαρίζω nor χελιδονίζω is *ever* used of oracles, as far as I am aware. As for "Ityn", that is a literary allusion to the nightingale's lament for her lover, Itys (see Aristophanes, Birds 213, and E. Fraenkel, *op.cit.*, p. 522, in vol. III) and thus a cry of grief, not ecstasy. The same is true of "ototoi", as a simple comparison with Aeschylus' Persae, 268 and 274, and Euripides' Phoenician Women, 1530, will show.

[31] Herodotus 8.135. The passage is cited as a parallel to glossolalia, apparently without note being taken of its exceptional nature, (for which see below) by E.R. Dodds, "Supernormal Phenomena in Classical Antiquity", in *The Ancient Concept of Progress and Other Essays*, Oxford, 1973, p. 202 n. 8, and briefly, without much comment, by K. Wicker, in H.D. Betz, ed., *Plutarch's Theological Writings and Early Christian Literature*, Leiden, 1975, p. 139. Inexplicably, Dodds links this passage with the

answered was the προφήτης, and that the answer was not understood except by Mys: he does not describe the language, except to say that it was not Greek. In his "Life of Aristides" he again says that the speaker was the προφήτης; this time he specifies that the answer was in Carian (ὁ προφήτης Καρικῇ γλώσσῃ προσεῖπεν . . .).[32] Finally, Pausanias gives the speaker as simply the god, and describes the oracle as being in διαλέκτῳ τῇ Καρικῇ.[33] The case is quite clearly treated as an extraordinary one by the ancient writers. Herodotus' mention of the amazement of the Thebans and Plutarch's explicit statement that the προφήτης normally spoke in the Aeolian dialect both reinforce the point: oracles normally spoke in plain Greek.

How did Oracles speak?

What little we do know of Hellenistic inspired or "charismatic" speech in the first century suggests strongly that the only manifestations of the phenomenon which were really well known to the ordinary man or woman were that form which was actually prevalent at Delphi, and that other form which Plutarch describes as follows: there exists

the tribe of wandering soothsayers and rogues that practised their charlatanry about the shrines of the Great Mother and of Serapis, making up oracles (χρησμοὺς), some using their own ingenuity, others taking by lot from certain treatises oracles for the benefit of servants and womenfolk, who are most enticed by verse and a poetic vocabulary . . .[34]

Homeric "Hymn to Apollo", line 162, for the claim that the *Delian* priestesses could "imitate the speech of all men". This suggestion is made despite the fact that the Delian festival referred to seems to have no oracular connections whatsoever. On the Homeric Hymn see further below. T.M. Crone, *Prophecy*, who otherwise rejects the concept of oracular unintelligibility, inexplicably links the Mys passage with Delphic practice, p. 36. M.E. Hart, *Tongues And Prophecy*, p. 11 is quite correct to say that "descriptions of the working of the oracle have not hinted at foreign languages for the gibberish (*sic*) that the Pythia utters".

There is only one other conceivable parallel of which I am aware for the idea of oracles speaking other languages: in the mid 2nd Century Apuleius begins the "Cupid and Psyche" section of his Golden Ass with a Latin response from Apollo of Miletus, which he claims was given directly by Apollo. But this is clearly a literary fiction. See H.W. Parke, *The Oracles of Apollo in Asia Minor*, London, 1985, pp. 75-6.

[32] Plutarch, On the Obsolescence of Oracles, Mor. 412 a, Life of Aristides, 19.1-2. In this latter passage he inexplicably places the events at the oracle of Trophonius.

[33] Pausanias, Description of Greece, 9.23.6.

[34] Plutarch, Mor. 407 c. Compare Tacitus, Annals 2.54, where the priest of Clarian Apollo is specifically noted as giving his oracles in verse "though ignorant generally of literature and metre". Whether or not Tacitus' account of Clarian procedure is correct, it

If this is understood to mean that the fortune-tellers described are "charismatic" in any sense, then the passage would seem to suggest that if there was any form of speech likely to convince ordinary people that the speaker was inspired, then it would be archaic and poetic, rather than glossolalic. However, it is not clear whether they are seen as "inspired", or as practitioners of augury. Regardless of this, the suggestion made above would appear to be substantiated by the fact that the Pythia's ceasing to give her oracles in verse was seen as a problem: hence Plutarch's essay on the subject.[35] Both at Delphi and elsewhere, poetry and archaic diction were expected.

---

testifies to the popular view of inspiration. On the use of collections of oracles, and selecting responses from them, see *New Documents Illustrating Early Christianity*, vol. 2, ed. G.H.R. Horsley, North Ryde, N.S.W., 1982, pp. 37-44, which also cites a number of late verse oracles. The Plutarch reference demonstrates that the use of such augural tools as the "Sortes Astrampsychi" goes back to the first century. His Life of Agesilaus 3 (cf. Xenophon, Hellenica 3.3.3) and Aristophanes, Birds 960ff., show that collections of oracles were in use well before the earliest extant examples of the collections themselves.
[35] Hence his eloquent apologia in Mor. 408f: "And as for the language of the Pythia, just as the mathematicians call the shortest of lines between two points a straight line, so her language (now) makes no bend nor curve nor doubling nor equivocation (ἀμφιβολία), but is straight in relation to the truth . . . yet it has afforded no proof of its being wrong." Perhaps the most impressive evidence that this was the dominant view of inspired speech is the vast bulk of preserved oracular responses, overwhelmingly in verse, scattered through most of Greek literature. On this well-known phenomenon see most recently H.W. Parke, *The Oracles of Apollo in Asia Minor*, London, 1985, pp. 28, 76-92, citing many examples from Didyma, and pp. 144, 146, 148, and 151ff., with examples from Claros. The epigraphic evidence is equally strong: for representative examples see *Didyma Inscriptions*, nos. 569-581. Note also that not all of these are obscure by any means: No. 577.5, though in poetic form, is perfectly clear. Whether verse actually *was* the form taken by most oracles (the point is disputed by Fontenrose, as noted above, and indeed, was disputed in Plutarch's time: see Mor. 403e-404b) is, however, irrelevant: clearly it was *believed* that this was the norm in the late Hellenistic and early Imperial periods. The idea that poetic diction is expected of the inspired is also explicitly stated in Mor. 623 a, where Plutarch suggests that "to the god-inspired (τοῖς ἐνθεαζομένοις) it is given to chant oracles in metre (χρησμῳδεῖν ἐμμέτρως) and few madmen can one find whose ravings are not in verse and song". Compare Mor. 566 d-e and 675 a, which describe the Sibyl prophesying in verse. See also Dionysius of Halicarnassus' description of prophetic poetry in A.R. 1.31.1. He calls the inspired lady "Themis", which is probably an etymology for the verb θεμιστεύω. Themis was also the name of the previous inhabitant of Apollo's Delphic oracle: see Mor. 566 d, and, for synopses of the differing stories of the oracle's prehistory, K. Latte, "The Coming of the Pythia", *H.Th.R.*, vol. 33, 1940, pp. 9-18, and R.E. Heine, "A Note on Lucan's Bellum Civile 5.79-81", *Classical Bulletin*, vol. 54, January, 1978, p. 44. Dionysius' story is repeated by Plutarch, Mor. 278 c. See also Pausanias, Description of Greece 10.5.6ff. and 10.7.3.

It would appear, therefore, that the attempt to parallel early Christian inspired speech from phenomena drawn from oracle cult procedure ought to be abandoned, in the form it has so far taken, as highly misleading. The respective terminologies are significantly different, and the phenomena under discussion have very little in common.

3. The Homeric Hymn to Delian Apollo

It has been suggested that there is one other source which provides a parallel between glossolalia and the cult of, not Delphic, but Delian Apollo. This is the "Homeric" Hymn to Delian Apollo, which vividly describes the ceremonies of the traditional Ionian festival of the sixth and fifth centuries B.C. According to the hymn, it is at Delos that

the long-robed Ionians gather with their children and shy wives. Mindful, they delight you [Apollo] with boxing and dancing and song, so often as they hold their gathering . . . And there is this great wonder (μέγα θαῦμα) besides - and its renown shall never perish -, the girls of Delos, hand-maidens of the Far-shooter; for when they have praised Apollo first (πρῶτον μὲν), and also Leto and Artemis (αὖτις δ' αὖ Λητώ τε καὶ ᾿Αρτεμιν) who delights in arrows, they sing a strain telling of men and women of past days, and charm the tribes of men. Also they can imitate (μιμεῖσθ' ἴσασιν) the tongues of all men and their clattering speech: each would say that he himself were singing, so close to truth is their sweet song.

The claim that the "great wonder" cited by the poet, that of the imitation of "the tongues of all men", is a miracle of speech or hearing parallel to Luke's report of the Pentecost miracle is made by H.J. Tschiedel, in an article written in 1975.[36] His argument may be summarised as follows:

The closing events of the Delian festival, the hymns to the gods and heroes and the "imitation" of the tongues of all men, are described as being a μέγα θαῦμα, and the description of the Ionians as resembling immortals

---

See also the other verbs which are specifically about poetic prophecy: θεμιστεύω: Plutarch, Mor. 406 b., 384 f., 1048 c (used of Apollo). θεσπίζω: Plutarch Mor. 402 b., 404 a, 421 b (προθεσπίζω); θεσπιῳδεῖν: to prophesy in verse, Plutarch Mor. 407 d quoting Euripides (a θεσπιῳδός was one of the key officials at the shrine of Clarian Apollo in the second and third centuries A.D.: see Chapter 8 below, and H.W. Parke, *op.cit.*, p. 147ff and 220-223.); θέσφατος: oracle, Dionysius of Halicarnassus, A.R. 4.4.2., 4.62.5 (the Sibyllines!).

[36] H.J. Tschiedel, "Ein Pfingstwunder im Apollonhymnus", *Zeitschrift für Religions- und Geistesgeschichte*, vol. 27, 1975, pp. 22-39. The passage is also cited by E.R. Dodds, "Supernormal Phenomena in Classical Antiquity", in *The Ancient Concept of Progress and Other Essays*, Oxford, 1973, p. 202 n.8., as noted above, footnote 31. Tschiedel's view seems to be accepted by G. Dautzenberg, "Glossolalie", col. 321.

likewise prepares the reader for some remarkable manifestation.[37] Yet nothing in the description of the hymns to the Gods and heroes really lives up to that expectation. The verb θέλγω, which is used of the effect of the songs on the audience, is translated "bezaubern", ("enchant" or "bewitch") by Tschiedel, which again suggests the supernatural. Of the events mentioned, only one can justify the poet's description: the "imitation of the tongues of all men". It must be understood as a Pentecost-like miracle of inspired speech or hearing.[38] Several parallels may be drawn between the poem and the account in Acts 2. Both recount events taking place at festivals. In both cases the crowds of people are of varied nationalities. Both speech-miracles are so described as to exclude natural explanation. In both cases the reaction of the hearers is to identify their own native languages. In both cases the content of the miraculous speech has to do with the praise of the god in question. The miracles both function so as to unify those who are present, breaking down national barriers. At a more sophisticated literary level, both passages act as transitions between descriptions of the earthly activities of the god, and descriptions of their continued influence from beyond the human realm.[39] Both cases are descriptions of epiphanies: the presence of the god continues, despite his physical absence. If it is objected that such a miracle is by no means normal for a sign of an epiphany among the Greek gods, Tschiedel replies that music and speech/hearing miracles

---

[37] H.J. Tschiedel, *art.cit.*, pp. 23-4, 36.

[38] H.J. Tschiedel, *art.cit.*, pp. 27-8 surveys a number of other suggestions, and argues that neither a simple mimetic performance (L. Weber) nor the survival of pre-Greek hymns into the Greek period (L. Weber, Wilamowitz) nor a polyglot assembly (Allen and Sikes) nor a group of multi-lingual maidens really explains the report which the poet gives. He argues (pp. 28-9) that at a literary level it is a report of a miracle of inspired speech, which must be understood at an historical level as a case of ecstatic gibberish from the choir, which, under the influence of the excitement of the occasion was believed by those in the audience to be their own languages. It was thus a "miracle of hearing" which was conceived of as a language miracle. Tschiedel goes on to suggest (without any historical argumentation: he simply asserts the case from unspecified modern cases of glossolalia) that the same was true at Pentecost. The case has, of course, been argued elsewhere: W.E Mills traces it back to Gregory of Nazianzen (who considered but did not accept it), and provides a brief survey of opinion before also rejecting it (*op.cit.*, pp. 60-61.

[39] In the case of the Hymn to Apollo, the description of the festival falls between the account of Apollo's birth and wanderings and his arrival at Olympia, and the subsequent work of his Delphic oracle. In the case of Acts, the Pentecost narrative links the story of Jesus' earthly life and work to the description of the continued ministry of his Apostles. Thus Tschiedel, *art.cit.*, pp. 33, 35, 38.

are thoroughly appropriate symbols for the presence of Apollo, god of music and inspired prophecy. (p. 37.) Both at Delos and Delphi, he argues, Apollo gives his people the power to understand inarticulate, ecstatic speech. At Delos this power is granted to the audience; at Delphi, it is the prerogative of the priests.

But the central point for Tschiedel's case which has not been established is simply this: is this passage an account of a miracle at all? I do not believe so. Not only is there insufficient evidence to suggest a miracle, but the passage makes far better sense without such an assumption. Tschiedel's argument assumes this point rather than attempting to prove it. Something is described as being a μέγα θαῦμα, and so a miracle must be found. But the term θαῦμα need not mean a miracle. In Homeric Greek, and in later Greek as well, it can mean "a spectacle", "something worth seeing", or "an amazing sight"; it is the effect on the viewer that the word focuses on, not the causation of the event in question.[40] In the context of the Hymn, "great spectacle" is probably a reasonable translation.

As soon as this point is understood difficulties begin to fall away. The fact that the three events described, the hymns to the gods, the hymns about "men and women of ancient times", and the "imitation of tongues" are all part of the μέγα θαῦμα, the spectacle of the festival, now makes sense, and we no longer have to argue that the "miraculous" aspect of the affair refers not to the events described in the same sentence, but only to the "tongues" described in a separate sentence. It cannot be objected that this ignores the "numinous" colouring of the passage, since this numinous quality is now seen to apply to the whole festival, not merely the "miracle" at the end. Nor

---

[40] See Iliad 18.83, Patroclus' armour is a θαῦμα, Iliad 11.287, where a beautiful woman, is a θαῦμα, Odyssey 6.306 and 13.108, where women weaving purple cloth is a θαῦμα, a "wonder", or "sight to see". Likewise the city of the Phaeacians and its buildings is a θαῦμα, Odyssey 7.45, and the fact that so fine a hound as Argos is lying in a heap of rubbish is a θαῦμα: it is a strange sight, Odyssey 17.306. For later references see Pindar, Nemean Ode 10.50, Aristophanes, Plutus 99, Plato, Republic 498 d. Even the phrase can be parallelled: an unexpected reverse in battle may be described as a μέγα θαῦμα, Iliad 13.99, as may the sight of someone you did not expect to see, Iliad 15.286, 21.54, or the disappearance of a foe in the thick of battle, Iliad 20.344. Only in the last case is the occurrence due to divine action. These are "amazing sights": their cause is irrelevant. A striking parallel may be found in Revelation 17.6, where John's vision of the Great Prostitute, Babylon, moves him to say: "Καὶ ἐθαύμασα ἰδὼν αὐτὴν θαῦμα μέγα". It is not the fact of a miraculous vision that strikes him with amazement, but rather the particular things he sees at one point of his vision.

can the verb θέλγω be made proof of the supernatural: not only does it apply most naturally to the "hymns about men and women of ancient days" rather than to what follows, but it is quite capable of a metaphorical sense as well as a magical sense, like the verbs "to charm" and "to enchant" in English.[41] The description of the Ionians as reminiscent of the immortals is simply a complement to their appearance and wealth, and need not be taken as a hint of wonders to come at all.

The second difficulty which dissolves is the fact that nothing in the passage suggests any divine inspiration whatever. There is no suggestion that the Delian girls are inspired to speak, or their listeners to understand. Despite Tschiedel's claim that both the Apollo-Hymn and the Acts account are written so as to exclude any possibility of natural causation, the Hymn is quite clear: the girls *know how to imitate* (μιμεῖσθ' ἴσασιν) the languages of men. They know how: they are not inspired; they imitate, rather than miraculously reproducing. The Hymn's language and context suggest some sort of mimetic performance far more naturally than they suggest a miracle.[42] The recognition of the listeners ceases to be the psychologically induced belief that they hear their own languages being spoken. It becomes instead a compliment to the skill of the girls' mimicry. The most recent translator of the Hymns comments as follows:

The Delian Maidens obviously followed a certain hierarchic order in their performance. They started with a hymn to Apollon, Artemis and Leto, the divine mother; then they sang a song in praise of heroes. Finally, in what must have been mimetic sketches in the various dialects of the pilgrims, they provided them with light-hearted entertainment. The sequence was thus in descending order (gods-heroes-men), and in typical Greek fashion the solemnity of the festival was tempered with a note of frivolity at the end.[43]

To my mind this descending order makes much better sense than Tschiedel's suggestion of a tension-filled miraculous climax.

Whether or not the suggestion made here is correct, several of Tschiedel's parallels will not do. First, the claim that both in Acts and the Hymn the "miracle" forms a transition between the earthly and heavenly life of the

---

[41] For such metaphorical usage see Odyssey 3.264, to charm someone with words, and esp. 17.514, 521, to charm with song or speech.

[42] Allen, Halliday and Sikes (*The Homeric Hymns*, Oxford, 1936, p. 225) suggest that rather than being conscious mimicry the "imitation" may be simply hymns in dialects, which the girls have presumably been trained to pronounce correctly. But the comment of the listeners fits conscious mimicry a little better. This solution is, however, still far more plausible than that of Tschiedel.

[43] A.N. Athanassakis, *The Homeric Hymns*, Baltimore, 1976, note on lines 157-64.

deity does not hold true for the hymn. After the "miracle", the poet asks to be remembered, and promises to carry the fame of Apollo and the festival far in his songs, and then goes on to mention his arrival at Delphi (line 183) *before* his arrival at Olympus is described. Second, the passage cannot form a bridge between Apollo's earthly wanderings and his heavenly (oracular) role. Here Tschiedel's argument is confused even in its own terms. It is not the case that normal Delphic practice included miraculous gifts of language, as we have seen. Further, his suggestion that it included miracles of *hearing* is mistaken on more than one count. First, he has not suggested that there actually *was* a miracle of hearing at Delos: merely that a psychologically induced *experience* of hearing gave rise to *belief* in a miracle. Not only so, but the suggestion that Delphic practice involved a miracle of hearing on the part of the προφήτης runs counter to all our evidence. There were no unknown languages, and the προφήτης was not inspired at all, as Plato makes abundantly clear. There is no close link at all between Delian and Delphic Apollo evident from a proper understanding of this hymn. Finally, the suggestion that the Pentecost miracle was in historical fact more one of hearing than of speaking may be correct, but by the very nature of our evidence such an assertion cannot be proven or disproved. It must remain mere assertion. Whether or not it is correct, it will not support a parallel between Acts and the Hymn to Apollo.

Chapter 6

Glossolalia, the Cults of Dionysus and Cybele,

and other Descriptions of Inspiration

The second major source suggested by modern writers for Hellenistic parallels to early Christian glossolalia is the field of the "Mystery Religions" generally, or, more explicitly, the cults of Cybele or Dionysus. Here the claim is made that the forms of inspired speech and enthusiasm which supposedly characterised these cults closely parallel apparently similar phenomena in early Christianity. Reference is often made to the wild cries and frenzy associated with the celebration of the rituals of these cults, which were sometimes public, though sometimes not. Very little of our evidence allows us to examine the self-awareness of devotees of these cults, or details of how they may have interpreted these phenomena. It is quite possible that the fairly stereotyped descriptions in our sources may skip over distinctions which the devotees of this or that god might have wished to make. For those distinctions we have little evidence. What is clear, however, from these stereotyped descriptions is that the Hellenistic world had a very clear image of what was involved. It is this image that we can examine.[1]

---

[1] For the suggestion, couched in general terms only, see *T.D.N.T.* vol. 2, 1935, E.T. 1964, pp. 449-460, esp. pp. 451, 457-8, where Oepke says " . . . the ecstatic experiences of the church rest basically on Jewish soil, as glossolalia belongs to Hellenistic". Günther Bornkamm speaks for many when he suggests that "speaking in tongues was regarded simply as an exalted form of prophecy. This corresponds to the picture of the prophet and giver of oracles which existed so plentifully in the syncretism of the Hellenistic period. In the portrayal of the enthusiasm of seers, ecstasy and raving were often made explicitly prominent." (*Early Christian Experience*, London, E.T. 1969, p. 38); G. Dautzenberg, "Glossolalie", cols. 229-30, argues that the allusion in 1 Cor. 12 is less to Dionysiac matters than to prophetic mania. See also C.K. Barrett, *The First Epistle to the Corinthians*, 2nd ed., London, 1971, p. 278; L.T. Johnson, "Norms for True and False Prophecy in 1 Corinthians", *American Benedictine Review*, vol. 22, 1971, pp. 29-45, esp. pp. 31-33, 35-36; F.F. Bruce, *Paul: Apostle of the Free Spirit*, Exeter, 1977, p. 260, J.D.G. Dunn, *Jesus and the Spirit*, London, 1975, pp. 242-3; U.B. Müller, *Prophetie und Predigt im Neuen Testament*, Gütersloh, 1975, pp. 31-32; D. Hill, "Christian Prophets as Teachers and Instructors in the Church", in Panagopoulos,

Like the oracle cults which we investigated in the previous chapter, the religious traditions of the "Mysteries" had long histories going back well into archaic Greek times. The evidence for the practices in which we are most interested, however, comes from three basic areas. The first of these is Euripides' play "The Bacchae", which established the pattern for the dramatic portrayal of Dionysiac religion for all subsequent writers. The second source is the historical tradition of the Hellenistic period, which depicts at various times and places both the founders of the various cults with which we are concerned, and the activities of their devotees. The third area is more diverse, being made up of the various descriptions in Hellenistic literature of the behaviour of persons believed to be under the influence of divine powers. I have reserved those passages most often cited as evidence for glossolalic phenomena for separate, detailed treatment in the

---

Vocation, p. 110; P. Roberts, "A Sign - Christian or Pagan?", *Expository Times*, vol. 90, no. 7, April 1979, pp. 199-203. The idea is developed in detail by Engelsen, *Glossolalia*, independently by Hart, *Tongues And Prophecy*, pp. 10-12, and more plausibly by R. and C.C. Kroeger, "An Inquiry into Evidence of Maenadism in the Corinthian Congregation", *S.B.L. Seminar Papers*, 1978, pp. 331-338. M.E. Boring, *Sayings*, p. 85, says: "For Paul, μαίνεσθαι (*sic*) (14.23) is a stinging rebuke, not a goal to be sought after, as it was in the Bacchic experience of the Dionysian cult . . . the prophet, like the speaker in tongues, is in control of himself and can be silent - though he may have to be reminded that this is the case . . . Paul's understanding of the prophetic experience is to be seen against the Old Testament-Jewish-Rabbinic background, rather than as a reflection of the Hellenistic enthusiastic view of prophecy." Though Boring is commenting more on ecstasy than on glossolalia, it is implicit throughout that he believes Paul to be correcting such a Hellenistic viewpoint among the Corinthians, which has led to their over-valuation of glossolalia and ecstasy generally. See most recently, but certainly no more persuasively, H.W. House, "Tongues and the Mystery Religions of Corinth", *Bibliotheca Sacra*, vol. 140, no. 558, pp. 134-150. The only dissenting voices I have found are T.W. Manson, "The Corinthian Correspondence (1)", from *Studies in the Gospels and Epistles*, ed. M. Black, esp. pp. 203-205, Gerhard Delling, *Worship in the New Testament*, trans. P. Scott, London, 1962, pp. 34-40, R.H. Gundry, "'Ecstatic Utterance' (N.E.B.)?", *J.Th.S.*, vol. 17, part 2, 1966, p. 303ff, and G. Dautzenberg, who does not spell out the criteria by which he believed the early Christians would have differentiated their own practices from those of their neighbours. Unfortunately Delling's critique of the parallel is theological: Christian glossolalia is not like Dionysiac phenomena because it is subservient to the aim of edification, rather than amoral ecstasy (pp. 39-40). Unfortunately this really reduces to: it is different because it is Christian. On less subjective ground, Manson (p. 204) argues that "Εὐοῖ is the cry by whose constant repetition the votaries of the god work themselves up into a frenzy or ecstasy. The shouting is one of the causes of the ecstatic condition, not a result of it. But in the glossolalia of the New Testament the falling into the ecstatic state (*sic*) comes first, and the strange utterances are the outward sign of the inward condition."

following chapter. Those passages which appear to have escaped general notice in the modern discussion will be treated, with the evidence drawn from the first two areas, in what follows.

The question to be asked as we approach this evidence is as follows: when our sources describe the abnormal states of mind that characterise the style of religion with which we are concerned, what are the symptoms by which they identify "inspiration", "frenzy" or "ecstasy"? And how are these visible manifestations of religious enthusiasm related to the alleged parallels within early Christianity?

1. Euripides' "Bacchae"

This most obscure of Euripides' great tragedies describes the causes, course and effects of an outbreak of Dionysiac madness among the women of Thebes during the reign of Pentheus. The outbreak was brought about by the refusal of King Pentheus to recognise the divinity of Dionysus, who had returned from great deeds in Phrygia and the East to his Greek homeland. Pentheus refused to allow the establishment of proper cultic honours to Dionysus, whom he considered an imposter usurping divine status on the basis of the legends concerning his miraculous birth and the death of his mother, Semelè. Arriving at Thebes with his entourage or θίασος of Asian women, Dionysus begins his revenge for this slight done to his honour. He drives the women of Thebes to a frenzy,[2] and they, leaving their homes, flee into the mountains, there to celebrate Bacchic rites with music and dancing. Dionysus himself engages in a struggle with King Pentheus, who aims to defeat his purposes, punish the women for what he sees as their wantonness, and expose Dionysus as a fraud. Entering the city in human form, Dionysus deludes Pentheus, suggesting that together they can spy on the women in the mountains, and probably catch them in the commission of all the kinds of immoralities which Pentheus believes will be the result of their adherence to this impostor of a god. As they go off together Dionysus puts him into a kind of trance as well,[3] so that he is unable to perceive clearly what is happening

---

[2]   This is described variously as μανία, and "being distracted in mind" (παράκοποι φρενῶν), line 33, being mad (ἐμμανεῖς), line 1094, and being seized (κατείχετ᾽), line 1124. Returning to their normal state of mind, they know nothing of their actions while in their frenzy, lines 1269-1272.

[3]   He is to be "driven out of his senses" (ἔκστησον φρενῶν) and these are to be replaced with frenzy (λύσσα), line 851. Note that, like the women, he remains conscious, but experiences hallucinations. On the difference between the state of the

around him, and brings him unknowingly close to the Theban women, who, at Dionysus' command, thinking him to be a wild beast, tear him apart and carry his head in triumph back to Thebes. Only there does their frenzy leave them, and they realise what it is they are carrying, though they have no memory of what went before.

Two different "frenzies" are described in the play. The first is that of the women, who in their inspired state celebrate the Bacchic rituals that Pentheus has forbidden. The second is that of Pentheus himself, as he is led to his death. Both share the factor of delusion: the women see Pentheus as a ravening wild animal, and he is unaware of the devices of Dionysus that leave him helpless in the hands of the women.[4] Both are thus characterised by thoroughly abnormal states of mind. In most other ways, however, they are different. The frenzy of the women, unlike that of Pentheus, is associated with extraordinary miraculous phenomena: supernatural strength, miraculous provision of food and drink, tongues of fire, and invulnerability.[5]

At this point, however, we must clearly distinguish between the phenomena of the frenzy of these "Maenads" and the Bacchic celebrations in which they are involved. In the situation of the play, the women are seized upon by frenzy and driven from the city in order to celebrate the forbidden rituals. Those rituals themselves involve the invocation of, and frenzy caused by, Dionysus, and it is with the physical manifestations of these that we are most concerned.

It is not without reason that many modern authors describe the frenzy that fell on the women of Thebes in Euripides' play as ὀρειβάσια, an outbreak of dancing in the mountains, though the term itself is rare, and does not occur in the text.[6] For although there is ecstatic speech in the Bacchae, the phenomenon which overwhelmingly characterises Dionysiac celebrations in the play is violent physical activity. Only four times, as far as I can see, are cries a prominent feature of the activities of the frenzied worshippers,

women and that of Pentheus, see R.S. Kraemer, "Ecstasy and Possession. The attraction of women to the cult of Dionysus", *H.Th.R.*, vol. 72, 1979, p. 67: "Those who accept the call of the god and surrender to the temporary possession suffer no harm, while those who struggle against the god invoke a second level of possession far more dangerous than the first."

[4] See particularly lines 1051-1075.
[5] See lines 690-711, 748-768, 1095-1136.
[6] See, for example, E.R. Dodds, *Euripides, Bacchae*, 2nd edition, Oxford, 1960, p. xiii, and A. Henrichs, "Greek Maenadism from Olympias to Messalina", *H.S.C.P.*, vol. 82, 1978, p. 149.

whereas energetic dancing features at least eleven times, and the frantic tossing of the head, with hair in disarray, is mentioned four times. Not only are the dances themselves mentioned, but the music that accompanies them is described at several points. Let us examine these passages in more detail.

Various kinds of cries are described at different points in the play. The Bacchic cry of "Euoi!" is the first to be noted.[7] However there is no suggestion in the text or in other sources that this cry is a word, the meaning of which is somehow esoteric, or part of a secret or foreign language: it functions simply as a ritual outburst, a shout of invocation or acclamation to Dionysus. He is also invoked as "Bromios" and "Iacchus",[8] which are in each case simply alternative titles for him.

Also commonly misunderstood is the passage where, defending his and Cadmus' intention to dance in Dionysus' honour, Teiresias explains to Pentheus that

A prophet is this god: the Bacchic frenzy and ecstasy are full-fraught with prophecy (τὸ γὰρ βακχεύσιμον καὶ τὸ μανιῶδες μαντικὴν πολλὴν ἔχει) . . . he makes his maddened votaries tell the future.[9]

It would be pressing the evidence too far to seize upon these lines as proof that prophecy was a regular part of Dionysiac rituals, though there is some later evidence that this was believed. Teiresias is not trying to suggest that prophecy (μαντική) is one of Dionysus' main roles. It is simply one more proof of his divinity, as the context makes clear. In Thrace he is worshipped as a god of oracles. His birth is of divine origin, his safety in childhood was ensured by Zeus, his followers tell the future, and his cry can panic armies. In other words, Zeus protected him in his infancy, and he shares attributes with Apollo, Pan and Ares: therefore he is divine. The prophetic element in Dionysiac frenzy is not much elaborated on, either in the play or in later tradition.[10]

---

[7] Line 142. The word is used as an adjective in lines 158, 238 and 579, and as a substantive in line 566, but it seems that these are secondary usages, derived from the cry itself. The word is thought to have no intrinsic meaning, but is so closely linked to its cultic usage that it can become an epithet of the god. See also Lysistrata, 1290ff., for the shouting of praise to Dionysus.

[8] Lines 446 and 725.

[9] Lines 298-301.

[10] Cf. E.R. Dodds, *Euripides, Bacchae*, 2nd ed. Oxford, 1960, pp. 108-110, where it is correctly argued that though Dionysus was known as an oracle god both in Thrace (Herodotus 7.111) and in at least one part of Greece (Pausanias 10.33.11), the dramatic significance of the lines does not depend on this fact. "Here he (Dionysus) is presented as

The only reference to a Dionysiac cry which seriously suggests linguistic unintelligibility is the mention of "Phrygian shouts" in line 159. Yet the point here is obvious: many of the women of the Dionysiac θίασος which makes up the chorus are Phrygian, and the rites they celebrate are of Phrygian origin. There is no suggestion that these shouts are in a foreign language because they are inspired, rather than simply being ritual invocations or acclamations, which happen to be in the language of origin of the cult members.

Turning now to the references to physical activity, we find that the rites which Dionysus demands are clearly characterised as dancing. He himself, in the first speech of the play, claims to have established his dances and rites (χορεύσας καὶ τελετάς) in many lands, before returning to Greece. Teiresias and Cadmus, who unlike Pentheus accept Dionysus' divinity, "will essay the dance", and wonder whether they "shall . . . alone of Thebes to Bacchus dance".[11] The rites which the Maenads are celebrating in the mountains likewise consist of dancing.[12] The musical instruments used are drums, cymbals and flutes.[13] Further, the dances are strenuous, and involve violent tossings of the head; even Pentheus, who is only mimicking Bacchic dances, explains to Dionysus that his hair is disordered because of the dancing. This is likewise a regular feature of the artistic portrayal of Maenads, though not to the exclusion of other types of portrayal.[14]

---

the cause of two unaccountable modes of behaviour" which, since they do not originate within normal human consciousness, must be "in the belief of antiquity, from a higher power". The claim that Dionysus is responsible for panic in armies is in parallel to this. It does not mean he is characteristically a war god, any more than an oracular god. The fact that he as a divinity had such powers does not mean that he normally bestowed them upon his followers. "These lines are a preparation for the description of such an incident in 761-4 . . . just as 298-301 may be taken as a preparation for Dion's concluding prophecy" (p. 110), and thus as a literary device within the specific context of the play, rather than an indication that prophecy was a characteristic feature of regular Dionysiac worship. Compare D.E. Aune, *Prophecy*, p. 21: "The ritual possession characteristic of some of the mystery cults was not the same phenomenon as divine possession enabling individuals to utter divine oracles, though the two were frequently confused in antiquity." See also the useful distinctions of Hart, *Tongues and Prophecy*, p. 10, who notes that "nothing seems to indicate that the Dionysian inspired prophecies are unintelligible, or that the oracles are given in answer to specific inquiry, at a specific time or place."

[11] Line 21 (Dionysus), lines 190-195 (Teiresias and Cadmus). See also lines 204, 219, 322-324.
[12] Lines 446, 511, 567ff, 862 and 1143.
[13] Drums, lines 59, 514, cymbals, line 514, flutes, line 128.
[14] Lines 930-931. See also lines 240-241, 862 and 695. On the artistic tradition see C.

I am aware of only one serious attempt to demonstrate that the "ecstatic" cries of the worshippers of Dionysus were understood as including glossolalic phenomena, and that, thus understood, they constituted an important part of the popular understanding of Dionysiac religion. This is the work of Engelsen, who argues that the common description of Dionysiac outcry as "Bacchic tongues" must be so understood.[15] The phrase in question, however, is very rare, and Engelsen himself can cite only one case, and even there, there is a more plausible explanation than the one he gives. Aristophanes, Frogs 353 ff, cited by Plutarch, Mor. 348 d, has the Chorus chanting for the expulsion from the scene of all those who have never "been trained in the Bacchic rites / of the tongue of bull-eating Cratinus". (γλώττης βακχεῖ᾽, Engelsen's translation). The suggestion is that Bacchic rites are understood as "rites of the tongue". A grammatically more precise translation, however, is that of Rogers, who writes that those under discussion are those who have not "shared in the Bacchic rites which old bull-eating Cratinus' words supply". The point is that the Chorus are satirically calling for the expulsion of all those who are not initiates in the mysteries of the comedy, part of the Dionysiac festival. The tongue is that of Cratinus, not of Dionysiac worship.[16]

Kerenyi, *Dionysos; Archetypal Image of Indestructible Life*, trans. R. Manheim, London, 1976, plates 69-71, 76a, 77, 85, 88b-d, 112c-d, and, for example, J. Boardman, *Athenian Red Figure Vases, The Archaic Period*, Norwich, 1975, figures 132, 136 and 218.

[15] Engelsen, *Glossolalia*, p. 21: "A Bacchic tongue (or mouth) is, then, an inspired tongue (or mouth). It is a tongue which is frenzied, which goes wild. It does not refer to 'glossolalia'. The term is broader and includes all Bacchic inspired speech." This point is merely one example in Engelsen's wider case, noted in chapter 2, that glossolalic phenomena were common in pre-Christian antiquity, and not distinguished from other forms of inspired speech until Paul made the distinction between "prophecy" and "tongues". It is a great pity that this entirely erroneous claim has begun to establish itself in the literature. It is accepted by both R.A. Harrisville, "Speaking in Tongues: a Lexicographical Study", *C.B.Q.*, vol. 38, 1976, pp. 41, 47, and by D.E. Aune, *Prophecy*, p. 199. For the claim that this reference suggests Bacchic glossolalia see also Behm, *T.D.N.T.*, vol. 1, 1932, E.T. 1964, p. 722, and, independently of Engelsen, though arguing briefly along similar lines, M.E. Hart, *Tongues and Prophecy*, pp. 10-11.

[16] Contra N.I.J. Engelsen, *Glossolalia*, p. 21. The translation of Rogers is taken from the Loeb Classical Library edition, p. 329. Plutarch cites a text very close to the original; no detail of this line appears to be in doubt. Cratinus was one of the "old masters" of the comic theatre, hence the point of the phrase. Against Engelsen, the point about the "bull-eating" seems to be that Cratinus had a reputation as a drinker (Horace, Epistles 1.19.1.), and "bull-eating" was an epithet of Dionysus, god of both wine and the theatrical festival. The independent but very similar discussion of this reference by M.E.

The only other passage Engelsen cites in support of his general point comes from Lycophron's Alexandra, where the prophetess's frenzy is described. Here, as elsewhere, he argues that since the speakers in the play cannot understand what the words of the prophetess mean, they must have been in some sense glossolalic. Yet in this case it is perfectly clear that the language in which the prophetess speaks is Greek, for within a few lines her words are being quoted at length. They are certainly obscure and ambiguous, but it is quite clear that their "frenzied" quality has nothing to do with the language in which they are spoken. Rather it describes the mental state of the speaker.[17] Engelsen's "Bacchic tongues" have no basis in the sources.[18] Frenzy in the classical Greek world is not accompanied by unintelligible speech.[19]

Hart, *Tongues and Prophecy*, p. 11 and note 17 (p. 111), also citing the Lysistrata, line 1290ff, is most misleading. N. Turner, *Christian Words*, Edinburgh, 1980, p. 459 n. 110 merely cites the passage, though disparaging its usefulness. G. Dautzenberg, "Glossolalie", col. 230, simply cites the passage without comment.

[17] Lycophron, Alexandra, lines 3-10 describe the obscurity of the prophetess's words. Lines 31-1460, the vast bulk of the rest of the poem, are made up of her words. Engelsen goes on to argue, (p. 21) that the verb βακχεύειν generally means "to rave like a Bacchant", i.e. to speak unintelligibly. This is not the case. As was noted above, in Chapter 3, the vast majority of uses of the word mean "to act like a Bacchant" in the most general sense, and as we have seen, Bacchic frenzy was not predominantly characterised by speech phenomena, but by violent physical activity. Very occasionally the verb refers to speech. Philo's de Ebrietate 123 once uses βεβακχευμένων of the singing around the Golden Calf in the Exodus story, but there is no suggestion of unintelligibility. The verb refers to the revelling generally. βακχεύειν means "to act like a Bacchant", and only secondarily "to sound like one". Compare A. Henrichs, art.cit., p. 147, who, speaking of married women in Hellenistic maenadism, says "they perform Bacchic rites (βακχεύειν), presumably not more than a reference to maenadic dances."

[18] It is true that Plutarch, in his Quaestiones Convivales 1, Mor. 613 c, says that "Dionysus is the looser and liberator of all things, and . . . especially he unbridles the tongue and grants the utmost freedom of speech" (μάλιστα δὲ τῆς γλώττης ἀφαιρεῖται τὰ χαλινὰ καὶ πλείστην ἐλευθερίαν τῇ φωνῇ δίδωσιν). But this means no more than that people chat more freely and happily with one another after they have had a few drinks, as Plutarch explicitly says in Quaestiones Convivales 7, Mor. 716 b.

[19] The conclusion that it was well known has also been drawn from the reference to "the Sibyl, with frenzied lips" (μαινομένῳ στόματι), Plutarch, Mor. 397 a, citing Heraclitus. (Thus Dautzenberg, "Glossolalie", col. 230.) But we have already seen that the prime symptom of this frenzy is poetic diction. "Sibylla was often inspired when she delivered oracles", according to Diodorus Siculus, 4.66.6. She was inspired in the tongue (ἐνθεάζειν κατὰ γλῶτταν), as were the so-called Bacchides. But the results were poetic, not glossolalic. See the references in the previous chapter.

2. Hellenistic Sources on "Enthusiasm"

Though the account of "maenadism" in Euripides' Bacchae gave classic literary form to the understanding of Dionysiac frenzy, it would be most unsafe to set the N.T. phenomena as parallels with those of a piece of imaginative literature written five centuries before the early Christian movement began.[20] The literature of the first century B.C. and the first century A.D. is rich with descriptions of "enthusiastic religion", and an examination of these descriptions provides a remarkably consistent picture.

Evidence for cultic enthusiasm is of two basic kinds. There are the legends associated with the foundations of the various cults, and historical, novelistic or poetic descriptions of people inspired by the gods of the cults.[21]

Further evidence may be drawn from the well-known legends surrounding the "cleft" at Delphi. Though the legend of the cleft and its vapours is certainly unhistorical, it was widely believed, and thus shaped and/or expressed the popular view of inspiration.[22]

We may also turn to descriptions of persons or events having to do with "inspired" or "enthusiastic" religion more generally, whether they be of the specifically oracular, or the more general kind. Within this category a special place must be given to Philo Judaeus' descriptions of his own experiences of "philosophic frenzy". Finally there are general statements which describe individuals or groups with the simile that they are "acting as if inspired".[23] As noted above, those few passages commonly quoted by

---

[20] The extended scholarly discussion on the problem of reconciling our knowledge of historical Dionysiac religion with the semi-mythical, dramatised poetic picture in the Bacchae is conveniently summarised in Henrichs, *art.cit.*

[21] Diodorus Siculus 3.57-59 (Basilea/Cybele), 4.3.3. (Bacchic revelries), 5.49.3 (Corybas), Plutarch, Mor. 249 e (the Thyads of Delphi), Mor. 364 e (an Osiran festival compared with Bacchic ones), Mor. 1091 (Bacchic frenzy generally), Dionysius of Halicarnassus 3.21.3 (an unnamed Roman girl), Livy, 39.8.5-8, 39.10.7, 39.13.12-13, 39.15.9-10. (the "Bacchanalian Conspiracy"), Catullus, Poems Nos. 63-64 (Dionysian worship). Compare also Demosthenes, de Corona, 258-60, Strabo, 10. 470-471 and Pausanias 2.7.5-6.

[22] Diodorus Siculus 16.26, Plutarch, Mor. 432-3. According to F.E. Brenk, the Delphian "vapours" (πνεύματα) are first mentioned by Lucan, Pharsalia, 5.111, 6.425, based on an analogy with the legends of the Cumaean Sibyl. See *In Mist Apparelled: Religious Themes in Plutarch's Moralia and Lives*, Leiden, 1977, p. 127, note 17.

[23] Diodorus Siculus 4.51.2 (Medea), 34/5.2.5ff and 34/5.2.24b (Eunus of Sicily), Plutarch Mor. 171 b and 417 c (the excesses of popular superstition), Mor. 278 c (Themis the prophetess), cf. Dionysius of Halicarnassus 1.31.1, Plutarch, Mor. 414 e (Eurycles), Mor. 1094 c (Archimedes), Philo, de Opificio Mundi 69, Migr. Abr. 35, 190, Vita Mosis 1.175, 1.294, 2.191ff, de Spec. Leg. 1.65, de Ebrietate 146, de Virtutibus

modern writers as paralleling early Christian glossolalia have been reserved for special treatment in the following chapter.

Legends of Cult Founders

Into the first category fall the legends of Dionysus, Cybele and Corybas retold by Diodorus Siculus. Diodorus, a convinced Euhemerist, sets out to show us how "people" like Basilea (who in other accounts is called Cybele) came to be recognised by mankind as gods or goddesses, and how the legends about them grew up. In the case of this Basilea, he specifically mentions the drums and cymbals that were used in the festivals that she instituted. In the version of the story which he reports in which she is known as Cybele he notes that she was the inventor of the multi-reed pipe. He then records that, when her lover died, she became frenzied (ἐμμανῆ), and, crying aloud (ὀλολύζουσαν) and beating on a drum, and with her hair hanging free, she travelled around[24].

Thus Diodorus accounts for several of the main features of the worship of Cybele with which he is familiar. The use of drums, cymbals and flutes is a recurrent theme in the orgiastic worship of Cybele, as is frenzied shouting and dishevelled hair.[25] In the same way Diodorus tells us of three (!) people by the name of Dionysus, who introduced various mysteries and initiations, because of which

it is lawful for the maidens to carry the thyrsus and join in the frenzied revelry, crying out 'Euai!' (συνενθουσιάζειν εὐαζούσαις).[26]

Descriptions of Cultic Rituals

That various forms of shouting, along with violent physical activity, were characteristic of Dionysian worship in our period is amply attested in our sources. The story told by Plutarch of the nocturnal wanderings of the Delphic "Thyads" and their reception in Amphissa illustrates the fact that women still left the towns to dance in the mountains.[27] Though this story does not necessarily emphasise the abnormal state of mind of the

---

217, Quaestiones in Gen. 3.9, Dio Chrysostom 1.2 (Alexander the Great), 1.55 (an allegorical figure of a lady who prophesied), 34.4 (behaviour of students of rhetoric).

[24] Diodorus Siculus 3.57-9.

[25] Cf. the picture of mendicant priests of Cybele given by Apuleius, Metamorphoses, 8.24, 27-28, and Lucian, de Dea Syria, variously.

[26] Diodorus 3.63ff., 4.3.3, and see the references in Henrichs, *art.cit.*

[27] Plutarch, Mor. 249 e, and cf. Pausanias 10.6.3.

participants in Dionysian rituals, it is normally assumed that ἐνθουσιασμός
is a feature of the rituals, and that this state is accompanied by violent
physical activity and/or shouting.[28] Several very clear statements of this are
to be found in Latin literature of the first century B.C. The best known of
these is the account given by Livy of the "Bacchanalian Conspiracy" of
187-6 B.C. Livy writes as follows:

There were initiatory rites which at first were imparted to a few, then began to be
generally known among men and women. To the religious element in them were added
the delights of wine and feasts, that the minds of a larger number might be attracted.
When wine had inflamed their minds, and night and the mingling of males and females,
youth with age, had destroyed every sentiment of modesty, all varieties of corruption
first began to be practised, since each one had at hand the pleasure answering to that to
which his nature was more inclined. There was not one form of vice alone, the
promiscuous matings of free men and women, but perjured witnesses, forged seals and
wills and evidence, all issued from this same workshop: likewise poisonings and secret
murders, so that at times not even the bodies were found for burial. Much was ventured
by craft, more by violence. This violence was concealed because amid the howlings
(ululatibus) and the crash of drums and cymbals (tympanorumque et cymbalorum
strepitu) no cry of the sufferers could be heard as the debauchery and murders
continued . . . they . . . would lead him to a place which would ring with howls and the
song of a choir and the beating of cymbals and drums . . . Men, as if insane, with
fanatical tossings of their bodies, would utter prophecies. Matrons in the dress of
Bacchants, with dishevelled hair and carrying blazing torches, would run down to the
Tiber, and plunging their torches into the water (because they contained live sulphur
mixed with calcium), would bring them out still burning. Men were alleged to have been
carried off by the gods who had been bound to a machine and borne away out of sight to
hidden caves . . . "there are men very like the women, debauched and debauchers,
fanatical, with senses dulled by wakefulness, wine, noise and shouts at night" . . . [29]

This account may be fruitfully compared with two poems of Catullus,
which give us vivid descriptions of a tapestry depicting scenes from the
worship of Cybele and Dionysus.

Away together, follow me to the Phrygian shrine of Cybele, to the Phrygian groves of
the goddess, where rings the clash of cymbals (cymbalum), where the tambourines
(tympana) keep sounding, where the Phrygian piper plays a deep note on his curved
reed, where the ivy-crowned Maenads violently toss their heads, where with shrill shrieks
(acutis ululatibus) they celebrate their inviolate rites, where the goddess's restless
company loves to bustle: thither it befits us to hasten, with impulsive tripping steps.'
When thus to her companions Attis had sung, a woman counterfeit, a band of devotees
suddenly yells aloud with tumultuous tongues (linguis trepidantibus ululat), again rings

---

[28] See, for example, Plutarch, Mor. 291 a, 364 e, 1091, Dionysius of Halicarnassus
3.21.3. and Dio Chrysostom 35.8.
[29] Livy, 39.8.5-8, 39.10.7, 39.13.12-13, 39.15.9-10.

the light tambourine (tympanum), again clash the hollow cymbals (cymbala), and with hurrying foot the swift rout makes for leafy Ida . . .

But elsewhere on the tapestry Iacchus in the bloom of youth was hastening with his troop of satyrs and Sileni Nysa-born, seeking you, Ariadne, and inflamed with love of you. At his bidding Maenads all about were raving frenziedly crying 'Evoe' in a tumult, 'Evoe' as they tossed their heads. Of them some were brandishing wands with ivy-covered tips, some were scattering the limbs of a heifer torn to pieces, some were girding themselves with writhing snakes, some were processing with mystic emblems in deep caskets, emblems which the uninitiated vainly long to learn, others with uplifted hands were beating on the tambourines (tympana) or stirring shrill tinklings (tinnitus) on cymbals of rounded bronze; many were causing horns (cornua) to blare out hoarse-booming blasts and the outlandish pipe to scream with a frightening note (barbaraque horribili stridebat tibia cantu). Such were the figures that sumptuously adorned the tapestry which clasped and clothed the couch with its folds.[30]

A pattern is clearly evident here. The features that are considered characteristic of the cults of Dionysus and Cybele are outbursts of shouting, the music of cymbals, drums and flutes, and frenzied dancing, sometimes also accompanied by frenzied cries. Livy's mention of the apparent miracle of torches that could not be extinguished by immersion also parallels a feature of Euripides' description of the Maenads - that supernatural phenomena were manifested in their presence. In the "Bacchae" these phenomena included superhuman strength and invulnerability, tongues of flame,[31] welling up of milk, water, honey and wine from the earth, and tameness of animals. It would appear that the trick of the torches was an

---

[30] Catullus, 63 lines 18-30, 64 lines 251-266. The translation in each case is that of G.P. Goold, *Catullus*, London, 1983, pp. 131 & 155. Compare also Lucretius' description of certain rituals of Cybele, in "On the Nature of the Universe", Book 2, lines 650ff.

[31] Euripides, Bacchae, lines 695-768. The tongues of flame mentioned in lines 757-8 are only one of the parallels cited by P.W. van der Horst in "Hellenistic Parallels to the Acts of the Apostles (2.1-47)", *J.S.N.T.* vol. 25, 1985, pp. 49-50. For the association between heavenly flame and "new age" themes in Roman iconography and literature see R. Oster, "Numismatic Windows into the Social World of Early Christianity: a Methodological Inquiry", *J.B.L.*, vol. 101, 1982, pp. 195-223, N.B. pp. 211, 212-4, 221, citing Vergil, *Aeneid* 2.634-729. His suggestion, though loosely argued, deserves further investigation. For Jewish parallels see p. Chag. 2.77b, 32, cited by M.E. Hart, *Tongues and Prophecy*, p. 27, and W.E. Mills, *A Theological / Exegetical Approach to Glossolalia*, Lanham, 1985, p. 53. On the use of gongs and cymbals see further H. Riesenfeld, "Note supplémentaire sur I Cor. XIII", *Coniectanea Neotestamentica*, vol. 12, 1948, pp. 50-53, with the references there, (and add Plato, Protagoras 329a) and the intriguing suggestion of W.W. Klein, "Noisy Gong or Acoustic Vase? A Note on 1 Corinthians 13.1", *N.T.S.*, vol. 32, 1986, pp. 286-289 to the effect that though the cymbala are certainly musical instruments, the "gongs" may be "resonating jars" used in theatres to help amplify voice and music.

attempt to demonstrate that miracles attended Dionysus' latter-day devotees as well. Naturally enough, miracles were very widely seen as authenticating the claim to divine inspiration in many differing contexts, as we shall see.[32]

The other parallel between Livy's account and that of Euripides that demands our attention is the mention of prophecy. Its appearance in the "Bacchae" has already been treated.[33] In Livy it is left undeveloped. It is mentioned as a distinctively male activity, paralleling the wild rushing of the torch-carrying women to the river, and may, for Livy, be simply another deplorable (and politically dangerous!) though not necessarily characteristic feature of the cult. It should be noted, however, that this feature of mantic inspiration is here imported into an account of Dionysiac inspiration. At a popular level the Hellenistic world did tend to link the differing forms of inspiration, which were distinguished, for example, by Plato, and to mix attributes between them. (See above, footnote 10.)

3. Oracular Enthusiasm?

This impression is reinforced by a reading of Vergil's and Lucan's descriptions, in their "Aeneid" and "The Civil War" respectively, of visits to oracles.[34] Here we must tread carefully, for in the case of the Aeneid we are dealing with conscious literary artifice, and in the case of the passage from the "Civil War" detailing the visit of Appius Claudius to Delphi there are serious problems to do with the historicity of the visit itself, and to do with the sources of Lucan's description of it.[35] One thing is quite certain,

---

[32] See especially A.B. Kolenkow, "Relationships between Miracle and Prophecy in the Greco-Roman World and Early Christianity", in *Aufstieg und Niedergang der römischen Welt*, Teil II. vol. 23, part 2, 1980, pp. 1470-1506.

[33] See, above, note 9, and compare Livy 38.18.9, where the priests of Cybele are also said to prophesy. Aune correctly argues that "Livy appears to have embellished the narrative by bringing one of the Galli's typical behaviours - ritual frenzy - into conjunction with their supposed prophetic activity." (*Prophecy*, p. 42.) Polybius, on whom Livy is dependent, does not mention the prophesying.

[34] Vergil, Aeneid 6.42-155, Lucan, de Bello Civile 5.67-225. See also the picture of the Pythia's activities in Lucian, Jup. Trag. 30, cited by D.E. Aune, *Prophecy*, p. 33.

[35] It is argued that the main problems with the historicity of the visit are that it is only mentioned by Lucan, Valerius Maximus (1.8.10) and Orosius (6.15.11), and that the circumstantial detail of the Oracle's closure in this particular period is not mentioned by Plutarch, our best source on matters Pythian. F.M. Ahl, *Lucan, an Introduction*, Cornell University Press, London, 1976 suggests that Juvenal, Satires 6. 533-6 and some of the scholiasts support Lucan. For a full discussion see Chapter 11. As to the sources of Lucan's description, Ahl argues that both Valerius' and Lucan's accounts probably

however: they provide no support for the theory that the Pythia spoke her oracles in an unintelligible form, to be interpreted by a προφήτης. Lucan's Pythia is frenzied, and a shriek should have marked the onset of her inspiration, but her actual words are (linguistically) perfectly clear. The same applies to Vergil's Sibyl.

Vergil

Vergil describes the prophecy of the Sibyl in the following terms (6.46ff):

(6.46:) As thus she spake before the doors, suddenly nor countenance nor colour was the same, nor stayed her tresses braided; but her bosom heaves, her heart swells with wild frenzy, and she is taller to behold, nor has her voice a mortal ring, since now she feels the nearer breath of deity. (77ff.) . . . But the prophetess, not yet brooking the sway of Phoebus, storms wildly in the cavern, if so she may shake the mighty god from off her breast; so much the more he tires her raving mouth, tames her wild heart, and moulds her by constraint . . . (98ff.) In such words the Cumaean Sibyl chants from the shrine her dread enigmas and echoes from the cavern, wrapping truth in darkness (dictis . . . horrendas canit ambages antroque remugit, obscuris vera involvens) - so does Apollo shake the reins as she rages, and ply the spur beneath her breast. Soon as the frenzy ceased and the raving lips were hushed, Aeneas the hero begins . . .

Lucan

In the account of Appius Claudius' visit to Delphi, Appius forces the unwilling Pythia into the sanctuary, where she, fearing actual inspiration, feigns it, but

(5.153ff.) her words, that rushed not forth with tremulous cry; her voice, which had not power to fill the space of the vast cavern; her laurel wreath, which was not raised off her head by the bristling hair; the unmoved floor of the temple and the motionless trees - all these betrayed her dread of trusting herself to Apollo.

Finally forced close to the "chasm", she does become inspired. The symptoms are graphically described.

(5.166ff.) as fully as ever in the past, he (Apollo) forced his way into her body, driving out her former thoughts, and bidding her human nature to come forth and leave her heart at his disposal. Frantic she careers about the cave, with her neck under possession; the fillets and garlands of Apollo, dislodged by her bristling hair, she whirls with tossing head through the void spaces of the temple; she scatters the tripods that impede her random course; she boils over with fierce fire, while enduring the wrath of Phoebus . . . first the

---

depend upon the tradition reported in Plutarch, *Mor.* 438 b. Fontenrose, *The Delphic Oracle*, Berkeley, 1978, pp. 208-210, though he notes the similarity with this tradition, argues that the source is Aeneid 6. 37-54. R.E. Heine demonstrates the eclectic nature of Lucan's treatment of Delphi in two short notes, "A Note on Lucan's *Bellum Civile* 5.79-81" and "A Note on Lucan's *Bellum Civile* 5.121", both in *Classical Bulletin*, vol. 54, January 1978, pp. 44-45.

wild frenzy overflowed through her foaming lips; she groaned and uttered loud inarticulate cries with panting breath; next, a dismal wailing filled the vast cave, and at last, when she was mastered, came the sound of articulate speech (extremaeque sonant domita iam virgine voces) . . . forth she rushed, driven from the temple. The frenzy abides; and the god, whom she has not shaken off, still controls her, since she has not told all her tale. She still rolls wild eyes, and eyeballs that roam over all the sky; her features are never quiet, now showing fear, and now grim with menacing aspect; a fiery flush dyes her face and the leaden hue of her cheeks; her paleness is unlike that of fear but inspires fear; her heart finds no rest after its labour; and, as the swollen sea moans hoarsely when the North wind has ceased to blow, so voiceless sighs still heave her breast.

The symptoms of inspiration, then, include violent tossings of the head and rushing about, hair standing on end, gasping breath, racing heartbeat, and frightening changes of facial and physical appearance. Shrieks and cries are characteristic of the onset of inspiration rather than the resultant state itself. Vergil's mention of the change in the Sibyl's voice is not parallelled at Delphi, however, as Plutarch explicitly disclaims the notion that such phenomena ought to be expected. Though we ought to note with care that in Vergil and Lucan the shrieks and cries are the result of the prophetess' resistance to inspiration, and that in Dionysiac cult they are invocations of the god, nonetheless the close relationship between this list and the symptoms of Bacchic inspiration, with its tossing heads, unbraided hair, wild rushing about and loud cries, is readily apparent.[36]

The Delphic Legend

We turn next to the legends surrounding the "discovery" of the Delphic chasm and oracle. Though we have several sources at our disposal, only one provides details of the behaviour of people believed to be under inspiration: Diodorus Siculus.[37] He explains that

as goats had been wont to feed about this (the chasm) because Delphi had not yet been settled, invariably any goat that approached the chasm and peered into it would leap about in an extraordinary fashion and utter a sound quite different from what it was

---

[36] W.E. Mills suggests (*op.cit.*, p. 21) that "after the priestess was unified with the god Apollo, she began to speak ecstatically. At times this speech was intelligible, and at others it was less coherent." What Mills has ignored is the question of which "times" these were. She was "less coherent" *before* she was "united with the god". On the change of voice, Plutarch, Mor. 397 c says "the voice is not that of a god, nor the utterance of it, nor the diction, nor the metre, but all these are the woman's . . . "

[37] The major sources for this legend are Diodorus Siculus 16.26, Plutarch, Mor. 433 c-d (which mentions only the inspired speech of those who discovered the oracle), Pausanias 10.5.7 (which mentions inspired speech in hexameters), and Strabo, 9.3.5.

formerly wont to emit (φθέγγεσθαι). The herdsman in charge of the goats marvelled at the strange phenomenon and, having approached the chasm and peeped down it to discover what it was, had the same experience as the goats, for the goats began to act like beings possessed (ἐνθουσιάζουσι) and the goatherd also began to foretell future events. After this as the report was bruited among the people of the vicinity concerning the experience of those who approached the chasm, an increasing number of persons visited the place and, as they all tested it because of its miraculous character, whosoever approached the spot became inspired (ἐνθουσιάζειν). For these reasons the oracle (μαντεῖον) came to be regarded as a marvel and to be considered the prophecy-giving shrine (χρηστήριον) of Earth. For some time all who wished to obtain a prophecy (βουλομενους μαντεύεσθαι) approached the chasm and made their prophetic replies to one another; but later, since many were leaping down into the chasm under the influence of their frenzy (ἐνθουσιασμός) and all disappeared, it seemed best to the dwellers in that region, in order to eliminate the risk, to man there as a single prophetess (προφῆτις) for all and to have the oracles (χρησμολογία) told through her . . .

Though Diodorus' account must be treated as totally legendary, since no Delphic "chasm" ever existed, his evidence is still important. It gives us his understanding of the symptoms of ἐνθουσιασμός. Those symptoms are the uttering of strange sounds, violent physical movement, and knowledge of the future. We should note that there are problems here, because although Diodorus' goatherds and inquirers are sufficiently frenzied to be in danger of throwing themselves down the chasm, they are nonetheless sufficiently sane to understand each other's oracles. Those replies were, we note in passing, perfectly comprehensible without the offices of an interpreter. Be that as it may, the evidence of Diodorus matches the general pattern noted above: the symptoms of inspiration are violent physical activity, loud cries, and knowledge of things beyond the reach of those not so inspired.

4. Other Descriptions of Enthusiasm

Our third major source of information is the least specific of the three. In retelling the story of the murder of Pelias by Jason and Medea, Diodorus notes that, as part of the plot, Medea disguised herself as an old woman and, carrying a statue of Hecate into the city,

acted like one inspired, and, as the multitude rushed together along the streets she summoned the whole people to receive the goddess with reverence . . . and while all the inhabitants were rendering obeisance to the goddess and honouring her with sacrifices, and the whole city, in a word, was, along with Medea herself, acting like people inspired (συνενθεαζούσης) . . .[38]

---

[38] Diodorus Siculus 4.51.2. To my mind the best parallel to this passage is the description in Lucian of the entry of Alexander into Abonouteichos, which is treated in detail in the next chapter.

Our Hellenistic sources include quite a number of such general statements, which in some cases do, but in others do not tell us what they think constitutes "acting as if inspired".[39] Plutarch, discussing the excesses of popular superstition, describes its "words and gestures, magic charms and spells, rushing about and beating of drums . . .", and cites Pindar for a description of days of ill omen, when "frenzy and shouting of throngs in excitement, with tumultuous tossings of heads in the air" were common. In the case of oracular inspiration, he says that "when its fumes (those of the prophetic current or πνεῦμα) rise to the head, (it) reveals many unusual movements and also words stored away and unperceived . . ." Discussing Archimedes, Plutarch notes that at one stage he leapt out of his bathtub shouting, "as if in a state of possession" (κατοχή) or "inspiration" (ἐπίπνοια)".[40]

Dio Chrysostom adds two passages for our consideration. In one of these he describes a lady whom he met one day in the woods. Of her he says that she

at once began to prophesy (προέλεγεν) . . . The manner of her prophesying was not that of most men and women who are said to be inspired (οὐχ ὥσπερ οἱ πολλοὶ τῶν λεγομένων ἐνθέων ἀνδρῶν καὶ γυναικῶν); she did not gasp for breath, whirl her head about, or try to terrify with her glances, but spoke with entire self-control and moderation . . .[41]

The parallels here with Vergil and Lucan are readily apparent. The gasping for breath, the violent movement of the head, and the changes of facial expression are all features of the three accounts. In another passage Dio raises another issue. Replying to some who are taunting him with madness, he says:

Yet is it not fitting, if you believe that I really am mad (μαίνεσθαι), that you should for that very reason listen to me? For you must not think that eagles and falcons foretell to mankind (προσεμαίνειν) what is required of them and that the counsel derived from such creatures is trustworthy because of its spontaneity and its divine inspiration, while refusing to believe . . . (me . . .)[42]

In other words, he argues, if he is mad then not he, but another, is responsible for his words, and therefore his detractors have no escape from

---

[39] Passages without explicit description include Diodorus 5.49.3 and Dio Chrysostom 1.2.

[40] Plutarch Mor. 171 b, 417 c. The passage cited is Fragment 208 of Pindar, Mor. 432 d. For Archimedes see Mor. 1094 c.

[41] Dio Chrysostom 1.55. For a similar description see Lucian, Jup. Trag., 30.

[42] Dio Chrysostom 34.4.

their importance. Inspired people are not responsible for what they may say. In that they are in the same category as the insane. But in the case of inspiration, it is clear that the inspiring power is responsible. In other words, the claim to inspiration is a legitimising claim: it allows a person to say with authority things which otherwise they might have no right to say.[43] Likewise it permits forms of behaviour which are otherwise unacceptable: women leaving the haven of the home, departures from normal sex-role stereotypes, especially those expressed in styles of clothing and adornment, and the violent expression of emotion.[44] Such "inspired" behaviour can, of course, be treated as fraudulent and illegitimate, as a wilful throwing-off of decency, as it is in the case of the Maenads as understood by Pentheus. When the claim to inspiration is used to legitimise behaviour which might threaten political institutions, rather than simply social norms, the claim then becomes a political matter, as in the case of the "Bacchanalian Conspiracy", and the Sicilian slave revolt, dealt with below. This "legitimising" aspect of claims to inspiration will concern us again.

Within Graeco-Roman society the most revolutionary aspect of the claim to inspiration can be illustrated from the Sicilian slave revolt, which was led

---

[43] This "diminished responsibility" of inspired persons is clearly implicit in accounts of oracular consultations in our sources. Nobody "blames" the Pythia, or the oracular system generally, for what they say or its consequences. To do so would be absurd. Oracles come from the gods, and it will do no good at all to blame *them*. Likewise it would simply not be sensible to punish the Maenads of Euripides for their slaying of Pentheus; indeed, it would be blasphemous, for the deed was Dionysus'. The same "diminished responsibility" applies to all forms of μανία: a person who is pathologically insane, or inspired (whether in the oracular, the poetic or the Dionysiac sense), or in the throes of love, cannot be held truly responsible for their actions. This applies whether the person was, as in the case of the Maenads, unconscious of the true nature of their actions, or, as in the case of the erotic passion mentioned in Plutarch, Mor. 763 a, merely carried away with passion. For the amazement of the Greeks at the power of love to break through all normal conventions see the story of Crates and his wife Hipparcheia, in Epictetus 3.22.76, and Diogenes Laertius 6.96-98. Thus the claim to inspiration can be not only a truth-claim; it can also be a disclaimer of responsibility. See, for example, Philo, Life of Moses 1.294, where Balaam defends his blessing of the Israelites with the simple statement that he had no choice: he acted under divine compulsion.

[44] This aspect of the "diminished responsibility" of the inspired has, along with reversals of normal social roles, been made the keystone of much recent sociological interpretation of Dionysiac religion. See especially R.S. Kraemer, *Ecstatics and Ascetics: Studies in the Functions of Religious Activities for Women in the Greco-Roman World*, Diss., Princeton, 1976. See also her brief treatment in "Ecstasy and Possession. The Attraction of Women to the Cult of Dionysus", *H.Th.R.*, vol. 72, 1979, pp. 55-80.

by a Syrian, one Eunus, who claimed dealings with the gods. Diodorus tells
the story as follows:

There was a certain Syrian slave, belonging to Antigenes of Enna; he was an Apamean
by birth and had an aptitude for magic and the working of wonders (ἄνθρωπος μάγος
καὶ τερατουργὸς τὸν τρόπον). He claimed to foretell the future (προλέγειν τὰ
μέλλοντα), by divine command, through dreams, and because of his talent along these
lines deceived many. Going on from there he not only gave oracles (ἐμαντεύετο) by
means of dreams, but even made a pretence of having waking visions of the gods and of
hearing the future from their own lips. Of his many improvisations some by chance
turned out true, and since those which failed to do so were left unchallenged, while those
that were fulfilled attracted attention, his reputation advanced apace. Finally, through
some device, while in a state of divine possession (μετὰ τινος ἐνθουσιασμοῦ), he
would produce fire and flame from his mouth, and thus rave oracularly about things to
come. He would place fire, and fuel to maintain it, in a nut - or something similar - that
was pierced on both sides; then, placing it in his mouth and blowing on it, he kindled
now sparks, and now a flame. Prior to the revolt he used to say that the Syrian goddess
appeared to him, saying that he should be king, and he repeated this, not only to others,
but even to his own master. Since his claims were treated as a joke, Antigenes, taken by
his hocus-pocus, would introduce Eunus (for that was the wonder-worker's name) at his
dinner parties, and cross-question him about his kingship and how he would treat each of
the men present . . . Going to Eunus they (the originators of the revolt) asked him
whether their resolve had the favour of the gods. He, resorting to his usual mummery
(τερατείας), promised them the favour of the gods, . . . they fell upon the city of Enna,
with Eunus at their head and working his miracle (τερατευομένου) of the flames of fire
for their benefit . . . Approaching Eunus, who lived not far away, they asked whether
their project had the approval of the gods. He put on a display of his inspired transports
(lit. the wonderworker, with ἐνθουσιασμός . . . stated), and when he learned why they
had come, stated clearly that the gods favoured their revolt . . .[45]

Such rare passages offer us an "occasional glimpse" into "the spiritual
underworld of antiquity".[46] Eunus claimed to interpret dreams, and claimed
to have been visited by the Syrian goddess. As time went on he claimed to
be privy to the counsels of the gods in a greater sense. His claim gained

---

[45] Diodorus 34/5.2.5, 34/5.2.24b. 34/5.2.41 mentions his μαντική. The mid-second
century account of Florus (2.7.), does not give the same detail, but notes that "a certain
Syrian named Eunus . . . counterfeited an inspired frenzy and waving his dishevelled hair
in honour of the Syrian goddess, incited the slaves to arms and liberty on the pretence of
a command from the gods. In order to prove that he was acting under divine inspiration,
he secreted in his mouth a nut which he had filled with sulphur and fire, and, by breathing
gently, sent forth a flame as he spoke . . ."

[46] The phrase is that of Morton Smith, from "Prolegomena to a Discussion of
Aretalogies, Divine Men, the Gospels and Jesus", *J.B.L.*, vol. 90, 1971, pp. 174-199,
esp. pp. 180-181. In discussion of a passage of Celsus cited by Origen, he says: "How
much truth was there in Celsus' statement? We can never be sure because the spiritual
underworld of antiquity - the world of wandering prophets and magicians and
miracle-workers - is known to us only by occasional glimpses."

credence from the accuracy of (some of) his predictions, and the "miracle" he was able to fabricate. As far as we can tell from our sources, the miracle of the fire-breathing was the only important "symptom" of his inspiration. His miraculous powers and more than human knowledge were, for his followers, proof of his divine commission, and were thus a legitimation of his leadership.

5. Philo on Inspiration

The evidence of Philo on the nature of inspiration and enthusiasm must be divided into two categories. First comes his evidence on the questions treated above: the visible symptoms of inspiration. Secondly we must examine his idiosyncratic view of the nature of "philosophic frenzy", and his own experiences of what he conceives of as divine inspiration.[47]

The "symptoms" which Philo links with divine inspiration in the Old Testament are a heightened excitement, the extent of which is not always clear, knowledge of divine truth, and a physical transformation of sorts. In some cases it would appear that the state of inspiration might properly be called "ecstatic": reason withdraws, or the person may appear to be drunk or crazy. In de Spec. Leg. 65 he notes that a prophet under inspiration has no power of apprehension at all. But in other cases, notably those where Philo retells a Biblical story, he does not attempt to embellish the narrative with dramatic seizures. What he does tell us is not specific enough for us to use the word "ecstatic" with any confidence: "Thus he (Moses) discoursed, still calm and composed, but, after a little, he became possessed (ἔνθους) and filled with the spirit (καταπνευσθείς) . . . " and prophesied.[48] As for the transformation effect,

whenever he was possessed (κατασχεθείη), everything in him changed to something better, eyes, complexion, stature, carriage, movements, voice. For the divine spirit (τοῦ

---

[47] For a recent detailed treatment of Philo's views on prophecy and inspiration against their Hellenistic context, see R.M. Berchman, "Arcana Mundi: Prophecy and Divination in the *Vita Mosis* of Philo of Alexandria", *S.B.L. 1988 Seminar Papers*, Atlanta, 1988, pp. 385-423. Berchman's paper is frustrating, because despite presenting much excellent comparative material, he argues with such a looseness of terminology and logic as to seriously vitiate several features of his case. For brief examples, see above, Chapter 5, notes 3 and 17. None the less, he demonstrates clear linkages between Philo and features of the philosophical tradition on prophecy and divination.

[48] Vita Mosis 1.175; knowledge of divine truth as the result of inspiration is implicit in virtually all of Philo's references to the subject. Inspiration is characteristic of the prophets as a class, Questions and Answers on Genesis 3.9.

θείου πνεύματος) which was breathed upon him from on high made its lodging in his soul, and invested his body with singular beauty, his voice with persuasiveness, and his hearers with understanding.[49]

Since Philo does not explain further, it is hard to know quite what to make of this. The nearest parallel I have been able to find is one of moral transformation, where Apuleius comments scornfully that the mendicant priests of Cybele act in certain ways to suggest to people that they are inspired by the goddess, "as if (forsooth) the presence of the gods were not wont to make men better than before", rather than (in Apuleius' view) to make them act in an absurd fashion.[50]

The portion of Philo's evidence which has most dominated the picture of "ecstasy" among modern writers is his discussion of his own experiences of philosophic contemplation. This is unfortunate, for it is here that he is at his most idiosyncratic. The difference between Philo's conception of the symptoms of inspiration and that conception in most of the material we have been discussing is that Philo is almost exclusively concerned with the mental symptoms: he does not really consider the question of visible, objectively observable symptoms at all. For him, the experience of ecstasy is the very height of the individual's understanding of reality. He implicitly identifies his own experience with that of the Biblical prophets, though never with the intention of asserting a like authority. It is simply that for him prophecy is one of the gifts given by God to the virtuous, along with self-control, self-sufficiency and wisdom.[51] Prophecy involves a unique state of mind:

> For no pronouncement of a prophet is ever his own; he is an interpreter (ἑρμενεὺς) prompted by Another in all his utterances, when knowing not what he does he is filled with inspiration (ἐνθουσιᾷ), as the reason (τοῦ λογισμοῦ) withdraws and surrenders the citadel of the soul to a new visitor and tenant, the Divine Spirit which plays upon the vocal organism and dictates words which clearly express its prophetic message.[52]

---

[49] de Virtutibus 217.

[50] Metamorphoses 8.28.

[51] According to Wolfson, "Prophecy is reserved for the refined man, the wise man, the just man, and the genuine lover of wisdom. With these qualifications of refinement, wisdom and justice any man is capable of attaining prophecy . . . there is no doubt that . . . the attainment of prophecy by those who are worthy of it is through an act of divine grace and selection." H.A. Wolfson, *Philo*, vol. 2, pp. 47-48. Wolfson cites as evidence Quis Rerum. 52.259-260, Quod Deus 1.3. and de Plantatione 6.24. Cf. also D.L. Tiede, *The Charismatic Figure as Miracle Worker*, S.B.L. Dissertation Series, Missoula, 1973, pp. 112ff; "Philo's conception of prophecy and the ecstatic state of the prophet is singular".

[52] Philo, de Spec. Leg. 4.48f. R.A. Horsley, "Spiritual Elitism", p. 228 suggests an

Philo's own experience of this inspiration he describes as follows:

under the influence of divine possession (ὑπὸ κατοχῆς ἐνθέου) I have been filled with Corybantic frenzy and been unconscious of anything (κορυβαντιᾶν καὶ πάντα ἀγνοεῖν), place, persons present, myself, words spoken, lines written. For I obtained language (ἑρμηνείαν), ideas (εὕρεσιν), an enjoyment of light, keenest vision, pellucid distinctness of objects, such as might be received through the eyes as the result of clearest shewing.[53]

Speaking more generally of the human experience of inspiration, he suggests that the human mind

carrying its gaze beyond the confines of all substance discernible by sense, . . . comes to a point at which it reaches out after the intelligible world, and on descrying in that world sights of surpassing loveliness, even the patterns and the originals of the things of sense which it saw here, it is seized by a sober intoxication like those filled with Corybantic frenzy (ὥσπερ οἱ κορυβαντιῶντες ἐνθουσιᾷ), and is inspired, possessed by a longing far other than theirs and a nobler desire.[54]

This experience can be a waking or a sleeping one; in Daniel, for example, prophecy was a matter of dream interpretation, but it need not always be so:

In deep sleep the mind quits its place, and withdrawing from the perceptions and all other bodily faculties, begins to hold converse with itself, fixing its gaze on truth as in a mirror, and, having purged away as defilements all the impressions made upon it by the mental pictures presented to it by the senses, it is filled with Divine frenzy, and discerns in dreams absolutely true prophecies concerning things to come (τὰς περὶ τῶν μελλόντων ἀψευδεστάτας διὰ τῶν ὀνείρων μαντείας ἐνθουσιᾷ). Thus it is at times. Or again it may be in waking hours. For when the mind, possessed by some philosophic principle, is drawn by it, it follows this, and needs must be oblivious of other things, of all the concerns of the cumbersome body.[55]

Here the link between the experience of the Biblical writers and Philo's own experience is particularly clear, as is the emphasis he places on the abnormal mental state of inspired persons: they "needs must be oblivious of other things, of all the concerns of the cumbersome body". This "sober intoxication" is a state of deep contemplation on the divine mysteries. Its results also include certain observable signs, however:

when grace fills the soul, that soul thereby rejoices and smiles and dances, for it is possessed and inspired, so that to many of the unenlightened it may seem to be drunken, crazy and beside itself. . . . For with the God-possessed not only is the soul wont to be

---

allusion to glossolalia in the last line of the passage quoted. It will hardly surprise the reader if I suggest that there is no evidence to support this conjecture.

[53] Migr. Abr. 35.

[54] de Opificio Mundi 70-71.

[55] Migr. Abr. 190.

stirred and goaded as it were into ecstasy but the body also is flushed and fiery, warmed by the overflowing joy within which passes on the sensation to the outer man, and thus many of the foolish are deceived and suppose that the sober are drunk . . .[56]

The primary symptoms of inspiration, then, are mental, but they do overflow into the visible realm; there they are commonly misunderstood.[57] Philo, however, provides us with little that parallels the kinds of symptoms we have seen as commonplace in the general Hellenistic tradition. For him, as for others, inspiration gives access to forms of knowledge otherwise unavailable. For him it is not accompanied by shouting and violent dancing or other movement; it is the contemplation of the philosopher, not the frenzy of the Maenad, that is inspired. For him Corybantic frenzy provides a useful metaphor, but no more than that. On the other hand his emphasis on the rapt mental state of the one inspired goes beyond what is otherwise common:

For ecstasy, as its very name clearly shows, is nothing else than the departing and going out of the understanding. But the race of prophets is wont to suffer this. When the mind is divinely possessed and becomes filled with god it is no longer within itself, for it receives the divine πνεῦμα to dwell within it.[58]

5. Summary

Philo stands as an exception to the general understanding of inspiration in the Hellenistic world. As we suggested at the beginning of this chapter, it is clear from these stereotyped descriptions that the Hellenistic world had a very clear image of what was involved in inspiration. This image included any, but not necessarily all of the following elements: violent physical

---

[56] de Ebrietate 146.

[57] The parallel with Acts 2, where the disciples are thought to be drunken due to their outburst of glossolalia, comes readily to mind. The idea that the inspired or the philosopher will appear to be drunk or mad has a long history, stemming back at least to Plato's analogy of the cave, where the philosopher, having finally come to understand ultimate realities, must return to the cave of illusions where most of humanity are still to be found, living among the shadows. There he appears to the inhabitants to be foolish and useless, having been rendered unable to live with "reality" as it is commonly understood.

[58] Questions and Answers on Genesis 3.9. Though this is particularly said to be true of prophecy, we must note that Philo discusses ecstasy more generally along the same lines as the rest of the Hellenistic tradition. He discusses four kinds of ecstasy; delusion, consternation, passivity and prophecy. (S. Sandmel, *Philo's Place in Judaism*, "augmented edition", Ktav, New York, 1971, p. 177 and note 346.) Clearly all four are paranormal states of mind, but only in the case of prophecy is the total absence of the rational faculty so strongly emphasised. In de Ebrietate 15 ordinary drunkenness is also said to produce ἔκστασις, but it is not clear if he sees this as a separate category.

activity, particularly frenzied dancing or rushing about; shouts and cries, sometimes in the form of intelligible cries of invocation; "supernatural" manifestations generally; more than human knowledge, and in many cases, considerable alterations to the frame of mind of those inspired. The modern term "ecstasy" might mean simply high excitement and exaltation; it might go as far as total lack of awareness of one's surroundings. To some extent our evidence suggests that the tradition blended elements that had originally been separate. Delphic prophecy came to be viewed (by those who had no direct experience of its occurrence) as frenzied, in parallel with the experience of the Dionysiac cult; Dionysus' devotees were said to prophesy.[59]

With this stereotyped image in mind, it would appear that the criticisms mounted by Manson and Gundry against the view that the inspired speech phenomena of Hellenistic popular religion closely parallel early Christian glossolalia are thoroughly justified. For one thing,

the N.T. contains no indications that glossolalia was induced artificially as in pagan religions by liquor, narcotics, frenzied dancing, rhythmic repetition of formulae, self-mutilation, or emotion-charged rituals,[60]

and though these methods of inducing frenzy are not uniformly found in all our cases of inspiration, some of them are reasonably common. For another, though it is perhaps an oversimplification to say that

The shouting (sc. in the Dionysiac cult) is one of the causes of the ecstatic condition, not the result of it. But in the glossolalia of the New Testament the falling into the ecstatic state comes first, and the strange utterances are the outward sign of the inward condition[61]

because it would appear that the shouting and wild cries could occur both at the onset of inspiration, and during the inspired state itself, it is certainly the case that the functions of Dionysiac shouts and Christian glossolalia as it is presented in our evidence were quite different. Dionysiac cries were invocations first, and acclamations as well. Christian glossolalia was not invocation, as Manson correctly states; nor does it appear to have been primarily acclamatory. Early Christianity had its ritual invocations and acclamations, such as "Amen", "Allelujah", "Hosannah", "Maranatha", "Abba" and "Kyrios Iesous", and it may be that here at least there is a point

---

[59] For a further suggestion that attributes of one form of ἐνθουσιασμός were imputed to other forms see D.E. Aune, *Prophecy*, pp. 42-3.

[60] R.H. Gundry, *art.cit.*, p. 307 n. 2.

[61] T.W. Manson, *op.cit.*, p. 204.

of contact between the early Christian phenomena of inspired speech and their Hellenistic environment. Certainly they are much better parallels than glossolalia.

Chapter 7

Glossolalia and Hellenistic Popular Religion,

and Exegetical Conclusions.

The third major source of Hellenistic parallels for glossolalia suggested by modern scholars is that described as "the spiritual underworld of antiquity".[1] It is claimed that glossolalia was a relatively common phenomenon in popular enthusiasm, and as such was readily recognisable to the ordinary man. The suggestion is unfortunately often argued with a heavier reliance on exegetical considerations relating to the New Testament, such as were mentioned above in Chapter 2, than on the actual citation of evidence. When evidence is explicitly cited, it is normally one or more of the following sources, which contain references to phenomena claimed to parallel early Christian glossolalia.

Lucian's "Alexander the False Prophet" reports that, when Alexander entered Abonouteichos, in his attempt to impress the people of the town with the divine origin of his oracular powers, he simulated a state of divine possession, thus:

whenever a person but turned up with someone at his heels to play the flute or the tambourine or the cymbals, telling fortunes with a sieve, as the phrase goes, they were all agog over him on the instant and stared at him as if he were a god from heaven . . . Alexander was a man of mark and note, affecting as he did to have occasional fits of madness and causing his mouth to fill with foam. This he easily managed by chewing the root of soapwort, the plant that dyers use; but to his fellow-countrymen even the foam seemed supernatural and awe-inspiring . . . In the morning he ran out into the market-place naked, wearing a loin-cloth (this too was gilded), carrying his falchion, and tossing his unconfined mane like a devotee of the Great Mother in the frenzy . . .

[1] The phrase, cited above and in the previous chapter, at footnote 46, is that of Morton Smith, from "Prolegomena to Discussion of Aretalogies, Divine Men, the Gospels and Jesus", *J.B.L.* vol. 90, 1971, pp. 174-199. The suggestion that glossolalia can be parallelled from this "spiritual underworld" goes back at least as far as Reitzenstein's *Poimandres*, Leipzig, 1904, pp. 57-58, and Harnack, *Über das gnostische Buch Pistis Sophia, Texte und Untersuchungen zur altchristlichen Literatur*, 7.2, Leipzig, 1891, pp. 87-89.

Uttering a few meaningless words like Hebrew or Phoenician, he dazed the creatures, who did not know what he was saying save that he everywhere brought in Apollo and Asclepius . . . and the whole population followed, all full of religious fervour and crazed with expectations.[2]

Origen's report of Celsus' description of prophecy in Palestine towards the end of the second century describes the mode of prophecy current at that time with the following words:

There are many, he says, who are nameless, who prophesy at the slightest excuse for some trivial cause both inside and outside temples; and there are some who wander about begging and roaming around cities and military camps; and they pretend to be moved as if giving some oracular utterance. It is an ordinary and common custom for each one to say 'I am God (or a son of God, or a divine Spirit). And I have come. Already the world is being destroyed. And you, O men, are to perish because of your iniquities. But I wish to save you. And you shall see me returning again with heavenly power. Blessed is he who has worshipped me now! But I will cast everlasting fire upon the rest, both on cities and on country places. And men who fail to realise the penalties in store for them will in vain repent and groan. But I will preserve for ever those who have been convinced by me.' Then after that he (Celsus, C.F.) says: 'Having brandished these threats they then go on to add incomprehensible, incoherent, and utterly obscure utterances, the meaning of which no intelligent person could discover; for they are meaningless and nonsensical, and give a chance for any fool or sorcerer to take the words in whatever sense he likes.'[3]

---

[2] Lucian, Alexander the False Prophet 9, 12-14. The closely related passage, Lucian's *Menippus* 7-11, has been completely ignored by scholarship, as far as I can see. It will be dealt with below. The passage from Alexander the False Prophet is used as evidence by the following scholars: H.D. Betz, *Lukian von Samosata und das N.T.*, Berlin, Akademie-Verlag, 1961, p. 140, who draws the parallel to the material from Origen cited below; T.W. Gillespie, "A Pattern" who on˙p. 80 translates the critical phrase of Lucian's description as "speaking some sounds without distinguishing mark" (ἄσημος), which is accurate, though overly literalistic. Gillespie summarises this viewpoint well when he says that "what Celsus (and Lucian) understood as the nonsense born of madness was accepted at the level of *Volksreligion* as the sure sign that a prophet was genuinely inspired by the god for whom he spoke . . . Put simply, among the common people 'tongues' was recognised as the divine legitimation of prophecy in the Hellenistic age." The passage is also cited as a caricature of prophetic mania by G. Dautzenberg, "Glossalalie", col. 230. Gillespie's general view is cited with approval by M.E. Boring, in *Sayings*, p. 84, and with qualified approval by D.E. Aune, *Prophecy*, p. 42, n. 221. The exegetical consequences of such a view are worked through in detail in Gillespie's thesis, *Prophecy and Tongues*. The essential point, for Gillespie, is that the problem in Corinth is due to the "pre-Christian encounter of the Gentiles of the congregation with the religious ecstasy of Hellenistic enthusiasm". (p. 37.) For the view that what Alexander was mimicking was not so much unknown languages, but rather simply nonsense syllables, and that these were a form of prophetic legitimation, see S.D. Currie, "Early Evidence", pp. 274 ff., and esp. p. 292 n. 14. Currie is not sure whether this provides a true parallel, because he is uncertain as to the actual nature of glossolalia.

[3] *Origen: Contra Celsum*, ed. H. Chadwick, Cambridge, 1965, pp. 402-3. The case is

The long strings of apparent nonsense syllables and mixtures of the religious terminology of different cultures often found as invocations of various divine or semi-divine powers in the magical papyri of the third and fourth centuries are sometimes mentioned, and it is suggested that these are either in some sense glossolalia, or else a related, though degenerate, phenomenon fossilised as part of the magical ritual.[4] Likewise the similar phenomena found in Gnostic writings such as the "Poimandres" and the "Pistis Sophia" are sometimes suggested as evidence for the wide spread of glossolalia in Hellenistic popular religion. We might cite, for example, the following passage of Engelsen, where, speaking of such phenomena, he says:

It is names of gods and powers, age-old cult cries, exclamations and acclamations, which have been preserved. But some of them seem to have their origin in impulsive ejaculations of unintelligible speech from mantic cults.[5]

---

argued in detail in the two works of Gillespie cited above; see especially the detailed references in his 1978 article, pp. 76-80., to the voluminous quantities written on this passage. Scholars identifying the phenomenon in question as glossolalia include Oepke, in Kittel, ed., *T.D.N.T.*, vol. 2, 1935, E.T. 1964, p. 458, Betz, *op.cit.*, p. 140, Georgi, *Die Gegner des Paulus im 2.Korintherbrief*, Neukirchner-Verlag, Neukirchen, 1964, pp. 120-121, implicitly Currie, "Early Evidence", pp. 292-293, Bornkamm, "Faith and Reason in Paul", *Early Christian Experience*, London, 1969, p. 38, N.I.J. Engelsen, *Glossolalia*, pp. 39-50, and Schmithals, *Gnosticism in Corinth*, trans. J.E. Steely, Nashville, 1971, pp. 276-277, who (naturally) takes it to be a Gnostic phenomenon, though he cites no evidence prior to the account of Marcus Gnosticus in Irenaeus, Adversus Haereses 1.13. G. Dautzenberg, "Glossolalie", col. 232, pronounces the question unsolved. See also U.B. Müller, *Prophetie und Predigt im Neuen Testament*, Gütersloh, 1975, pp. 31-2, who makes the accurate observation that Corinthian *prophecy* cannot have been glossolalic, like that cited by Celsus, or Paul would not have described it as speech "with the mind".

[4] See J. Behm, "Γλῶσσα", in Kittel, *T.D.N.T.*, vol. 1, p. 723. Behm cites PGM XIII's display of the languages of various heavenly beings. G. Dautzenberg thinks there is possibly a distant link to be drawn here, "Glossolalie", col. 231. See also S.D. Currie, "Early Evidence", p. 293, n. 15, but, in line with Currie's uncertainty about the nature of glossolalia, the parallel is not pressed. Wire, *Women Prophets*, pp. 141-2, is likewise cautious, though more positive. In M. Smith, "Pauline Worship as Seen by Pagans", *H.Th.R.*, vol. 93, 1-2, 1980, pp. 241-249, esp. pp. 245-247, by comparison, M. Smith's confidence is boundless.

[5] Engelsen, *Glossolalia*, pp. 47-49, and see Behm, in *T.D.N.T.* vol. 1, 1932, E.T. 1964, p. 723, Harnack, *loc.cit.*, Reitzenstein, *loc.cit.*, and, more recently though with little supporting argument, M.E. Hart, *Tongues and Prophecy*, p. 19, and H.H. Hunter, "Tongues-Speech: a Patristic Analysis", *J.E.Th.S.* vol. 23, 1980, p. 128. Other sources about Gnostic inspired speech include Irenaeus, *loc.cit.*, cited in Epiphanius, Panarion, 34, and Hippolytus, Elenchus 4.39ff. These latter three sources are analysed with care by J. Reiling, "Marcus Gnosticus and the New Testament: Eucharist and Prophecy", from *Miscellanea Neotestamentica* vol. 1, ed. T. Baarda, A.F.J. Klijn and W.C. van Unnik,

The various references to Montanist prophecy in the ecclesiastical writers are sometimes cited, with the suggestion that the form taken by this outbreak of prophecy was heavily influenced by Montanus' own pre-Christian experience in Phrygian ecstatic religion. Some note that he is said by Jerome to have been a priest of Cybele, by others to be a priest of Apollo. The implicit claim seems to be that Montanist prophecy took some form analogous to glossolalia.[6] This is based on the normal view of Eusebius' description of Montanist prophecy, and its generally acknowledged "ecstatic" nature:

a recent convert called Montanus, when Gratus was proconsul of Asia, in the unbounded lust of his soul for leadership gave access to himself to the adversary, became obsessed, and suddenly fell into frenzy and convulsions. He began to be ecstatic and to speak and to talk strangely, prophesying contrary to the custom which belongs to the tradition and succession of the church from the beginning . . . he raised up two more women and filled them with the bastard spirit so that they spoke madly and improperly and strangely, like Montanus.[7]

These, then, are the sources brought forward by modern authors. The single most important point to be noted, as we turn to examine these suggested parallels, is that *the overwhelming majority* of these references come from the mid-second century or later. In the light of the problems to do with changing views of paranormal phenomena in Hellenistic culture between the first century and the end of the second, mentioned in the Introduction, the lateness of the evidence cited above must raise very real doubts. If a strong thread of evidence of a demonstrably pre-Christian date could be shown to exist, then it might be legitimate to link this later evidence

---

Leiden, 1978, pp. 161-179. The suggestion of G. Dautzenberg, "Glossolalie", col. 231, that the case for a parallel (albeit distant) between glossolalia and the phenomena in the papyri is reinforced by the occurrence of a Pentecost-like speech miracle in the Delian Festival of Apollo seems to me to be extremely unlikely: nearly a millennium separates the two sets of phenomena, if nothing else. The evidence of the "Homeric" Hymn to Apollo has been dealt with above, in Chapter 5.

[6]   See, for example, C.L. Rogers, "The Gift of Tongues in the Post-Apostolic Church", *Bibliotheca Sacra*, vol. 122, no. 486, April-June 1965, pp. 134-143, esp. pp. 139. See also Currie, "Early Evidence", pp. 286ff., Bornkamm, *op.cit.*, p. 36, n. 31, M.E. Hart, *Tongues and Prophecy*, pp. 105-6, W.F. Orr and J.A.R. Walker, *1 Corinthians*, New York, 1976, pp. 305ff, and H.W. House, "Tongues and the Mystery Religions of Corinth", *Bib. Sac.* vol. 140, part 558, 1983, p. 137.

[7]   Eusebius, H.E. 5.16.7-10, 11. This is the passage most commonly cited for detail about the nature of original Montanist prophecy. Of course, Tertullian provides great amounts of corroborative detail. See H. Güntert, *Von der Sprache der Götter und Geister*, Halle, 1921, p. 28, Rogers, *op.cit.*, p. 141, Engelsen, *Glossolalia*, pp. 44-45, Bornkamm, *op.cit.*, p. 38 note 31.

with it, though considerable care would still be necessary. So far, however, very little convincing pre-Christian evidence has been adduced.

1. The Magical Papyri

The magical papyri may be rapidly dismissed, as having no demonstrable link with early Christian glossolalia whatsoever. Very few of the magical papyri so far discovered date from earlier than the third century of the Christian era, and though we know that such documents existed in the first century from Acts 19.19 and other references[8], we have very few examples of such early documents, and their real flowering came in the fourth century. It is true that a number of magical papyri are to be dated to the first century A.D. or earlier, and some of these do contain "nomina barbara".[9] It is also true that such magic is deeply traditional, and we could safely presume such early documents, even if they were not extant.[10] But these invocations and incantations, which make up so much of the magical papyri, are not conceived as language, do not need, or receive, interpretation, and neither are they seen as in any sense revelatory. They are invocations, and (if inspiration is in view at all) they are part of the process intended to *lead* to

---

[8] For example, Suetonius, Life of Augustus 31, where the Emperor orders the destruction of two thousand magical documents, and Juvenal, Satire 6 (cited by G.P. Corrington, "Power and the Man of Power in the Context of Hellenistic Popular Belief", *S.B.L. 1984 Seminar Papers*, pp. 257-262, p. 260), lines 133, 548, and 610, on magical, astrological and other occult practices in the late first century in Rome. See also the careful treatment in C.E. Arnold, *Ephesians: Power and Magic; the Concept of Power in Ephesians in light of its Historical Setting*, Cambridge, 1989, pp. 14-34.

[9] See, for example, PGM XVI, dated 1st Century B.C. in H.D. Betz, ed., *The Greek Magical Papyri in Translation*, Chicago, 1986, p. 252, and also PGM LXXII, Betz p. 298, dated 1st or 2nd century A.D.

[10] See A.D. Nock, "Greek Magical Papyri", in Z. Stewart, ed., *Essays on Religion and the Ancient World*, vol. 1, p. 187, D.E. Aune, "The Apocalypse of John and Graeco-Roman Revelatory Magic", *N.T.S.* vol. 33, 1987, p. 483, and H.D. Betz, "The Formation of Authoritative Tradition in the Greek Magical Papyri", B.F. Meyer and E.P. Sanders, eds., *Jewish and Christian Self-Definition*, vol. 3, London, 1982, pp. 161-170.

inspiration; they do not result from it.[11] Neither are they spontaneous: they are incantations to be recited or inscribed precisely as they are written.[12]

2. Heavenly Languages

There may be a distant connection between glossolalia and magic via the concept that there are heavenly as well as earthly languages, but the idea that it is appropriate to praise and invoke the gods and other supernatural beings using these languages is much harder to parallel. While the concept of heavenly languages has a long pedigree in Greek thought, the deduction that therefore one ought to attempt to address the gods or other divine powers in these languages (or by their names in these languages) cannot be shown to have pre-Christian origins. Indeed, this idea seems only to develop considerably later.

I would argue, contrary to H. Güntert,[13] who does not distinguish the two ideas, and also contrary to most more recent writers, that this dual concept, of divine languages *and* human use of them, originates within what might loosely be called mystical Judaism, and works its way only slowly into Hellenistic sources, and thence finally into magical practice. Despite his claim that such a Hellenistic concept must lie behind both 1 Cor. 12-14 and Acts 2, Güntert produces no convincing evidence. His insistence that it is *divine* languages only that lie behind the New Testament concept of

---

[11] For useful summaries of the evidence of the magical papyri see J.M. Hull, *Hellenistic Magic and the Synoptic Tradition*, London, 1974., ch. 3, and, for details on the dates of the various documents, pp. 25-26. See also the useful discussion of various features in C.E. Arnold, *loc.cit.* Protests against the easy equating of the phenomena have been raised, most notably by T.W. Manson, in *Studies in the Gospels and Epistles*, ed. M. Black, Manchester, 1962, p. 204: "The complicated mess of alphabetic permutations and combinations, interlarded with battered relics of divine names, which appears in the papyri is the product of perverted ingenuity rather than religious ecstasy. It is not glossolalia, whatever else it may be . . ." Likewise D.E. Aune, "Magic in Early Christianity", *A.N.R.W.* II.23.2., pp. 1507-1557, esp. section VII, pp. 1549-1551, is critical of the identification. One of the magical papyri most commonly cited is the great Paris Magical Papyrus, published by C. Wessely in *Griechische Zauberpapyri von Paris und London*, Vienna, 1888. It is normally dated around A.D. 300. The other is Preisendanz's PGM XIII, cited by Behm, above.

[12] See the detailed instructions in the documents cited by Hull, *op.cit.*, pp. 42-4. The same point applies to the "Ephesia Grammata", the incantatory formula attributed to Branchus, the legendary founder of the oracle of Didyma, reported in (among other places) Clement of Alexandria, Stromata 5.8.48. They are totally formulaic: it is these very words which must be used. D.E. Aune, *art.cit.*, p. 1550, doubts the clear distinction between spontaneity and formula, but the difference is still there: glossolalia is *not* consciously ritualised - quite the reverse! - and the magical invocations *are*.

[13] *Op.cit.*, pp. 26-31.

glossolalia, and that Acts' interpretation of the Pentecostal tongues as human languages must be a later elaboration due to the author's love of the miraculous, ignores the fact that Paul clearly speaks of "the tongues *of men* and angels", and discusses the intelligibility of tongues generally with the analogy of the problem of communication between foreigners.[14] Why Luke should consider a "human language" miracle more noteworthy than one of divine languages, and hence re-interpret Pentecost in this light, is not explained. Though some first and second-century writers show an awareness of the idea of divine languages, deriving the concept from Homer, who spoke of the difference between the names given to places by men and by the gods,[15] my reading of the Hellenistic sources of the immediate New Testament environment has found no evidence for the *dual* idea that they existed *and* were understood as being a matter of importance for communicating *from men to the gods*. Why should there be such a problem? Men do not know divine languages, but there is no suggestion at all that the gods do not know those of men!

On the other hand, some authors display no interest in the idea of divine languages at all. Philo's "On the Confusion of Tongues" and Josephus' account of the Babel story contain no hint of such a concept. Philo's discussion of the mode of God's speech to Abraham in his Questions and Answers on Genesis 4.140 argues that God "speaks without uttering words and talks . . . without audible voice". Despite Philo's consistent use of the term ἑρμενεύς for prophets (for which see above, Chapter 3), there is never any suggestion that the word is being used in its literal sense, to mean "translator". Plutarch, speaking of Socrates' daimon and its mode of communication with him, shows no acquaintance with such a concept when he discusses the possibility that what Socrates heard was "not a spoken language, but the unuttered words of a daemon, making voiceless contact with his intelligence by their sense alone . . . Their thoughts have no need of nouns and verbs, which men use . . . " (Mor. 588e - 599c). Plutarch goes on to discuss popular beliefs that he himself does not hold, but again there is no mention of daimonic languages. The concept is also absent in the account of the heavenly journey of Timarchus in Mor. 590 ff.; though Timarchus has a heavenly guide, and has conversations with several heavenly beings, there is

---

[14] See Chapters 3 and 4, and the very pertinent comments of R.H. Gundry, " 'Ecstatic Utterance' (N.E.B.)?", *J.Th.S.* 17. part 2, 1966, pp. 299-307.

[15] As was noted in Chapter 5, at notes 28 and 29, Dio Chrysostom, Discourses 10.23, 11.22, and Clement of Alexandria, Stromata 1.21 even suggest that the obscurity (ἀσάφεια) of oracles may be the result of bad translations.

no suggestion that anything but Greek was used. It is likewise absent from Fragment 176 of the Moralia, describing "post-mortem experience", and Mor. 944a-b, where the cries to one another of the sub-lunar souls are mentioned, *despite* the fact that these souls or spirits are believed to be responsible for the transmission of oracles. Finally, there is no mention of any such idea in such scanty descriptions as we have of the experience of initiates into the "Mysteries".[16] We must conclude, then, that the concept of the use of divine languages for prayer does not help us understand magical practice, and is not one that commends itself as a parallel to glossolalia. The concept is not represented in our pre-Christian evidence, nor for some time after the arrival of Christianity on the world scene. Not only so, but as we have seen in Chapter 3, above, the attempt to argue that glossolalia was *primarily* understood as angelic languages (often on the basis of two words in 1 Corinthians 13) must be judged a failure.

3. Gnosticism

The same chronological point made about the magical papyri applies to the suggested Gnostic parallels. Once again, absolutely no pre-Christian evidence has been cited, and even more so than in the case of the magical papyri, the presumption that the second-century evidence may be based on, and thus read back into, first-century or earlier traditions requires hard evidence to substantiate it. At least magical formulations such as the "Ephesia Grammata" of Branchus, mentioned in note 12 above, themselves demonstrably ancient, are part of a widespread tradition traceable throughout our period. Are the Gnostic phenomena? Regardless of this issue, the evidence of Irenaeus certainly does bring us considerably closer to the first century. On the other hand, it also brings us into circles thoroughly penetrated by a Christianity which did know of glossolalia as a still relatively common experience.[17] Hence we may not simply presume that Marcus Gnosticus' understanding of inspiration draws on a pre-Christian Hellenism. The particular phenomena suggested as parallels, however, have yet to be examined.

Irenaeus describes for us a case that he suggests is typical of the style of Marcus' attempts to gain himself a following. After outlining the kinds of "wonder-working" with which Marcus convinced people that he had great

---

[16] See Apuleius, The Golden Ass, 11.23. For a discussion of the Jewish evidence see Appendix 1.

[17] As I have argued in Chapter 4, contra Rogers, *art.cit.*, pp. 138-140, Irenaeus can only be understood as saying that he does know of glossolalia as an orthodox Christian experience, though not one he has had himself.

and supernatural powers, he offers the following version of Marcus' "prophetic initiation". Marcus would say to the woman in question:

I want you to enjoy a share of my grace, for the Father of all continually beholds your angel before his face. Now the place of your angel is among us, and it is fitting that we should be joined together. First receive Grace, from me and through me. Prepare yourself as a bride expecting her bridegroom, so that you may be what I am, and I what you are. Set the seed of the light in your bridal chamber. Accept from me your groom, hold him and be in him. Behold, Grace has descended upon you: open your mouth and prophesy.

But the woman replies, "I never prophesied; I don't know how to prophesy." Then he offers some invocations a second time, to the amazement of the deceived woman, and says to her, "Open your mouth and say whatever comes, and you will be prophesying."

Excited and taken in by what has gone before, with her soul overheated in the expectation of being able to prophesy, her heart beating wildly, she dares to speak inanities, to say everything which comes to her, rashly and emptily, flushed with the warmth of that vain spirit; and henceforth she regards herself as a prophet . . .[18]

As Reiling demonstrates, there are many features in this passage reminiscent of the apocryphal gospels and of magical practice, as well as of Plutarch's description of the psychological state of inspiration in "On the Obsolescence of Oracles", Mor. 432f.[19] The critical question, however, is whether the phrases "she dares to speak inanities, to say everything which comes to her, rashly and emptily" ought to be understood as evidence of glossolalia. There seems to be no clear evidence to suggest this. Irenaeus knows of glossolalia, and like Paul describes it as unknown languages.[20] He does not draw such inferences here, but describes what was said, with obvious polemical intent, as "inanities ($\lambda\eta\rho\dot{\omega}\delta\eta$), . . . everything which comes to her, rashly and emptily ($\pi\dot{\alpha}\nu\tau\alpha$ $\kappa\epsilon\nu\dot{\omega}\varsigma$ $\kappa\alpha\dot{\iota}$ $\tau o\lambda\mu\eta\rho\dot{\omega}\varsigma$)". These terms are far more likely to mean that the content of what was said was not worth hearing than that the words were incomprehensible.[21]

---

[18] Irenaeus, A.H. 1.13. The passage is cited by Currie, "Early Evidence", p. 290-291, and by Schmithals, *Gnosticism in Corinth*, trans. J.E. Steely, Nashville, 1971, p. 276-277. The sources are analysed with greater care by Reiling, *art.cit.*

[19] J. Reiling, *art.cit.*, pp. 164ff. See also the parallel description of enthusiasm in Philo, de Ebrietate 147.

[20] Irenaeus, Adversus Haereses 3.10.6., Eusebius H.E. 5.7.6.

[21] M. Turner, "Spiritual Gifts Then and Now", *Vox Evangelica* vol. 15, 1985, p. 19 also suggests that "incoherent *prophetic* speech", not glossolalia, is what we are dealing with here. Reiling compares the description in the passage with that of the false prophet in Hermas. $K\epsilon\nu\dot{\omega}\varsigma$ simply means "vain" or "empty", of course, as it does in the next line, describing the spirit that possesses the woman, and $\tau o\lambda\mu\eta\rho\dot{\omega}\varsigma$ tells us nothing about the nature of what was said. $\Lambda\eta\rho\dot{\omega}\delta\eta$ and its cognates mean "frivolous" or "silly", and are often used in Philo for the foolishness of the drunken: see de Plantatione 143-4, de

Engelsen cites a passage from the "Pistis Sophia", a Coptic document which in its present form can hardly be dated earlier than the third century, where the risen Christ, speaking with his disciples, prays, invoking his divine Father:

Then Jesus stood with his disciples beside the water of the ocean and pronounced this prayer, saying: "Hear me, my Father, thou father of all fatherhoods, thou infinite Light: αεηιουω. ϊαω. αωϊ. ωϊα. ψινοθερ. θερνοψ. νωψιτερ. ζαγουρη. παγουρη. νεθμομαωθ. νεψιομαωθ. μαραχαχθα. θωβαρραβαυ. θαρναχαχαν̅. ζοροχοθορα. ϊεου. σαβαωθ."

As Jesus was saying these things, however, Thomas, Andrew, James and Simon the Canaanite were in the west, with their faces turned to the east. But Philip and Bartholomew were in the south, with their faces turned to the north. The rest of the disciples and women disciples however were standing behind Jesus. But Jesus was standing before the altar.

And Jesus cried out as he turned to the four corners of the world with his disciples, and they were all robed in linen garments, and he said: "ϊαω. ϊαω. ϊαω." This is its interpretation: iota, because the All came forth; alpha, because it will return again; omega, because the completion of all things will happen.

When however Jesus had said these things, he said: "ϊαφθα. ϊαφθα. μουναηρ. μουναηρ. ερμανουηρ. ερμανουηρ." which is: "O Father of all fatherhoods of the infinite ones, hear me for the sake of my disciples whom I have brought into thy presence that they may believe every word of thy truth. And do thou perform everything about which I shall cry out to thee, because I know the name of the Father of the Treasury of the Light."[22]

Engelsen, citing Horner, comments that the strange words are

"not gibberish as at first sight they appear to be, but a jumble of Hebrew, Egyptian and perhaps Persian words, copied and recopied by scribes ignorant of these languages until they are all but unrecognizable" . . . It is names of gods and powers, age-old cult cries, exclamations and acclamations, which have been preserved. But some of them seem to have their origin in impulsive ejaculations of unintelligible speech from mantic cults.[23]

It must be simply said, however, that Horner's comment (quotes mine) is far more plausible than Engelsen's conjecture that follows it. For it is pure

Ebrietate 4, 6, 123, 126, 197. Dionysius also uses it in this sense, A.R. 11.18.1. Plutarch uses the word of the nonsense of gossips, de Garrulitate, Mor. 502 c, 504 b, 512 d, and of the ravings of madmen, Quaestiones Convivales, Mor. 623 a, and less strongly 769 a, and of the nonsense of drunks, Quaestiones Convivales, Mor. 715 c, d, 716 d. Cf. also Dio Chrysostom 9.8, 32.49, 33.56. "Inanities" is a good translation. Clearly the *content* of what was said is the point.

[22] *Pistis Sophia*, ed. C. Schmidt, translated and with notes by V. Macdermot, Leiden, 1978, pp. 354-356. Engelsen, *Glossolalia*, pp. 49f, quotes only one paragraph of an older translation, but as far as I can see no material point of difference affects the argument. The relationship between the types of words used here and those to be found in the magical papyri is clear.

[23] N.I.J. Engelsen, *Glossolalia*, pp. 47-49, as cited above at note 5. The quotation is from G. Horner, *Pistis Sophia*, London, 1924, p. xxiv.

conjecture, entirely unsupported by evidence. I know of no evidence that manticism resulted in such speech.

Quite clearly we are dealing here with a phenomenon which has only tenuous links with glossolalia. It is not conceived of as being a language. Although it needs interpretation, that interpretation is more symbolic than linguistic. Although it may be inspired, it is conceived of as invocation, not praise. Like the material from the magical papyri, it is formulaic rather than spontaneous, and has far closer links with inspired invocations or acclamations such as "Abba" and "Maranatha", than with glossolalia as it is presented to us in Acts and the Epistles.[24]

The only passage of which I am aware in which Gnostic literature evidences an interest in heavenly *languages*, as opposed to isolated and symbolic words or phrases, is the following extract from the Corpus Hermeticum. It describes the transformations that take place in the soul of the true Gnostic at death. Having shrugged off his material form, he ascends through the various levels of the heavens until

. . . he ascends to the substance of the eighth sphere, being now possessed of his own proper power; and he sings, together with those who dwell there, hymning the Father; and they that are there rejoice with him at his coming. And being made like to those with whom he dwells, he hears the Powers, who are above the substance of the eighth sphere, singing praise to God with a voice that is theirs alone (or: with a certain sweet voice) . . .[25]

It must be noted that though the Gnostic hears the songs of the powers, in the φωναί that are theirs alone (if that is the correct reading), he does not sing with them. He sings with those of the eighth sphere, directly below. Their language is not described at all. Though the next stage of the process is to become one of the powers, the consequence of joining in their singing is not mentioned; neither is the process of acquiring a φωνή like theirs. Finally we must remember that the whole process described takes place at death: it is not part of this life at all. In the light of these observations, and the late date of this document, any claim that we have here a substantive parallel to early Christian glossolalia must appear extremely far-fetched. What we may have here, depending on the reading of the text, is at best the late development of the common concept that heavenly beings have their

---

[24] See the section in Chapter 6 on invocations and acclamations in the "Mystery" cults.

[25] The first translation offered is that of W. Scott, *Corpus Hermeticum* vol. 1, London, 1924, p. 129, section 26a. Nock and Festugière, however, read ἡδείᾳ for Scott's ἰδίᾳ, thus suggesting the second translation. (*Hermes Trismégiste*, Paris, 1972, Vol. 1, p. 16, line 9.) The acceptance of this reading would, naturally, weaken the case for a parallel even further.

own languages; nothing here suggests that such languages are desirable for prayer, even as evidence of spiritual achievement.[26]

4. Montanism

The suggestion that Montanist ecstatic prophecy reflects the same postulated Hellenistic background, though chronologically as plausible as any other, collapses under even slight scrutiny. If Montanist prophecy was in any sense analogous to glossolalia it is quite remarkable that no ancient writer ever noticed or commented on the fact. Though it is certainly true that Montanist prophecy was characterised by ecstasy (in the modern sense), and occasionally by oracular obscurity, there is no unambiguous evidence whatsoever that it took glossolalic form.[27] Indeed, the evidence of Eusebius, who knows of collections of Montanist oracles, and actually cites the contents of some of them,[28] makes it luminously clear that these oracles were delivered in plain Greek. Nor is there any suggestion at all, so far as I

---

[26] Indeed, certain sections of Gnosticism would have found the whole concept of glossolalia as a higher form of prayer incomprehensible. The Gnostic concept of certain pure sounds being a higher form of language than normal speech, and the related idea that certain heavenly beings speak only in vowel sounds (for which see, for example, the *Gospel of the Egyptians*, trans. A. Böhlig and F. Wisse, section 44, in *The Nag Hammadi Library in English*, ed. J.M. Robinson, Leiden, 1977, p. 197), is based on speculations about the epistemological value of language as such. For such thinkers, silence, not miraculous gifts of language, is the highest expression of prayer. On this issue see now R.J. Mortley, *From Word to Silence*, vol. 2, Bonn, 1986, pp. 25ff, and compare the "Martyrdom of Peter", ch. 39, cited by S.D. Currie, "Early Evidence", p. 279.

[27] Of recent writers only W.C. Klein, "The Church and its Prophets", *Anglican Theological Review*, vol. 44, no. 1, 1962, p. 15, and H. Hunter, *art.cit.*, p. 129 seems to have noticed the lack of evidence.

[28] Eusebius, H.E. 5.16.17-19. Various modern authors have made collections of these oracles; the most recent known to me is that of W. Tabbernee, *The Opposition to Montanism from Church and State*, Diss., Melbourne University, 1978. He unfortunately continues the identification of Montanist prophecy as at least partially glossolalic: see p. 548. M.E. Hart (*Tongues and Prophecy*, p. 106), N. Turner (*Christian Words*, Edinburgh, 1980, p. 462) and C.G. Williams (*Tongues of the Spirit*, Cardiff, 1981, p. 38) also suggest the parallel, Hart doing so despite noting that Maximilla's and Montanus' preserved oracles were quite intelligible. The word ἑρμηνευτής does occur in one Montanist oracle, cited in Epiphanius, Haer., 48.13.1, (also cited by Aune, *Prophecy*, p. 315) which may be taken to mean that Maximilla not only spoke her oracles, but also explained their meanings. However, it seems more likely that the three terms "adherent, revealer and interpreter" are seen as parallel terms for Maximilla's role. Certainly it would be forcing the usage here to infer the kind of interpretation required by glossolalia. Thus also E. Fascher, *Prophetes*, p. 222.

am aware, that they achieved this form by way of any complementary gift or process of interpretation.

However, Eusebius' description of Montanus' prophecy has been used to argue for a parallel with glossolalia, and to this we now turn. Engelsen has argued that

the piling up of strong expressions, πνευματαφορέομαι, κατοχή, παρεκστασις (*sic*), and ἐνθουσία leaves no doubt about Montanus' ecstatic experience, in which he also prophesied and uttered strange sounds, as is shown by the expression λαλεῖν καὶ ξενοφωνεῖν.

Speaking of Eusebius' comment on Montanus that

he raised up two more women and filled them with the bastard spirit, so that they spoke madly (ἐκφρόνως) and improperly (ἀκαίρως) and strangely (ἀλλοτριοτρόπως), like Montanus,

Engelsen says:

Also the prophetesses utter unintelligible sounds when they prophesy.[29]

Unless this is simply a grammatical error, and Engelsen intends us to understand that the prophetesses speak unintelligibly as Montanus is also *said* to do, this statement is completely unsupported by evidence. "Madly" (ἐκφρόνως) implies nothing about the linguistic nature of what was said, but merely indicates the mental state of the speaker. "Improperly" (ἀκαίρως) likewise adds nothing to the case. "Strangely" (ἀλλοτριοτρόπως) is a rare term, cited only from this one passage in Lampe, but the related term ἀλλότριος, common in the Patristic period, means quite simply "strange" or "alien", and is commonly used of heretical teaching. In this case it may have to do with, not the form, but the content of what was said.[30] Even if this is not the case, the term is far too imprecise to be the basis of an argument that glossolalia is meant. As for ξενοφωνεῖν, despite Engelsen's comment, it means "to speak like a foreigner" only in the most basic etymological sense. It is also a rare word, but means, in Lampe's opinion, "to speak strange things" or "to astonish by strange words or teaching", so that it is again the content of what was said, not the form, that seems to be under consideration.[31]

If Lampe is right, then, there is no clear evidence at all that Montanist prophecy resembled glossolalia, and a good deal of evidence that it did not.

---

[29] Engelsen, *Glossolalia*, p. 44; Eusebius, H.E. 5.16.9, Engelsen, *loc.cit.* Very similar views are expressed by Güntert, *op.cit.*, p. 28, and M.E. Hart, *Tongues and Prophecy*, p. 106.

[30] So Lampe, *A Patristic Greek Lexicon*, Oxford. 1961.

[31] *Ibid.*

Rather, it resembled Delphic enthusiasm in that the inspired speech that resulted from it was intelligible, and "Dionysiac" enthusiasm in its (in the modern sense) ecstatic or frenzied nature; it seems to fall half way between the two.

5. Lucian

The evidence of Lucian and Origen is of a different calibre, and requires fuller analysis. These two sources must, however, be treated separately, in order to test the assumption that they describe similar phenomena.

H.D. Betz speaks for many when he argues that Alexander's unintelligible speech is to be understood as a report of glossolalia. He believes that Lucian misunderstands the phenomenon, thinking that it was meant as a miracle of speech, whereas Betz himself believes it to have been a glossolalic utterance, a legitimation of the discovery of the "egg of Asclepius".[32] Engelsen likewise argues that

Alexander is presented as an ecstatic, and he prophesies and utters meaningless words. Although Lucian does not have a term for inarticulate or unintelligible speech, Betz is well within the evidence when he refers to it as glossolalia.[33]

The evidence itself, however, quoted at note 2 above, requires closer analysis. What features of it have led scholars to suggest that glossolalia is what is being (inaccurately) reported here? The first is the use of the term ἄσημος in association with the verb φθέγγομαι, "to utter", which is sometimes used of oracles, to indicate the unintelligibility of what Alexander said. The second is the comment of Lucian that these "unclear" words resembled Hebrew or Phoenician. The third is the general comment that the people to whom he spoke "did not know what he was saying save that he everywhere brought in Apollo and Asclepius". Finally, there is the general context, which clearly indicates that Alexander is mimicking inspired frenzy. But I submit that the combination of the adjective ἄσημος and the lack of understanding of the populace does not demonstrate that the phenomenon was glossolalic. These portions of the evidence can be explained quite adequately on the assumption that Alexander was mimicking the kind of inspiration and frenzied cries of invocation and acclamation that were commonplace in the Dionysiac cult, and in magical rituals. The comment that "he everywhere brought in Apollo and Asclepius" also suggests that his speech was of this type. The adjective ἄσημος is itself the most general of terms, with a range of meanings from "vague" to "inarticulate", as its use for

---

[32] H.D. Betz, *Lukian von Samosata und das Neue Testament*, Berlin, 1961, p. 140.

[33] N.I.J. Engelsen, *Glossolalia*, p. 40.

"without distinguishing marks" of the human body in the papyri demonstrates. In this present context it simply means "unclear" or "indistinct".[34] The verb ἀποφθέγγομαι, as Behm and Haenchen correctly note,[35] means primarily "speak out loudly and clearly"; "to make a pronouncement", with some sense of the importance and sententiousness of what is being said. Though it is commonly used of oracles, it is their formal nature as pronouncements that is in view, rather than their inspired character. It is at least as commonly used for witty or pithy sayings, "apophthegms". Certainly the term does not indicate unintelligibility; that is a mistaken inference from the mistaken view that oracles were normally unintelligible.

---

[34] The term is never used in the N.T. Aeschylus Prom. 662 uses it of χρησμοὺς ἀσήμους δυσκρίτως τ' εἰρημένους, riddling oracular speech; Herodotus 1.86.4 uses it of "dark sayings" such as that of Croesus about Solon; Philo, de Migratione 79, uses it of ideas not yet put into words. Plutarch, Mor. 564b, mentions the "inarticulate sounds (φωνὰς . . . ἀσήμους), mingled with outcries" uttered by the souls of the dead, and even uses the term for the obscurity of Pythagorean symbolism (Fragment 202). The term can thus take a wide range of meanings, from "indistinct" through to "riddling", or "inarticulate". It can even be used of a flock of sheep that are "unmarked", as it is in Philo, de Fuga 9.

[35] For ἀποφθέγγομαι see Behm, in Kittel, *T.D.N.T.*, vol. 1, 1932, E.T. 1964, p. 447, I.H. Marshall, "The Significance of Pentecost", *S.J.Th.*, vol. 30, 1977, p. 357, and Haenchen, *op.cit.*, p. 168, note 3. The four New Testament passages fit this mixed context well; see Acts 2.4, 2.14, 4.18, 26.25. The suggestion of Boring, *Sayings*, p. 32, that the use of this term is further evidence of a prophetic consciousness among early Christian writers seems to me to be inconclusive. W.G. Rollins makes a similar suggestion in H.D. Betz, ed., *Plutarch's Theological Writings and Early Christian Literature*, Leiden, 1975, p. 109 and 123, though Mor. 405d, 421b and 434e speak against the point he makes. It would be hard to argue that the term is one for inspiration in the case of Acts 26.25, and also, for example, in Diodorus Siculus 16.27.1, which, though in the context of a discussion of the origins of the Delphic Oracle, simply means "to utter". Cf. Dionysius of Halicarnassus A.R. 16.26.2, Philo, de Vita Mosis 2.33, Plutarch, Mor. 506b, 589c, Life of Lycurgus 19.1, Life of Brutus 2, Lucian, Zeuxis 1, Diogenes Laertius 1.63, 73, 79, and Philostratus, Life of Apollonius 1.19, in most of which it is the pithy or sententious nature of what is said that is in view. The view of Engelsen, *Glossolalia*, p. 83-84, that it means "short eruptive outbursts given in an excited state of mind " or that "it alludes to short eruptive sentences delivered in a staccato, even loud form" seems to me to be purest conjecture. The closely related verb φθέγγομαι can likewise be used both with and without oracular connotations, but never carries the concept of unintelligibility: rather the reverse! See its use in Plato, Philebus 28b (in the same sentence as the word προφήτης, but not even remotely oracular!), and in Philo, de Migratione 81, Quis Rerum 25, de Mutatione 242, de Abrahamo 61, de Iosepho 248, de Vita Mosis 2.200, 206, de Decalogo 93, de Spec. Leg. 1.53, 2.198, 3.174.

The critical question is that of the identification of the words said to be ἄσημος as Hebrew or Phoenician.[36] I submit that, once again, this can be explained adequately by comparison with the kinds of utterances familiar from the Dionysiac cult, and later from the magical papyri and Gnostic writers, where "nomina barbara" (outlandish, foreign-sounding and obscure words) were commonplace. In Lucian's time we are far closer to the bulk of our extant evidence of such phenomena than with the New Testament writers, and the parallel is far more likely. I suggest that what Alexander used to bemuse the populace of Abonouteichos with was an amalgam of many elements, from Pythagorean, Dionysiac and magical rituals and legends. In the light of the continuing absence of clear Hellenistic parallels, I see no compelling reason to identify the phenomena with an hypothetical pre-Christian form of glossolalia.

The point is, I think, strengthened by an examination of Lucian's Menippus, sections 7-9. This passage, though closely related to the Alexander passage, has curiously escaped detailed treatment in the modern literature. The Cynic philosopher Menippus determines to visit the underworld. He is assisted in this by a Chaldaean μάγος, who casts the spells both to begin and to continue the journey. According to Lucian,

He would make a long address which I could not follow very well, for like an incompetent announcer at the games, he spoke rapidly and indistinctly (ἐπίτροχον τι καὶ ἀσαφὲς ἐφθέγγετο). It is likely, however, that he was invoking certain spirits (δαίμονας) . . . Meanwhile the magician held a burning torch and no longer muttered in a low tone but shouted as loudly as he could, invoking the spirits, one and all, at the top of his lungs; also the Tormentors, the Furies, "Hecate, Queen of the Night, and eery Persephoneia". With these names he intermingled a number of foreign-sounding, meaningless words of many syllables (βαρβαρικά τινα καὶ ἄσημα ὀνόματα καὶ πολυσύλλαβα).

Here again we find the terms ἀσαφής and ἄσημος, the verb φθέγγομαι, the description of words as foreign-sounding, and meaningless polysyllables, linked together in an occult context. But here again that context is explicitly one of invocation, *not* inspiration, and there is no suggestion that the words used are either a real human or divine language, or that they can be interpreted, in any sense. They are magic charms, pure and simple. It is quite possible, on this evidence, that Christian glossolalia might be mistaken for

---

[36] This passage is, to my knowledge, the *only* example from the period under discussion of inspired speech (or, in this case, fraudulent mimicry of it) being described as *resembling* an actual language, but one unknown to the hearers. Both Betz and Engelsen suggest that this is Lucian's editorial comment, rather than a report of what may have been thought at the time.

such incantations by outsiders, but it seems most unlikely that any Christian would think in such terms. The anti-magical bias of the great bulk of the movement would make it more likely that Christians would do their best to resist the identification. Not only so, however: the whole conception of what glossolalia was would militate against the identification.

6. Origen, Contra Celsum

The evidence of Celsus, cited by Origen, is of similar importance. Here the case has been put in the greatest detail by T.W. Gillespie, who argues as follows. The three-part form of the prophecies reported by Celsus is (1) an "I am" statement, in this case "I am God/a son of God/a divine Spirit"; (2) an "I have come" statement, which introduces the main message or content of the prophecy and (3) a "prophetic confirmation" in the form of glossolalia.[37] The same pattern may be detected, he argues, in the situation on which Paul comments in 1 Corinthians 12-14.

Beside the exegetical difficulties that such a view creates, there are two problems here. The first is the very real possibility that the prophets Celsus is describing are Christian prophets.[38] If this is the case, then the evidence is worthless as a Hellenistic parallel for Christian prophecy.

The other problem is the more critical. How clear is it that Celsus' description of the "prophetic confirmation" must mean glossolalia? His highly negative terminology includes the terms ἄγνωστα, πάροιστρα and πάντη ἄδηλα, as well as ἀσαφῆ γὰρ καὶ τὸ μηδέν. Unlike Lucian, there is no direct suggestion that the utterances resembled foreign languages. Nor need the terms used imply this. Though ἄγνωστος can be used of foreign languages[39], it usually means simply "vague" or "obscure". Πάροιστρος certainly can mean "frenzied", though its meaning may not always be this strong, but we have seen already that frenzy need not mean unintelligibility.

---

[37] T.W. Gillespie, "A Pattern", p. 75.

[38] That the prophets described by Celsus are Christian is suggested by Chadwick, op.cit., p. 403, citing W.L. Knox, Hellenistic Elements in Primitive Christianity, 1944, p. 83 n. 2, Oepke, op.cit., p. 458, Bornkamm, op.cit., p. 38 and Engelsen, Glossolalia, p. 42, citing Reitzenstein. Gillespie seems not to even consider the issue, though he admits that several factors make it possible that the account is a satire of Christian prophetic practice: see Gillespie, "A Pattern", p. 79, note 26. Dautzenberg, "Glossolalie", col. 232, doubts that the issue can be settled at all.

[39] The term ἄγνωστος is occasionally used of foreign languages, as in Aeschylus, Agamemnon, 1051. However the broader usage is more normal - see, for example, Sophocles, Antigone, 1001, where in a context of divination the adjective is used of the indistinct sounds of birds.

Ἄδηλος is a very general term, meaning simply "unclear" or "indistinct", as the parallels in Luke 11.44 and 1 Corinthians 14.8 make clear.[40] Likewise ἀσαφής can mean "indistinct", "dim", "faint" or "obscure".[41]

In his polemical way, Celsus is heaping scorn on the utterances of these prophets as being meaningless. It is far from certain that he is saying they were linguistically unintelligible. Engelsen's comment is that, as in early Christianity, "the prophet or another person gave an interpretation of the unintelligible part of the speech . . . Celsus looks upon it only as an opportunity for the prophet or one of his followers to put in whatever meaning he thinks appropriate . . . "[42] But Celsus' language is most naturally taken as describing something quite unlike the interpretation of glossolalia. He appears to be describing the kind of interpretation that takes an ambiguous, obscure (though intelligible) oracular utterance, and explains the point of its riddles and allusions.[43] In other words, he could well be

---

[40] See also Philo, de Sacrificiis 91 (not of words), and de Spec. Leg. 1.200 which has the general sense of "obscure", and Quis Rerum 303, of the deliberate obscurity of sophists who do not wish to be pinned down. Dio Chrysostom uses the term to mean "obscure" in the general sense of ideas or instances, not words, in Discourses 61.8 and 70.7; in 64.8 it has to do with people's notability: obscure origins mean one is not one of the great.

[41] Like ἄδηλος, ἀσαφής can be used of indistinct notes played on musical instruments: see Aristotle, de Aud. 801 b 21, or, poetically, it can be used of the indistinct "voice" of a ruined monument, only part of which can be read: Epigrammata Graeca, ed. G. Kaibel, repr. 1965, no. 1003 line 6. "Formless and meaningless" (Gillespie) is probably a little too precise. It can signify linguistic unintelligibility, as it does in Dionysius of Halicarnassus, A.R. 5.47 and Josephus, A.J. 12.36, and it is used of oracles in Plutarch, Mor. 407c, 409c, 409f. It is never used in the N.T., but later becomes a standard term for obscurity of Scripture. Generally, however, it simply means "unclear" or "indistinct", as it does in Philo, de Iosepho 10, of Pharaoh's dreams, Plutarch, Mor. 853c, and 652d, where one of the signs of drunkenness is said to be slurring of speech, ἀσάφεια γλώττης. Dreams can be ἀσαφής, (Dio Chrysostom 11.129), people with heavy accents no longer speak σαφῶς (Dio Chrysostom 36.9), and the kind of deliberate mumbling that attempts to cover a lie is also described as ἀσαφῶς (Dio Chrysostom 11.27). Philo also uses the term in this sense of sophists, in Quis Rerum 302. Musonius Rufus, on the other hand, uses both terms of difficult philosophical problems in Book 1. line 19, (see the text and translation of C.E. Lutz, *Yale Classical Studies*, vol. 10, 1947, p. 33) and suggests that to the gods all things are clear. Only humans, therefore, have need of philosophical reasoning to clarify difficult points.

[42] N.I.J. Engelsen, *Glossolalia*, p. 43.

[43] This point is also noted by M. Turner, *art.cit.*, pp. 19-20. The Greek of this period does have terms which can be used of linguistic unintelligibility: τὸ συνετὸν means "intelligibility" in Plutarch, Mor. 406f; in Euripides' Ion 1205 ἀσύνετος is used of the scream of a poisoned bird. In Phoenician Women 1731 the Sphinx's riddle is an αἴνιγμ'ἀσύνετον, which shows that the word could also be used of oracular ambiguity

describing the kind of literary, as opposed to linguistic interpretation that was applied at a popular level to the ambiguities of the Delphic Oracle. He could equally well be describing the exposition of Christian or semi-Christian apocalypticism, with its obscure and esoteric imagery. His suggestion that the nonsensicality of the utterances "gave a chance for any fool or sorcerer to take the words in whatever sense he likes" seems to me to point strongly in this direction. The contrast between the suggestions that "no intelligent person" can make sense of them, but that "any fool or sorcerer" can find ways to make use of them, strongly indicates that the terms "incomprehensible, incoherent and utterly obscure . . . meaningless

---

in Classical Greek. However, later references suggest that this was not its primary meaning in our period. See the Scholia on Aristophanes, Frogs line 1286, where the scholiast, speaking about Aristophanes' use of nonsense syllables, uses ἀσυνετοποιόν for "making unintelligible". Diodorus Siculus 13.58.2. uses the term of the unintelligible speech of foreign troops. But neither Lucian nor Celsus use the term at all in the passages under discussion. Most important is the term ἄναρθρος, which means inarticulate; Diodorus Siculus 3.17.1 uses it of the inarticulate songs of the Ichthyophagi; Plutarch, Life of Marius 19, uses it of the inarticulate battle cries of the Ambrones (ἄναρθρον ἀλαλαγμὸν); in Life of Caesar 63.8 he describes Calpurnia's "indistinct words and inarticulate groans" in her sleep (ἀσαφεῖς δὲ φωνὰς καὶ στεναγμοὺς ἀνάρθρους); Plutarch Mor. 613e asks whether people's contributions to dinner conversation will be articulate or not (παντελῶς ἄναρθρος). Voices can be ἄναρθρος, Mor. 994e, as can the noise of drums; see Philo, de Fuga 22. Cf. also the term ἀδιάρθρωτος, Plutarch Mor. 378c, referring to imperfect and inarticulate reasonings about the gods. On the other side, ἔναρθρος is used (Plutarch, Mor. 589c) of articulate speech: i.e. speech that is both linguistic in nature and sufficiently clear to be understood. Cf. Plutarch Mor. 738b, 973a and 1131d also. The fire seen by the gathered Israelites at Mount Sinai sent forth "an articulate voice" (φωνὴν . . . ἔναρθρον), by which the Law of Moses was proclaimed. (Philo, de Decalogo 33, cf. de Praemiis 2.) "The flame became articulate speech" (διάλεκτον ἀρθρουμένης) de Decalogo 46. The noise of the crowd of Israelites at the base of the mountain is spoken off as φωνῆς ἀνάρθρου καὶ ἀσήμου (de Vita Mosis 2.164). In all of this it is highly significant that the terminology is never, so far as I am aware, used in reference to oracles to indicate the kind of unintelligibility that is supposed to accompany inspiration. Philo also discusses the process by which speech is articulated within the mouth in de Somniis 29. Greek also has available to it a verb which is occasionally used for "to make unintelligible sounds", τερετίζω. Though its primary meaning is simply "to make a noise", and it is usually used of inanimate things or birds, when used of people it means "to babble" or such. Liddell and Scott, however, know of only three usages in this sense: Aristotle, Ath. Pol. 83 a 33, Procopius Gaz., Ep. 33, Philodemus, Po. p. 228 H. See also Plutarch. Mor. 1010a and 1034e, which are not in Liddell and Scott. Greek also has a word for stammering, and for faltering, inarticulate speech (ψελλός, ψέλλισμα, for which see, for example, Plutarch, Mor. 650d: the LXX sometimes uses it for the language of foreigners, as in Isaiah 29.4 and 32.4) but as far as I am aware none of these terms is ever used of oracular or other inspired speech, for the very good reason that such speech did not come in a stammering, inarticulate form.

and nonsensical" (if we adopt Chadwick's strong translation) are to be understood as polemic against the *content* of the utterances. Celsus is saying that they are the sort of oracular speech that is so vague that it means nothing, and can be made to mean anything.

In brief, then, there are major objections against the view that Celsus' report of prophetic utterance at the end of the second century in Palestine provides us with a parallel for early Christian glossolalia. But even if my objections are judged to be insufficient, it must still be noted that we have no demonstrably pre-Christian evidence of such parallel phenomena. In the light of the kinds of cultural changes occurring in this period, discussed in Chapter 1, unless such evidence can be cited, the inconclusive evidence of Lucian and Celsus from the middle and late second century is simply not sufficient for us to infer the existence of a widespread tradition of glossolalia in Hellenistic religion in the pre-Christian period.

7. Summary

Our search of the Hellenistic world for parallels for the early Christian phenomenon of glossolalia has led to several major conclusions. The major positive conclusion is this: we have seen in these last three chapters that the Hellenistic period knew of several related, though differing traditions of inspired or charismatic speech. The first of these which we treated was that identified with the oracle of Apollo at Delphi, which was neither "ecstatic" nor unintelligible, and which was commonly characterised by oracular obscurity. The form which the oracles took was stereotyped, and the authority which they held in the minds of their recipients was often linked to, for example, their archaic or poetic form. That was what was expected of oracles, and, in some circles at least, failure to produce such forms was perceived as a problem. "Ecstasy" or "frenzy", however, the physical manifestation of the "inspired" state, was not a major feature of Delphic inspiration manticism.[44]

The second form was that identified with the enthusiastic worship of Dionysus and Cybele, which included ritual and invocatory outcry with its enthusiasm, but was not seen as being primarily oracular. Montanist

---

[44] "Since bizarre behaviour on the part of those regarded as possessed frequently occurred outside the strictures of normal social or religious institutions, such behaviour functioned as a legitimation of the supernatural nature of the experience in the absence of built-in institutional guarantees. Ecstatic behaviour, as we shall see, was a much more pronounced characteristic among those ancients who claimed divine inspiration but who had no permanent connection to a traditional oracle sanctuary." Thus D.E. Aune, *Prophecy*, p. 34. Though this statement does make sense of the bulk of our evidence, it is hard to see how Lucan's view of Delphi and Virgil's description of the Sibyl could be explained.

prophecy witnessed to a later intermediate type, "ecstatic" but intelligible, which seems like a blending of Hellenistic and distinctively Christian ideas and practice. Lucian's description of Alexander's behaviour seems to draw mainly on the "Dionysiac" tradition, with Pythagorean and magical elements thrown in, though his later oracular practice was modelled on a popularised version of Delphic practice. Celsus' description of late second-century prophetism seems to draw more from the tradition of oracular obscurity than from the tradition of "ecstasy". Gnosticism's tradition of unintelligible speech shares with the magic tradition the nature of invocation, and seems to be closer to the Dionysiac tradition than any other single source; it has, however, its own more philosophically sophisticated rationale. In this latter group of phenomena we see "inspired" speech acting as a major factor in the legitimation of forms of cult or forms of behaviour: the frenzy of the initiate of the Mysteries is a sacred thing to be held in awe, "ecstasy" legitimated Montanist prophecy, and "behaving like one inspired" or using magical ritual was a way to grasp and hold popular attention when setting out to found a new cult.

The second major conclusion is that the Christian glossolalic tradition, though it shares elements with these, is substantially different. It is seen as revelation and praise, not as invocation. It is seen as spontaneous and communicative, not ritual and inarticulate, and as such is interpreted. Though spontaneous as opposed to formulaic, it is not characterised by "frenzy" or "ecstasy", though, as Boring aptly comments, some practitioners did need to be reminded of that. Further, its "inspired" nature was not regarded (by Paul at least) as sufficiently authoritative to make it a legitimising force for other forms of belief or practice. Inspired speech (both glossolalic and prophetic, as we shall see) was subordinated to the community and the Gospel, not vice versa.

The major errors of much scholarship on this topic have been two: a willingness to generalise across the centuries, which has led to the use of second and third-century evidence to explain the background to first-century phenomena; and secondly, the blurring of the distinctions between the distinct, though related, traditions outlined above. Compounded with the "overtranslation" of general terms such as ἄδηλος and ἀσαφής, this second problem has led to the identifying of the various phenomena, and to the erroneous conclusion that glossolalia was a well recognised phenomenon in the Hellenistic world.

The related negative conclusion is that nowhere in the world of pre-Christian Hellenism has a substantial parallel for early Christian glossolalia been found. Those phenomena claimed to be parallels in the modern scholarly debate have suffered from either or both of two major defects: they have been drawn from periods and sources which do not predate Christianity, and the phenomena themselves can be shown to be substantially different from glossolalia as it was understood and/or practised within early Christianity. Of course, what we know about that phenomenon in early Christianity is limited, and, at times, of uncertain interpretation, but the two sets of phenomena are substantially different.

On this basis we can argue that any attempt to show that either the terminology or the phenomena of glossolalia are to be understood on the basis of Hellenistic parallels is fundamentally unlikely to succeed. It is most unlikely that the problem with which Paul finds himself dealing in 1 Corinthians 12-14 is based on the supposed pre-Christian religious experience of his converts. This conclusion applies both to the form of the hypothesis which suggests that actual pagan practices were being imported into the life of the Corinthian congregation, and to the more subtle reconstruction which suggests that glossolalia was being valued by the Corinthians by analogy with supposedly similar phenomena of which they would have been well aware. It is to early Christianity itself, and indeed to its earliest period, that glossolalia must be traced. The most we can say of the parallels is that there was a chance that non-Christians, hearing glossolalia for the first time, might presume that it was a form of magical invocation. The reasons for the disagreements between Paul and his Corinthian converts over the phenomenon, however, will have to be sought in other factors than those outlined above. It is to this problem that we now turn.

8. The Problem in Corinth, Revisited

In Chapter 2 I surveyed the various interpretations that attempt to link the problem of inspired speech with the other issues in 1 Corinthians. I argued that neither of the two prevalent theories as to the root cause of Paul's disagreement with his Corinthian converts really explained why glossolalia and prophecy had become issues in that disagreement. The last three chapters have dealt with the third theory, the possible influence of Hellenistic enthusiasm. At a methodological level, however, the first two hypotheses suffer from a second major problem. This is the fact that Paul tells us *nothing* directly about what the Corinthians *thought* about inspired speech. He does, however, tell us what they were *doing* that he objected to, and (sometimes by implication, sometimes directly) something about why he objected. In my view this point needs to be taken up in detail in order to explain the origins of "the problem in Corinth."

What Paul Objected To.

The Corinthians were doing at least three things to which Paul objected. (1) They were allowing glossolalia to be widely practised in the assembly without interpretation, which Paul believes to be unhelpful to those assembled. (2) They were allowing this practice to continue even when there were unbelievers or outsiders present. (3) They were practising prophecy in a way that discouraged the congregational testing of prophetic statements, and individuals wishing to exercise prophetic gifts were competing in some way with one another for opportunities to do so. In the case of (1) Paul lays down a maximum of three glossolalic episodes, and even those only if there is a reasonable expectation (so I would suggest we should interpret 14.27b-28) of an interpretation.[45] In the case of (2) he deprecates glossolalia in favour of prophecy. In the case of (3) he limits the number of prophetic episodes, as with glossolalia, to two or three, and insists on congregational discernment.[46]

At the behavioural level, then, that was the problem as Paul saw it. But what is it, precisely, that he objects to in this behaviour? First, he believed that within the community this sort of behaviour and the attitude behind it exalted one work of the Spirit (glossolalia) above others, and did so at the expense of the community whose benefit, in his view, is the aim of the gifts anyway. This is surely the point of 1 Corinthians 12.12-31. Second, this behaviour exalted those who practised glossolalia, and (in their view, Paul implies) proclaimed their standing within the community as pneumatics. In

---

[45] On this also see Hart, *Tongues and Prophecy*, p. 260, who suggests that the gift of interpretation may have been "more or less a permanent gift", and thus a glossolalist would know whether an interpretation was likely simply by checking whether an interpreter was present. Such a suggestion must remain speculative. The alternative, that Paul is offering only a rough rule of thumb, to the effect that, if after two or three glossolalic episodes no interpretation is forthcoming, the glossolalists should be silent, seems to me to be more likely.

[46] There is a slight distinction between his limit in the two cases. There are to be two or three glossolalists *at most*, and two or three prophets, absolutely. This is to be the case so that "you can all prophesy, one at a time". On this passage see below, in Chapter 10. On the question of who may take part in the discernment of prophetic utterances (the whole congregation, the whole male congregation, or only those who are themselves prophets) see also Chapter 10. The issue of how one might relate the opening problem in 1 Corinthians 12, the cry "Jesus is anathema", to the other issues discussed is simply too complex to be handled here. With no scholarly consensus as to the likely status of the cry itself (actual statement made by a believer, hypothetical Pauline alternative to "Jesus is Lord", etc.) let alone its likely background, the issue will simply be bracketed off here. One might well add a fifth problem: that of the behaviour of some of the women in the congregation. But that issue will also be dealt with separately, below.

doing so they caused (or exacerbated) gradations of status within the community. To this Paul replies that tongues are not a special sign of anything for believers, and certainly not of pneumatic status, if that is conceived of as an elite status within the community. Tongues is at best a sign for unbelievers, and a negative one at that. But the development of this point will have to wait for the fuller consideration of 1 Corinthians 14.20-25 below. Third, if this sort of behaviour is practised in the presence of unbelievers, its effect is to alienate and exclude them. Fourth, this approach to the practice of prophecy leads to disorder, the exclusion of some in favour of others, and a consequent loss of possible benefit to the community. All of these practices appear to have been defended (or else Paul assumed they *would* be, on receipt of his letter) with the claim to prophetic or pneumatic status by those involved. I would suggest that this claim was theologically a separate matter: inspired speech happened to be one of the concomitants of the claim to pneumatic status, but it was not its defining theological characteristic. To all this Paul lays down that the Spirit regulates as well as freeing, and acts communally, not individualistically.

Since neither of the major theological explanations of the disagreement discussed in Chapter 2 seems capable of providing an adequate background for the dispute over inspired speech, and Paul's critique of the Corinthians focuses so exclusively on their practice, I would propose an alternative framework from which to understand the dispute.

It has long been argued for a variety of reasons that in Corinth Paul, representing an egalitarian and/or communal view of Christianity, is in conflict with an elitist view. The recent researches of R.A. Horsley and J.A. Davis show (convincingly, in my view) the kind of theological framework within which the Corinthian elitists legitimised their claim to elite status. But these scholars have been unable to show how the issues of inspired speech in Corinth were related to this theological framework. All our evidence suggests that glossolalia was a characteristically Christian form of behaviour. Why then had its use become contentious? In my view the most probable (though still hypothetical) answer is as follows.

The Corinthians learned of glossolalia, and learned to practise it, from Paul himself. There is no reason to doubt his claims to glossolalic proficiency, nor, since he founded the church, to look further for the original source of the practise in Corinth. Perhaps the influence of what Sweet calls "Palestinian piety"[47] strengthened the esteem in which the practice was held

---

[47] J.P.M. Sweet, "A Sign for Unbelievers: Paul's Attitude to Glossolalia", *N.T.S.*, vol.

in Corinth, but this is not certain. But from the beginning the Corinthians learned of glossolalia as a habit of the great leaders of the Christian movement. If they had available to them the traditions about the Day of Pentecost later committed to writing by Luke, these could only have confirmed their high estimate of the gift. Paul may have taught restraint and what he teaches about interpretation of glossolalia in 1 Corinthians in his 18 months or so in Corinth, or he may have had no need to do so: we do not know. But in his absence the elitist tendencies of some members of the congregation came to the fore. Glossolalia, and perhaps to a lesser extent prophecy (both practices related to direct communion with God, authoritative revelation and the great figures of the early days of both Christianity itself and their own congregational life), easily suggested themselves as the marks of a spiritual elite. They became, in the minds of the elitists, decisive evidence of the work of τὸ πνεῦμα τὸ ἅγιον in the truly mature Christian. The term πνευματικός, then, as a Corinthian slogan, originates with experiences of πνεῦμα interpreted in terms of an elitist theology.[48] Paul may previously have laid down his own understanding of the term: if not, he certainly does so in 1 Corinthians. The self-proclaimed πνευματικοί/τέλειοι made glossolalia a mark of elite status. It is against this view that Paul's polemic in 1 Corinthians 12-14 is directed. Whereas some of the Corinthians had made their gifts the mark of their "mature" or "perfect" status, he argues that when perfection *really* comes (and that will not be until Christ returns) all such charismatic endowments will cease.[49]

Returning to the main issue at hand, we may now ask what it was about the Corinthian use of glossolalia that Paul specifically objected to. In my view the problem may be formulated as follows. For Paul glossolalia was simply one manifestation of the work of the Spirit among other manifestations. It was not the highest of these; nor, necessarily, was it the lowest.[50] It was simply one among many. As such its function ought to have

---

13, 1966-67, pp. 240-257, esp. p. 246.

[48] Thus M.E. Isaacs suggests that "in Hellenistic Judaism πνεῦμα and σοφία were closely associated, and could be used synonymously." and that the πνευματικοι "were claiming superior knowledge and a greater share of the divine πνεῦμα". (*The Concept of Spirit*, London, 1976, pp. 77, 138.)

[49] Compare N.I.J. Engelsen, *Glossolalia*, p. 138.

[50] Though most scholars emphasise that Paul lists glossolalia last or next to last in all his lists of charismata, this "order" may well be polemically motivated, rather than being a true reflection of Paul's normal view.

been the building up of the assembly as a whole: such upbuilding ought to include both numerical increase, by way of the attraction, retention and conversion of interested non-believers, and also the edification of those who already believed. Some of the Corinthians, however, had made glossolalia a criterion by which (a) believers might be identified from among non-believers, the boundaries of the community being thus clearly defined, and (b) the truly mature, the πνευματικοί or τέλειοι, might be identified from among their lesser brethren. Thus the boundary within the community between elite and non-elite members was defined. In other words, they had used it as a form of behaviour that differentiated between "insiders" and "outsiders", both with regard to the community in relation to the wider world, and with regard to relationships within the community itself.[51] Such a view explains Paul's double objection to glossolalia used without interpretation: it excludes and alienates "unbelievers and those who do not understand", and does not "build up" believers.

I suggest further that in Paul's view the "unbelievers" in question would describe glossolalia as "raving", not because it was familiar to them as a sign of divine inspiration, but precisely because it was not. As a thoroughly strange and inexplicable phenomenon, it would probably be interpreted by them as evidence of some form of divine activity. As such it might be frightening, off-putting, or merely strange, but it would most certainly act to exclude them from the fellowship of the Christian assembly.[52]

---

[51] See the similar suggestion of J.H. Neyrey, "Body Language in 1 Corinthians: the Use of Anthropological Models for Understanding Paul and his Opponents", *Semeia* vol. 35, 1986, pp. 129-170, esp. p. 151: "When someone speaks in unintelligible tongues, the result is an artificial but deleterious re-drawing of boundaries within the group: 'I shall be a foreigner to the speaker and the speaker a foreigner to me' (14:11) . . . if outsiders and unbelievers observe this unregulated practice . . . they will be confirmed as outsiders . . . speaking in tongues can function to re-draw boundaries within and around the group . . ."

[52] This view is thoroughly in accord with the usage of the terms μανία and μαίνομαι in our period. Though the terms can be used of the kind of "raving" brought on by divine inspiration, they are also, and predominantly, used of simple irrationality and insanity. In the great majority of cases (in whichever category) such behaviour is frightening and repellent rather than attractive. The terms are used of divine inspiration in Plato's *Phaedrus*, 245, of course, and also by Plutarch, Mor. 821b, describing Cassandra's prophetic frenzy. In this case, however, as in Dio Chrysostom 4.112 and 27.2, the sense is pejorative despite the religious context. Cassandra prophesies, and people say that she is merely raving. Μανία brought on by the gods can be a curse rather than a blessing as in Plato: see Diodorus Siculus 3.65, 16.42.2, Plutarch, Mor. 249b, e, and 432d, citing Euripides' *Bacchae* 298; for the "breath of madness" spread by ivy among those susceptible to ἐνθουσιασμός see Mor. 291a and 671c, where the sense is more neutral.

This, then, I suggest, was the origin of the dispute between Paul and his Corinthian converts. It was not so much a matter of theology, but of small group practice and dynamics, upon which the beginnings of a theological position had been constructed. With this in mind we turn, finally, to the exegetical puzzle of 1 Corinthians 14.20-25.

9. 1 Corinthians 14. 20-25 and the "Sign for Unbelievers"

We must now turn to this, the most difficult passage figuring in the debate over the function of glossolalia. Opinions on the meaning of this passage abound, and virtually every possible position has been taken up.[53] The points at issue are as follows.

First, how seriously does Paul take the context of his quote from Isaiah 28.11? If he is quoting with full regard to context, then the "sign" he is discussing almost certainly must be a sign of judgement against God's erring

---

The same is true in Mor. 397a, where the Sibyl is described (cf. Mor. 758d). Divine frenzy is only regularly seen as a good thing in Philo, for whom see de Migratione 84, Quod Deus 138, Quis Rerum 249, 264, 266, de Fuga 168, de Mutatione 39, and de Somniis 1.254 and 2.2. Even Philo, however, uses it with negative connotations: see de Somniis 36, 56, 2.98, de Vita Contemplativa 14.

On the other hand the terms are regularly used of irrationality of other kinds, virtually always with negative connotations. It can be used of simple irrationality, as in Plutarch, Mor. 321f, 1047e, Dionysius of Halicarnassus, A.R. 3.7.4., 3.8.3. 11.43.3, 19.16.5; of wilful irrationality, Philo, de Spec. Leg. 58, and extreme stupidity, Philo, Legatione 183, 192. It can be used of irrationality due to strong emotion generally (Dionysius of Halicarnassus, A.R. 6.49.5, 7.15.2, 7.25.2, 7.42.4, 7.44.4, 7.50.2, 8.31.2, 9.58.4), and anger (A.R. 8.50.1, Plutarch, Mor. 361d, 551a), battle rage (A.R. 5.24.2, 5.46.4, 7.48.3, Plutarch, Mor. 609f, 759a), lust or erotic love more specifically (A.R. 11.33.1, Plutarch, Mor. 451e, 746f, 756b, 769b, and Fragments 135, 136), jealousy (Plutarch, Mor. 267d), or grief (Plutarch, Mor. 609f). It can also be used of drunkenness (Diodorus Siculus 4.4.4, 4.4.6, 4.11.1, 4.55.4, 4.65.7, 4.66.6, 4.68.4, 5.26.3, 5.50.5, 5.55.6, Plutarch, Mor. 503d, 657a, 791b, Philo, de Plantatione 147-8), melancholia (Plutarch, Mor. 856c) or of pathological insanity (Plutarch, Mor. 18b, 299e, 462b, 469d, 474e, 501b, 519e, 623, 641, 693a, 704e, 706e, 963d, e, 1123d; Dio Chrysostom 10.27, 17.9, 32.44, 56, 61, 34.4, 38.17, Diodorus Siculus 9.4.2, 10.6.3, 10.14.1, 14.71.3, 24.3.3, 30.9.2, Dionysius of Halicarnassus, A.R. 11.16.4, 11.37.6, 16.44.3). In Dio Chrysostom it has uniformly negative connotations (see 4.83-4, 9.8, 9.9, 11.16(x2), 12.8, 17.20, 32.5, 32.24, 32.28, 32.41, 32.44, 32.61, 32.75, 32.87, 32.89, 32.94, 34.2, 35.7, 57.8, 64.2, 65.12, 66.6, 66.25, 75.10, 77/8.8-9, 41-2). The same would appear to be generally true of Josephus: see Jewish War 1.352, 2.395, 3.375, 7.332.

[53] J.P.M. Sweet, *art.cit.*, B.C. Johanson, "Tongues", W. Grudem, "1 Corinthians 14.20-25: Prophecy and Tongues as Signs of God's Attitude", *Westminster Theological Journal*, vol. 41, No. 2, Spring 1979, pp. 381-396, and D.A. Carson, *Showing the Spirit*, have summaries of many views on the difficult 1 Cor. 14.20-25. Almost the only view they do not canvass is the possibility that the term μαίνεσθε may have positive connotations.

people, for that is what the Isaiah 28.11 passage discusses.[54] This would raise the problem that his application of the quotation has to do with the reaction to the "sign" of complete unbelievers - not erring believers at all.[55] If he is quoting with little or no detailed reference to the context of Isaiah then the options available are far more open.[56] He may, for example, simply be picking up the negative connotations of the passage, and nothing else.

Second, in what sense does Paul think tongues are a "sign" for unbelievers (v.22)? Are they a sign of divine grace, of divine activity, divine judgement, or are they merely confusing and off-putting? Are they a sign of conversion, an initiatory sign, as in Acts?[57] Or is the verse a rhetorical

---

[54] The most sophisticated versions of this approach are those of O.P. Robertson, *art.cit.*, and Grudem, *art.cit.* Grudem's is the better reconstruction, because he avoids the problem that the unbelievers in Corinth are not likely to be predominantly Jews. He also explains the difference between the Isaiah quotation and the Corinthian situation (for which see below) better than most. He says the Corinthians ought not to give the unbelievers this "sign" - the sort that will alienate them from the Gospel - because they do not deserve it (pp. 391-2). They have not rejected the Gospel the way the people referred to in Isaiah 28.11 had. (A similar suggestion is made by W.F. Orr and J.A.R. Walker, *1 Corinthians*, New York, 1976, p. 305ff.) As noted above, Grudem also takes the important step of suggesting that it is not tongues *per se* that are the problem. It is *uninterpreted tongues*. "Paul is not talking about the function of tongues in general but only about the negative result of one particular abuse of tongues, namely, the abuse of speaking in public without an interpreter . . ." (p. 393) when there are unbelievers present. "Uninterpreted tongues are a sign to unbelievers of God's displeasure and impending judgement (vv. 21-22a), and Paul, not wanting the Corinthians to give unbelievers this sign, discourages the childish (v. 20) use of uninterpreted tongues in the Corinthian church meeting (v. 23)." Grudem does not raise the issue of what the unbelievers might think, confining himself to Paul's critique of the Corinthians, which, it would seem, is a theological rather than a practical one. One weakness of his position is that it does require a great deal of Old Testament knowledge of the Corinthians if they are to understand Paul's point.

[55] Thus, correctly, P. Roberts, "A Sign - Christian or Pagan?", *Expository Times*, vol. 90, no. 7, 1979, p. 200.

[56] B.C. Johanson notes ("Tongues", p. 182), that Paul has linked the "but even then they will not listen to me" to the unintelligible tongues, whereas both the Massoretic Text and the LXX relate this hardened attitude to the statement "this is rest, give rest to the weary . . ." i.e. to an intelligible message. P. Roberts, like Grudem, points out (*art.cit.*, p. 200), that in Isaiah the unbelievers have repeatedly heard and rejected God's message, and there is nothing to suggest this in the Corinthian case. Unlike Grudem he argues that Paul is therefore unlikely to be taking the Isaiah context too seriously. An alternative view is that of Sweet, *art.cit.*, who thinks that the quotation from Isaiah is an anti-Jewish testimonium to the effect that strange tongues are a sign of judgement on Jerusalem's unbelief, picked up by the Corinthians and now re-used against them by Paul. I have suggested at least one criticism of this view in Chapter 3.

[57] As suggested by J. Ruef, *Paul's First Letter to Corinth*, London, 1977, p. 152.

quotation of the Corinthian position, to which Paul is replying, μὴ γένοιτο?[58] Or does the term "sign" have a special meaning here?[59]

Third, ought we to understand prophecy as a sign as well, using the evident parallelism within verse 22 to import the term a second time? In other words, is Paul arguing that, contrary to Corinthian views, *prophecy*, not tongues, is a sign for believers, or is he arguing that while tongues are a sign, prophecy has another function than that of a sign?[60]

Fourth, what is the problem with the reaction of the outsider? Is μαίνεσθε a rebuke, "You are raving", or a qualified recognition of divine or daemonic activity, "You are possessed"? Clearly if it is the second, there is a possibility that Paul brings it forward as a partially positive comment on the part of his hypothetical unbeliever, recognising the presence of the

---

Prophecy, on the other hand, is seen as a sign for believers as they go on in their Christian lives.

[58] This is Johanson's solution to the puzzle. I would suggest that it can only be checked by looking at other rhetorical questions asked by Paul to see whether Johanson's criteria for detecting rhetorical questions are reasonable. But of the approximately fifty rhetorical questions in 1 Corinthians, only this one hypothetical example uses the term ὥστε, Johanson's suggested clue, and of all the usages of this term by Paul, twenty by my count, only one other, Gal. 4.16, is part of a rhetorical question. Johanson's suggestion must therefore be judged highly speculative. It seems to me to be a good example of the exegesis of desperation that led J.B. Phillips (*The New Testament in Modern English*, London, 1972, p. 363, p. 552 note 5) to presume that the text of these verses must be corrupt. Gillespie, *Prophecy and Tongues*, p. 127, suggests that "tongues is a sign" must be a Corinthian slogan. Paul, he says, would never have formulated such a statement because he is generally negative about signs. I would suggest, however, that Paul is not negative about signs as such: what he is negative about is *seeking* signs - see 1 Corinthians 1.22. For the more positive attitude see Romans 15.19, 2 Corinthians 12.12.

[59] Thus, for example, T.M. Crone, *Prophecy*, p. 215, notes 20, 21, who argues that "sign" in the passage actually means "cause": tongues cause unbelief, prophecy causes belief. For this meaning, however, he has to appeal to usage of the term in Epicurean and Stoic philosophy, and interpret "unbelievers" and "believers" as "unbelief" and "belief". Though this is a very creative solution, it does run counter to Paul's detailed descriptions of "some who do not understand or some unbelievers". The term "unbelievers" in v. 22 does most naturally link up with the same term in v. 23. Further, the term "sign" is not otherwise used in this sense in Paul. "Sign" normally means a miracle of some sort, pointing beyond itself for its significance.

[60] For understanding prophecy as a sign, in parallel with glossolalia: W.A. Grudem, *art.cit.*, pp. 389-392, who presents a most thorough and persuasive case. Against: O.P. Robertson, *art.cit.*, p. 52. F.W. Grosheide, *Commentary on 1 Corinthians*, London, 1954, p. 333, suggests that prophecy is a sign for believers that they still enjoy the grace of God; he makes no attempt to link this with the statements in v.24. F.F. Bruce, *1 and 2 Corinthians*, London, 1971, p. 133, similarly argues that prophecy is a sign for believers in the sense that it produces believers. Compare also the view of Ruef, noted above.

supernatural. Hence the "sign" would not be totally negative, though it would still be less than ideal.[61]

The greatest single problem in the passage, however, is the manifest contradiction within two sets of Pauline statements. He calls (uninterpreted) tongues a sign for unbelievers, and then says they will react to it in a way he wishes to discourage, and calls prophecy a sign for believers (or, less likely, something else than a sign, but still for believers) and discusses most of all its effect on unbelievers. Various scholars have attempted to solve this dilemma by different means. Hans Conzelmann suggests that Paul is simply writing imprecisely: "the wording of v. 22 is overdone for the sake of rhetoric . . . naturally, speaking with tongues is a sign *also* for believers . . . and prophecy has an effect *also* on unbelievers . . ."[62] But this is to presume to correct Paul rather than to try to understand him. Charles Isbell suggests that the statement is a straw man; "Paul's own opinion on the matter was exactly the opposite."[63] Others argue that Paul means that tongues are a sign that *produces* or confirms unbelief, or a sign for *future* unbelievers; prophecy, likewise, is a sign that produces belief, or is for those about to become believers.[64] Though such suggestions have the virtue of rescuing

---

[61] Thus, for example, Roberts (*art.cit.*, p. 201) says that "Tongues are the proof of divine activity for which non-Christians look." T.W. Gillespie suggests, *Prophecy and Tongues*, pp. 124-6, that "If "tongues" produces the response "*You* are possessed [by God]", prophecy brings forth the confession, "*God* is surely present among you." . . . " M.E. Hart, *Tongues and Prophecy*, p. 240, thinks μαίνεσθε is a positive comment, while S.D. Currie, "Early Evidence", p. 275, says "The observer might not be able to decide whether the utterances are lunatic or mantic, frenzied or oracular." R. and C.C. Kroeger, "An Inquiry into Evidence of Maenadism in the Corinthian Congregation", *S.B.L. Seminar Papers*, 1978, p. 334 suggest that μαίνεσθε here is a reference to Dionysiac ecstasy. Surprisingly, Nils Engelsen, who believes that glossolalia was a widely recognised phenomenon in the period, does not take up this interpretation, though the internal logic of his argument might have led him to do so. (N.I.J. Engelsen, *Glossolalia*, pp. 166-168.) Instead he argues that glossolalia is a sign which confirms the unbeliever in his state of unbelief.

A related minor question is whether this response of the unbeliever is due to hearing glossolalia as such, or the tumult of numbers of glossolalists speaking together. It seems quite likely, in view of Paul's ordinance in 14.27 that glossolalists should speak in turn , that this kind of tumult might be encountered in Corinth, but the question of whether *this* is what produces the μαίνεσθε cannot be answered with any certainty.

[62] H. Conzelmann, *1 Corinthians*, trans. J.W. Leitch, Philadelphia, 1975, p. 242.

[63] C.D. Isbell, "Glossolalia and Propheteialalia: a study of 1 Corinthians 14", *Wesleyan Theological Journal*, vol. 10, 1975, p. 18. I do not see how such a position can be maintained without some clear evidence (such as a Pauline μὴ γένοιτο) to suggest it.

[64] A sign that confirms unbelief: N.I.J. Engelsen, *Glossolalia*, pp. 166-8; a sign for future unbelief: W.C. Klein, "The Church and its Prophets", *Anglican . Theological Review*, vol. 44, 1962, p. 8. According to Sweet, *art.cit.*, p. 242, note 6, T.F. Glasson

Paul from himself, they do so at the cost of reversing the plain meaning of the passage. Others argue that while tongues are a (negative) sign for unbelievers, confirming them in their unbelief, prophecy functions as a sign for believers precisely in the effect that it has on unbelievers.[65] In its simple form, this suggestion likewise seems a little casuistic. It can, however, be better supported.

It seems to me that there are two sides to Paul's statement. On the one hand, the effect of prophecy on unbelievers is, in Paul's view, a sign for believers in a quite specialised sense. The unbeliever's confession, "God is truly among you", is strongly reminiscent of Isaiah 45.14 and Zechariah 8.23, where the realisation of the nations around about Israel that God is truly among his people is one of the signs of the fulfilment of God's promises to them.[66] In this sense the unbeliever's confession, provoked by prophetic conviction of his sins, is a sign to believers of the eschatological presence of God among his people.

On the other hand, Paul's insistence that prophecy is a sign for believers can be taken as a continuation of his case for preferring prophecy to glossolalia over the previous two and a half chapters. Prophecy is far more the sign for believers than is glossolalia. The confusion in Paul's case springs from his mixing of two strands of argument in the one passage. One strand is his preference for prophecy due to its intelligibility, and therefore its utility for edifying the congregation, a case he has been developing in a sustained fashion since the beginning of chapter 14. The second strand is the contrast between the effects of glossolalia and prophecy on unbelievers. The two

---

and J. Héring take a similar position. J.D.G. Dunn, *op.cit.*, p. 231, argues that glossolalia is a sign for unbelievers in the sense that it confirms them in their unbelief.

[65] Thus Grudem, *art.cit.*, p. 392. A similar view is taken by C.M. Robeck, Jr., "The Gift of Prophecy in Acts and Paul, Part 2", *Studia Biblica et Theologica*, Vol. 5, no. 2, October 1975, p. 52, who argues that the conversion and praise that prophecy elicits from the unbeliever are what constitute prophecy as "a sign for believers"; likewise J.D.G. Dunn argues that prophecy confirms believers in their belief, including the confirmation of their faith afforded by the effect of prophecy on unbelievers: it converts them (*op.cit.*, p. 231 and note 161); thus also P. Roberts, *art.cit.*, p. 202. The meaning of the term "sign" is thus based around the sense of "confirmatory sign".

[66] The importance of the fact that the unbeliever's confession is reminiscent of the Isaiah and Zechariah passages was pointed out to me in conversation by Dr. Paul Barnett. Though the commentaries of Grosheide, p. 333, Barrett, p. 327, Bruce, p. 133, and Conzelmann, p. 243, as well as J.D.G. Dunn, *op.cit.*, p. 231, all cite these references, and in some cases add others (Daniel 2.47, Sirach 1.30), none of them draws out the implications of this fact for the exegesis of the passage; of other recent discussions only Sweet, *art.cit.*, pp. 245-6, and D. Hill, "Christian Prophets as Teachers or Instructors in the Church", in Panagopoulos, *Vocation*, p. 113, and *Prophecy*, p. 124, mention the reminiscence at all. Their brief treatments are very valuable.

strands are intertwined in this passage, producing the difficulties we have
outlined above.

It seems to me, on this basis, that, out of the multiple options available,
the following is the most plausible reconstruction. First, Paul cites Isaiah
28.11 with very little regard for the nuances of the context. His form of the
passage, unlike any textual witness known to us, specifically links "but even
then they will not listen to me, says the Lord" with the hearing of
unintelligible speech.[67] Paul's understanding of part of the problem in
Corinth (the observed fact that uninterpreted tongues in the presence of
unbelievers leads them to reject what they see and hear) has consciously or
unconsciously shaped his quotation of Isaiah, in order to make precisely that
point: "they (outsiders) will not listen to you, or to what you say about God."
Second, he must therefore be understood as arguing that tongues function as
a sign in the way suggested by his form of the Isaiah passage. They are a
sign, a miracle of some kind, yes (perhaps he is quoting the Corinthians; it
does not matter), and they do signify the presence of God and his activity. In
line with his other, earlier theme, however, he says that they are a sign more
appropriate for unbelievers than for believers. But unbelievers will say that
you are raving. Whether they believe this raving to be (in our terms)
insanity, magical ritual or divine inspiration, they will be put off by it,
excluded, perhaps even frightened, and will not listen further.[68]
Uninterpreted glossolalia will function, then, as a *negative* sign, a sign of
judgement or similar. Prophecy, on the other hand, is also a sign. But (in line
with the whole argument of chapters 12-14) it is to be preferred. *It*, rather
than uninterpreted glossolalia, is a sign appropriate for believers. It is
intelligible, it edifies. And, what is more, because it is both intelligible *and*
revelatory, not merely revelatory, the unbeliever will hear and understand

---

[67] The consequences of Paul's quoting Isaiah in a totally non-standard form is glossed
over in the otherwise excellent treatment of W. Grudem, *art.cit.*, p. 386-7; the best
discussions of this point are those of Sweet, *art.cit.*, p. 243ff, and Johanson, "Tongues",
p. 182, as noted above.

[68] In the light of the conclusions of chapters 5-7, I would judge that it is highly unlikely
that unbelievers hearing the kind of glossolalia Paul is commending for the first time in a
Christian context would recognise it as a familiar phenomenon. It is possible that the
tumult of a large number of Corinthians speaking in tongues simultaneously would
remind them of the frenzy of Hellenistic cult groups, but overall it seems more likely to
me, especially in the light of the usage of the terms μανία and μαίνομαι, treated above,
that the thoroughly negative reaction "you are all crazy" is what Paul thought
would occur.

things which will, by the insight they offer into his own life, wring from him a confession of the presence of God.[69] Such a confession is a sign of the eschatological promises of God coming to fulfilment among his people. Paul offers the Corinthians two alternatives: a sign of judgement that will exclude outsiders while benefitting no-one but the glossolalist, and a sign for believers of the fulfilment of the promises of God, *in* the response of unbelievers.

The reader will of course note that my solution must put up with the term "sign" being used explicitly in one sense in v. 22a, and then being implied in another sense in v. 22b. It might likewise be argued that it breaks up the close thematic unity of vv. 20-25. I believe, however, that this unity can only be maintained at the expense of the wider unity of chapter 14, and at the expense of the passage remaining nonsensical. The solution offered is not without difficulties, but seems to me to be the best reading of the passage.[70] It takes Paul's description of the problem in v. 23 seriously, accounts for the form of his quotation of Isaiah, requires no term to be used in an unparalleled sense, and takes seriously the prophetic reminiscence in v. 25.

This concludes our discussion of glossolalia and its role both in the conflict between Paul and his Corinthian converts and in early Christianity more generally. We turn now, after the Appendix, to a discussion of that form of inspired speech which Luke did not clearly distinguish from glossolalia, and which Paul preferred to it: Christian prophecy.

---

[69] It is more likely that this happens because the content of some of the prophecies is the secrets of his heart (as in the case of Jesus and the Samaritan woman at the well, John chapter 4), than that he is so impressed by what he overhears of the general tone of proceedings that he discerns the presence of God (as at Pentecost) which is the view of D.A. Carson, *Showing the Spirit*, p. 116. Verse 25 seems decisive here.

[70] W. Grudem has shown persuasively that the term σημεῖον can take this kind of double sense in the LXX (*art.cit.*, pp. 389-90); it is therefore less of a step to argue that it may be implied in a second sense in v. 22b. Of all the commentators Barrett's suggestion is perhaps closest to that offered here: he comments that the passage "is certainly obscure; his thought clears up as he turns to the practical demands of the church's evangelistic task." (*op.cit.*, p. 327.) Barrett cites Isaiah and Zechariah too, but makes no use of the references.

Appendix

Proposed Jewish Evidence.

Alongside the "consensus" argument criticised in detail in the preceding three chapters, there are those who argue that the unintelligibility of glossolalia as a form of ecstatic speech, and its characterisation as angelic languages, find their closest parallels within intertestamental Judaism. The first aspect of the argument is well summarised by Harrisville, who says that

these parallels appear to support the contention that for the O.T. and Inter-testamental Jewish community, glossolalic utterance was not regarded as a category separate from the ecstatic per se. A reading of Philo, e.g., tends to reinforce this position. On the other hand, with the exception of the parallels in Jub. and the Test. Judah from which it may be inferred that inspired speech constituted intelligible utterance, the remainder ranges from references to a modicum of intelligibility (1 Enoch, Similitudes 40) to the unintelligible or inarticulate (1 Enoch 71.11 and the Martyrdom of Isaiah 5.14), thus yielding soil for the development of a term exclusively applied to ecstatic speech.[1]

The evidence presented for this conclusion is Jubilees 25.14, Test. Judah 25.3, 1 Enoch 40, 71.11, 4 Maccabees 10.21, and Martyrdom of Isaiah 5.14, and from Philo, Quis Rerum 249, 259, 264-266, de Spec. Leg. 4.49, de Vita Mosis 1.274 and de Decalogo 32-33, 46. It must be said simply that *none* of these passages, not even Enoch 71.11 or Martyrdom of Isaiah, suggests either an unintelligible form of "ecstatic" speech (or the human use of heavenly languages).[2] It is hard to see how Harrisville's point can be maintained from the evidence he has cited.

---

[1] R.A Harrisville, "Speaking in Tongues: a Lexicographical Study", *C.B.Q.*, vol. 38, 1976, p. 47. Harrisville refers here, of course, to the work of Nils Engelsen.

[2] The Testament of Judah refers to the fact that in the eschatological state, when "Abraham and Isaac and Jacob will arise unto life" (25.1) "there will be one people of the Lord and one tongue" (25.3, *The Testaments of the Twelve Patriarchs, a Commentary*, H.W. Hollander and M. de Jonge, Leiden, 1985, pp. 228-230). For Enoch see the recent translation, with critical notes, of M. Black, *The Book of Enoch, or, 1 Enoch*, Leiden, 1985, pp. 45, 68, 199-201 and 251-252, though Black makes no reference to glossolalia. While Isaiah was being executed "his mouth spoke with the Holy Spirit" (the translation is that of M.A. Knibb, in J.H. Charlesworth, ed., *The Old Testament Pseudepigrapha*, vol. 2, p. 164) but that phrase is far too general to be used as proof of "the unintelligible

Of all the evidence brought forward by Harrisville (and Engelsen), only one piece is even likely to prove persuasive as a parallel to early Christian glossolalia. This is the short section of the Testament of Job, chs. 48-51, where Job's daughters receive their inheritance from their father. This inheritance consists of three cords or sashes, wonderful in appearance, which the daughters put on. What happens next is described as follows:

> Thus, when the one called Hemera arose, she wrapped her own string just as her father said. And she took on another heart - no longer minded toward earthly things - but she spoke ecstatically (ἀπεφθέγξατο δὲ) in the angelic dialect (τῇ ἀγγελικῇ φωνῇ), sending up a hymn to God in accord with the hymnic style of the angels. And as she spoke ecstatically, she allowed "The Spirit" to be inscribed on her garment.

> Then Kasia bound hers on and had her heart changed so that she no longer regarded worldly things. And her mouth took on the dialect of the archons (τὸ μὲν στόμα αὐτῆς ἔλαβεν τὴν διάλεκτον τῶν ἀρχόντων) and she praised God for the creation of the heights. So, if anyone wishes to know "The Creation of the Heavens", he will be able to find it in "The Hymns of Kasia".

> Then the other one also, named Amaltheia's Horn, bound on her cord. And her mouth spoke ecstatically (ἀποφθεγγόμενον) in the dialect of those on high (ἐν τῇ διαλέκτῳ τῶν ἐν ὕψει), since her heart also was changed, keeping aloof from worldly things. For she spoke in the dialect of the cherubim (ἐν τῇ διαλέκτῳ <τῶν> Χερουβὶμ), glorifying the Master of virtues by exhibiting their splendour. And finally whoever wishes to grasp a trace of "The Paternal Splendour" will find it written down in "The Prayers of Amaltheia's Horn".

> After the three had stopped singing hymns, while the Lord was present as was I, Nereus, the brother of Job, and while the holy angel also was present, I sat near Job on the couch. And I heard the magnificent things, while each one made explanation (ὑποσημειουμένης) to the other. And I wrote out a complete book of most of the contents of hymns that issued from the three daughters of my brother, so that these things would be preserved. For these are the magnificent things of God.[3]

or inarticulate" Indeed, in context, it would appear to mean simply "he spoke the truth". The visions of the Ascension of Isaiah are greatly concerned with the praise of God at the various levels of the heavens, and with Isaiah's praise of God as he ascends (see 8.13, 8.17, 9.32, 9.33, 9.40-41, 10.19), but *at no stage* is it suggested that he takes on or learns the type of praise, or the language of praise, of the angels.

[3] The translation given here is that of R.P. Spittler, in *The Old Testament Pseudepigrapha*, vol. 1, ed. J.H. Charlesworth, London, 1983, pp. 864-867. The translation "speak ecstatically" (ἀπεφθέγξατο, (ἀποφθεγγόμενον) is tendentious: as far as I know there is no use of the term ἀποφθέγγομαι which requires us to understand it as having to do with the psychological state of the speaker at all. Rather it indicates (as has been argued above) the significant nature of what is said. It is often, but far from exclusively, used of oracles, but again the emphasis is on what is said, and its nature as a formal pronouncement, rather than on the oracular origins of the statement. See Chapter 7 footnote 35 for detailed references.

Spittler, Engelsen, Dautzenberg and most other authors see here a clear parallel with glossolalia. U.B. Müller, for example, is so certain of both the parallel, and of the Hellenistic origins of glossolalia, that he argues that the Testament must be seen as a Hellenistic Jewish work, on the basis of this passage (as well as others).[4] Before such conclusions may be legitimately drawn, however, several questions will have to be answered. The date of the Testament, for example, is a widely contested issue. Likewise open is the question of whether it has suffered interpolation by later (Christian?) hands. If it cannot be proven to be pre-Christian, or if there is serious reason to suspect Christian or other interpolation in the critical chapters, then the Testament's value as an independent parallel falls away.

It is here, unfortunately, that consensus fails us. Spittler is not willing to be more specific about the Testament's date than "First Century B.C.-First Century A.D."[5] Various authors he cites put the Testament in the second century, or the pre-Christian era. On the interpolation question, Spittler suggests that

the Testament may have been reworked in the second century by Montanists. Eusebius (HE 5.17.1-4) preserves the argument of an unnamed anti-Montanist who demands to know where in the range of Biblical history any precedent appeared for ecstatic prophecy. The descriptions of Job's daughters speaking in ecstasy . . . may have been a Montanist move to supply such a precedent.[6]

There are two weaknesses in this suggestion. The first is the suggestion that what Job's three daughters are doing would be seen as prophecy by a Montanist. None of our records suggest that Montanist prophecy was understood as hymnic: those samples which remain are remarkably prosaic. Likewise, as I have argued above, there is no evidence that glossolalia was practised among the Montanists, or that they understood their prophecy to include angelic languages.[7] On the same line, Montanism seems to know of

---

[4] U.B. Müller, *Prophetie und Predigt im Neuen Testament*, Gütersloh, 1975, pp. 31-37. Naturally, if the evidence for pre-Christian glossolalia is as slight as I have suggested, such an argument would have to be completely revised. Müller seems to me to have been forced to an untenable position. Our only close parallel for glossolalia is this passage, and it is primarily a Jewish, not a Hellenistic piece of work.

[5] R.P. Spittler, *op.cit.*, pp. 829, 833. See the list of opinions there, and in J.H. Charlesworth, *The Pseudepigrapha and Modern Research*, Missoula, 1976, p. 135.

[6] R.P. Spittler, *op.cit.*, p. 834.

[7] See Chapter 7. Spittler's supporting argument (p. 834), that the work appears to be reflected in one of Tertullian's pre-Montanist works, is inconclusive and double-edged. That Tertullian knew of the work before he became a Montanist (if he did) says nothing about its possible editing by Montanists, before or after. In his unpublished Doctoral

no parallels for the "sashes" or "strings" worn by the daughters; neither does the Testament mention the Spirit/Paraclete, so characteristic of Montanist prophetic self-understanding. The suggestion of Montanist style ecstasy is not borne out by the language of the writer: Montanist writers do not use the term ἀποφθέγγομαι to denote ecstasy, and neither does anyone else. In other words, nothing in the passage suggests Montanism.[8] Secondly, there is no suggestion that the girls' mutual explanation (if that is what it is, ὑποσημειουμένης) of their songs to one another is in any sense a parallel to the interpretation of tongues. *Pace* Dautzenberg, "Glossolalie", col. 233, the term is simply not clear enough for that.[9]

There is therefore no clear evidence to suggest a Montanist redaction of the Testament. It remains quite possible, however, that there was a Christian or Gnostic (τὴν διάλεκτον τῶν ἀρχόντων!) redaction at some period. Once again, it is the inconclusiveness of the dating of the Testament that hampers us here. It is not proven that the Testament must be pre-Christian; neither is it proven that, if it is contemporary with early Christianity, it is free from editorial influence from within early Christianity. Any claim that the Testament gives us independent evidence of the existence of pre-Christian glossolalia must somehow surmount these two related obstacles to establish its case. What the Testament *does* provide, however, is clear evidence that the concept of angelic languages *as a mode of praise*

---

thesis, portions of which Dr Spittler kindly sent to me, he further argues that the designation of God as πατήρ parallels the Montanist oracles, and that the prowess of Job with the κιθάρα may parallel Montanus' description of inspiration on the analogy of a plectrum on strings. It seems to me, however, that this title for God is too generally Christian, and this description of inspiration is too much a stereotype to be seen as distinctly Montanist (see Chapter 5, notes 9 and 27 for references to inspiration with musical metaphors), and that the link is tenuous at best. Spittler admits that an origin among the Therapeutae seems more plausible for the major part of the document, but feels surer of a Montanist origin at least for Chapters 48-50. He also admits that several features of these chapters, such as the semi-magical "sashes" and the interest in angelology, are a little hard to parallel closely in either setting. For this (in my view, inconclusive) argumentation, see R.P. Spittler, *The Testament of Job: Introduction, Translation, and Notes*, Diss., Harvard, 1971, pp. 58-67.

[8]   See also the critique of Spittler's "Montanist redaction" hypothesis by P.W. van der Horst, "The Role of Women in the Testament of Job", *Nederlands Theologisch Tijdschrift*, vol. 40, no. 4, 1986, pp. 273-289, esp. pp. 283-4.

[9]   Kraft, et.al., *The Testament of Job according to the SV Text*, Missoula, 1974, translate the term "noted things down". The term is very unclear.

to God was an acceptable one within certain circles.[10] As such it is our nearest parallel to glossolalia.

The only other recent treatment of the question of angelic or divine languages within Judaism to cite fresh evidence is that of G. Dautzenberg.[11] He argues that the link in Jewish angel-speculation between angels and people of prayer provides the conceptual background for the idea of praying in angelic languages, and cites Daniel chs. 7-12, 4 Ezra chs. 10-13, B. Baba Bathra 134a, the Apocalypse of Zephaniah 8, Slavonic Enoch 17.19 and various passages from the Qumran writings. In all of this we find some evidence for humans relying on angelic knowledge, some for the concept of the angels having their own languages, but only one more piece of evidence for the use of such languages by humans. This of the Apocalypse of Zephaniah.[12] In the course of describing "Zephaniah"'s cosmic wanderings, he describes his praying with a group of angels, as follows: "I myself, prayed together with them; I knew their language, which they spoke with me."[13] So this passage goes with Test. Job., as having a concept of prayer or praise using angelic languages. As distinct from the Test. Job., however, the Apocalypse of Zephaniah seems not to have undergone a Christian redaction. Its dating is, like the Testament's, very unclear. It cannot come from later than A.D. 175, and, according to its most recent translator, may be as early as A.D. 70; it may be even earlier.[14]

---

[10] The suggestion of Engelsen, that in the Testament the "glossolalia" of the three women is understood as prophetic (in the Lucan sense) because "Job and his daughters are able to see into the hidden world, both present and future" (Engelsen, *Glossolalia*, pp. 52ff.) is unsupported by the text. While it may be that they can see into the hidden world, there is no suggestion that their knowledge extends to the present or future. That they use their languages to sing God's praises is the important point.

[11] G. Dautzenberg, "Glossolalie", cols. 232-235.

[12] Daniel and 4 Ezra have their respective heroes relying on angelic explanation of apocalyptic visions. According to Talmud tractate Baba Bathra, Jochanan ben Zakkai's studies included "the language of the demons, the whispering of the palms, the language of the ministering angels and the great matter [the Throne Chariot] and the small matter". (Baba Bathra 134a, trans M. Simon, I.W. Slotki, Vol. 2 of the Soncino edition, 1976. Compare Sukkah 28a.) There is, however, no suggestion that he learned these languages through vision or inspiration, or that he used them for prayer: they are simply evidence for the breadth of his learning. Slavonic Enoch 17.19 has angelic singing, but no suggestion as to what language they may have been using. The Qumran references appear to add nothing significant to the case.

[13] O.S. Wintermute, Apocalypse of Zephaniah, ch. 8, from *The Old Testament Pseudepigrapha*, vol. 1, London, 1983, ed. J.H. Charlesworth, p. 514.

[14] O.S. Wintermute, in J.H. Charlesworth, ed., *op.cit.*, p. 501. The *terminus* is

We have, then, within Judaism, only two substantial parallels for the concept that humans might, under inspiration, learn and use the languages of the angels for prayer. Neither of them is of demonstrably pre-Christian date. One of them has probably undergone Christian or Gnostic redaction. Both come from apocalyptic tradition. It may be the case, then, as Harrisville suggested, that "something akin to glossolalia" was practised among "those who nourished apocalyptic hopes". The thread of evidence for such a case is, however, very slender. What we must ask is, is it sufficient to justify the suggestion that Paul and his converts (and the rest of primitive Christianity) believed glossolalia to be exclusively or predominantly angelic languages, as Güntert, Dautzenberg and others have suggested? Clearly, given the background, Jewish and Graeco-Roman, they could have believed this. The question is, did they?

Here I think the answer must be no. Neither in the Hellenistic nor the Jewish background have we found sufficient evidence to overthrow the case that early Christians uniformly believed glossolalia to be the power to speak in otherwise unlearned human languages. They may have believed that angelic languages were included, but the evidence that they did is not strong. It consists of Ellis' controverted case about angelic intermediary spirits, Dunn's suggestion that heavenly mysteries are what glossolalists speak, the reference in the Acts of Paul, Test. Job. if it is (in its current form) Christian (rather than, for example, Gnostic), and Paul's phrase "tongues of (men *and*) angels". This is not a great deal of evidence. It seems to me that the most we can claim is this. With some such background in mind, Paul argues that even if one could, hypothetically, reach such a point of righteousness or vision as to speak in the tongues of angels, without love it would do no good. One, or perhaps two, Christian writers picked up the concept in later times. But this is the strongest conclusion that may reasonably be drawn, with any confidence, from the evidence we have examined.

---

established by the quotation of the Apocalypse by Clement of Alexandria.

Chapter 8

Early Christian Prophecy and its Hellenistic Parallels:
Definitions and Terminology

As we turn to discuss early Christian prophecy and its relationship with prophetic phenomena in the wider Graeco-Roman world it rapidly becomes apparent that our task is different and more complex than that undertaken in the previous chapters. There the question was simply: does "inspired" speech in the Graeco-Roman world characteristically take a form that is linguistically unintelligible? Is inspired speech in Graeco-Roman religion conceived of as a miraculous gift of language? Though definitional questions were unavoidable, they did not unduly complicate the issue. In the case of prophecy, however, they require careful discussion. Likewise, due to the enormous range of the material which might be included under the heading "prophetic", this section of my case will not attempt to be exhaustive. It should be regarded rather as an exploratory treatment, attempting to eliminate a number of false hypotheses and to provide a firmer basis for continuing work.

1. Matters of Definition

In his programmatic essay for the Society for Biblical Literature's Seminar on Early Christian Prophecy, M.E. Boring suggested as follows:

As its first major task, the SBL Seminar on Early Christian Prophecy will explore the phenomenon of prophecy in the Hellenistic world prior to and apart from its manifestation in early Christianity. Each major body of relevant materials will be investigated in terms of the data and understanding(s) of prophecy it offers, in order to bring to sharper focus the manifestations of the prophetic phenomenon in the world into which Christianity was born.[1]

This is precisely the task which the next three chapters undertake, with one proviso. As was noted in the Introduction, we will consider here on the Christian side only those forms of Christian prophecy testified to in Luke-Acts and the letters of Paul, the most easily accessible body of explicit evidence.

---

[1]   "What Are We Looking For?: Toward a Definition of the Term 'Christian Prophet'", *S.B.L. Seminar Papers*, 1973, Missoula, 1973, pp. 142-154; esp. p. 142.

Boring's own discussion of the various kinds of definition is excellent; his suggestion for a working set of definitions for the task in hand, however, requires consideration.

Since the Seminar intends to study early *Christian* prophecy, the working definition of "prophet" should be formulated on the basis of the Christian sources themselves. This will leave open the question of the "uniqueness" of the phenomenon, i.e. whether and to what extent something identical, similar or analogous to it was present before and/or alongside it in the Hellenistic world. But of course even if Christian prophecy should prove to be unique in some features, the definition should not be composed only around these features, unless it is they that constitute Christian prophecy as *prophecy*. Otherwise, no light at all will be shed on the phenomenon from non-Christian sources . . .[2]

There are two problems here. The first is that while the above statement may be useful, it does ignore the possibility that definitions formulated from the Christian sources may not be appropriate in the Graeco-Roman world. In a cross-cultural analysis such as this, the definitions of the sources themselves *on both sides of the comparison* must be taken into account, as well as whatever definitions we may ourselves adopt, if the comparison is not to be jeopardised.[3]

Nor is this merely a theoretical problem. As we shall see, even at the level of terminology there are fundamental differences between the early Christian usage of the term προφητεία and the usage of that term in the wider Graeco-Roman world. Further, the differences are not "merely" semantic, but indicate the very different conceptual frameworks within which the terms were used. In the New Testament προφητεία is used by Paul (9 times, including twice in the Pastorals) for the ability or gift of prophesying: speaking inspired messages given to one by the Holy Spirit. It does not occur in Hellenistic literature until Lucian (Alexander 40), as has been noted often enough, but it does occur in inscriptions of our period, including first-century ones, for the period of time during which one held the annual

---

[2] M.E. Boring, *art.cit.*, p. 146.
[3] In his book, *Sayings of the Risen Jesus*, Boring makes use of what he describes as a "functional definition" which, though sensible and helpful, does not correspond fully with what Paul or Luke calls a prophet, as he several times notes (i.e. pp. 30-31). We must remember that early Christianity did *not* describe every form of inspired speech as prophetic. We have a responsibility to take notice of this fact, or we will not be doing justice to our sources. Luke's and Paul's implicit definitions are not the only ones possible, but they are not to be ignored.

office of prophet at Didyma and other shrines, or else for that office itself.[4] In early Christianity "prophecy" was the *ability* to speak messages received under inspiration. In the Hellenistic world this ability would have been called μαντική. "Prophecy" was an official position in the hierarchy of oracular centres, and had nothing directly to do with inspired speech at all. In early Christianity προφητεύειν designates the activity of delivering an oracle (Paul 10 times, Luke 6 times). In the Hellenistic world it means "to hold the office of προφήτης". Even on this limited basis it becomes clear that using a definition formulated only on the basis of the early Christian evidence would be most misleading. Both fields of evidence must be allowed to speak to us in their own terms.[5]

This leads to the second point. Boring's proposal, and his working definition that follows, are formulated in terms of "Christian prophets." In my view there are two strong reasons why working definitions ought to be formulated with reference to "Christian prophecy", that is, the function, as well as the person exercising it. The first reason is that Boring's definition assumes that in early Christianity prophecy is characteristically exercised by those called prophets, which may or may not have been the case.[6] If we

---

[4]   E. Fascher, *Prophetes*, pp. 8-9, 53-4, and H. Krämer, in G. Friedrich, ed., *T.D.N.T.*, vol. 6, 1959, E.T. 1968, p. 784. See, for examples of its use in this sense, *Didyma Inscriptions*, nos. 222 (2nd C AD, trans. "two years before his prophetship"), 331 (early imperial, "he fulfilled his prophetship with piety"), 337 (early imperial, "he completed his prophetship . . ."), 350 (1st C AD, "having completed his prophetship"), 351 (1st C AD, "in the year of his prophetship"), 358 (1st C AD, "he took the office of prophet"), 360 (AD 50-84, "he took over the prophetship"), 365 (1st C AD, "he promised to hold the prophetship for the second time"), 366 (1st C AD, "undertaking both the prophetship and the magistracy"), 382 (130-138 AD, "due to his holding the office of prophet"), 384 (a & b, 2nd C AD), 377 (2nd C AD, "taking the office of prophet unallotted"), 389 (2nd C AD), 404 (3rd C AD, "in the year in which he held the prophetship"). For an Egyptian example see Papyrus Tebtunis 294, dated 146 B.C., where a tender is made for the προφητεία and the rights and privileges pertaining thereto: see also below for more examples.

[5]   The terminological confusion, discussed in Chapter 5, continues. Thus, R.M. Berchman, in his "Arcana Mundi: Prophecy and Divination in the *Vita Mosis* of Philo of Alexandria" (*S.B.L. 1988 Seminar Papers*, Atlanta, 1988), pp. 385-423, argues (p. 387) that "*propheteia* is a type of *manteia*; the prophet a kind of *mantis*." For differing reasons, Hellenistic Greeks, Jews, and Christians would *all* have disagreed with this piece of definition.

[6]   Those challenging this assumption include M. Turner, "Spiritual Gifts Then and Now", *Vox Evangelica*, vol. 15, 1985, p. 14: "Paul . . . reserved the honoured title of 'prophet' for the recognised *specialist* in prophecy, while allowing that all at Corinth

examine the function as well this problem is avoided. The second reason is that a "functional" definition will lead us much further when we come to consider the Graeco-Roman evidence, as we shall see.[7]

Beyond this point, however, I am in substantial agreement with Boring as to the procedure to be adopted, at least in the formulation of working definitions. We must begin with those people and phenomena specifically designated prophets and prophecy respectively in each sphere, and then set out to analyse the characteristics of the activity and persons. What will very rapidly become apparent are the real differences between the ways in which prophecy was conceived in the two cultures with which we are concerned. It will therefore first of all be necessary to go over a certain amount of

---

might prophesy one-by-one." Turner continues: "All may *seek* prophecy, for none are excluded *a priori*, but God will not in fact distribute any one gift to all." (p. 15) See also the discussion by D.E. Aune, *Prophecy*, pp. 196-201. Compare J.D.G. Dunn, *Jesus and the Spirit*, London, 1975, p. 281: "Prophetic authority was not confined to the prophets. Only an apostle could exercise apostolic authority; but anyone might prophesy. Paul clearly expected that other members of the assembly other than the prophets would be inspired to prophesy (cf. 14.5, 24, perhaps 31); . . . the authority lay in the prophesying and not in the prophet." E. Best, "Prophets and Preachers", *S.J.Th.*, vol. 12, 1959, p. 142-3 (with others) suggests a steady institutionalising of the charisma: "at first there does not seem to have been an exact class of prophets; at different times different people prophesied. But long before the end of the first century we find the emergence of such a definite class. In the church in Corinth, as described in Paul's first letter, this process would appear to have been in progress; on the one hand the possibility remains open that anyone may prophesy, insofar as Paul urges his readers to desire prophecy rather than glossolalia; on the other hand there are also those within the church who are looked upon as prophets and are so called. . . . the outburst of spiritual activity beginning at Pentecost produced a definite class of prophets, who may be considered an order of ministry within the early Church." This issue will be dealt with in detail below.

[7]   This fact is well illustrated by comparing the approaches of Crone and Aune. Crone focuses his investigation on occurrences of the term προφήτης, and as a result ends up with very few closely parallel prophets. The reasons for this will become apparent below. Aune, on the other hand, looks at a much wider field. His definitions, simply put, are that "Divination may be defined as the art or science of interpreting symbolic messages from the gods. Often these symbols are unpredictable or even trivial. Oracles, on the other hand, are messages from the gods in human language, received as statements from a god, usually in response to inquiries." (*Prophecy*, p. 23) This is reasonably clear: prophecy is that field of human endeavour which has to do with receiving messages from the gods, by whatever means. On this basis he examines "consultation oracles" of various sorts, their personnel, both "diviners" and "mantics", and the various minor types, only very few of whom are ever described as προφῆται. In other words, Aune's definition is far more a "functional" one, whereas Crone's is (in Boring's terms, *art.cit.*, p. 144) based on the "label approach".

well-ploughed ground to do with the history of the προφήτης terminology, in order to correct some emphases of older studies, to take account of new evidence, and to clear up one or two recent misconceptions. The first of these is the claim that in the Hellenistic period the term προφήτης was widely used to designate ecstatics who prophesied, and that this usage is illuminative of the early Christian usage. Another is that the term was used in our period for wandering teachers / wonder-workers, and that, again, this usage is valuable for our understanding of the relationship between early Christianity and its environment.

2. The Terminology in Outline

I argued above, in Chapter 5, that the conventional picture of the role of the προφήτης at Delphi had been seriously misunderstood. Instead of being the interpreter or versifier of the Pythia's ravings, he was an official spokesman, with little active role in the oracular process itself. It is now time to examine the role of προφῆται more closely. Treatments of the terminology abound: of these the best is probably T.M. Crone, *Prophecy*. The consensus of opinion is that the term προφήτης went through several reasonably clear stages of usage. These we may summarise as follows:

(1) In Classical Greece, i.e. from Pindar down, the term προφήτης and its cognates could have three meanings, all fairly clearly related to the etymological sense of the word, "spokesman" or "announcer". It could be used of a certain class of officials at oracular shrines, pre-eminently at Delphi, who, though not necessarily inspired themselves, mediated the oracles of others.[8] It could also be used of those inspired persons who both received and proclaimed oracles from the gods, provided that the focus of the term is understood to be on their function as *proclaimers* of such oracles, rather than as inspired receivers of them.[9] Finally, it could be used

---

[8] This usage has been fairly thoroughly discussed in Chapter 5, and, provided this mediation is restricted to public proclamation, is not affected by the arguments there.

[9] Thus, correctly, H. Krämer, in G. Friedrich, ed., *T.D.N.T.*, vol. 6, 1959, E.T. 1968, p. 790: "While the functions of both [sc. προφήτης and μάντις] . . . are allotted to different persons, they may often fall to the same person, and in this case they denote different aspects . . ." The most common case of this dual role is, naturally, the Delphic προφῆτις: the term is rarely used in this dual sense in the masculine form in this period. Outside the case of the Pythia, the more normal term is μάντις. Exceptions include Teiresias (Pindar, Nemean Odes, 1.60) and the unnamed προφήτης of Ptoan Apollo who spoke to Mys of Caria, mentioned in Chapter 5; see also Plutarch, Mor. 431 b.

in a less technical sense of any official spokesman, be he speaking on behalf of gods, Muses, or others.[10]

(2) In the Hellenistic period all three usages outlined above continued. Two major developments also occurred, both of which have given scholars pause. The first of these is the use of the term προφήτης by the Greeks for certain high-ranking Egyptian priests. The puzzle here is that these priests seem to have no particular connection with specifically oracular matters.[11] The second development is the adoption of the term by the translators of the Septuagint for the Hebrew term *nabi*. It is not clear why this term, only

---

[10] Thus Pindar calls on the Muse to give him oracles (μαντεύω, Μοῖσα,) that he may proclaim them (προφατεύσω δ' ἐγώ) in Fragment 150, compare Nemean Odes 1.60. Likewise in Nemean Odes 9.50, the drinking bowl is described in a metaphorical sense as προφήτης of the song of triumph. Likewise in Euripides' Bacchae, 210ff, Cadmus offers to act as Teiresias' προφήτης in a completely non-oracular sense. The term also occurs in this sense in Aristophanes Birds 972, where a χρησμολόγος, or oracle-monger, is satirically permitted to style himself προφήτης of Bakis, the legendary "male Sibyl". Once again, the term here means neither more nor less than "spokesman".

[11] The first known literary usage in this sense is in Manetho, cited by Josephus, Apion 1.249. Other references may conveniently be found in H. Krämer's article in G. Friedrich, ed., *T.D.N.T.*, vol. 6, 1959, E.T. 1968, p. 794, in Crone, *Prophecy*, pp. 37-9, or, for the considerable papyrological evidence, in F. Preisigke, *Wörterbuch der griechischen Papyrusurkunden*, Berlin, vol. 2 (1925) p. 427, and vol. 3 (1931) p. 383, and S. Daris, *Spoglio Lessicale Papirologico*, vol. 3, Milan, 1968, p. 1351. For the puzzlement see, for example, Erman, cited in E. Fascher, *Prophetes*, p. 76: "Warum die Griechen sie so benannten, ist noch zu untersuchen." Fascher himself suggests the title may first have been applied to the priests who supervised the oracle of Ammon in Libya, and then applied by extension to others of similar rank. R. Reitzenstein, *Hellenistic Mystery Religions*, trans. J. Steely, Pittsburgh, 1978, p. 33, argues that "revelation and the non-mediated vision continued . . . to be the outcome and the climactic point of the true cultus; he beholds God, and God speaks through him; only thus could the Greek designation of *prophet* have been chosen for the highest class of priests." But this view is based on an impossibly anachronistic view of pre-Ptolemaic Egyptian religion, and, as we have seen, misrepresents the role of the προφήτης in the Greek world as well. H. Krämer cites two possible explanations without comment, but neither really solves the problem; see *art.cit.*, p. 794. T.M. Crone describes this as "a most perplexing problem", and says "it is not at all clear why they were called προφῆται", when they have "no oracle connections", *Prophecy*, pp. 37, 38. His own suggestion (p. 39) is that it is possible that the word had lost its specifically oracular connotations by this period, and was simply used as a priestly title. T. Callan, "Prophecy and Ecstasy in Greco-Roman Religion and in 1 Corinthians", *Nov.T.*, vol. 27, 1985, pp. 125-140 esp. pp. 132-3, argues that the term's widespread (*sic*) use as a synonym for μάντις is the most reasonable explanation. He greatly exaggerates the importance of this usage, however, as will be argued below.

secondarily concerned with inspiration, was used for those who were first and foremost inspired prophets.[12]

It is also in this period that we are faced with an explosion in the amount of epigraphic and papyrological material related to προφῆται. While, to our great surprise, no inscriptions related to προφῆται have as yet been found at Delphi, one has been found at Thera which mentions the Delphic προφῆτις.[13] Inscriptions related to other προφῆται have been found at Acraiphia in Boeotia, at Argos, Miletus and Didyma / Branchidae,[14] Chalcedon, Tanagra, Lindus, Corope in Magnesia, and, naturally enough, in various parts of Egypt.[15] They are also found in Rome itself,[16] at Marseilles,[17] Patara,[18] Claros,[19] and elsewhere. The great majority are

---

[12] Crone suggests, *Prophecy*, p. 14, that "it could have been that the first *nabi* passages to be translated concerned temple prophets (cf. Zechariah 7:3), and the προφῆται in Greece were first of all cult officials. More probably, however, the translators thought first of the major prophets as preachers and announcers of the will of God, and this function is well described by the basic meaning of προφήτης."

[13] Fascher, *Prophetes*, p. 41. The inscription is I.G. 12.3, No. 863. The question as to why no inscriptions have been found at Delphi will be treated below.

[14] Fascher, *Prophetes*, pp. 41-51, Krämer, *art.cit.*, p. 789, Crone, *Prophecy*, pp. 35-39. See also the important article of L. Robert, "Inscriptions de Didyme et de Milet", *Hellenica* XI-XII, 1960, pp. 440-489, where twelve inscriptions making use of the term are gathered and discussed along with others from Didyma and Miletus, and the references to earlier discussions there. Most important, however, are the recently published corpus of Didyma, *Didyma Inscriptions*, in which approximately 190 inscriptions out of the 701 listed make use of the term in one way or another, and H.W. Parke, *The Oracles of Apollo in Asia Minor*, London, 1985.

[15] For Egypt see most especially the papyri, for which references up till 1968 may be found in F. Preisigke, *loc.cit.*, and S. Daris, *loc.cit.* See also the article of A. Bülow-Jacobsen, "The Archiprophetes", in *Papyrologica Bruxellensia*, vol. 19, part 4, 1979, pp. 124-131, where the usage of this term (confined, in the papyri, to the Roman period and later) is examined.

[16] For Rome, see *Inscriptiones Graecae ad Res Romanas Pertinentes* (ed. C. Cagnat, Paris, 1911-22), vol. 1, Nos. 32, 109, 144 and 157.

[17] For Marseilles see I.G., vol. 14, part 2, section 3, p. 643.

[18] For Patara, which like Didyma claimed to have to do with the birth of Apollo: *ibid.*, vol. 3, number 680; see also Herodotus 1.182.

[19] For Claros see *Inscriptiones Graecae ad Res Romanas Pertinentes*, vol. 4, ed. G. Lafaye, Paris, 1927, reprinted Rome, 1964, nos. 1586-1589, and C. Picard, *Éphèse et Claros*, Paris, 1922, pp. 219ff, L. Robert, *Fouilles de Claros*, which is unavailable to me, D.E. Aune, *Prophecy*, (briefly only), p. 28, and most recently H.W. Parke, *op.cit.*, and the discussion below.

prophets of Apollo or of one of the Egyptian gods, in which case they fall in a separate category.[20]

(3) In early Christian literature the term was applied to those directly inspired members of congregations who claimed to speak on behalf of either the risen Christ or the Holy Spirit. The claim has recently been made that this Christian usage was facilitated by the fact that "In later Hellenistic times . . . frenzied enthusiasts were often called προφῆται, prophets were described as mantics."[21] Alongside this usage the earlier usages continued, with increasing evidence of the loose, metaphorical use.[22]

This overall consensus must now be examined. The first point to be made is that, in strict terms, very little of the pre-Hellenistic evidence is relevant to our concerns. As M. Turner correctly argues, "we can base no conclusions on the results of study of word-formation or etymology . . . we are only interested in . . . what the words meant in Paul's day."[23] Previous scholarship, however, has based many conclusions on such study, some of which require consideration in detail.

3. The Classical Period

The consensus as to the first stage of the history of the term would seem to be essentially correct. Contrary to the assertions of scholars such as Callan,[24] there are actually very few references to προφῆται as inspired persons in this early period, and in virtually every case they are inspired persons who also *announce* their own oracles. While Callan claims (p. 128) that "In connection with oracles προφήτης usually designates one who may

---

[20] One exception is the prophet of Zeus Arion noted by E.N. Lane, *Corpus Monumentorum Religionis dei Menis*, III (1976), p. 24, cf. p. 38. The great majority, however, fall into one of the two categories noted above.

[21] Boring, *Sayings*, p. 82. A similar claim is made even for the early Hellenistic period by Engelsen, *Glossolalia*, p. 57.

[22] See the references at note 30, below. On this metaphorical use see particularly W.A. Grudem, *Gift*, pp. 39-43, who argues that the wide spread of this usage militates against any automatic assumption in the N.T. world that a προφήτης was an authoritative divine messenger. This issue will be treated for both the New Testament and at the level of the Hellenistic evidence below.

[23] M. Turner, "Spiritual Gifts Then and Now", *Vox Evangelica*, vol. XV, 1985, p. 10. Similar points are widely made: see, for example, M.E. Boring, "What Are We Looking For? Toward a Definition of the Term 'Christian Prophet'.", *S.B.L. Seminar Papers*, 1973, Missoula, p. 144.

[24] "Prophecy and Ecstasy in Greco-Roman Religion and in 1 Corinthians", *Nov.T.*, vol. 27, 1985, pp. 125-140, and see below.

more precisely be called μάντις, i.e. the inspired medium through whom the god communicates . . .", the summary of Fascher is still far closer to the truth: μάντις and προφήτης are complementary terms, not equivalents. "Mantis und Prophetes ergänzen sich also. Mantis ist einer, der etwas sieht. Sofern er diese Geheimnisse den Menschen mitteilt, ist er Prophetes."[25] I know of only one passage, from Plato, where προφῆται are discussed with the focus on the process of reception of their messages, rather than on the announcing of them, and this will be discussed below.

Herodotus

Given that more than forty Delphic consultations are recorded by Herodotus, it is striking that in only one of these is the προφήτης even mentioned. In Book 9.93 one Evenius is said to have inquired at both Dodona and Delphi, asking the gods' προφῆται his question. It is possible that Dodonite terminology is here being assimilated to that of Delphi, though we cannot be certain. We might assume that the προφῆται were the officials to whom questions were formally submitted. As we saw in Chapter 5, however, there is little other evidence to support this hypothesis.[26]

Herodotus' only unambiguous mention of the Delphic προφήτης comes in Book 8, 36-37, where he tells the story of the miraculous destruction of the Persian column sent to attack the shrine during the great Persian invasion. Here he notes that all the Delphians had left the site to go into hiding, with the exception of sixty men and the προφήτης. These stayed

---

[25] E. Fascher, *Prophetes*, p. 13. Compare also the summary of Krämer, *art.cit.*, p. 790, cited above, and that of Crone, *Prophecy*, p. 37: "its primary reference is to the function of announcing or proclaiming the answer of the god to the enquirer whether directly or indirectly." The summary of Aune, that "While the term *mantis* is not synonymous with the terms *prophetes, hypophetes* or *promantis* (not every *mantis* is a *prophetes*, though every *prophetes* is a *mantis*), the last three terms are essentially synonymous" (*Prophecy*, p. 29) is mainly true, but the assertion that "every *prophetes* is a *mantis*" is completely false. Though the Delphic προφῆτις is also a μάντις, the Delphic προφῆται are never so described. Cf. J. Fontenrose, *The Delphic Oracle*, Berkeley, 1978, p. 218: "In most instances a προφήτης is not himself a μάντις . . ." The error is repeated by R.M. Berchman, in the article cited above at note 5.

[26] T.M. Crone, *Prophecy*, p. 22, on the other hand, suggests that Dodona may have imitated Delphi by introducing priestesses at an early stage, and that these προφῆται may have been assistants to the priestesses. For further treatment of the personnel at the oracle of Dodona see below. The case of Evenius and that of Xouthus in Euripides' Ion, ll. 413-416, cited above in Chapter 5, are the only ones known to me where the προφήτης receives the question from the inquirer.

behind, and witnessed the miracles that saved the temple. No hint whatever is given as to the προφήτης' official role. He is merely a high official who remains at the temple.

Herodotus has only two other references to the προφήτης of other oracular shrines. In 7.111 he mentions the shrine of the Bessi, who act as προφῆται, and explicitly states that it is a πρόμαντις who utters the oracles. In 8.135 he tells the story of Mys the Carian at the shrine of Ptoan Apollo, treated above in Chapter 5; we saw there that Herodotus again attributes the reply to a πρόμαντις whom he later also describes as a προφήτης, Plutarch (twice) says it was a προφήτης and Pausanias does not specify.

Plato

With the groundwork laid, we are now in a position to return to the terminology of Plato, where the discussion of Chapter 5 began. The Timaeus and Phaedrus passages have dominated scholarly attention, and it is time to set them in the wider context of Plato's complete usage of the term.

In Philebus 28b Socrates is chosen to act as προφήτης of a philosophical discussion group. In the dramatic context, this clearly means that he is to lead the discussion, and no more. He will speak for the group, to the group.

In Republic 366b poets, satirically described as προφῆται of the gods for their role in forming peoples' early theological opinions, are under discussion. The conclusion to which Plato is leading is that they will have to be expelled from any truly just society, for misleading the people. Once again (self-appointed) "spokesman" is the sense here.

In Phaedrus 262d the cicadas, whose song has formed the backdrop to the discussion, are humorously described as προφῆται of the Muses, who have presided over the discussion. Perhaps, says Socrates, they have given us our inspiration. The sense here is "mediator", and we ought not to press the light-hearted comment further.

In the Alcibiades II (a dialogue of doubtful authenticity), 148d-150a, a visit to the Oracle of Ammon in Libya is described. The προφήτης is mentioned twice as the official spokesman of the shrine, and the god.

In the "Myth of Er", at the end of the Republic (617-619), Socrates tells the story of a descent into the underworld. The souls of the dead go before Lachesis to be judged and assigned their next incarnation. The assignment is organised along the lines of a "lot oracle". A προφήτης lines the souls up before Lachesis, makes a speech, and then throws the "lots" down among the souls, for them to choose their new lives for themselves, according to their own folly or wisdom. His role here is consistent with what we have seen of προφῆται as convenors and supervisors of oracle sessions.

In Charmides 173c, Socrates argues that if σωφροσύνη is given the right to evaluate (note: *not* interpret) μαντική, then τοὺς . . . ἀλαζόνας ἀποτρέπειν (charlatans will be deterred), and ἀληθῶς μάντεις will be established as our προφῆτας τῶν μελλόντων. Μάντεις, those receiving oracles, inspired or augural, become προφῆται when they speak what they have seen and heard. Sane people must decide who they believe.

In Phaedrus 244a, discussed above in Chapter 5, the Delphic προφῆτις and other μάντεις are discussed as examples of valuable μανία. The social benefit of their μανία is gained when their inspired messages are publicly proclaimed.

Finally, in Timaeus 72, the character Timaeus argues that "it is customary to set the tribe of prophets to pass judgement upon these inspired divinations (τῶν προφητῶν γένος ἐπὶ ταῖς ἐνθέοις μαντείαις κριτὰς ἐπικαθιστάναι νόμος); and they, indeed, themselves are named μάντεις by some people who are wholly ignorant of the truth that they are not μάντεις, but ὑποκριταί of the mysterious voice and apparition (which μάντεις hear or see, C.F.), for whom the most fitting name would be προφῆται . . . μαντευομένων (spokesmen of the things divined).

This is the one and only passage in Plato, or *anywhere else* in Greek literature, where προφῆται are given the role of evaluating and judging the statements of μάντεις. It does not reflect known cult practice anywhere. Here, I think, normal oracular practice is bent to serve Plato's philosophical intentions. Just as προφῆται customarily speak for oracles, and supervise their deliberations in a formal sense, so now they will do so in a more philosophically responsible fashion.

With the one exception of the Timaeus, then, Plato's usage falls comfortably into the pattern we have seen elsewhere. Unfortunately the Timaeus passage, and one aspect of Phaedrus 244, have been permitted to dominate the entire discussion, with misleading results.

Summary

In brief then, the term προφήτης is not in this period primarily a term having to do with inspiration. It is a term which is used of high officials whose particular task was to act as the official spokesmen of oracular shrines. It was used of inspired persons such as the Pythia only in so far as they were seen as representing one other than themselves, while the question of the source of their authority, their inspiration or lack of it, was not expressed in the use of this term. At Delphi (regularly) and at Dodona (occasionally: Strabo 7.7.12 and 9.2.4, as well as possibly Herodotus 9.93) it was used in the feminine of the oracular priestesses, who also announced their own oracles. They were τοὺς προφήτας of the god: the προφῆται were the προφῆται of the shrine. It was also used in a derivative sense of any person speaking officially on behalf of another. Naturally, the question of inspiration did not arise in this context.

4. The Hellenistic period

As stated above, all three categories of usage may be found continuing in the literature of the Hellenistic period. Προφήτης still designates officials at oracular shrines, whether Delphi,[27] Ammon in Libya,[28] or others. It can still be used of inspired persons, though I would contend that this is again more a matter of their role as spokesmen than of their inspiration. Nothing requires us to believe that inspiration was believed to be a defining quality of προφῆται.[29] Finally, the term is widely used in this period in its looser sense, in which one person is designated a spokesman of another in a non-official capacity, or a person or discipline is called the spokesman of a semi-divine being or abstraction.[30] But the usages which one might describe as "metaphorical" are not the ones which scholars have found to be

---

[27] For Plutarch references see Chapter 5, note 20.

[28] Plutarch, Sayings of Kings, Mor. 180 d, Diodorus Siculus 17.51.3-7.

[29] Again, see Chapter 5, and the detailed discussion below.

[30] See, for example, Diodorus Siculus 1.2.2 and 21.17.4, where "History" is described as the προφῆτις of truth; Dio Chrysostom describes poets as προφῆται of wisdom in Discourse 7.101, and of the Muses in Discourse 36.42. In fact Fascher is quite correct to point out that Dio's use of the term is uniformly metaphorical, having to do with philosophers and poets: see *Prophetes* pp. 22-23. Plutarch has one of the characters in his Pythian Discourses described as a προφήτης of Epicurus, Mor. 397 b, and as noted above, in Mor. 792 f he describes an old man as "leader and προφήτης of the sacred rites" of civic life: he was an example in both deed and word, and in that sense a spokesman. Similarly Sextus Empiricus describes Timon as the προφήτης of Pyrrho and his philosophy, Adv. Math. 1.53, and Lucian has Diogenes describe himself as a prophet of truth and boldness in "Philosophies for Sale" 8.

problematic. We must now examine the Egyptian, Septuagintal and epigraphic evidence in more detail.

Egypt

The problem is that the Greek term προφήτης applied in the Ptolemaic period to a whole class of Egyptian priests who, though they may occasionally have oracular duties, are most certainly not characteristically oracular officials. Native Egyptian priesthoods in Ptolemaic Egypt were made up of three broad ranks, which were then further subdivided. The Egyptian titles for these three broad classes of priests may be translated as "God's servant" (hem neter) for the upper ranks, "Divine father " for the second ranks, and "Pure one" (wab) for the lower echelon. It is with the first of these groups that we are concerned, for the title for all such "God's servants" was uniformly translated as προφήτης. This was so for those of the highest grade, (commonly rendered into English as "First prophet") and for the second, third, fourth or lower grades of "God's servants". Within these grades only one official, the "God's servant who reports" (hem neter wechem) had any oracular function: he was the priest charged with officially proclaiming oracles which had been given within the temple. Why then was the title προφήτης used for all such "God's servants"? A persuasive solution for this problem has been advanced by Kees.[31] He argues that whereas in the 18th and 19th Dynasties the title "God's servant who reports" was one of the titles of High Priests, "First god's servants", by the later period (22nd Dynasty) it had become the title of a separate official. In the Ptolemaic period, and even earlier, it was no longer even a separate office, but merely a function, which might be exercised by the "First prophet" or by some other "prophet", but not by a priest of lower rank. Only "God's servants" could be "God's servants who report". While in major temples it would be the "First prophet" who would officiate, smaller temples, which might only have one first rank priest anyway, would assign the task to one less exalted. According to Kees, then, the title "God's servant" was translated as προφήτης by the Greeks because it designated that rank of priests from which the official reporter or spokesman of an oracular response might be chosen. He was a προφήτης because he was of a rank sufficient to be

---

[31] H. Kees, "Der berichtende Gottesdiener", *Zeitschrift für ägyptische Sprache und Altertumskunde*, vol. 85, 1960, pp. 138-143. For a simple statement of the background to the problem see A. Bülow-Jacobsen, *art.cit.*, p. 130.

called upon to exercise the function of προφήτης. As we have seen in part, and as will be argued in more detail below, such a view is entirely compatible with the normal Greek view of the function of the προφήτης.[32]

It should be noted in passing that there can be no question of these priests being in any sense inspired, or the interpreters of inspired speech. Egyptian oracular practice knew of no such phenomenon, but was exclusively a matter of technical divination. The most common method was the placing of a written query before the image of the god in question, borne on the shoulders of a number of lower priests. The affirmative or negative response was deduced from the movement of the statue either towards or away from the written query. The view of Diodorus Siculus (27.50-51) that the bearers of the statue were inspired is a piece of Hellenistic rationalisation - if that is the right word.[33]

The Septuagint

We turn now to the Septuagintal usage, which has an *a priori* claim to be the most likely background to the New Testament terminology. We have seen above that the choice of the term προφήτης to translate the Hebrew *nabi* is not an obvious one. While "temple prophets" are occasionally mentioned in the LXX, they are clearly not the majority referent of the term *nabi*, which first and foremost signified the "free" prophets of Yahweh. The

---

[32] For a clear exposition of Egyptian oracular practice see J. Cerny, "Egyptian Oracles", in *A Saite Oracle Papyrus from Thebes*, ed. R.A. Parker, Providence, 1962, ch. 6, pp. 35-48. My thanks go to Dr Boyo Ockinga of Macquarie University and Prof. K.A. Kitchen of Liverpool University, who helped me to clarify my understanding of the Egyptian evidence. It is interesting to note that a passage of Epiphanius, Expositio Fidei 12 (*P.G.*, vol. 42, 803-4), discussing heresiarchs and other faction leaders, compares them with the Persian Magi, the Egyptian προφῆται, certain Babylonian priests called Gazareni, the Indian Brahmins and the Greek hierophants. All of these are simply high ranking priests: there is no suggestion that *any* of them have oracular functions.

[33] Compare Quintus Curtius 4.7.24, and, for the oracle of Hierapolis, Lucian, de Dea Syria 36. T.M. Crone's claim that the pseudo-Platonic author of the "Alcibiades" (148d-150a) says that "the god of the oracle spoke through the mouth of the prophet . . . the author was obviously thinking about some kind of direct inspiration as in the case of the Pythia . . ." (*Prophecy*, p. 35) is a misunderstanding of the passage. Though Alexander was told only what the god had said, this was because the προφήτης said to him "Thus says Ammon", a formula that tells us nothing about the method of divination whatever. Strabo 17.1.43, though critical of literary parallels with Homer, is quite explicit: "the oracular responses were not, as at Delphi, . . . given in words, but mostly by nods and tokens (συμβόλοις)", a description which fits very well with the model of Egyptian divination given above.

question is: what terms did the Septuagint translators have available to them? The answer is, very few. Only χρησμολόγος, ἐγγαστριμῦθος / ἐγγαστρίμαντις, μάντις, and πρόμαντις really suggest themselves as terms for inspired speakers of divine oracles. But χρησμολόγος overwhelmingly speaks of one who carries about and expounds oracles delivered at another time and place. Ἐγγαστριμῦθος and its related terms carried far too many negative connotations.[34] Μάντις was pre-eminently the term applied to those who told the future through "inductive divination", and since the time of the classical prophets all such methods of divination had been out of bounds for the strict Yahwist.[35] Only προφήτης, "official spokesman", was free of these problematical connotations. As the term for one authorised to deliver a statement on behalf of another, it suited at least part of the Hebrew concept of the prophet well.

Epigraphy

The epigraphic and papyrological field is the one area where large amounts of new information have become available since the early surveys of our problem were completed. As was noted above, there are now literally hundreds of inscriptions and papyri relating to προφῆται from the late Hellenistic and early Roman periods. Indeed, so wide is the field that it can only be touched on briefly. Purely for reasons of space I will not be dealing with the papyrological evidence here, since it requires a full study in its own right. I suggest that it will in all probability have to do exclusively with the Egyptian high priests styled προφῆται by the Greeks, and will therefore be of minimal direct interest to us as evidence for wider Hellenistic ideas.

The inscriptions of the great oracle centres are another matter. If there is a general popular concept of the role of those designated προφήτης from which to find parallels for the New Testament usage, here is where we should begin to search for it. Oracle cults had a very high profile in the Greek and Roman worlds, and the προφῆται of these shrines were among

---

[34] On the χρησμολόγος see the discussion of the case of Boring below. On the ἐγγαστρίμυθοι see the LXX, and below, in Chapter 11. For a fuller treatment of the Septuagint evidence see W.A. Grudem, *Gift*, pp. 34ff.

[35] Deuteronomy 1.10, 2 Kings 17.16ff, Isaiah 8.19, Jeremiah 14.14, Ezekiel 12.24, 13.7. J. Reiling points out, "The Use of ΨΕΥΔΟΠΡΟΦΗΤΗΣ in the Septuagint, Philo and Josephus", *Nov.T.*, vol. 13, 1971, p. 154, that the term μάντις is never used neutrally in the LXX, but always with pejorative connotations.

their highest officials. The evidence of Didyma, the single most extensive and coherent body of information, will be examined in detail.[36]

We know that in the second and third centuries A.D. the shrine at Didyma had at least three officials who had to do with giving oracles: the προφήτης and two with the title Θεοπρόπος, one called a ποιητής and another simply ἱερεύς.[37] I know of nothing further about the ποιητής, though his title is highly suggestive, but the evidence for the προφήτης is substantial. From at least the first century B.C. two προφῆται were appointed at Didyma annually,[38] the choice from a small field of candidates being made by lot.[39] It was regarded as a particular honour to be appointed "unallotted", i.e. unopposed.[40] Though election may have been theoretically open to quite a wide circle, in fact the position of προφήτης was dominated by a fairly small group: the ruling elite of Roman Miletus.[41] The titles of those who set up inscriptions commemorating their term/s of office as προφήτης read like lists of major positions in both local and provincial affairs. Among those who held the position I have counted one Asiarch (Inscription 369) and several relations of Asiarchs, eleven Stephanephoroi (the highest annual position in the Milesian hierarchy),[42] and then (in no particular order), eight Agonothetes, eight more Agonothetes of the Great Didymeian festival and one of the Augustan Games, two Agoronamoi, two Archiprytaneis, three Boularchs, three Tamiae, five Strategoi (one of whom had held the position twice), eighteen Gymnasiarchs, four High Priests of the Augusti, two high priests of Ionia (one of whom had also been High Priest of Augustus), four "patrons of the (Milesian) Senate", and five who had taken part in international embassies. Twenty inscriptions showed that their owners had held four or more high public offices. Only three had held the post of

---

[36] On the officials at Didyma see now also J. Fontenrose, *Didyma: Apollo's Oracle, Cult, and Companions*, Berkeley, 1988, pp. 45ff.

[37] *Didyma Inscriptions*, No. 552. A Θεοπρόπος is otherwise normally a delegate *to* an oracle or other shrine, particularly in Ionic Greek: see Herodotus 1.48, and Liddell and Scott.

[38] *Didyma Inscriptions*, Nos. 298, 314, 359.

[39] *Didyma Inscriptions*, Nos. 555, passim.

[40] *Didyma Inscriptions*, Nos. 377, 388, 395.

[41] Between 34 B.C. and 10 A.D. we have a list of ten προφῆται from only four families, in Inscription 322.

[42] *Didyma Inscriptions*, Nos. 120, 163, 222, 333, 350, 356, 377, 385, 409, 460, 571 and possibly 289.

προφήτης more than once.[43] Perhaps three others demand particular attention. Inscription 318 tells us of Lysimachos the son of Sopolis, who lead the embassy to Rome in 39/8 B.C. which resulted in Miletus being permitted to re-establish its ancestral democratic constitution. He also led an embassy to Ptolemy of Egypt, and was clearly one of the leading figures of his time.[44] Second, Claudius Chionis recorded in his inscription a remarkable career which for him seems to have culminated in holding the post of προφήτης and ἀρχιπρύτανις in the same year. He had already been an Eparch (Prefect) in Rome, a Military Tribune in Alexandria, and private secretary to Messala, proconsul of Asia, as well as holding local posts as choregus and gymnasiarch (several times). Most prestigious of all, he had been on embassies for the Emperors, and had been High Priest of the Augusti in Miletus.[45] Third, and perhaps most striking, we have the anonymous worthy who proudly proclaimed himself to have been the fifth ever Roman Senator to be chosen from the whole of Asia, and the first and only one so far from Miletus and Ionia, and High Priest of the Augusti.[46]

Such was the class of persons who at Miletus were thought worthy to be προφήτης of Apollo. What is surprising about this wealth of data is how little it tells us about the role of the προφήτης. The focus of the inscriptions is uniformly on positions held, honours voted, contributions towards building projects and festivals, ancestry, and the occasional personal note. But what did the prophet actually do in his duties as prophet? We have only occasional hints. Nothing whatsoever suggests any personal experience of inspiration or revelation. Indeed, one προφήτης notes with pride that he is an Epicurean philosopher: if he took this at all seriously, he most certainly could not have believed in the process of divination, and his role at the

---

[43] *Didyma Inscriptions*, Nos. 357, 358 cf. 365, 395.

[44] Compare H.W. Parke, *op.cit.*, p. 69.

[45] Inscription 366. J. Delamarre, "Notes Epigraphiques", *Revue de Philologie*, vol. 19, 1895, pp. 131ff., argued that this inscription ought to be dated in the early third century, denying that the Messala in question could be the proconsul of the final few years of Augustus. He provided no evidence for this point, however, and McCabe and Plunkett date the inscription in the first century.

[46] *Didyma Inscriptions*, No. 323, dated somewhere in the first century A.D. R.J.A. Talbert argues that there were virtually no Senators from Asia until after the accession of Vespasian, *The Senate of Imperial Rome*, Princeton, 1984, p. 31. See the discussion in H. Halfmann, *Die Senatoren aus dem östlichen Teil des Imperium Romanum bis zum Ende des 2.Jh. n. Chr.*, Göttingen, 1979, p.108.

oracle could only have been a formal one.[47] We know a little about the garb of the προφήτης in office (Inscription 555 mentions a wreath, though that is hardly surprising), and that he was himself in a position to inquire of the oracle (Inscription 551), and was occasionally addressed by the oracle (Inscriptions 409, 551, 555, 579).[48] But we do not know what official it was who addressed him in the name of the god. In plain terms, the main business of the oracle, the giving of oracular responses, hardly features at all in the inscriptions of the προφήται. Where the duties of the προφήτης are specifically mentioned they are *uniformly financial*. One could fulfil one's duties as prophet "piously towards the gods and philanthropically towards the citizens"[49] and since the inscription goes on to record a monetary distribution by the προφήτης in question, there can be little doubt what that means. Three inscriptions explicitly note expenditure as having been undertaken as part of the office of προφήτης, and in several others the suggestion, though only implicit, is very strong.[50] We also know that when no-one was able to take up the position of προφήτης (or possibly no-one could afford to due to the expense involved), Apollo himself was officially declared to be προφήτης.[51] Finally, in A.D. 101/2 the post was taken by the Emperor Trajan himself.[52]

---

[47] *Didyma Inscriptions*, No. 279. His Epicureanism, of course, may not have been thorough-going (his evident involvement in local politics strongly suggests it was not! Epicureans generally took little or no part in politics at all, though for a notable exception see Athenaeus 5.215), but the example is still striking. Compare the statement of Parke, *op.cit.*, p. 42: "Clearly such a short-term official could not be expected to act as the vehicle of the god's inspiration." and see also his similar statements in "The Temple of Apollo at Didyma", *J.H.S.*, vol. 106, 1986, pp. 121ff.

[48] *Didyma Inscriptions*, No. 555 has the προφήτης Herakleon Nikiades greeted by Apollo as he takes office. But even here, strangely, this event is not the focus of attention. The emphasis is placed far more heavily on the honour of being selected by lot than upon being welcomed as prophet by the god.

[49] *Didyma Inscriptions*, No. 337, cf. No. 372.

[50] Explicit: *Didyma Inscriptions*, Nos. 163, 377, 382. Implicit: Nos. 360, 365, 366, 372 noted above. Compare Parke, *op.cit.*, p. 42: "As it also acquired over the years expensive obligations, such as feasting the townsfolk at his cost on stated festivals, in practice the prophetship tended . . . to fall into the hands of a group of leading families . . ."

[51] This expedient was adopted as early as the first century B.C., as well as later. See *Didyma Inscriptions*, Nos. 293, 296, 317.

[52] See *Didyma Inscriptions*, No. 474.

In summary, the position of προφήτης at Didyma would appear to have been perhaps the highest religious honour to which a citizen of Didyma could aspire, but its duties were ceremonial and financial, like those of so many other official positions in local government under the Roman Empire. As far as we can tell it required no particular specialist religious qualifications, let alone what we would call "personal spirituality". It was a position of high honour from which the powerful were expected to undertake public works or other benefactions for the Temple itself, or the community at large. The epigraphic evidence, rich though it is in such detail, tells us virtually nothing about the functioning of the Oracle itself.[53]

Though the evidence is limited, there seems no reason to argue that the ceremonial duties of the προφήτης at Didyma were other than those suggested by his title: acting as official spokesman of the shrine, by publicly announcing the results of oracular consultations or by making other public statements on behalf of the shrine.[54]

One other feature of the evidence requires our attention. Three inscriptions certainly, and another possibly mention a προφῆτις, though they give no clues whatsoever as to her duties and relationship to the

---

[53] As far as I am aware there are only two exceptions to this picture. One is Inscription 390, which mentions a spontaneous oracle given to a προφήτης, most probably in the early third century. Such an event, if it actually occurred, and is not merely "a fantastic piece of self-advertisement" (H.W. Parke, *op.cit.*, p. 88,) is quite unique at Didyma, and extremely rare anywhere in the historical period. The other is a piece of description in a poem set up to commemorate the building of a fountain in the shrine itself in the late third century. It says that μαντική is "beloved of the Nymphs, who pour out the divine πνεῦμα upon προφῆται." The mention of Nymphs is perhaps reminiscent of Plutarch's attribution of oracles to δαίμονες, but the concept of πνεῦμα θεῖον being poured out onto προφῆται in particular is quite unique. The reference is, however, very late, and may be either simply a piece of poetic looseness of expression, or evidence for the poet's knowledge of the Biblical text or Christian or Jewish writings, where such terminology is common. H. Kleinknecht suggests ("Πνεῦμα", *T.D.N.T.*, vol. 6, 1959, E.T. 1968, p. 347) that "Here πνεῦμα θεῖον might well be an apologetic concept . . . in opposition to the spiritual utterances of Christianity", and this may be true, though there is no way to be sure.

[54] Compare Parke, *op.cit.*, pp. 214-215. Prophetesses are also known from other areas, though they are rare: see C.I.G. 3796, (= R. Merkelbach, ed., *Die Inschriften von Kalchedon*, Bonn, 1980, p. 56, No. 61), *Dialectorum Graecarum Exempla Epigraphica Potiora*, ed. E. Schwyzer, Leipzig, 1923, No. 633, p. 302, and *Tituli Asia Minoris*, vol. 3, ed. R. Heberdey, Vienna, 1941, No. 870, p. 263. On prophetesses at Didyma see below.

προφήτης.[55] She may be, as Parke has suggested, the equivalent of the Pythia at Delphi. She may equally be a woman filling the role of προφήτης in exactly the way her male colleagues did. Unfortunately we simply do not have the evidence to decide.

Having surveyed the epigraphic evidence from Didyma we are in a position to ask one final question before embarking on the next stage of our investigation. What was the relationship between the prophet and the other officials of oracular shrines? Here our evidence is too varied to allow for firm general conclusions. At Didyma, for example, priesthoods were lifetime appointments, and the prophetships were two annual appointments made by lot from a limited selection of candidates. We do not know whether one had to be a priest to be eligible to be prophet, though the question may be soluble through a thorough study of the inscriptions. At Dodona the three προμάντεις/προφήτιδες were also described as priestesses, but we have insufficient evidence to analyse the male side of the hierarchy.[56]

At Delphi it has been suggested that "The office of the prophet was exercised by one of the priests of the shrine, but whether all the priests were in turn prophets is not certain . . ."[57] Certainly there were two or more

---

[55] *Didyma Inscriptions*, Nos. 178, 450, and possibly 533; the text of the graffito mentioned by Parke, *op.cit.*, is not available to me. The suggestion of Parke, *op.cit.*, p. 42, cf. p. 213ff, *art.cit.*, pp. 124ff, that "as at Delphi" the προφήτις was the inspired medium of the god was until recently based only on the Delphic parallel, but a recently found inscription, reported by J. Fontenrose, *Didyma: Apollo's Oracle, Cult, and Companions*, Berkeley, 1988, p. 55, has made it certain. The remainder of Parke's reconstruction of the oracular procedure at Didyma, pp. 210ff., must remain speculative. The evidence of Iamblichus on which it is loosely based is late, and his sources are unknown to us. In a rare slip, D.E. Aune, *Prophecy*, p. 28, note 65, says there was a πρόμαντις at Didyma. He cites Origen, Contra Celsum, 1.70 and Iamblichus, de Mysteriis 3.11, but Origen mentions only a προφήτις, and Iamblichus speaks of a γυνή χρησμῳδός and a προφήτις (twice). In any case Aune is correct to say that she is never mentioned in the inscriptions by the title πρόμαντις. The most common title for women in the functioning of the oracle is ὑδροφόρος. Beyond the raw facts of the titles in a late source we have little to go on, and as we have argued above, drawing parallels between the different shrines is a dangerous procedure. There is certainly no evidence that the προφήτης at Delphi was elected in anything like the way it was done at Didyma, and certainly the social status of the role was different at the two shrines. Despite the recently discovered inscription, we must remain equally uncertain about the details of the background and role of the προφήτις.

[56] See T.M. Crone, *Prophecy*, pp. 21ff, and Strabo 7.7.12 and 9.2.4.

[57] T.M. Crone, *Prophecy*, p. 33. Footnote 64 continues: "Plut. Quaest. Conviv. viii 1 (717d) seems to imply that all the priests were προφῆται.". This suggestion is followed

prophets at the shrine, but here we have no inscriptional evidence to help us. At other shrines the evidence is even more fragmentary. Only one pattern suggests itself to me as even a tentative hypothesis. It seems possible that generally speaking προφήτης was the title of those particular persons (priests at Delphi) chosen to publicly report oracular sessions. This may have been on an occasional basis as at Delphi (perhaps a roster: we cannot be sure), or on an annual basis, as at Didyma. If this hypothesis can be accepted, it would throw extra light on the question of the Egyptian προφῆται, who were likewise priests exercising a specialist function. The question as to why the Greeks chose the term προφήτης to refer to these officials would then be no puzzle at all, as the task of the Egyptian προφήτης would correspond exactly to that of his Greek counterpart. It would likewise explain the lack of Delphic inscriptions, as the προφῆται would not set up inscriptions under that title, but simply as priests. The hypothesis remains speculative, however, and we will have to wait for further evidence to come to light to verify or falsify it.

5. Recent Characterisations of Hellenistic "prophets"

Inspired and frenzied prophets.

Despite the clear evidence for the contemporary usage of the term laid out above, it is still widely argued that in the later Hellenistic period, προφήτης was a common term for inspired speakers. As noted above, M.E. Boring claims that

In classical times there had existed a distinction between μάντεις, who were enthusiastic, ecstatic recipients of revelation from the divine world, and προφῆται, who were basically interpreters and proclaimers of revelation. Μάντις has an ecstatic element in the root idea of the word itself that is completely lacking in προφήτης . . . even in classical times this theoretical distinction was not always maintained . . .

In later Hellenistic times this distinction was hardly maintained at all, and as frenzied enthusiasts were often called προφῆται, prophets were described as mantics.[58]

---

by Aune, *Prophecy*, p. 28 and note 50, citing W.R. Halliday on the Plutarch reference, but the implication Crone makes is not convincing. That *some* of the priests were also prophets is indicated by the case of Nicander, as Crone correctly notes, citing de Defectu Oraculorum 51 (Mor. 438b) and Plutarch's de E. apud Delphos generally.

[58] M.E. Boring, *Sayings*, p. 82. According to H. Krämer, *art.cit.*, p. 791, this identification is first made by Iamblichus. That is much too late to be of interest to us.

A very similar case is made by T. Callan, who argues that, for the period in which we are interested, the term προφήτης could function as an equivalent for the term μάντις. He argues that this was its prevalent use.[59] The claim, however, cannot withstand detailed analysis. Boring is mistaken at several points.

First, it may be true that "Μάντις has an ecstatic element in the root idea of the word itself", but it is not relevant. It is simply not true that "μάντεις... were [sc. exclusively or even mainly] enthusiastic, ecstatic recipients of revelation from the divine world". The term μάντις is commonly used of people who are plainly totally non-inspired diviners. Μάντις and πρόμαντις are both terms used regularly of both "technical" diviners and "inspired" diviners, and the term's etymology tells us nothing about its later usage.[60]

Secondly, we have seen in Chapter 5 that it is not true that προφῆται were "interpreters" of divine revelation. That is a misunderstanding based on no evidence whatever of actual oracular practice, and only one passage in Plato.[61] Elsewhere in his writings Plato's distinction is the normal one:

---

[59] T. Callan, *art.cit.*, p. 130: "Although προφήτης is used most often to designate the medium of an oracle, it is also used frequently to refer to other spokesmen." But Callan produces only one piece of direct evidence for this suggestion: Phaedrus 244 a-b, discussed below, which specifically discusses only one προφῆτις: the Delphic Pythia. As we have seen, this cannot be taken as typical at all.

[60] Compare D.E. Aune, *Prophecy*, p. 21: "The presence of abnormal behaviour of the type associated with possession trance and possession cannot be inferred from the root meanings of such terms as *mania, enthousiasmos, entheos, katoche,* or the like . . ." and p. 35: "This etymological derivation, however, contributes little or nothing to our knowledge of most diviners in the Greco-Roman period." For examples of the use of the term μάντις of purely technical diviners see Dionysius of Halicarnassus, A.R., 9.6.3, 9.40.1 and 9.55.2, where it is his term for the Roman augurs. Though they are normally called οἰωνιστής or similar (for which see H.J. Mason, *Greek Terms for Roman Institutions*, Toronto, 1974, p. 116.), their business is described as μαντική. In fact the term μάντις is overwhelmingly used of technical diviners, with the exception of Delphic μαντική, and seers of the ancient past such as Cassandra and the various Sibyls. This is doubtless due to the fact, dealt with in detail below, that technical divination was the dominant form of μαντική in the Hellenistic period everywhere except at the great oracle centres. The only exceptions of which I am aware are one in Plutarch and one in Pausanias, dealt with below, and Dio Chrysostom 1.54ff (dealt with in Chapter 6, above), which is clearly a literary fiction. It tells us that such people existed, but gives no actual examples.

[61] The passage, of course, is the much discussed Timaeus 71e-72b, for which see Chapter 5, and above. Is Plato referring to Delphic practice at all? It is possible he is,

μάντεις are those who receive messages from the gods and προφῆται are those who proclaim them. On occasion the one person may fill both roles.[62] In the early Hellenistic period, then, the classical distinction still held. The question is whether this remained the case.

Thirdly, we must note that the Timaeus passage itself does not support Boring's suggestion that "In later Hellenistic times this distinction was hardly maintained at all, and as frenzied enthusiasts were often called προφῆται, prophets were described as mantics." Though Plato argues that "some ignorant people" confuse the two, we should note that he reports that they call προφῆται μάντεις: nothing at all suggests that they call frenzied people προφῆται, which is precisely the point Boring wishes to establish. Further, it is hard to believe that any educated person in "later Hellenistic times" did even this once Plato had spoken on the subject![63]

Fourth, we must ask what actual examples of frenzied people or mantics being called προφῆται Boring can produce. They are as follows: the Pythia in Lucan's account of the visit of Appius Claudius to Delphi, Pharsalia 5.61ff, the Sibyl in Vergil's Aeneid 6.45-51, (both dealt with in Chapter 6), Alexander of Abonouteichos in Lucian's Alexander the False Prophet, and Philo's account of the Old Testament prophets. But the first two references are both in Latin, where (naturally) the term προφήτης is not used at all (the

since Aune notes, *Prophecy*, p. 39, that the discussion is part of one following on the Delphic maxim, "Know Thyself". But Aune correctly adds that "Nowhere else is the Pythia described . . . as having visionary experiences . . . he may be combining two or more kinds of inspired divinatory phenomena." H. Krämer (*art.cit.*, pp. 787-8) also correctly notes that "the inner motif of this description and evaluation of the σώφρων προφήτης is Plato's concept of the philosopher; for this reason one must exercise caution in drawing conclusions as to the actual practice at Delphi."

[62] As noted above, this point was correctly understood by H. Krämer, *art.cit.*, p. 790. In Charmides 173c, for example, the distinction is perfectly clear: μάντεις are the προφῆται of the future. T.M. Crone's citation of the passage from the Charmides (*Prophecy*, p. 34) to support the contention that "the prophet in Plato's Timaeus 71e-72b was to assess critically what was uttered in ecstasy" and that these references "reveal the *general* function of the Greek prophet" is very misleading: though the Charmides does speak of μαντική having to be guided by σωφροσύνη, nothing at all suggests that this σωφροσύνη is embodied in a "rational" προφήτης. No other evidence than the Timaeus passage itself supports such a conclusion. The Charmides passage does not suggest that rational judgement of μαντική will lead to proper interpretation of genuine oracles; it suggests such evaluation will put frauds out of business!

[63] Pausanias certainly sticks to the classical usage: in 10.33.11 the people of Amphicleia receive dream-oracles from Dionysus, who they call their μάντις; the ἱερεύς who utters them under inspiration (ἐκ τοῦ θεοῦ κάτοχος) is a πρόμαντις.

Latin vatis is used in both passages for both the god and his priestess): even if it were, it would not prove his point, as in each case the lady in question filled the role of both μάντις and προφῆτις. In the case of Alexander we have a μάντις who became a προφήτης by founding an oracular shrine and appointing himself chief official of it: his pretence of frenzy and inspiration happens before he becomes a προφήτης. His operations as a προφήτης are totally devoid of frenzy and inspiration, even if we discount the obvious bias of Lucian: he becomes the chief priest of the shrine, leading the ritual and making public proclamation of oracles. In his wandering period Lucian calls him a γόης: he would probably have claimed the title μάγος or μάντις. Finally, Boring argues that "Philo considers the authors of all Old Testament books to be prophets, who receive their revelations in Dionysian ecstasy . . ."[64] But as we have seen in Chapter 6, this is something of a misunderstanding of Philo's view of inspiration. Furthermore, it is hardly evidence of what was widespread in the late Hellenistic world: Philo's readership was extremely limited outside Jewish and Christian circles.

Fifth, Boring's general statement, that "Plato, Lucan, Lucian, Vergil and Philo only illustrate a point that could be documented many times over: prophecy was generally an enthusiastic, ecstatic phenomenon in the Hellenistic world"[65] must be examined. First, Boring has shifted his ground. His statement might or might not be true of "prophecy" in some modern sense, but it is certainly not true of those called προφῆται in the sources he has cited, which is the point he set out to establish. Second, προφητεία is certainly *not* "an enthusiastic, ecstatic phenomenon": it is the solemn business of the highest ranked official at oracular sanctuaries. Third, not even all μαντική in the Hellenistic world was "an enthusiastic, ecstatic phenomenon". In fact, as we shall see, very little of it at all could be so described. Boring's error seems to me to be another example of reliance on what Aune calls "the Greek ecstatic model" of prophecy,[66] and its deleterious effects on New Testament scholarship.

The only direct piece of evidence for the contention that the term προφήτης was widely used as a synonym for μάντις in the Hellenistic

---

[64] M.E. Boring, *Sayings*, p. 83.
[65] Ibid.
[66] D.E. Aune, *Prophecy*, p. 17, citing D. Hill.

period that T. Callan brings forward is the famous passage from Plato's Phaedrus, 244, as follows:

the greatest of blessings come to us διὰ μανίας, when it is sent as a gift of the gods. For the προφῆτις at Delphi and the ἱέρειαι at Dodona when they have been in frenzy (μανεῖσαι) have conferred many splendid benefits on Greece . . . and if we should speak of the Sibyl and all the others who by prophetic inspiration (ὅσοι μαντικῇ χρώμενοι ἐνθέῳ) have foretold many things to many persons . . . we should speak a long time . . . The ancients, then, testify that in proportion as prophecy (μαντικὴ) is superior to augury (οἰωνιστικῆς), both in name and in fact, in the same proportion madness (μανίαν), which comes from god, is superior to sanity (σωφροσύνης), which is of human origin. Moreover, when diseases and the greatest troubles have been visited upon certain families through some ancient guilt, madness has entered in and by oracular power (προφητεύσασα) has found a way of release for those in need . . . [67]

Here, in a discussion of the role of the prophetic priestesses of Dodona and Delphi, Plato argues for the virtues of inspired frenzy (μανία). Since the Pythia is described as a προφῆτις Callan argues that προφῆται are characteristically frenzied. But once again this ignores the fact that the Pythia has a double role. In respect of the shrine she serves, she is a (προ)μάντις. In respect of Apollo, the great μάντις, she is a προφῆτις. Since it is μαντική that is under discussion, we may safely argue that it is the προφῆτις' role as a μάντις with which Plato is concerned. As for the priestesses of Dodona, no other evidence suggests that they were frenzied or inspired. The Hellenistic evidence (discussed below) is unanimous that they practised various forms of technical divination. It is thus quite hard to know what to make of Plato's statement. We have several options: he may be using the term μανία in a less specific sense, such as might be consistent with inductive divination, or he may be speaking only generally, with little attention to the fine details of Dodonite practice: he may be reflecting a popular view that differed from actual practice. It is even possible that in his period there was inspired divination at Dodona, though I know of no other evidence that might suggest this. Finally, it is possible that the sharp distinction between technical and inspired divination is simply not applicable here, though again, none of our other evidence suggests so. Whatever the solution to this puzzle, however, the προφήτης terminology is perfectly consistent with the picture outlined above: Callan has added nothing to the case of Boring.

---

[67] T. Callan, "Prophecy and Ecstasy in Greco-Roman Religion and in 1 Corinthians", *Nov.T.*, vol. 27, 1985, pp. 129-130.

Finally we must examine certain evidence that Boring has not cited. We noted above, in Chapter 5, that in four passages Plutarch spoke of the inspiration of people that he describes as προφῆται. In Mor. 412 a he describes the giving of an oracle to Mys, the Carian, by the προφήτης of Ptoan Apollo. In Mor. 414 e Plutarch severely criticises a popular theory of the inspiration of prophecy, arguing that it would be foolish to suggest that the god himself actually enters the bodies of his προφῆται. The argument has no particular Delphic reference, but given that Plutarch was himself a Delphic priest, it does more than suggest that people did believe that persons called προφῆται, including those at Delphi, were inspired. In Mor. 431 b. he discusses the causes of the inspiration of prophets and prophetesses in general. Finally, in Mor. 438 a he discusses the inspiration (ἐνθουσιασμός) of those who prophesy (προφητεύουσιν) generally.

It seems to me that all four of these passages can be understood quite adequately within the framework laid out above. One person could occupy the role of both μάντις and προφήτης, and when this happened, their inspiration could be discussed. Nothing forces us to give up the classical distinction between the two roles. Indeed, one reading of Aelius Aristides' To Serapis 47-49 (and cf. Peri Rhetorike 11-13) would strongly suggest that precisely the same distinction was drawn in the mid-second century, between προφῆται who happened to be mantic (who spoke under an inspiration similar to that of the poets, and thus spoke in verse) and προφῆται who were not mantic (most probably technical diviners) who, like the Pythia (in this later period) and the priestesses of Dodona, prophesied in prose, as was also the case with the dreams given by Asclepius and Serapis.[68] Μάντις is the term for an inspired person. A μάντις *may* also be a προφήτης, if he/she proclaims his/her own oracle as well as receiving it. But it is the proclaiming, not the reception, that constitutes him or her a προφήτης/προφῆτις.

---

[68] The interpretation of this passage is, however, very difficult. Depending on how strictly Atticist Aristides is, he may be saying that those προφῆται who are mantics speak in verse (using the classical sense of ὁπόσοι), or he may simply be saying that prophets (who are mantic) speak in verse (using the looser Koine sense). The context seems to me to favour the former interpretation, which suggests a distinction between prophets who are mantic and prophets who are not (perhaps technical diviners), but dogmatism would be most unwise.

Finally we should consider once more the case of the oracular priestesses of Dodona. It seems likely that there were προφῆται at Dodona in the classical period (Herodotus 9.93), but we know nothing of their role. The priestesses who are called προμάντεις by Herodotus (2.55) in the classical period are called τὰς ἱερείας, προφῆται and τὰς προφήτιδας by Strabo in the first century (7.7.12 and 9.2.4.). Might this provide some basis for Boring's hypothesis? No: for Strabo never calls them μάντεις, and there is precious little evidence that they were inspired. The bulk of our evidence suggests that in our period their methods of divination were purely inductive.[69] Insofar as the priestesses practised such divination (or any other kind) they were properly termed μάντεις or προμάντεις; insofar as they announced the conclusions of their divination they were properly termed προφῆται.

In summary, very little if any evidence supports the claim of Boring and Callan that in the Hellenistic period the term προφήτης was widely used for inspired persons. Even if some of the arguments brought forward here are not decisive, it must be clear that the overwhelming majority of usages of the term have to do with persons who were not inspired or frenzied in any sense. It is therefore highly unlikely that this hypothetical sense for the term προφήτης has any bearing at all on the question of early Christian prophecy.

Prophets as wandering teachers

The second claim mentioned at the beginning of this survey as requiring our attention is that implied by the work of T.M. Crone. As was noted in Chapter 2, Crone sets out to show that certain features of the claims and lifestyle of some Hellenistic wandering preachers are useful parallels to the phenomena of early Christian prophecy. Strongly implied by this case is the claim that certain of these wandering teachers were described as προφῆται, and that this usage of the term allows us to better understand its application to Christian prophets.[70]

---

[69] All of our evidence, that is, except Plato's Phaedrus reference treated above. See Pausanias 8.23.5 (the oak), Strabo 7 fragment 1 (observing the flight of birds), Cicero, de Divinatione 1.34 (the use of the lot) and the archaeological evidence of the site itself, for which see T.M. Crone, *Prophecy*, p. 23, and Aune, *Prophecy*, p. 52.

[70] That the claim is implied, though it is nowhere stated, is suggested by two considerations, one general and one specific. At the general level, Crone's entire case is developed around the occurrences of the term προφήτης. This is both its strength and

The individuals Crone chooses for close investigation are Apollonius of Tyana, Alexander of Abonuteichos, Pythagoras and Peregrinus Proteus. For each of these four (with the exception of Pythagoras, who is only touched on briefly) he gives a brief summary of our evidence, noting the phenomena that suggest that they ought to be seen as prophets. Before we examine this in detail, however, one chronological point ought to be made. Though Pythagoras belongs to the fifth century B.C., Apollonius to the first century A.D., and Alexander and Peregrinus to the mid-second century A.D., *all* our evidence for their careers comes from the late second century or after: more than a century distant from the N.T. phenomena. Crone presents no evidence at all that relates to the immediate environment of the New Testament. He is aware of the problem, and when it comes to actual comparison of the types of "prophetic" figures in each culture, uses his parallels only with respect to the second-century Christian phenomena.[71] He likewise admits that only two of these figures are explicitly described as προφῆται,[72] though he believes his case is strengthened by the fact other philosophers are described as προφῆται (in the metaphorical sense on which we have touched above). At the level of the terminology, then, the implied claim mentioned above remains, and it is this which we must examine.

For Apollonius we know that he was widely regarded as a "magos", and that Philostratus' "Life" is partly intended to disprove the idea. He travelled as a popular teacher, collecting students as he went. He is reported to have worked miracles, foretold the future and manifested superhuman knowledge, and to have spoken by divine impulse. His wisdom is seen as divinely given. He is, however, never described as a προφήτης.

For Alexander we have the hostile account of Lucian (treated above in Chapter 7), which none the less contains much valuable material. Lucian describes Alexander's career as a religious confidence-trickster, giving circumstantial details of his fraudulent cult-foundation at Abonuteichos. Crone notes that

---

its weakness. More specifically, Crone is at pains to show that several of the figures he examines *are* described as προφῆται. As we shall see, this is highly misleading.

[71] T.M. Crone, *Prophecy*, p. 286. It ought to be noted, however, that he does claim, without detailed argumentation, that "there are sufficient indications to conclude that this Hellenistic counterpart exercised an influence on the Christian prophet already in the first century".

[72] T.M. Crone, *Prophecy*, p. 39.

He announced his discovery (of the "egg of Asclepius") to the city in a frenzy, uttering meaningless sounds . . . which Lucian compares to Hebrew or Phoenician. This frenzied state was undoubtedly meant to be a sign of Alexander's inspiration. He also invented a myth for the founding of the oracle in which he is designated as the προφήτης (Alex. 22).[73]

But then Crone gives away a significant weakness in his case, by admitting that

Although Lucian is primarily interested in Alexander's activity at the oracle in Abonuteichus, he spent the earlier part of his life as a wandering preacher and wonderworker . . . this serves as an example of how indefinite were the lines between cult personnel and popular teacher in the middle of the second century.[74]

But surely the point is that Alexander is *not* designated a prophet until he founds the oracle and settles down: at no stage is he a "wandering prophet". First he wanders. Then he settles down, and appoints himself prophet. That he was able to found a successful oracle marks him out as extraordinary, and one suspects that "the lines between cult personnel and popular teacher" were not nearly as vague as Crone suggests.[75]

Crone's final case, Peregrinus Proteus, is extremely important for his argument, for not only does Peregrinus wander, but he is known as a prophet in Christian groups. He eventually loses his status due to his luxurious lifestyle. Crone points to him as a parallel with the wandering prophets of the Didache, but the parallel with Hermas is in some ways at least as close. However, there is a critical weakness in Crone's case here. For Peregrinus is not a Hellenistic "prophet" at all! He is a Hellenistic wandering preacher who at one point in his career was a *Christian* prophet, and a lapsed Christian prophet is hardly a Hellenistic parallel for Christian prophecy. Crone's material is valuable, and can certainly be used with profit to develop parallels with Christian prophecy; the fact that Lucian notes that Peregrinus was known as a prophet is an important fact. But he is nowhere described as a prophet during the non-Christian part of his career.

There is, then, no evidence to suggest that the term προφήτης was used as a title for wandering teachers and philosophers. The suggestion that the early Christian usage of the term is in some way indebted to a wider usage

---

[73] T.M. Crone, *Prophecy*, p. 50.

[74] *Ibid.*

[75] H. Krämer is more correct when he says (*art.cit.*, p. 795) that "Historical seers and prophets not connected with an oracle are never called προφῆται but χρησμολόγοι or the like."

than the classical that was becoming current in the Hellenistic world cannot be supported. It would seem that the most likely background for the early Christian usage of the term προφήτης should be sought in the Septuagint and the Judaism of the synagogues, rather than in the Hellenistic environment of early Christianity.

6. Summary

On the basis of the above argumentation I would suggest that it is clear that the attempt to find parallels between early Christian prophets and those described as προφῆται in the Hellenistic world is not particularly useful. As I suggested at the beginning of this chapter, the differences between the way προφῆται were seen and their roles understood in the two cultures are simply too great. If we are to find any meaningful points of contact between early Christian prophecy and prophecy and oracles in the Graeco-Roman world, it is the phenomenon of prophecy itself, rather than those called prophets, around which the attempt must be organised.

Chapter 9

Christian Prophecy in Luke-Acts and the Letters of Paul

We turn now to an attempt to characterise early Christian prophecy as we find it in the writings of Luke and Paul. Our task is to deal with several major related issues to do with early Christian prophecy, which may be summarised briefly as: "What?", "Where and When?" and (in the next chapter) "Who?". Under "What?" we will try to establish what the characteristic activities were that early Christians described as prophecy. As was noted in Chapter 3, Luke's and Paul's understandings of the nature of prophecy differ in some details, and these will be dealt with here. Under "Where and When?" we will inquire as to the normal setting of early Christian prophecy, the typology of early Christian prophets, and the period of time over which prophecy was a common phenomenon in Christian groups. Under "Who?" in the next chapter we will deal with an issue already raised in the previous chapter: the degree to which early Christian prophecy was a matter of "specialist prophets", and the degree to which prophecy was a gift available to any or all early Christians; we will also inquire whether particular groups were either widely encouraged, or forbidden, to prophesy. This will lead to a discussion of the question of the legitimation and evaluation of prophecy within early Christianity. Finally we will again attempt to ask the question: what was it that had led to disputes breaking out between Paul and his congregation in Corinth about the nature of prophecy? This question will be dealt with from the New Testament evidence alone, before we turn, in Chapter 11, to consider whether parallel phenomena in the wider Greek and Roman world cast any light on the question.

1. What was early Christian prophecy?

In Chapter 8, above, I argued for a definitional procedure closely related to that adopted by M.E. Boring.[1] This procedure began with actual

---

[1] "What Are We Looking For?: Toward a Definition of the Term 'Christian Prophet'", *S.B.L. Seminar Papers*, 1973, Missoula, 1973, pp. 145-6.

occurrences of the term prophecy (or related terms) in our sources, and then set out to find what activities and functions were seen as characteristic of what was called prophecy. Using this procedure, a core of material will be built up, around which related activities can be linked more or less directly to prophecy.

It is gratifying to see recent research reaching a reasonable degree of consensus as to the nature of prophecy. Max Turner summarises his own view and that of several recent writers as follows:

> For Paul prophecy is the reception and subsequent communication of spontaneous, divinely given *apokalupsis* . . . the declaring of a revelatory experience.[2]

For Luke, however, matters are not quite so clear-cut. It is clear that both Luke and Paul believe prophecy to be a matter of speaking under the inspiration of the Holy Spirit. For Luke, however, virtually any speech inspired by the spirit may be described as prophetic, whereas Paul subdivides such speech into several types, of which prophecy is only one. We will deal with Luke's view first.

Though the speeches of Elizabeth to Mary in Luke 1.42 and Simeon with Jesus' parents in Luke 2.28 are not explicitly described as prophecy, despite the fact that they are "filled with the Holy Spirit" (Luke 1.41) or "moved by the Spirit" (Luke 2.27), Zechariah's speech in 1.67 is so described, when he is likewise "filled with the Holy Spirit". Anna's thanksgiving in Luke 2.36ff is attributed to her as a prophetess. In Acts the Pentecostal glossolalia is described by Peter as prophecy (Acts 2.4, 14-17) and its content (the "wonders of God") is likewise the content of the glossolalia of Cornelius' household in Acts 10.44ff;[3] in Ephesus glossolalia and prophecy are closely

---

[2] M. Turner, "Spiritual Gifts Then and Now", *Vox Evangelica*, vol. XV, 1985, pp. 10-11. Thus also, in essence, G. Friedrich, in *T.D.N.T.*, "Προφήτης", and J.D.G. Dunn, *Jesus and the Spirit*, London, 1975, p. 228: "For Paul prophecy is a word of revelation. It does not denote the delivery of a previously prepared sermon; it is not a word that can be summoned up to order, or a skill that can be learned; it is a spontaneous utterance, a revelation given in words to the prophet to be delivered as it is given." Likewise Grudem, *Gift*, pp. 116, 142. The view of Grudem that the fact of revelation does not necessarily mean absolute authority (pp. 69-70, 116-119), even if correct, in no way compromises the revelatory nature of prophecy as such. Nor does Grudem intend such implications to be drawn; cf. p. 118: "The "revelation" which comes to the prophet is thought by Paul to be of divine, not human origin" and p. 143: "if there is no *apokalypsis*, there is no prophecy . . ."; cf. p. 140ff. generally. He argues that in the NT the term comes to be used specifically of the type of revelation related to Christian prophecy, rather than other kinds of revelation (p. 134).
[3] The suggestion of G. Friedrich, *T.D.N.T.*, vol. 6, 1959, E.T. 1968, p. 854, that Peter's Pentecost sermon should be characterised as προφητεύειν, which thus "has missionary

linked. This much we have dealt with in Chapter 3, above. For Luke, as for the Didache (10.7 and 15.1), inspired prayer and praise would appear to be prominent among the activities characterised as prophecy.[4] The content of that prayer and praise usually has to do with the unfolding of God's purposes. Thus there is very little distance between this function of prophecy and the other which is prominent in Acts: prediction of coming events (Agabus in both Acts 11.27ff and Acts 21.10ff.). More will have to be said about prediction as an aspect of Christian prophecy later in this chapter.

Paul, on the other hand, sharply distinguishes between glossolalia and prophecy. Nor is this merely a polemical outworking of his dispute with the Corinthians. His differentiation of the charismata is characteristic of his whole thought on the matter. Glossolalia and prophecy are also to be distinguished from "words of knowledge" and "words of wisdom", which are also mutually distinct, though the nature of the distinction is certainly not clear to us.[5] "Gifts of healing", for him, are to be distinguished from "miraculous powers", though to us the categories seem to have an obvious overlap. But to return to prophecy: for both Luke and Paul it would appear to be true that prophecy is public proclamation of a revelatory experience, and predominantly a verbal one at that. Revelations for one person only are not normally called prophecy; prophecy is public. Nor is the telling of a vision described as prophecy, so far as I am aware.[6] For Paul prophecy is normally "immediately inspired": that is, in normal circumstances the public proclamation ought to follow immediately on the reception of revelation.[7]

---

significance" is a serious misreading of the Acts passage. Peter (and / or Luke) regards the Pentecostal glossolalia as the fulfilment of Joel's prophecy, not his own sermon.

[4] G. Friedrich's suggestion, *loc.cit.*, that a similar link is to be found in Paul, is based only on 1 Thessalonians 5.17-20 closely linking prayer and prophecy. The link does not seem particularly close to me.

[5] Scholars' attempts to distinguish between this pair of gifts have been singularly unconvincing. T.W. Gillespie, for example ("A Pattern", p. 85), points out that C.K. Barrett and J. Héring draw precisely the opposite conclusions as to what the two terms mean, and what distinguishes them. (The same point is made in his thesis, *Prophecy and Tongues*, p. 68.)

[6] Thus Paul does not describe his "visions and revelations" of the third heaven as prophecy, nor what God said to him about the consequent "thorn in his side". This distinction also seems to hold in Acts 27.21ff, where Luke has Paul recount a revelation, but does not describe it as prophecy. The same point applies to dreams.

[7] 1 Corinthians 14.30, a passage which will be discussed in detail below. W.A. Grudem also notes in this context that while ἀποκάλυψις is a necessary condition of prophecy, it is not a sufficient condition: ἀποκάλυψις only becomes prophecy when it is publicly proclaimed. See *Gift*, pp. 133ff, p. 139-40, citing e.g. Romans 1.17-18 and Philippians 3.15 for revelations that are not described as prophecy. M.E. Hart, *Tongues and Prophecy*, p. 284, D. Hill, in "Christian Prophets as Teachers or Instructors in the

For Luke this may also be the case, but we do not have the explicit evidence to be certain.[8]

Luke's definition of prophecy, then, is relatively broad and less precisely laid out than that of Paul.[9] But neither writer offers an explicit definition of prophecy, and we must remember that those given above are tentative, based on implications drawn from narrative (in the case of Luke) and occasional comments which may be situationally or polemically conditioned (in the case of Paul). We must not expect absolute terminological precision of our sources, which are occasional writings, not philosophical treatises.

If this is what Luke and Paul believed prophecy to be, our next three questions are: (1) what did early Christians *do* when they prophesied? (2) what purposes did they believe that this form of speech served? (3) in modern perspective, what was the function of prophecy in early Christian groups?

What did early Christians do when they prophesied?

The short answer is that they made statements which they claimed were made not on their own authority, but on the authority of God/Christ/the Holy Spirit.[10] But this is far from adequate. They were not the only ones within early Christianity to make statements backed up by such claims, nor does the short answer tell us what kinds of statements these might have been, or in what form or forms they might have been brought forward.

With Luke we are in a position to make some immediate statements. They praised the "mighty works" of God, predicted coming events, and (presumably) selected individuals for special tasks, helped in the solving of disagreements, and gave guidance in the making of other kinds of decisions.[11] We have, however, very little information as to how this was

---

Church", in Panagopoulos, *Vocation,* and D.E. Aune, *Prophecy,* note 54 to p. 255, similarly argue that prophecy is public proclamation.

[8] We have no evidence as to when Agabus, for example, received his revelations. Indeed, it is often hypothesised that he made his two journeys, to Antioch and to Caesarea, in order to deliver revelations received previously. This is possible, but must remain speculative, as Luke simply does not say.

[9] M.E. Hart notes correctly that "distinguishing between the various utterances which he (sc. Luke) attributes to the Spirit is difficult" (*Tongues and Prophecy,* p. 82). Thus while Zechariah's speech inspired by the Spirit is called prophecy, Peter's speech in Acts 4.8 is not so described, despite the fact that Peter is "filled with the Spirit" at the time.

[10] Cf. Aune, *Prophecy,* p. 204: "The prophet was unique among early Christian leaders in that, unlike other functionaries, he claimed no personal part in the communication which he conveyed." See also M.E. Boring, *art.cit.,* p. 149, W.A. Grudem, *Gift,* pp. 118, etc.

[11] For these last three see Aune, *Prophecy,* p. 192. I say "presumably" because in the

done, as Luke's reports are simply too condensed. In Antioch we know that Agabus stood up (apparently in a congregational meeting) to deliver his message, but we have no direct report of his words. In Caesarea he simply approached Paul and his companions and delivered his message, with its associated "acted parable", and though the context suggests a meeting of some kind (21.12), we know nothing more. The "prophetic" speech of the disciples at Pentecost and the later cases where prophecy is linked with glossolalia strongly suggest a spontaneous overflowing of excited praise, but tell us little else.

For Paul the situation is both better and worse. It is worse because we have no examples whatever of prophetic speech explicitly so called. It is better because we have his comments on how prophecy ought to be handled and the results it ought to have within a congregational setting, in 1 Corinthians 14. It is hard to know, however, how far these are conditioned by the particular situation in Corinth. What is reasonably clear is that with the exception of the matter of inspired prayer and praise, treated above, Paul's evidence suggests a view of prophecy very similar to Luke's. For example, though Luke never explicitly describes the revealing of the secrets of men's hearts (linked firmly with prophecy by Paul in 1 Corinthians 14.24-5) as prophecy, he clearly believes that such things occurred within the Christian community (Acts 5.1-10, 8.20-24, 13.9-11), and they certainly would fit within what we know of his definition of prophecy as inspired speech.

Predictive Prophecy?

To take a more contentious example: it has been denied, though there is strong circumstantial evidence that, like Luke, Paul believed that prophecy included (though it was in no way limited to) the prediction of the future.[12]

---

passages to which Aune refers, the Spirit is given as the origin of what was said, but no prophet is explicitly mentioned. W.A. Grudem argues, *Gift*, p. 78, that Acts 11.28, where speech "by the Spirit" is attributed to a prophet, is sufficient parallel to make the identification. If Luke does not count these examples as prophecy, we do not know what happened at all. On Agabus' prediction of famine, we should note that since J. Jeremias, "Sabbathjahr und neutestamentliche Chronologie", *Z.N.W.*, vol. 27, 1928, pp. 101ff, it has been common to argue that Luke has here "historicised" what was originally an eschatological prediction to do with the woes to precede the return of the Messiah. T.M. Crone, *Prophecy*, p. 96, is correct to argue that this view is pure hypothesis. It is in any case irrelevant for us, as we are concerned with Luke's view of prophecy. Crone also thinks (p. 198) that Agabus is the only example of a predictive prophet in the NT. He also argues that while "there can be no doubt that the Christian prophets made predictions of specific future events . . . we should not . . . make this the specific prophetic aspect of his activity." (p. 294) In this he is doubtless correct.
[12] G. Friedrich and M.E. Hart deny, for example, that Paul's idea of prophecy includes

While it is true that Paul's discussion in 1 Corinthians nowhere discusses prediction, the following points strongly suggest that he did see it as a prophetic function.

First, it was the uniform view of Judaism that the Old Testament prophets had been, among their other tasks, predictors of the future. This is also Paul's own view, as passages like Romans 1.2, 9.25f, 1 Corinthians 15.4 and 54 make perfectly clear. It is not just that certain passages in Scripture have application in his own time, due to the patterns inherent in God's saving activity ("as it is written"): in his view what God had done in Christ had been predicted long ago.[13]

Second, this was also the uniform view of the other New Testament writers. The note of prophetic fulfilment is seldom absent for long in Matthew's gospel, and, though it is less prominent in Mark and Luke, it is still there.[14] Likewise 1 Peter 2.6-8 and 2 Peter 3.2-4 testify to this view of prophecy. Jude 14 adds to this consensus, and verses 17-18 make the apostles predictors also.

---

prediction. Friedrich denies that the verb προφητεύειν is ever used of prediction, which, though correct, ignores Paul's use of προλέγειν, etc., for which see below ("Προφήτης", T.D.N.T., vol. 6, 1959, E.T. 1968, p. 829). More precisely, Hart, *Tongues and Prophecy*, p. 310, says that Paul never calls the prediction of *earthly* events prophecy. The distinction between the prediction of earthly and eschatological events seems a little fine-spun, however, in the light of the other evidence. In favour of Paul's view of prophecy including prediction are, for example, C.M. Robeck, "The Gift of Prophecy in Acts and Paul", *Studia Biblica et Theologica*, vol. 5, no. 2, 1975, p. 50; D.E. Aune, *Prophecy*, pp. 253ff, 258-9. Aune would certainly disagree with Hart, arguing that Paul himself predicts things both to do with the immediate and the eschatological future (pp. 258-9).

[13] On the Jewish side, see, for example, J. Blenkinsopp, "Prophecy and Priesthood in Josephus", *J.J.S.*, vol. 25, 1974, pp. 242ff, and J.T. Squires, *op.cit.*, pp. 129ff. See also, and most recently, L.H. Feldman, "Prophets and Prophecy in Josephus", *J.Th.S.* vol. 41 no. 2, 1990, pp. 386-422, esp. p. 396-400, and note 48, who argues that for Josephus, prediction is the one major feature of prophecy which *does* survive into his own time. The interpretation of the national past and the expounding of the present will of God which characterised the Biblical prophets are the features of prophecy which have ceased. For Paul the distinction between "fore-telling" and "telling forth" the will of God is simply not relevant. Of course Paul (and Josephus!) believes that the future is the future of God's plan, and His morally-charged action in history. But it remains the future none the less. The two categories are not mutually exclusive. It is likewise fruitless to argue that New Testament prophecy only includes prediction conditional on the moral response of the hearers: neither of Agabus' prophecies fits that model at all, and, as we shall see, Paul's evidence provides no evidence for the suggestion.

[14] See Mark 1.2, 7.6, 12.9, 13.24, 14.27, Luke 3.4f, 4.21, 7.27, 10.24, 20.17, 22.37: the list is in no way exhaustive.

Third, the sub-apostolic authors see the prophets of the Old Testament as predictors of the future work of God. The point hardly needs demonstration in detail: we need only cite, as examples, Justin's Dialogue with Trypho, especially 90.2 and 114.1, his First Apology, ch. 31, Irenaeus' Demonstration of the Apostolic Preaching, 5, 30, 34ff, his Adversus Haereses 4.34ff, and Tertullian's Apology, 18.5.

In the light of this unanimity, I suggest that it would be extraordinary if Paul did *not* think prediction was part of prophecy. We now turn to his own evidence.

Paul himself uses the terms προλέγω and προειπεῖν for prediction in 1 Thess. 3.4, 4.6, and Galatians 5.21. That he does so is strong evidence that he saw prediction as part of his own apostolic role, and though the contexts in which he uses the verbs do not have other oracular terminology, Aune has made a case for these passages being oracular.[15] We might add to this evidence the prediction in 1 Thess. 4.14-18, which is "by the word of the Lord", though Aune argues persuasively that in all likelihood it is not a prophecy given to Paul himself. In any case Paul clearly thought that predictive revelations were made within early Christianity.[16] It seems to me that in view of the consensus of our other sources that prediction was one function of prophecy, and of Paul's failure to provide us with an alternative category within which to place it, the onus of proof is definitely on those who would argue that Paul did not see it so.

Beyond this point we enter a field where descriptions of early Christian prophecy according to Paul are various, and there seems little to choose between them. G. Friedrich has described it as Spirit-endowed counsel,[17] D. Hill as inspired pastoral (as opposed to evangelistic) preaching, expressed in sustained utterance,[18] W. Grudem as the public proclamation of a revelation, the aim of which is the benefit of the congregation,[19] and D.E. Aune most simply as "Christian discourse presented with divine legitimation".[20]

The reason that all of these descriptions are credible is basically that our evidence is limited to what can be deduced from 1 Corinthians 14. From this evidence we know that if Paul's instructions were followed in Corinth,

---

[15] D.E. Aune, *Prophecy*, pp. 253ff.
[16] Romans 11.25-27, 1 Corinthians 15.51ff, and the passages cited above.
[17] G. Friedrich, "Προφήτης", *T.D.N.T.*, vol. 6, 1959, E.T. 1968, p. 855.
[18] D. Hill, "Christian Prophets as Teachers or Instructors in the Church", in Panagopoulos, *Vocation*, pp. 116-18 and 112.
[19] W.A. Grudem, *Gift*, pp. 143-4, 184.
[20] D.E. Aune, *Prophecy*, p. 338.

prophets stood to speak, addressed the congregation with their revelation, possibly added some comments "of their own", and were then seated. After each contribution, or possibly after a number of contributions, the prophecies were discussed and evaluated in the meeting.[21] Virtually any formulation consistent with these data would be acceptable.

Prophecy, Preaching and Teaching

There are, however, two areas in which our definition of "what happened" can be improved upon. Both have to do with the relationship between the functions of prophecy and preaching and teaching more generally. The first matter is simply this: what distinguished prophecy from other forms of speech such as preaching and teaching, as far as the early Christians were concerned? The second develops from an answer to the question: did Christian prophecy characteristically take the form of the (inspired) exegesis of the Old Testament?

On the first question, of what distinguished prophecy from other forms of speech, scholars have taken two differing lines. For David Hill, for example, the distinction between prophecy and teaching more generally conceived is that "the characteristic emphasis of the teacher may be found in his expository work: that is different from, but not opposed to, prophetic revelation . . ."[22] In arguing this case Hill is in line with much older scholarship which set out to distinguish prophecy and preaching in terms of their respective "functions". Prophecy has to do with new revelation, not the human development of previous revelation or other material.[23] It seems to

---

[21] That they possibly added interpretative comments is suggested by a reading of Acts 21.4, and also the priority Paul gives to new revelation: presumably he gives priority to revelation over interpretative comment or related exhortation, rather than to one revelation over another. See C.M. Robeck, *art.cit.*, pp. 26-28 and, for a different interpretation of the same suggestion, W.A. Grudem, *Gift*, p. 78, p. 81 note 150. The question as to who could take part in the ensuing discussion and evaluation of revelations is dealt with in detail below.

[22] D. Hill, "Christian Prophets as Teachers or Instructors in the Church", in Panagopoulos, *Vocation*, pp. 114 and 123. Compare the important observation of Grudem, *Gift*, pp. 142-3, esp. p. 142 note 47, that revelation in the New Testament leads to prophecy, not teaching.

[23] In this case "function" would appear to have no technical meaning; Hill and others are simply saying that prophets and teachers did different things. E.M.B. Green similarly argues that "The men of the first century knew preaching and teaching when they heard it, and they knew prophecy as well. The two were quite different. . . . It is one thing to prepare one's address in dependence on the Spirit, and to preach it in the power of that same Spirit; it is quite another thing to find the Spirit taking over and speaking directly from Christ through you, in words you had never intended to use at all." (*I Believe in the Holy Spirit*, Grand Rapids, 1975, pp. 170-171.) W.H. Mare argues not only that the two

me that such a view would fit very well with Paul's discussion of prophecy and teaching, where members of a congregation contribute "some revelation or knowledge or prophecy or teaching" (1 Cor. 14.6) These four elements should be seen as "two alternate pairs . . . *propheteia* is the outworking of *apokalupsei*, while the ultimate outgrowth of *gnosei* is *didache*."[24]

Others, however, argue that this attempt to distinguish between prophecy and preaching on the basis of their respective functions has been much overdone, and that the two "offices" are the ends of a continuous spectrum: thus M.E. Boring, speaking of prophecy and teaching, says that

Among recent writers there seems to be a fresh perception of the way the functions of prophecy and teaching shade into each other, with the result that the prophet is now seen as much more a teaching figure than formerly.

Boring admits, however, that this definition may not always fit the terminology of our sources. Elsewhere he suggests that

The better way to state the point is in terms of the *way* traditional materials are used by prophetic and non- prophetic figures. The prophet presents all that he utters as a prophet as the immediately inspired present address of the deity to his community. This message may well include material taken from tradition and the prophet's own reflection, consciously or unconsciously, with or without re-interpretation, but it is not presented as

---

roles are clearly distinguished in 1 Corinthians 12, but that in Ephesians "not only is the prophet listed separately from the teacher, but the latter is now connected with the larger concept of pastor (Eph. 4.11.)". See "Prophet and Teacher in the New Testament Period", *B.E.Th.S.*, vol. 9, no. 3, 1966, pp. 139-148, esp. p. 148. E.E. Ellis, "Prophecy in the New Testament Church - and Today", in Panagopoulos, *Vocation*, p. 51) argues that the distinction between prophets and teachers is that prophets have access to divine mysteries, and thus that the experiential source of their knowledge is different. James Dunn, *Jesus and the Spirit*, London, 1975, p. 228, suggests that "For Paul prophecy is a word of revelation. It does not denote the delivery of a previously prepared sermon; it is not a word that can be summoned up to order, or a skill that can be learned; it is a spontaneous utterance, a revelation given in words to the prophet to be delivered as it is given." Likewise W. Grudem, *Gift*, p. 116, 142. He argues that in the NT the term comes to be used specifically of the type of revelation related to Christian prophecy, rather than other kinds of revelation. (p. 134)

Of course, as M.E. Boring notes, *art.cit.*, p. 149, revelation need not be divorced from tradition: the prophet's message, even though revealed to him, may well contain traditional material. As he says, it is therefore not true that "if he uses tradition he is not a prophet". But this does not affect the arguments above.

[24] C.M. Robeck, *art.cit.*, part 2, p. 42, footnote 28. Compare Part 2, pp. 48-9: "for Paul, the gift of prophecy differs from preaching in that its content is not kerygmatic, and it differs from teaching in that teaching relies upon knowledge and exposition while prophecy comes from fresh revelation." W.A. Grudem, *Gift*, pp. 138-9 argues that the parallelism is implicit only, and ought not to be made to bear much weight: this seems to me to be an evasion of the clear force of the passage.

material which a past authority once said, but as what the deity now says. The same material may be presented by the non- inspired teacher or preacher, but with the formal and functional difference that this claim to immediate inspiration is not made.[25]

A similar view to that of Boring and Aune, but this time related specifically to preaching instead of teaching, was argued in 1971 by T.W. Gillespie, who suggested that the terminology of the kerygmatic and paraenetical preaching in Paul

does not prohibit an intellectual distinction between the two in analytical thought, yet does tend to discourage the view that they were artificially separated in actual practice. The paraenesis is best conceptualised as the unfolding of the same divine mercy announced in the kerygma, as "the exposition of the accomplished salvation act" . . .

. . . "He who prophesies" is thus one who preaches the gospel. This observation makes it possible to infer the content of prophecy from the theological meaning Paul attributes to the terms εὐαγγέλιον and εὐαγγελίζεσθαι. Whereas the kerygma proclaims the gospel according to the essential contours of its meaning, prophetic wisdom explicates through revelation the fullness of meaning that is only implicit in the kerygma; it unfolds and develops the as yet unexpressed content of the gospel.[26]

In other words, there is no functional distinction between the two. If taken at face value, Gillespie's second statement is going to far. Gillespie does show that the terms οἰκοδομή and παράκλησις can apply to both the missionary preaching and what we might call pastoral preaching. He has shown, and indeed common sense would suggest, that the two areas would have considerable overlap. But overlap is not identity. It is not at all legitimate to infer the content of one from the other. There may be some overlap, but at present we are not able to say what it might be. This point is emphasised by the fact that, with the exception of 1 Cor. 14.24-25, we have no Pauline evidence of prophecy being discussed in relation to unbelievers at all. Prophecy, as it is understood in Paul's letters, and as it is described in Acts, is overwhelmingly described as being an "in house" phenomenon.

---

[25] Boring, *Sayings*, p. 79, 80, and "What Are We Looking For? Toward a Definition of the Term 'Christian Prophet' ", *S.B.L. Seminar Papers*, Missoula, 1973, p. 149. The approaches of T.M. Crone, W.A. Grudem and D.E. Aune are very similar. For Crone, *Prophecy*, p. 291, "the *specific* characteristic of *prophetic* preaching" was that "The prophet was conscious of a degree of inspiration which allowed him not only to voice his own opinion but to speak the judgement otherwise reserved for the Lord himself." For Grudem, "prophecy cannot be distinguished from other speech activities simply by means of its functions, for there is no one function that will serve as a distinguishing characteristic" (*Gift*, p. 183). For Aune "the distinctive feature of prophetic speech was not so much its content or form, but its supernatural origin. Christian prophetic speech, then, is Christian discourse presented with divine legitimation . . ." (*Prophecy*, p. 338.)
[26] T.W. Gillespie, *Prophecy and Tongues*, p. 93, p. 102, p. 220.

But Gillespie has clearly qualified what he means by "inferring the content of prophecy" in the first and third statements quoted above. He only means that the content can be inferred in the most general sense, for the content of prophecy will be "the unfolding of the same divine mercy announced in the kerygma", "the exposition of the accomplished salvation act", and hence logically derivable from them. But this in no sense shows that Paul believed their functions to be identical. It shows only that he expected them to serve one similar generally conceived purpose.

In both these ways, then, scholars have argued that prophecy and teaching/preaching are not to be separated on functional grounds. Though several legitimate points have been made, it seems to me that the view itself is an over-reaction. The distinction between prophecy and preaching / teaching can be maintained along both lines. Prophecy is presented in the New Testament as inspired messages, and doubtless prophets believe it to be so. Preachers (and teachers) present their material as reports of past events, past revelations, and as the considered results of their own expository labours. But there is more than this. If one examines the use of the various verbs (ἀγγέλλω, κηρύσσω, etc.) usually translated by the English "to preach", they are overwhelmingly used of the proclamation of *past* revelation. Prophecy, on the other hand, is proclamation of revelation only just received. To put it another way, today's prophecy is tomorrow's preaching or teaching.[27]

Furthermore, we must note that, despite Gillespie's case, both the content and the audiences for prophecy and preaching are different. In both Acts and Paul prophets speak to the church, not to the world: preaching is normally addressed to the world, not the church. Prophecy is "for believers"; the one passage in which its effect on unbelievers is noted, 1 Corinthians 14.20-25, has been dealt with in Chapter 7, above.[28]

---

[27] See the similar statements of E. Best, "Prophets and Preachers", *S.J.Th.*, vol. 12, 1959. He defines the difference between the two "offices" by way of the more than human knowledge of the prophet, his direct inspiration, and his predictive function, pp. 146-150. Thus also M.E. Hart, *Tongues and Prophecy*, p. 313: "the content of the prophetic word is dependent on revelation, that of the teacher upon truths already accepted in the church."

[28] Max Turner suggests, *art.cit.*, p. 13, that prophecy is a sign for believers that is "transparent, too, to the unbeliever (vv. 24f.)". But even this is not as precise as the formulation in Chapter 7. Cf. D. Hill, *Prophecy*, p. 218; J. Reiling, *Hermas and Christian Prophecy*, p. 13: "The apostles preach the gospel to unbelievers, the prophetic ministry is primarily church centered." Likewise M.E. Hart, *Tongues and Prophecy*, p. 315; James Dunn, *Jesus and the Spirit*, London, 1975, p. 227. Likewise C.M. Robeck, *art.cit.*, p. 36: "At no time is the message of any prophecy in Acts the *kerugma*." T.M.

We also need to note that the predictive function of prophecy clearly separates it from other forms of speech. Prediction, based as it is on no human source of knowledge, cannot be the role of the teacher. In the New Testament it is not attributed to the preacher either, but only to prophets.

Finally we should note that "preaching" is not a category used by Paul, as far as we can see, in the same way that "prophecy" is. He nowhere calls preaching a charisma, and does not include "preachers" in his lists of those God has established in the churches.[29]

The attempt to distinguish prophecy and preaching / teaching has thus led to considerable clarification of the question of the nature of prophecy. We may summarise our understanding of Christian prophecy according to Acts and Paul as follows: prophecy is the reception and subsequent public declaration of (usually) verbal revelation. Such revelation is normally spontaneous (we have no clear examples of it happening in response to inquiries) and the subsequent declaration is normally immediate. Regardless of the novelty or familiarity of its content, the speaker conceives it to be revealed truth, rather than the results of his own thought processes. A person receiving a revelation which they believed to be for "public consumption" would normally stand in order to claim the right to speak. Prophecy might include, but was not limited to, the prediction of the future: it might equally be unsolicited guidance, exhortation, or remonstration. It was not normally the basic gospel proclamation itself, but might commonly be some application of its principles to a particular situation.

Prophecy and "Charismatic Exegesis"

Having dealt with the relationship between prophecy and preaching /teaching, we can now ask the question: did early Christian prophecy characteristically take the form of the (inspired) exposition of the Old Testament? The claim has been made on two bases. The first is

---

Crone also argues that "it [sc. prophecy] included few of those elements which we normally ascribe to the κήρυγμα . . . this is understandable in the light of prophecy's normal context within the community of believers." (*Prophecy*, p. 291) David Hill obscures this point when he argues that because the παράκλησις terminology is used in 1 Thessalonians 2.12 of evangelistic preaching, we may presume that "the New Testament attributes to prophets in the church the task, not only of kerygmatic proclamation, but of warning, instructing and correcting the congregation and individuals on the fringe . . ." (*Prophecy*, p. 129) Nothing in 1 Thessalonians describes what Paul and his associates did there as prophetic. See also the discussion of παράκλησις below.
[29] M.E. Hart (*Tongues and Prophecy*, p. 314) points out that Paul never mentions a gift of preaching. She speculates that this may be because preaching is directed mainly to outsiders, while gifts are mainly to do with insiders. Compare, however, the related passage in Ephesians 4.11ff, where evangelists are included.

circumstantial only. It is argued that in the immediate environment of the New Testament writers, (1) the Old Testament prophets were understood by first-century Judaism as interpreters of earlier revelation, (2) contemporary revelation (in first-century Judaism again) was widely believed to take the form of the interpretation of Scripture,[30] and (3) the term προφήτης was used in the Hellenistic world of persons whose divinatory methods included the inspired interpretation of collections of oracles.[31] The second basis is the more direct argument that the New Testament evidence itself suggests that "charismatic exegesis" was one of the forms characteristically taken by Christian prophecy.

The first and second points, that in the intertestamental period revelation was often seen in terms of Scriptural interpretation, would appear to be incontestable (though such revelation, if seen as continuing, was only rarely described as prophecy). The third, more precise claim that in the Hellenistic world the term προφήτης was occasionally used of persons who gave inspired interpretations of old oracles, has recently been made in order to suggest that "it is helpful to know that . . . 'prophet' and 'interpreter of scripture' were very congenial concepts." To support this statement, M.E. Boring (*Sayings*, p. 97) argues that

Plutarch, for example, describes an oracle-giver who reads from a manuscript but receives his inspired interpretations of this manuscript directly from the deity, so that he is in this sense a προφήτης, a proclaimer of new revelations.

This claim is made with reference to Fascher, *Prophecy*, pp. 25-6. But the argument is mistaken at several points. First, Fascher makes his claim on the basis of Aristophanes' "Birds", lines 972ff, not with reference to Plutarch. Second, Fascher does not claim that the χρησμολόγος is a προφήτης on the basis of inspired interpretations of his oracles. He claims it on the basis

---

[30] "only those prophets whom the Law needed in its self-development were recorded and given a place in salvation history . . . the prophets of the classical period are at root no more than interpreters of the Law speaking with the authority of the Spirit and charged to unfold only what the Law contains." (R. Meyer, *loc.cit.*, p. 818.) Meyer also cites examples from among the Essenes, Qumran, the Pharisees and the Zealots, as well as Philo. In this case, he argues, personified "Wisdom" is the origin of prophecy, and any truly wise man is a prophet. Philosophic contemplation and prophetic inspiration are identified, and, once again, biblical interpretation is central to this re-interpreted concept of prophecy. For Philo, of course, this is so because the Law is the very font of Wisdom. On all this see pages 812-823. Compare also T.M. Crone, *Prophecy*, pp. 59-61, pp. 107ff, pp. 138-9, J. Blenkinsopp, *art.cit.*, esp. p. 242.

[31] M.E. Boring, *Sayings*, p. 97.

of the text, in which the χρησμολόγος, citing one of his oracles, describes himself as a προφήτης. Third, though Fascher is claiming that the χρησμολόγος' interpretation of his collected oracles is inspired, there is nothing in the text to justify this hypothesis. The χρησμολόγος does claim to be impelled by the god to speak at one time rather than another, but nothing suggests that he believes his interpretations to be divinely given in any sense. This is implicitly admitted by Fascher, who says that "(er) . . . seine Deutung sicherlich ebenso als "göttlich" bezeichnen würde" (p. 26). In Plutarch, Life of Agesilaus, 3, and Xenophon, Hellenica 3.3.3, as well as Aristophanes' "Knights" 997ff and "Peace" 1045ff. there are other accounts of χρησμολόγοι, but still no suggestion that their interpretations of their selected oracles are inspired, or (with the exception of Birds 972 ff,) that they are called προφῆται by anyone. That such wandering soothsayers could on occasion appropriate the title, or could satirically be described as doing so in the fifth century, is not strong evidence that the term was regularly applied to them in the Hellenistic period. In so far as I am aware, the only evidence of χρησμολόγοι speaking oracles of their own, rather than of ancient mantics, is Herodotus 1.62 (6th Century B.C. reference), 8.96 (possible only: it is not clear whether the prophecy is inspired or merely recounted), Philo, de Spec. Leg. 4.52, and Pausanias 1.34.4.[32] Of these only Philo and Pausanias are close enough to our period to take seriously. While Philo says that such people use divination under the name of προφητεία, there is no way to check the semantic detail of this claim, since as we have seen in Chapter 8, above, the term is not used in extant secular Greek prior to Lucian. The Pausanias passage and the first Herodotus passage seem to be the only unambiguous passages where persons speaking under inspiration are designated χρησμολόγος. In the case of the Philo passage we do not know that they claimed the title προφήτης, though it is possible; certainly neither the title nor the claim to inspiration were characteristic of the χρησμολόγος.[33] J. Fontenrose is surely correct when he summarises the evidence as follows:

---

[32] Dio Chrysostom 13.36 is not relevant: Dio claims that "These same pronouncements (sc. as the ones I have just made as a philosopher) you will find were made both by Sibylla and by Bakis, if it be true that the two of them proved to be good χρησμολόγοι and μάντεις." The term μάντις is quite appropriate for both Sibylla and Bakis. In this context χρησμολόγος seems to be imported from those who normally hawked the oracles of those two legendary seers.

[33] Cf. D.E. Aune, *Prophecy*, p. 44.

Chrêsmologos and *mantis* are overlapping terms for a speaker of oracles . . . But the *mantis* as diviner, interpreter of omens and dreams, is not likely to be called a *chrêsmologos*; and the man who did not speak oracles through direct inspiration from a god, but possessed a collection or book of oracles that a god or former *mantis* had reputedly spoken was not called *mantis* but only *chrêsmologos*.[34]

As we have seen, the evidence that such people were called προφῆται is very slight indeed.

The possibility that prophecy might have been understood in terms of scriptural interpretation remains, however, on the basis of the Jewish evidence. We must therefore examine the New Testament to see whether the case can be substantiated. The main protagonists for such a case are E. Earle Ellis, E. Cothenet, and M.E. Boring.[35]

The weakness of Ellis' position is that he can find no cases in Acts (his chosen field) in which anyone both functions as an expositor of Scripture and is described as a prophet. He quotes Peter's three early sermons in Acts as evidence, but nowhere is Peter described as a prophet. Nor, for that matter, is the role of biblical exposition *ever* directly linked with a person being described as a prophet in Acts. Certainly people such as Silas and Barnabas are pictured as preaching from the Bible, but never in close association with the term "prophet". The only two instances of Christian prophecy we have from Luke in any detail, those of Agabus in Acts 11.27-28 and 21.10-11, are completely lacking in Biblical citation or allusion. Ellis' strongest case is made around the speech of James in Acts

---

[34] J. Fontenrose, *The Delphic Oracle*, Berkeley, 1978, p. 153. D.E. Aune (*Prophecy*, p. 40) claims "That Onomakritos had been caught forging an oracle may suggest that some *chrêsmologoi* . . . were inspired diviners who produced their own oracles and yet attributed them to such ancient and legendary worthies as Orpheus, Musaeos, Sibyl and Bakis." This seems to me to be most unlikely. Forgeries were made because, in order to gain credence, oracles normally had to come from one of the legendary figures above. Anyone believing himself or herself able to prophesy would have claimed to be able to do so. For other chresmologues see Herodotus 5.90-91, 7.6, and cf. Pausanias 1.22.7, 5.43.

[35] See Ellis' article, "The Role of the Christian Prophet in Acts", in *Apostolic History and the Gospel*, ed. W.W. Gasque and R.P. Martin, Exeter, 1970, pp. 55-67, reprinted and developed in detail in *Prophecy and Hermeneutic in Early Christianity*, Grand Rapids, 1978, pp. 129-144. Here it makes up part of Ellis' extensive thesis on the "prophetic" leadership of early Christianity and the forms of Biblical interpretation common within it. Compare Cothenet, "Les prophètes chrétiens comme exégètes charismatiques de l'écriture", in Panagopoulos, *Vocation*, pp. 77ff. M.E. Boring has taken the kind of case developed by Ellis and Cothenet and developed it further. Thus he argues that "As a prophet, Paul functioned as an interpreter of the Scriptures to the church for the last times. He interprets the Old Testament in the light of contemporary eschatological events . . ." (*Sayings*, p. 100) Compare D.E. Aune's criticism of this general case, *Prophecy*, p. 342-6.

15.16-21. Here James' exposition of Amos 9.11 is strongly reminiscent of Paul's exposition of the "mystery" of the inclusion of the Gentiles in Ephesians 3. Nowhere, however, is it suggested that James is speaking as a prophet! The most that could be argued (*pace* Aune, *Prophecy*, pp. 191-192) is that Luke believed that the guidance of the Spirit was at work at some point in the discussions. One might speculate that Christian prophets spoke in the debate, and that this is the origin of the phrase "it seemed good to the Holy Spirit and to us", but the phrase itself is the only evidence. Certainly, on my understanding of Luke's general definition of prophecy, any "inspired" interpretation of the Bible *could* be called prophecy. It is therefore all the more noteworthy that Luke does not so describe it.

Ellis notices the difficulty posed by Luke's unwillingness to describe people as prophets, but thinks this can be explained on the basis of the overlap between the roles of apostles and prophets. However, he has not been able to demonstrate any explicit link between the role of the "prophet" and biblical exposition. Luke does not seem to have seen such a task as characteristic of the prophet's role. It ought to be noted in passing that Luke never describes Paul himself as either apostle or prophet, and most characteristically calls Paul's role teaching.[36]

It is therefore ironic that an argument very similar to that of Ellis can be made out quite strongly in the case of Paul's understanding of prophecy. While Paul does not define the prophet's role in terms of exegesis any more than does Luke, he does make strong links between the revelation of "mysteries" and the exposition of the Bible. And the revelation of "mysteries" is characteristic of the prophet's role, as well as the apostle's: cf. 1 Cor. 13.2, 14.6, 29-30, Eph. 2.19-20, 3.4-6. There are definitely two and possibly four occasions in his letters where Paul expounds "mysteries" (Romans 11, 1 Cor. 15.51-57, and Ephesians 3.3-9 and Colossians 1.26-27, if these are Pauline), and in the first two, which are undoubtedly Pauline, his teaching is closely linked with passages from the Bible. For example, in Romans 11 vv. 25-26, Paul informs the Roman congregation of the "mystery" of the eschatological salvation of "all Israel". Aune describes this as "In all of Pauline literature . . . perhaps the clearest example of the prophetic or charismatic exegesis of the OT."[37] But to me the strongest

---

[36] See J.D.G. Dunn, *Jesus and the Spirit*, London, 1975, pp. 171-2, 186. Dunn does allow exposition to be part of the prophet's role, due to a failure to distinguish between "inspired interpretation" (which we must probably allow), "prophetic interpretation" for which there is little or no evidence, and just plain interpretation.

[37] D.E. Aune, *Prophecy*, p. 252. Cf. E.E. Ellis, *Paul's Use of the Old Testament*, Grand Rapids, 1957, p. 139.)

evidence for the claim is to be found in Romans ch. 16 vv. 25f (presuming this to be Pauline), where Paul offers praise to God as follows:

Now to him who is able to establish you by my gospel and the proclamation of Jesus Christ, according to the revelation of the mystery hidden for long ages past, *but now revealed and made known through the prophetic writings* by the command of the eternal God . . ."

If the Gospel is *now* made known through the prophetic writings, it is entirely plausible that this revelation (φανερωθέντος) is to be thought of as prophetic.

From these passages, with the explicit linkages they draw between the revelation of mysteries and the exposition of the Bible, we can conclude safely that as far as Paul himself is concerned, the inspired interpretation of the O.T. may be at least one part of the role of a prophet. The question remains, however, as to what extent it is a constitutive part, and to what extent a merely auxiliary one. Does the prophet cite Scripture because it is meditation over it which forms the background to his revelatory experience? Because he sees his role as the inspired exegesis of it? Or simply because, having received his revelation, he, or others who use his material, naturally turn to the Bible for corroborative, explanatory (and in the case of Romans 11, tendentious) detail? That is the question that must be answered, before we can speak with confidence of "charismatic exegesis". And that is the point, I would contend, where our evidence gives out. How are we to tell the difference between charismatic or prophetic exegesis and exegesis of the less inspired kind?

To put the question another way: we noted above that M.E. Boring has argued that "As a prophet, Paul functioned as an interpreter of the Scriptures to the church for the last times. He interprets the Old Testament in the light of contemporary eschatological events . . ."[38] But is it "as a prophet"? This Boring and Cothenet have not proven. Boring's argument, citing Ellis, that in four places where Paul cites the Bible in forms that differ from both the MT and the LXX, the words λέγει κύριος are inserted in the text. Since this phrase is the mark of OT prophetic statements, Ellis and Boring suggest, we have here the "free peshering" of the Bible by Christian prophets. Aside from the multitude of sins covered by the phrase "free peshering", the argument has one striking weakness. There is no direct evidence whatever that *Christian prophets* used it as an indicator of their prophetic consciousness. D.E. Aune has shown that there is no need to understand the

---

[38] *Sayings,* p. 100. Compare E. Cothenet, *art.cit.,* in Panagopoulos, *Vocation,* pp. 77ff.

"says the Lord" phrase as anything more than a tag indicating the source of the quote as being the Bible.[39]

E. Cothenet, on the other hand, argues that Acts 13.16-41 is a prophetic sermon, due to its nature as παράκλησις and the promise / fulfilment schema around which it is structured. But such a schema is prominent in virtually all early Christian preaching: what makes it prophetic? And while the term παράκλησις is used of prophetic speech, it is by no means restricted to it.[40]

That Christian prophets (or at the very least, Christian inspired teachers such as Paul) made free and creative use of the Bible is not in question. Whether it can be detected by way of λέγει κύριος formulae, and whether or not such Biblical exposition was a defining characteristic of their role is a question which has not been examined by Boring. When he goes on to argue that the use of such quotations by Paul is "a convincing corroboratory bit of evidence for the prophetic aspect of Paul's own ministry" his argument has simply become circular.[41]

But even if it could be shown that biblical exposition were a major part of the role of Christian prophets, that would still be completely unhelpful in allowing us to distinguish what made Christian prophets' use of the Bible different from the use of the Bible by Christian non-prophets. The suggestion of Ellis and Boring simply fails at the level of logic to tell us what was distinctive about *prophets*. To describe Peter's speech in Acts 2 as προφητεία[42] is simply tendentious. Does Luke so describe it? No: that is

---

[39] Aune, *Prophecy*, pp. 343-5. On this point see also Hill, *Prophecy*, p. 106-7. D.A. Carson points out further (*Showing the Spirit*, p. 92) that similar quotations in the Epistle of Barnabas are called teaching, not prophecy.

[40] E. Cothenet, "Les prophètes chrétiens comme exégètes charismatiques de l'écriture", in Panagopoulos, *Vocation*, 1977, pp. 77-107. A similar error occurs in the cases of M.E. Hart, *Tongues and Prophecy*, p. 79, and T.M. Crone, *Prophecy*, p. 290, when they argue that in Acts the function of prophecy must include the exposition of Scripture because Acts 13. 15-43 links παράκλησις with Paul's synagogue exposition in Pisidian Antioch. But it is the synagogue leaders who ask for a word of παράκλησις. Surely Luke is not suggesting that *they* expected prophecy! Cothenet likewise puts forward 1 Corinthians 10.1-11 and 2 Corinthians 6.14-18, but all the above points apply. See also my discussion of the παράκλησις terminology, below.

[41] M.E. Boring, *Sayings*, p. 101.

[42] *Ibid.* On the other hand Boring is quite correct to say that "Luke's descriptions of those he specifically designates as prophets give no indications that prophets function as interpreters of Scripture, . . .", *Sayings*, p. 101. Likewise David Hill says that "it would be invalid to limit prophecy to the interpretation of Scripture or to assume that the

Luke's description of the glossolalia that preceded it! Presumably most if not all early Christians speculated about the relationship between their own beliefs and the Bible. What, if anything, made the prophets distinctive?

So two points of logic as well as the lack of direct evidence forbid us to conclude that early Christian prophets were characteristically expositors of the Bible, and that this (specifically prophetic) "charismatic exegesis" was a critical factor in the development of early Christian theology. First, we have no way of knowing what might have characterised specifically prophetic exposition, as opposed to any other kind. Second, if Paul *is* to be understood as a prophet, we do not know whether the prophet cites Scripture because it is meditation over it which forms the background to his revelatory experience, because he sees his role as the inspired exegesis of it, or simply because, having received his revelation, he, or others who use his material, naturally turn to the Bible for corroborative and explanatory detail.

Summary

According to Luke and Paul, Christian prophecy was the reception and immediately subsequent public declaration of spontaneous, (usually) verbal revelation, conceived of as revealed truth and offered to the community on the authority of God/Christ/the Holy Spirit. It might include, but was not limited to, the prediction of the future: it might equally be unsolicited guidance, exhortation, or remonstration. It was not normally the basic gospel proclamation or κήρυγμα itself, but might commonly be some application of its principles to a particular situation. Here Max Turner's careful statement is applicable: the content of prophetic speech is "particularistic knowledge - not merely general principles that could be deduced, for example, by illuminated reading of the Torah, or from the Gospel tradition or from the apostolic Διδαχή."[43] It was distinguished (in Paul's thought at least) from teaching and preaching in both form and content, though overlap was obviously possible. Finally, though the "prophet" might well cite the Bible, either in the words of the prophecy itself, or (in my view, more likely) in his/her comments upon it, we have no evidence that "inspired interpretation"

Christian prophets were bound to a particular method or tradition of interpretation . . ." (*Prophecy*, pp. 199-200)

[43] "Spiritual Gifts Then and Now", *Vox Evangelica*, vol. XV, 1985, p. 12. Turner's definition seems to me to remain generally valid in the second and third centuries, with the exception of Montanism: see C.M. Robeck, Jr., "Canon, *Regula Fidei*, and Continuing Revelation in the Early Church", in J.E. Bradley and R.A. Muller, eds., *Church, Word and Spirit: Historical and Theological Essays in Honor of Geoffrey W. Bromiley*, Grand Rapids, 1987, pp. 65-91.

of the Bible was a constitutive part of prophecy for either Luke or Paul.[44] There may well be what we may call inspired or "charismatic" exegetes at work in the Christian communities, and their methods, in all probability, were as Ellis and others describe them. But what our evidence does not allow us to do is simply identify them with those described by Luke and Paul as "prophets".

2. The "Function" of Prophecy.

With this issue settled, we can now ask: what purposes did they believe their prophesying served? The question of the function of early Christian prophecy has been confused due to lack of definition. For some scholars "function" seems to mean "intended result": thus the function of prophecy is said to be edification, encouragement, or upbuilding. For others it seems to mean "characteristic activity". In these cases the function of prophecy is said to be the conveying of messages from the divinity, or similar. Others ask the question of function from a sociological perspective. These seem to mean by function something like "function within the structures and processes of community formation and maintenance." The issues raised by the second definition have been treated above. Here we will separate the questions raised by the first and third approaches into two. (1): What purposes did the early Christians believe prophecy served? and (2): What purposes do scholars now attribute to it from a modern perspective?

The first question can be answered relatively quickly, at least for Paul. There is widespread agreement that his statement that "everyone who prophesies speaks to men for their strengthening, encouragement and comfort . . . he who prophesies edifies the church" (1 Cor. 14.3-4) must be the basis of all discussion on the matter. There is also agreement that the statement cannot be read apart from its context in the discussion of

---

[44] For a similar conclusion reached on different grounds see D.E. Aune, *Prophecy*, p. 339ff. David Hill's attitude is a little unclear. In his article in Panagopoulos, *Vocation*, p. 108ff, esp. pp. 123-6, he seems to allow exegesis a role, but not the defining or characteristic role. In *Prophecy*, p. 100, however, he argues that "Undoubtedly, this discovery of the "meaning" of Scripture belonged to the prophetic charism: at least part of the ministry of prophets in the New Testament was the interpretation of the Old." But see his qualification of this on p. 104. Compare the less ambiguous position of T.M. Crone, *Prophecy*, p. 200: "we have no clear evidence in the New Testament of Christian prophets interpreting scripture in the manner of the Jewish teacher." The summary of C.M. Robeck cited above is, I think, to be accepted: "for Paul, the gift of prophecy differs from preaching in that its content is not kerygmatic, and it differs from teaching in that teaching relies upon knowledge and exposition while prophecy comes from fresh revelation." See "The Gift of Prophecy in Acts and Paul, part II", *Studia Biblica et Theologica*, vol. 5, no. 2, 1975, 2, pp. 48-9.)

glossolalia, where the speaker "does not speak to men but to God . . . he utters mysteries with [his] spirit . . . he who speaks in a tongue edifies (only) himself".[45] In other words, Paul's discussion is polemically conditioned by the contrast between prophecy and glossolalia. But the real problem is that, once all the lexicographical work on the terms "strengthening, encouragement and comfort" has been done, we still know very little. We know the other contexts in which the terms are used, but almost nothing about what members of a first-century Christian group might have found strengthening, encouraging or comforting; still less do we know in which areas of these fields prophets might be expected to specialise.[46]

In a similar vein, D.E. Aune says:

> . . . after we have listed the various characteristic activities of Christian prophets, we are still left with a great many unanswered questions . . . Why did Christian prophets, if the summary of their activities above is essentially correct, focus so much of their efforts on exhortation, admonition and encouragement? . . . One very important set of questions, and one with which none of the five general presentations deals, pertains to the *social* functions of Christian prophets. Indeed, each of the questions which were just enumerated is basically sociological in orientation . . .[47]

Aune is correct, and he has identified one of the most fruitful areas of inquiry. Our second question, then, is: what social function within early Christianity did prophecy serve? The question will become particularly important when we come to compare early Christian prophecy with its Hellenistic counterpart, as we have considerable evidence to do with the social functions of oracles in the Hellenistic world.

3. The Social Functions of Early Christian Prophecy

Aune goes on to distinguish between two general models of prophetic function drawn from anthropological study: "central" and "peripheral" mediation. "Central mediation" is that form of prophecy which is structurally tied to the central institutions of a given culture. "Peripheral mediation" is

---

[45] See the detailed discussions of T.W. Gillespie, *Prophecy and Tongues*, pp. 86-101, T.M. Crone, *Prophecy*, pp. 204, 212-3, 226, 291, M.E. Hart, *Tongues and Prophecy*, pp. 76-79, D. Hill, *Prophecy*, pp. 122ff, 128-9, and W.A. Grudem, *Gift*, pp. 181ff. Unfortunately the predominant weakness of some of this research has been the tendency to identify παράκλησις with prophecy, so that not only is παράκλησις seen as the result of prophecy, but it is also seen as an infallible sign of the presence of prophecy. Paul urges the Corinthians to "try to excel in gifts that build up the church" (14.12) of which prophecy is only the prime example in the contrast with glossolalia; he wants "all things" done for edification (14.26), not just prophecy.

[46] J. Reiling (citing M.A. Chevallier) is likewise critical of the overuse of the terminology: "they are not even specific characteristics of Prophecy." (*Hermas and Christian Prophecy* p. 13.)

[47] D.E. Aune, *Prophecy*, p. 19.

that less institutionalised form which normally functions on the borders of "respectable society". In the Graeco-Roman world these two forms correspond to (for example) the official colleges of augurs and haruspices, and the travelling mantic or chresmologue. Perhaps Eunus, the Syrian slave-cum-revolutionary, discussed in Chapter 6, represents the extreme of this type. Citing R. Wilson, "Prophecy and Society in Ancient Israel", Aune (*Prophecy*, p. 20) develops the following analysis:

Peripheral mediation has several social functions: (1) the attainment of social status, (2) a means of bringing about social change, and (3) a means of maintaining social stability. Central intermediaries, on the other hand, are "primarily responsible for maintaining their societies and for promoting community welfare". This is accomplished by their mediations in providing divine legitimation for the existing social order and by their functions in easing social tensions.

Though this model seems to have real application to the Graeco-Roman world, and may also be of use in the analysis of ancient Israelite prophetism, it seems to me to have very limited application to the study of Christian prophecy in the first century. This is so because, as Aune himself admits, our data are so scanty on (a) the details of the functioning of prophecy, and (b) the institutional structure/s of early Christianity. For early Christianity is not a "culture" in the sense that these definitions require. It is a peculiarly intense form of sub-culture, with its own rules, sanctions and legitimisations. These are naturally "central" to its own life, though utterly "peripheral" to the wider Graeco-Roman world. As a result the above categories are likely to become merely confusing unless used with great care. But even more importantly, "early Christianity" barely exists as a recognisable social institution. What exists in the first century is a number of early Christian groups, with widely differing and rapidly changing institutional frameworks.[48] These range from the conscious attempt of Paul to develop a "charismatic community", with very little fixed structure or hierarchy, dependent rather on a high degree of mutual involvement and shared values, through the Jerusalem church with its widely recognised "pillars", to the emerging monarchical episcopate visible in the Ignatian epistles. It is clearly quite unreasonable, in this situation, to expect generalisations about the function of Christian prophecy to have any but the most limited application.

Aune's form-critical analysis allows him to go further and posit the following types of oracles, which could be used to fill out the standard

---

[48] Thus Aune: "It is therefore far from certain that the institutional complexion of early Christian congregations maintained any kind of consistent structure . . ." (*Prophecy*, p. 20, cf. pp. 194-5.) "Strong group boundaries coupled with a relatively low degree of internal social structure" characterised early Christianity (p. 216).

"function" definition.[49] They are oracles of assurance (including announcements of salvation), prescriptive/paraenetic oracles, very occasionally oracles of judgement, legitimation oracles (including oracles of commendation), and eschatological theophany oracles. There are, of course, composite and complex types. Finally Aune would be happy with only three basic types: paraenetic salvation-judgement announcements, paraenetic oracles of assurance, and amplified oracles.[50]

Such a typology would allow us to make certain generalisations about the social functions of early Christian prophecy; these would, however, be only as valid as the form-critical and other considerations that produced the typology. That, unfortunately, is an issue far beyond the scope of a piece of work such as this. But I think certain points would apply regardless of the validity of Aune's methodology.

It seems to me that early Christian prophecy does not yet have, in the N.T. period, a clearly defined social function or set of social functions. The reason for this is inherent in its relatively unstructured, non-institutionalised form. As we shall see, a good deal can be said about the social functions of Graeco-Roman prophecy, because it was highly structured, and well integrated into its wider society. Early Christian prophetism, on the other hand, seems to have been diverse, unstructured, and not particularly well integrated into its context: that is to say, it was obviously capable of being a disruptive, as well as an integrating force within Christianity.[51] It was also capable of a variety of functions theologically defined, and not at all points sharply distinguished from other forms of speech, though reasonable definitions can be developed. Paul, of course, tells us in some detail how he believes prophecy ought to function, and to what ends, but that is because he is in conflict with the Corinthians, who disagree. Nor was Corinth the only place where conflicts arose about prophecy in early Christianity. 1 Thessalonians witnesses to a very different problem; the denigration of prophecy. Matthew's Gospel gives indirect evidence of a church under threat from "false prophets", and the Epistle of Barnabas, the Didache and the "Shepherd" of Hermas, not to mention the documents of Montanism, all show that prophecy was commonly a problem. It would appear that the forms that prophecy took, and the authority it commanded, did not lend

---

[49] D.E. Aune, *Prophecy.*, pp. 321ff.

[50] D.E. Aune, *Prophecy.*, pp. 325-6.

[51] Compare D.E. Aune, *Prophecy.*, p. 203: "The evidence . . . suggests that the prophet was never integrated into the organisational structure of local churches . . ."; early Christian prophecy was "a relatively unstable and unstructured institution within early Christianity" (p. 231). "The institution of Christian prophecy, it appears, does not readily lend itself to categorical conceptualisation . . ." (p. 231)

themselves well to integration into the structure of the early Christian communities.

In summary, then, we are not yet in a position to make definitive statements about the "function" of early Christian prophecy, sociologically considered. We know far too little about it and its context to allow such statements to be more than guesses dressed up as generalisations. But we do know a good deal about the particular forms it took at different times and places, and the ways in which it was conceived by its practitioners and audience. The typology suggested by Aune is, I think, helpful, provided that we remember that the terms "central" and "peripheral" can only relate to one culture or subculture at a time. Perhaps the conflict between Paul and the Corinthians could even be conceived as a conflict between central (Pauline) ideas and peripheral (Corinthian) ones: but such an analysis would be dangerously value-laden. In my view, if we are to pursue sociological and anthropological models in our study of Christian prophecy (and indeed, early Christianity more generally), they will have to be models related to small-group behaviour and sectarian dynamics rather than models of large scale, highly structured societies.

4. Where and When did early Christian prophecy occur?

Having completed our discussion of our first major question, "What?", we turn now to the second, "Where and When?". Here we will inquire as to the types and normal setting of early Christian prophecy, and the period of time over which it was a common phenomenon in Christian groups. The "where?" part of the question involves two closely related issues. The first has to do with the typology of early Christian prophets. The second is the question of the setting of early Christian prophecy.

Types of Early Christian Prophecy

For most scholars early Christian prophecy, like Gaul under the Romans, is divided into three parts. There are said to be wandering Christian prophets, who travel from place to place, staying for differing periods with Christian groups as they go.[52] The evidence suggested includes the accounts

---

[52] It was, of course, the work of Harnack on the Didache that popularised this side of early Christian prophecy. In recent scholarship this category has come under attack from a number of quarters. The most direct attack is that of M.E. Boring, who argues that there is almost no clear evidence of wandering prophets within early Christianity, and that Harnack's understanding of the Didache is seriously faulty. (Boring, *Sayings*, pp. 58-63.) The point is debatable, but I personally find Boring's summary, that "the "wandering" aspect of early Christian prophecy has been greatly exaggerated in the secondary literature and, while not absent, is by no means typical" (p. 62) thoroughly

of Agabus in Acts, the Didache, and the discussion of false prophets in Matthew. There are said to be Christian prophets resident within congregations whose ministry does not normally extend beyond those congregations. They are evident both in Acts and in Paul's letters. Finally there are those Christians who, though they are not considered "prophets" in any regular or official sense, none the less occasionally prophesied. If this form of prophecy was common, or the dominant form of prophecy within a congregation, it could be described as "congregational prophecy". The evidence here is the theological conception of the New Testament writers that in some sense "all the Lord's people are prophets", and the discussion of prophecy in 1 Corinthians, and in the "Shepherd" of Hermas.

For many scholars a correct description of early Christian prophecy has been a matter of finding the correct mix of these three forms, or arranging them in a broad chronological sequence.[53] What is actually needed, however, is a thorough re-examination of the categories, especially numbers one and three.

"Wandering Prophets"

What would constitute a prophet's "wandering"? If it is sufficient that he or she travel from place to place, then wandering prophets and other wandering charismatics may be found aplenty in early Christianity. But it is not sufficient. In both cases in which Agabus is mentioned in Acts "wandering" is a most inappropriate description of what he does. The place of origin is specified: in the first case, Jerusalem, and in the second case, Judaea. Now the fact that a place of origin is specified at all is interesting.

acceptable. A second, and far more significant, development is the questioning of the definition of "wandering" by P. Bowers and D.E. Aune, discussed below.

[53] The surveys of opinion of J. Reiling, *Hermas and Christian Prophecy*, Chapter 1, and C.M. Robeck, *art.cit.*, seem to me to be the best and most balanced. The summary of Robeck, p. 39, that "the prophet and the gift of prophecy in the early Church appear to have been part of a very complex situation, but the oldest form was probably congregational prophecy . . . the distinctions are often blurred in the reality of prophetic activity" is eminently reasonable. As to the stages of the development, in opposition to the earlier view of Harnack, T.W. Gillespie, *Prophecy and Tongues*, p. 5, conjectures that they developed from local to peripatetic as local prophecy diminished. Similarly J.D.G. Dunn, *Jesus and the Spirit*, London, 1975, p. 171 notes that "prophets as opposed to prophecy first appear in itinerant form". M.E. Hart, *Tongues and Prophecy*, p. 355, argues that congregational prophecy is both the earliest stage of the development, and the ideal as far as Paul is concerned. She also proposes a scheme of the likely development, which is, however, largely speculative. D.E. Aune points out the interesting fact that the term "prophet" is mostly used in the plural in the NT, and in the singular in the post-apostolic writings. He suggests (*Prophecy*, p. 196) that this may indicate that we ought to expect groups of prophets in the New Testament period, and individual prophets later.

That Agabus is later noted as still being based in Judaea years later is also important. For while it is quite clear that he and his fellows at Antioch did have a ministry which extended beyond their church of origin, it is not proven that their normal ministry was "wandering". Twice Agabus is noted as having made a specific journey. That does not in any way demonstrate that he was an *itinerant* prophet, let alone one who wandered "at random" from place to place. The same applies to the prophets with whom he went to Antioch. The third case regularly cited is that of Judas and Silas in Acts 15.22ff:

Then the apostles and elders, with the whole church, decided to choose some of their own men and send them to Antioch with Paul and Barnabas. They chose Judas, called Barsabbas, and Silas, two men who were leaders among the brothers . . . Judas and Silas, who were prophets themselves, said much to encourage and strengthen the brothers. After spending some time there, they were sent off by the brothers with the blessing of peace to return to those who had sent them.

A careful reading of the text immediately shows that we have here a very special set of circumstances. Two Jerusalem prophets are specifically chosen and commissioned to accompany the *normally* itinerant Paul and Barnabas, who are *not* called prophets (though Barnabas' name might suggest that he was one). They go to one place, Antioch, and stay there for some time before returning to Jerusalem. They do not travel around: they simply move from Jerusalem to Antioch for an unspecified period, and then return. They do so specifically to help with the implementation of the "Jerusalem Decree", and though we may doubt that this is all they did, there is no evidence for any other major role. In Acts, then, it is to be seriously doubted whether we have any evidence for "wandering prophets" in the sense of itinerancy. The same is true of Paul's letters. For him prophets have a congregational ministry: I see no evidence of any wider task.[54]

---

[54] D. Hill, *art.cit.*, p. 110 and *Prophecy*, p. 218 , argues that Paul gives us no evidence of wandering. Likewise against the notion are H. Greeven, "Propheten, Lehrer, Vorsteher bei Paulus", *Z.N.W.*, vol. 44, 1952, p. 9, and H. von Campenhausen, *Ecclesiastical Authority and Spiritual Power in the Church of the First Three Centuries*, trans. J.A. Baker, Stanford, 1969, p. 61. C.M. Robeck, *art.cit.*, part 1, using a different definition, argues that prophets (as opposed to those who prophesy occasionally) are normally itinerant in Acts: "While prophets were normally attached to a specific congregation, they had freedom to move from place to place . . . for this reason it is possible to term them itinerants . . ." (p. 35.)

Further, if we extend our discussion to prophets more generally defined (perhaps "wandering charismatics" would now be a better term) in order to construct a model of the Pauline mission (as Ellis has done, for example, in *Prophecy and Hermeneutic in Early Christianity*, Grand Rapids, 1978) we come up against other problems. Paul Bowers has pointed out that it is simply not true that Paul "wanders". While it appears to have been true of most Hellenistic "missionaries" that "the pattern of their movement had

The lack of clarity in the scholarly discussion summarised above has led D.E. Aune to suggest an alternative typology of prophetic activity.[55] His categories include (a) prophets who prophesy in a prophetic group, (b) prophets who belong to a wider prophetic group but who have separate ministries within their own congregations, and (c) solo prophets. He also distinguishes between (a) special-purpose travel, such as that undertaken by Agabus, (b) John as a prophet being widely known in Asia Minor, having authority in an area wider than a single congregation, and (c) prophets who adopted an ascetic life-style and wandered like the Cynic philosophers and other "wandering preachers" of the Hellenistic world, such as Dio Chrysostom and Peregrinus Proteus.[56] This typology is a considerable improvement over the simple category of "wandering prophet", as it takes account of factors to do with the life-style of the prophet which are otherwise glossed over. The results it produces, however, are virtually identical to those suggested above. Aune's own summary is that

migrations of such prophetic figures . . . were only incidental to their prophetic roles. The itinerant prophets described in Acts were not aimless wanderers but appear to have travelled to certain places for the specific purpose of exercising their prophetic gifts . . .[57]

So much, then, for the moment, for "wandering prophets". The category will need to be examined again in the context of parallels between Christian and Hellenistic prophecy. Our task, however, is briefly to examine the third category; "congregational prophecy". Here again David Aune has recently taken a hand in the debate. This time, however, he has done so not to propose a new set of categories, but to argue that the whole conception of "congregational prophecy" is a category mistake.

"Congregational Prophecy"

As background we must note that the evidence for the idea of "congregational prophecy" falls into two categories. There is evidence that

---

no special purpose, however much purpose the movement itself had" it is certainly not true of Paul. Again in Bowers' words, "They wandered; Paul progressed." ("Paul and Religious Propaganda in the First Century", *Novum Test.*, vol. 22, no. 4, 1980, pp. 316-323, esp. p. 319.) Nor is it valid to describe Paul and his co-workers as "itinerant" in any strict sense, as that term implies some kind of repetitive movement around a limited area: itinerants must have an itinerary! Early Christian prophets travelled occasionally. The Pauline mission travelled purposively. The distinction must be borne in mind, especially as we turn to parallels with the wider Hellenistic world.

[55] D.E. Aune, *Prophecy*, p. 198.

[56] D.E. Aune, *Prophecy*, p. 212-3. It is with this third category, with its possible parallels to Graeco-Roman phenomena, that scholarship seems to be most concerned. See Aune's survey, p. 211ff, esp. p. 213.

[57] D.E. Aune, *Prophecy*, p. 215.

suggests that the belief existed that, due to the endowment of the Holy Spirit, "all the Lord's people are prophets", fulfilling of the prophecy of Joel. There is also evidence that some early Christians tried to give such a belief practical form in the way prophecy was managed within their communities. Aune, however, is highly critical of the concept, arguing that

The notion that early Christianity was conscious of the Spirit dwelling in the midst of the community so that the gift of prophecy, strictly speaking, was not and could not be monopolized by particular individuals, is a theological rather than a historical statement . . . We therefore conclude that some, but not all, early Christians acted as inspired mediums of divine revelation and that these individuals alone received the label "prophet". To regard all Christians as potential prophets is a theological dictum which cannot be confirmed or denied by historical or literary criticism . . .[58]

But while virtually all scholars are agreed that *for Luke* there was at least a theoretical sense in which all believers, having the Spirit, were prophets, the question which Aune's critique raises is, to what extent was this belief ever actualised in practice? Did it inform any patterns of behaviour to do with the use of prophecy, or did it remain (like the doctrine of the priesthood of all believers in most modern Protestant churches) a mere article of faith, largely irrelevant to day to day practice?[59] If it did so remain, or is merely an implication drawn by modern scholars that the early Christians themselves would not have drawn, then Aune's statement is justified. But my point is slightly (but critically) different. Aune is quite correct to claim that it cannot be the case that all Christians were "potentially prophets". No positive evidence suggests such a position, and the designation of certain individuals as prophets, as well as Paul's rhetorical question in 1 Corinthians 12.29, is

---

[58] D.E. Aune, *Prophecy*, p. 6. Compare p. 200, and 201. This is only true, of course, if such a view is not expressed or implied in the sources. If it is, then the statement may well be historically meaningful.

[59] As Aune correctly notes, *Prophecy*, p. 24, Plutarch expresses the view that all people are potential mantics, due to the inherent mantic power of the individual soul. Philo once makes a similar statement (Philo, In Flaccum 186). Stating that Plutarch or Philo held this view is an historical statement. The same is true of Paul and Luke. The question is, did Plutarch or Philo see it being put into use? Could just anyone be a μάντις at Delphi? Clearly not. The belief did not affect traditional practice. About the only consequence of the belief was the further belief in the portentous nature of dreams and portents at the approach of death (Cicero, de Div. 1.4.12, 1.20, 1.33, 2.11, Philo, Plutarch Mor. 432 c). Anyone could have significant dreams. If Paul's position is similar, then the idea of "congregational prophecy" is purely a theological one, though still a belief that Paul held, and thus a proper object of historical study. Likewise Reiling's case is not only that "all Christians are potential prophets", but that *Hermas* would have believed so (Panagopoulos, *Vocation*, p. 75).

against it. But there is important evidence that *for Paul*, all Christians were capable of prophesying occasionally. At any point the Spirit might speak through any believer with all the authority of the Lord. That is what I mean by "congregational prophecy". Any one might occasionally prophecy; those who did so regularly or in a notable fashion became known as prophets in the stronger sense.[60] If this position can be maintained, then Aune's critique of the concept of "congregational prophecy" must be judged defective.

Summary

I would contend, then, that while there is no evidence to suggest that Luke or Paul believed that prophets were characteristically travellers, whether wandering or itinerant, there is evidence for the other two forms of prophecy that made up the classical three-way division, namely "intra-congregational" prophets, and congregational prophecy. That early Christian prophecy was practiced by specialists designated "prophets" within individual communities is not in doubt: the evidence for prophecy as an endowment of the "charismatic community" will be presented in detail in the next section.

The Setting of Early Christian Prophecy

After the long and controversial discussions of the previous few pages, it is a pleasure to be able to report that the strong consensus that the setting of early Christian prophecy was the assembled community appears to be incontrovertible. There is virtually no evidence to suggest that Christian prophecy was practiced outside the gathering together of Christian groups. The only exceptions to this of which I am aware are the accounts of the Pentecostal glossolalia and "initiatory" experiences of prophecy mentioned by Luke, and dealt with in Chapter 3, above, and these examples are clearly noted by Luke himself as being exceptional. Not only is prophecy exercised within the community, but as we have seen, it is also addressed *to* the community, not to the wider world. In the one case in our evidence where prophecy has an effect on an outsider, (a) it is an outsider who is visiting the community, and (b) the experience draws him into the community. Though our evidence is scanty and often inferential, these points appear to hold right across the spectrum. By the mid-second century this view of prophecy has

---

[60] This definition is closer to that of W.A. Grudem (*Gift*, pp. 234ff) and J. Reiling, *Hermas and Christian Prophecy*, Leiden, 1973, pp. 9ff, and "Prophecy, the Spirit and the Church", in Panagopoulos, *Vocation*, pp. 73-75, than that of Aune, who seems to use the phrase to designate a situation where all believers were equally likely to prophesy, so that the term "prophet" ought not to be applied to any one person more than to another.

been formalised by Hermas, who lays down that the prophet who does not exercise his gift within the gathered community is a false prophet.[61]

The Historical Extent of Prophecy

Having settled the question of "where", we are now in a position to ask "when?". Over what period of time was prophecy common in early Christian groups, and what led to its demise?

Here a general consensus pertains according to which prophecy was common in the "apostolic" period (say down to about A.D. 70), very rare in the immediate sub-apostolic period (70-100), and occasionally present thereafter until the rise of Montanism made all such phenomena highly suspect: after 170 prophecy is often said to be extremely rare.[62] But contradictions are apparent within this view. It is clear from a great volume of evidence covering a wide area that prophecy was present in the second-century church and later;[63] there is reasonable evidence that it was

---

[61] J. Reiling, "Prophecy, the Spirit and the Church", in Panagopoulos, *Vocation*, p. 61, and *Hermas and Christian Prophecy*, pp. 122ff, 163. N.B. Acts 13.1-3, "while they were liturgizing": thus Robeck, *art.cit.*, part 2, pp. 43, 44. Likewise T.M. Crone, *Prophecy*, p. 212, "as far as our sources allow us to conclude, prophecy in the Pauline Churches was exercised chiefly in the course of the liturgy", cf. p. 295. On Agabus see also p. 197. D. Hill, *Prophecy*, pp. 119-120 cites R.P. Martin and J.M. Robinson to the effect that 1 Thessalonians 5.16-22 gives us evidence of the structure of an early Christian "order of worship", thus confirming that the "Sitz im Leben" of prophecy was congregational worship. R.L. Fox, *Pagans and Christians*, London, 1986, p. 381, note 22, suggests a date for Hermas in the 90s A.D.

[62] For this view see, for example, G. Friedrich, *T.D.N.T.*, vol. 6, 1959, E.T. 1968, pp. 859-60, H. von Campenhausen, *op.cit.*, Chapter 8, p. 191, T.W. Gillespie, *Prophecy*, pp. 5-6, M.E. Boring, *Sayings*, pp. 36-7, D. Hill, *Prophecy*, pp. 182ff, 191.

[63] See Justin Martyr, Dialogue with Trypho 39, 51, 82, Ignatius, Trallians 5, and Ephesians 20, Ep. Barnabas 16.9, Ep. Polycarp 5.2, Martyrdom 16, and Hermas 11, as well as the Didache 13.1, Irenaeus, A.H. 2.32.4, 3.11.9, 5.6.1 and 5.7.3-5, and Origen, Contra Celsum 1.46 and 2.8. For particular known Christian prophets we have Polycarp of Smyrna, Melito of Sardis, Ammia of Philadelphia, Quadratus, and Cerinthus, all of whom are explicitly described as prophets in early Christian literature. For this list see D.E. Aune, *Prophecy*, p. 196. He adds: "This rather meagre list could be slightly expanded with the addition of the names of those early Christians who prophesied or who apparently regarded themselves as prophets though they were not labelled as prophets by others (so far as we know) or by themselves. These would include Paul, John the Seer, Ignatius of Antioch, and Hermas of Rome." To this we should probably add Peregrinus Proteus, who, according to Lucian, Peregrinus 11 and 16, was considered by the Christians to be a prophet while in his "Christian stage". If the hypothesis of Michael Green, to the effect that the first-person singular used in the conclusion of Melito's Paschal Homily is an indicator of prophetic inspiration, is accepted, then we also have a full-blown example of prophetic speech, such as we certainly do not have for the first century. See E.M.B. Green, *Evangelism in the Early*

still a powerful and independent force, not yet tied to the institutional structures of the emerging episcopate.[64] If it was in fact absent in the immediate sub-apostolic period, it must have undergone a remarkable renaissance thereafter![65] To such views the article of M.A.G. Haykin, "The Fading Vision? The Spirit and Freedom in the Pastoral Epistles",[66] is a welcome corrective. The view that prophecy continued to flourish in the late second century is persuasively documented for Irenaeus of Lyons by C.M. Robeck, Jr., who cites, along with a number of other passages, Irenaeus' *Demonstration of the Apostolic Teaching* 99:

And others too do not admit the gifts of the Holy Spirit, and reject from themselves the charism of prophecy, being watered whereby, man bears fruit of life to God. And those are the ones spoken of by Isaias; *for they shall be,* he says, *as a leafless terebinth, and as a garden without water.* And such men are of no use to God, in that they can bear no fruit.[67]

After the repudiation of Montanism by the mainstream church, however, the situation does change.[68] Prophecy does not vanish, but it is more and

Church, London, 1970, pp. 201-2. The papyrus to which Green refers, P. Bodmer XIII, is discussed in Van Haelst, *Catalogue des papyrus littéraires juifs et chrétiens,* Paris, 1976, as No. 678. O. Perler and J.I.H. McDonald make similar suggestions, Perler (*Méliton de Sardes sur la pâque,* 1966, p. 24ff) before, and McDonald ("Some Comments on the Form of Melito's Paschal Homily", *Studia Patristica* XII, 1971, pp. 111-112) after Green's suggestion, but apparently independently. T. Halton, in "Stylistic Device in Melito, *Peri Pascha*", in *Kyriakon,* ed. P. Granfield and J.A. Jungmann, Münster, 1970, vol. 1, pp. 249ff, esp. p. 255, discusses the rhetorical devices of the passage, but does not comment on the question of prophecy.

[64] For this see J. Reiling's convincing exegesis of Hermas 11, as well as the comments of Irenaeus and, less immediately, John Chrysostom, Homily on 1 Corinthians no. 32, "every church had many who prophesied".

[65] It is on this basis that it seems quite reasonable to reject the suggestion of, among others, Friedrich, *art.cit.,* p. 860, to the effect that 2 Peter reflects the situation where prophecy is no longer a living force in the church. He argues that since the writer quotes Scripture rather than Christian prophets in defence of its eschatology he can no longer have access to such prophecy. But such an argument can hardly be applied to Paul, who both in Romans and 1 Corinthians both quotes O.T. prophecy and cites a "mystery". It is hard to see how 2 Peter could be dated after A.D. 170, which is what Friedrich's case would seem to require.

[66] *Evangelical Quarterly,* vol. 57, no. 4, 1985, pp. 291-305. D.E. Aune's position, *Prophecy,* p. 189, is a little better, as he argues that prophets had an integral role until the end of the first century, and were steadily marginalised from then on, especially after the repudiation of Montanism.

[67] The passage is cited by Robeck, "Irenaeus and 'Prophetic Gifts'", in P. Elbert, ed., *Essays on Apostolic Themes,* Massachusetts, 1985, pp. 104-114, p. 111, and cited above in the translation of J.P. Smith, *St. Irenaeus, Proof of the Apostolic Preaching,* Maryland, 1952, p. 108-9.

[68] Montanism is itself evidence of continued prophetic activity. See now C.M. Robeck,

more seen as a gift only available to great saints and those (such as martyrs) of impeccable orthodoxy. By the fourth century discussion of prophecy by anyone not so qualified gave rise to grave doubts, as the case of Priscillian makes clear. While he believed that charismatic prophecy was still very much current, and available to both men and women, his Italian contemporary Filastrius labelled such claims heresy.[69] But even by the end of the second century some people were treating prophecy as a past phenomenon.[70] In the fourth century, however, Eusebius was still happy to quote an anti-Montanist writer to the effect that charismata continue "until the end of the age throughout the church".[71] Whether this point of view was a purely theoretical one or not, the statement could still be made. Likewise in the mid-fourth century Cyril of Jerusalem, in his Catechetical Lectures 17.37, seems to believe that some of his hearers may still receive the gift of prophecy.[72]

Christian prophecy, then, was a widespread and powerful force within early Christianity for more than a century. Over this period it underwent changes and developments, but the evidence of, for example, Hermas 11, makes it clear that even in the mid-second century the ideal of congregational prophecy could be upheld. This is so despite the fact that prophecy is, for Hermas, controversial. His response to what he perceives as false prophecy is not tighter and more "institutional" control of prophecy, but an emphasis on the communal responsibility for prophecy. In most other

---

Jr., *Prophecy in Carthage: Perpetua, Tertullian and Cyprian*, Cleveland, 1992.

[69] See H. Chadwick, *Priscillian of Avila*, Oxford, 1976, pp. 79-80.

[70] Hippolytus, de Antichristo 2.31 (Migne, *P.G.* vol. 10, col. 729), for example, seems to see things this way. A similar view is also implied in Origen's Commentary on Matthew 28 (= Philocalia 6, in the *Ante-Nicene Fathers Library*, vol. 10, p. 425, trans. J. Patrick, Grand Rapids, 1969), and the Muratorian Canon, 78-9 (text in A. Souter, *The Text and Canon of the New Testament*, London, 1913, pp. 208-210, esp. p. 210).

[71] H.E. 5.17. This was, of course, what Paul believed (see the discussion of the phrase "when the perfect comes" above in Chapter 4, and add to the references there C.M. Robeck, *art.cit.*, part 2, p. 48, and W.A. Grudem, *Gift*, pp. 210ff.), and Irenaeus, Clement of Alexandria, Origen (with modifications) and Tertullian concurred. See footnote 20 in Chapter 4.

[72] For a detailed and sensible treatment of continuing prophecy, and dreams and visions, which does not, however, distinguish the verbal from the visionary elements, see now R.L. Fox, *Pagans and Christians*, London, 1986, pp. 375ff and esp. 410ff. For the gift of predictive prophecy and its availability to martyrs see p. 474, and pp. 487-8, and the careful discussion of the ways in which such prophecies were handled by the churches in C.M. Robeck, Jr., "Canon, *Regula Fidei*, and Continuing Revelation in the Early Church", in J.E. Bradley and R.A. Muller, eds., *Church, Word and Spirit: Historical and Theological Essays in Honor of Geoffrey W. Bromiley*, Grand Rapids, 1987, pp. 65-91.

writers of the second century, however, we see the signs of a growing institutionalism.

The Decline of Prophecy

Why, then, does prophecy decline in importance? It is not sufficient to argue that increasing institutionalism in the church left no room for prophecy.[73] Prophecy could adapt: it became, for example, increasingly tied to "institutional" leaders such as bishops. In ancient Israel "charismatic" prophecy co-existed with a strong institutional cult for several centuries, so there is nothing that can demonstrate *a priori* that prophecy is incompatible with growing institutionalism. There were always several possibilities. Prophecy could be integrated within the new institutional framework (as it apparently was in Hermas' church, and had been in the case of the Temple-prophets of Israel); it could be subsumed within the new structures of the churches (as seems to happen when it becomes more and more the prerogative of bishops, as part of their teaching function), or it could remain in opposition to the institutional structures (as it did in ancient Israel in the case of the "classical" prophets, and as in the case of Montanism). Finally, it could simply cease to be a common experience within Christianity.

Clearly the conflict between orthodoxy and Montanism is partially responsible, though it cannot be a full explanation. Irenaeus, for one, resisted the temptation to throw the baby out with the bath-water (A.H. 3.11.9, Demonstration, 99). Prophetic conflict need not lead to the decline of prophecy: once again, it did not do so in ancient Israel. It seems to me, then that we do not yet have any convincing explanation for the decline of Christian prophecy. In some places it does seem to have been subsumed into new structures, and in others to have become well integrated with them. But the question of causation eludes us: the evidence is simply not clear.

We have now completed our discussion of early Christian prophecy with reference to the questions "What?", and "When and Where?". We turn now to the question of "Who?", which cannot be separated from the question of "Why?": in this case, why did Paul and his Corinthian converts come into conflict over the question of prophecy.

---

[73] For this theory see, most recently, D.E. Aune, *Prophecy*, p. 189.

Chapter 10

Prophecy in Corinth.

In the previous chapter I suggested that there were two grounds on which the concept of "congregational prophecy" might be defended. I argued firstly that if the concept that any Christian might occasionally prophesy were one that Luke and/or Paul held, rather than a modern extrapolation from their beliefs that they themselves would not have made, then it would properly be a subject of historical analysis. I argued secondly that such a belief would be not only a legitimate subject for study, but one of great interest, if it could be shown that it was a belief that either grew out of or had effects on the practice of the communities with which they were associated. In this chapter, then, our first task is to answer the question "Who?": who prophesied in early Christianity?

1. Who Prophesied?

While there is widespread agreement that the term "prophet" is used of a limited group within the New Testament churches, those who made use of the gift of prophecy most regularly and in the most noteworthy fashion[1],

---

[1] See, for example, C.M. Robeck, Jr., *art.cit.*, part 2, p. 37, p. 44; D. Hill, in Panagopoulos, *Vocation*, p. 110, M.E. Boring, *Sayings*, p. 63-4: "early Christianity was a prophetic community in which the line between prophets and non-prophets was not firmly drawn . . . without being an official 'order', they were a recognizably distinct group within the early church . . ." W.C. Klein, "The Church and its Prophets", *Anglican Theological Review*, vol. 44, no. 1, 1962, p. 4, is even less happy with the concept of a prophetic "order": ". . . the New Testament neither states nor implies that prophets constituted, or belonged to, a distinct order . . ." While this may be true to the extent that "the prophets" had no particular prerogatives (other than their more regular exercise of prophecy) unavailable to the non-prophet, the suggestion of D. Hill, *Prophecy*, p. 120, that "The frequency of reference to Christian προφῆται in these chapters (sc. 1 Cor. 12-14) may imply . . . that it was in Corinth that those who prophesied first emerged and were treated as a relatively fixed group within a congregation" ought to be used as a balance. Hill cites 1 Cor. 12.28, 29, and 14.37 in support of his claim. It seems to me that a good deal of the debate about the existence of a "prophetic office" or "prophetic order" is a matter of semantics only. The problem is that scholars are not agreed as to what might constitute an "office" as opposed to a "function". Aune's comment that there

there is little agreement as to what extent "prophecy" as a gift was believed to be open to all believers, or to the congregation itself, conceived of as a charismatic or prophetic community. The issue may alternately be expressed as follows: to what extent was prophecy characteristically conceived of as the domain of its regular practitioners, "prophets", and to what extent was it conceived of as a congregational asset, exercised by whichever member of the congregation the Spirit happened to use?

Once again a distinction must be made between Luke and Paul. It is widely agreed that for Luke, at least, there is a sense in which all Christians, having the Holy Spirit, are able on occasion to speak under the inspiration of that Spirit. The Pentecost account in Acts 2 is critical here. Now "all the Lord's people are prophets" at least in that sense. But the evidence is not limited to this one passage and its implications. The case is strengthened by the very firm link between "the Spirit" and prophecy in Judaism.[2] "The

---

is no evidence "that they possessed personal or professional qualifications or talents other than the ability to prophesy" ought to be taken into account here. I would argue that to say that an office of prophet existed you would need to show that it could exist (notionally) without a prophet holding it: it could be vacant and need filling. M. Turner suggests (*art.cit.*, pp. 33-34, citing Brockhaus, *Charisma und Amt*, pp. 24ff) several criteria for office: an element of permanency, recognition of that office by the church, formalisation of that office with ceremonial (whether laying on of hands, letters of authority, or other) and remuneration. In my view such a definition asks far too much organisational sophistication of this very early stage of the development of Christian groups. Probably the fairest statement is that of G.W.H. Lampe, "Grievous Wolves (Acts 20.29)", in B. Lindars and S.S. Smalley, eds., *Christ and Spirit in the New Testament*, Cambridge, 1973, pp. 253-268. He suggests that "there seems to have been a definite, though to us obscure, distinction between occasional prophesying by 'ordinary' church members, on the one hand, and the exercise of a ministry by 'specialist' prophets, on the other." The two exceptions in all this are W.A. Grudem and D.E. Aune. Grudem argues that Paul uses the term προφήτης simply to designate any person at all who might occasionally prophesy, *Gift*, pp. 231ff. He does, however, admit a narrower meaning of the term, pp. 233ff, p. 256. Aune, *Prophecy*, p. 199, argues that Paul may recognise a distinction between regular and occasional prophets, but that he does not exhort all to desire prophecy: only those who have gifts of inspired speech, which they may not previously have differentiated into prophecy, glossolalia and other types. Here, of course, he is drawing on the work of Engelsen, which is to be rejected. Paul is exhorting all to desire to prophesy, (14.1), and even if the issue in Corinth has been provoked by a few, a pneumatic elite, Paul's advice is proffered to the whole congregation: see 14.39-40, for example.

[2]   On the Acts passage see M.E. Hart, *Tongues and Prophecy*, p. 72: "it seems clear that ideally all believers may at some time prophesy . . . at least ideally the Spirit is the Spirit of prophecy and the community is a community of prophets . . ." Given that Luke's

Spirit" was widely understood as "the Spirit of Prophecy": in this context it would be remarkable if Luke did not draw the conclusion that all who had the Spirit were at the very least potential prophets. But Luke gives us very little evidence that he saw this belief worked out in the daily life of the churches he describes in Acts.[3]

The case of Paul is different. Paul believes, as does Luke, that every believer has the Holy Spirit. The inferential case made out above therefore applies here as well. But there is considerable evidence that Paul expects to see this principle put into practice in certain concrete ways.

definition of prophecy is broader than Paul's, this statement is correct. Though "it would be very difficult to show that Luke believed all Christians prophesied in the narrow sense . . . " (M. Turner, *art.cit.*, p. 14-15), this is only true because Luke did not believe in prophecy "in the narrow sense". Cf. W.A. Grudem, *Gift*, p. 235. D. Hill, *Prophecy*, p. 96, argues that the link between the Spirit and prophecy for all believers is also visible in Acts 4.31 and 10.44ff. Once again, allowing for Luke's definitions, this appears to be valid. On "prophets" and "prophecy" in 1 Corinthians see pp. 137-8 of Hill, *Prophecy*. For Acts note also the statement of James Dunn: "there does seem to be something of a distinction between prophet and prophesying evident within the Acts material . . ." (*Jesus and the Spirit*, p. 175.) On the Jewish background see M.E. Isaacs, *The Concept of Spirit*, London, 1976, p. 13: "The association of spirit with the prophetic activity was common in post-exilic Judaism", and p. 89: "the Spirit is primarily the prophetic spirit which we find so prominent in the writings of Hellenistic Judaism." James Dunn, op.cit., pp. 170-1, also notes the Rabbinic references to "all the Lord's people" being prophets in Numbers Rabbah on Numbers 11.17, though T.M. Crone doubts that this and similar passages are early enough to represent first century thought, *Prophecy*, p. 69, but notes that the Sibylline Oracles (3.582) seem to express the belief in a general outpouring of prophecy in the last times. Crone also points out (*Prophecy*, p. 142) that "Like the Rabbis, Josephus practically equates the spirit with prophesy. Thus when the spirit comes upon someone, he begins to prophesy . . . in several O.T. traditions where the LXX speaks of the spirit, Josephus refers to prophecy." See also the works of Blenkinsopp, Meyer, and Gillespie referred to in Chapter 3, footnote 15.

[3]　Apart from the evidence that Luke believed that new converts might prophesy as they received the Spirit for the first time, there is perhaps some ambiguous evidence in Paul's comment in Acts 20.23 that "in every city the Holy Spirit warns me . . ." that trouble awaits at Jerusalem. The prophecy of Agabus in 21.10ff would appear to be the culmination of this process, but in the earlier case, though prophecy is probably what is being referred to, no particular prophets are named. This could be taken to indicate that it was prophecies by ordinary Christians, rather than by particular specialist prophets, that Paul received. The same might well be argued of Acts 13.2 and 16.6, but in all three cases the suggestion would only be speculative. The difference between Paul and Luke on this point may be a problem if one assumes, as I do, that the author of Acts is Luke, the companion of Paul. The problem does not appear insurmountable, however. Luke gives us very little information about the details of the working of prophecy at all, so the lack of evidence on this particular point is hardly surprising.

First, he exhorts the Corinthians to "eagerly desire spiritual (gifts), but rather that you may prophesy." (1 Corinthians 14.1.)[4] There is no suggestion that this exhortation is directed at any group smaller than the entire congregation, and thus Paul must be understood to be encouraging the whole congregation to seek to be able to prophesy. The same is true in 1 Corinthians 14.39.[5]

---

[4]   This seems to me to be the best understanding of this passage. In four places in chs. 12-14 Paul uses the term ζηλοῦτε: 12.31, 14.1, 14.12 and 14.39. It has been argued that the term can be read as either indicative or imperative in 12.31, and since it is clearly indicative in 14.12, ought to be read in 12.31 as indicative, "you eagerly desire the 'greater' gifts". The argument is inconclusive, however, as 14.1 can hardly be indicative. See D.L. Baker, "The Interpretation of 1 Corinthians 12-14", *Ev.Q.*, vol. 46, 1974, pp. 224-234, for the suggestion, but the view of T.L. Wilkinson, "Tongues and Prophecy in Acts and 1st Corinthians", *Vox Reformata*, No. 31, Nov. 1978, pp. 6-7., W.A. Grudem, *Gift*, p. 56, and D.A. Carson, *Showing the Spirit*, pp. 55-8, that we ought to read both 12.31 and 14.1 as imperative seems far preferable. See, most recently, J.F.M. Smit, "Two Puzzles: 1 Corinthians 12.31 and 13.3: a Rhetorical Solution", *N.T.S.* vol. 39, 1993, pp. 246-264.

It has also been argued that the verb itself ought to be understood as "to practise zealously" rather than "to eagerly desire". (W.C. van Unnik, in the long unpublished paper noted by J. Reiling, in Panagopoulos, *Vocation*, pp. 65-66, who approves, and M. Turner, *art.cit.*, p. 32, who argues that the suggestion is possible but contextually unlikely. As noted in Chapter 2, the paper has recently been published posthumously, as "The Meaning of 1 Corinthians 12.31", *Nov.T.*, vol. 35, part 2, 1993, pp. 142-159.) This would leave us with altogether too many possible alternatives for comfort. But 12.31 can hardly be read as "you are zealously practising the greater gifts" without considerable irony, and the reading seems unlikely in 14.1 as well. If we read this meaning with the imperative sense, "practise these gifts zealously", then Paul's attitude is not really very different from that expressed by "desire them eagerly". The only real difference would be that in the first case Paul would be allowing that the gifts the Corinthians were already practising were "higher gifts", and in the second he would be urging them to aspire to such gifts. Again the imperative seems preferable.

Finally, D.A. Carson, *Showing the Spirit*, p. 101, points out the adversative sense of μᾶλλον (14.1), thus suggesting the translation "but rather" instead of "especially".

[5]   See, for example, E. Best, "Prophets and Preachers", *S.J.Th.*, vol. 12, 1959, p. 142: "The possibility remains open that anyone may prophesy . . . " As noted above, D.E. Aune, *Prophecy*, p. 199, argues that Paul does not exhort *all* to desire prophecy: only those who have gifts of inspired speech, which they may not previously have differentiated into prophecy, glossolalia and other types. But again there is no indication of this in the text, which would appear to be directed to the entire congregation. Aune also points out the interesting fact that the term "prophet" is mostly used in the plural in the NT, and in the singular in the post-apostolic writings. He suggests (*Prophecy*, p. 196) that this may indicate groups of prophets in the N.T. period, and individual prophets later. It may suggest even more than that in terms of congregational prophecy, but we cannot be sure.

Second, he describes a situation where, with unbelievers present, "everybody is prophesying" (14.24). Though there is doubtless hyperbole here, the question is, how much? The all-inclusiveness of the prophesying is heavily emphasised: "he will be convinced *by all* that he is a sinner and judged *by all*". Third, Paul notes that if certain rules of procedure are adhered to, "you can *all* prophesy in turn so that you may all be instructed and encouraged" (1 Cor. 14.31). Clearly the constant repetition of πάντες cannot be accidental: Paul is deliberately emphasising a point. We will return to this passage in detail below.

There exists, then, a reasonable *prima facie* case that Paul believed it possible for a high proportion of the Corinthian congregation to participate in prophecy: all should seek it, not just those who were known as prophets. Not all would become prophets in any regular or formal sense, but all could occasionally contribute in this way.[6] This case must now be examined in detail.

Apart from the critique of Aune discussed above, the view with the most radical consequences for "congregational prophecy" in recent scholarship is probably that of Earle Ellis.[7] In a series of individual papers, now gathered together into one volume, Ellis develops a coherent thesis about the nature of the leadership of the early Christian movement. In brief, Ellis is arguing that there existed within the early Christian communities an elite cadre of missionary workers, whose exegetical and hermeneutical work was central to the development of the movement's self-understanding. They were

---

[6] C.M. Robeck argues that "congregational" prophesy is in view in Romans 12.6, because "he (sc. Paul) sees prophecy as a gift given to individuals who will exercise it at the appropriate times" (*art.cit.*, part 2, p. 37). Likewise he argues that because Paul counsels the Corinthians (14.1) to seek to be able to prophesy, rather than to become prophets, this congregational form is in view (p. 47). This view seems to me to be placing too much emphasis on the precise wording (verb rather than noun), though in combination with the evidence offered above it is certainly suggestive. In favour of congregational prophecy being an important element in Paul's view of prophecy on various other grounds are M. Turner, *art.cit.*, pp. 14-15, J.D.G. Dunn, *Jesus and the Spirit*, London, 1975, p. 281, and *Unity and Diversity in the New Testament*, London, 1977, p. 178, E. Best, "Prophets and Preachers", *S.J.Th.*, vol. 12, 1959, pp. 142-3, all of whom are cited in more detail on this point in footnote 6 to Chapter 8: see also H. von Campenhausen, *Ecclesiastical Authority and Spiritual Power in the Church of the First Three Centuries*, trans J.A. Baker, Stanford, 1969, pp. 61ff.

[7] E.E. Ellis, *Prophecy and Hermeneutic in Early Christianity*, Grand Rapids, 1978, Chapters 1 and 2.

referred to by Paul as "the (or my, or our) brother/s", "fellow worker/s", "deacons", etc.[8] The terms "brother" and "brothers" are widely used in early Christianity to refer to any believer, but Ellis argues that when used with the article, the term refers to this missionary and teaching elite.

Further, Ellis argues that these people are characteristically described as πνευματικοί, or as being those endowed with "pneumatic" gifts, which, he suggests, are (again, characteristically) gifts of inspired speaking and teaching, such as prophecy and preaching.[9] From this he goes on to argue that "the brothers" addressed in some of Paul's letters are also πνευματικοί: they constitute the internal leadership of the congregations. On this basis he suggests that certain Pauline letters, and portions of letters, may be directed specifically towards these leadership groups. He treats 1 Corinthians 11 as a prime example. Thus he can argue that its teaching is directed towards this group of pneumatics, as opposed to the congregation in general, and account for the supposed differences in teaching between this passage and 1 Corinthians 14.33-36 by positing different audiences.[10]

This otherwise plausible reconstruction contains two logical jumps. Ellis has shown that "the brothers", etc., normally indicates Paul's associates. But he has in no way shown that "brother" is sufficiently clearly a technical term that we may presume that when it is used in the vocative (as it is, for example, in Romans 1.13, 7.1,4, 10.1, 11.25, 12.1, 15.14, 16.17, 1 Corinthians 1.10, 11, 26, etc.) it addresses the "pneumatic" leadership within a congregation.[11] Indeed, when not used "absolutely", the term normally

---

[8] E.E. Ellis, *op.cit.*, pp. 6-15.

[9] E.E. Ellis, *op.cit.*, p. 22. Ellis does admit, in "Prophecy in the New Testament Church - and Today", in Panagopoulos, *Vocation*, p. 51, that "Prophecy occurs in the early church both as the occasional utterance of members of the congregation and as the continuing ministry of a relatively few persons within it." But those relatively few are what he is interested in. On the opposite end of the spectrum, D. Hill suggests that it is possible that "in Corinth alone of the Pauline congregations . . . those who prophesied emerged and were treated as a distinct group within the church . . ." ("Christian Prophets as Teachers and Instructors in the Church", in Panagopoulos, *Vocation*, p. 109).

[10] E.E. Ellis, *op.cit.*, p. 27 and footnote 25.

[11] In only one case that I can find (Romans 16.23) does the term apply to persons acting as representatives from *within* a congregation. Yet this is precisely the meaning which Ellis needs to find in abundance if he is to support his case. A good example of the usage of the term for the (informal) leadership of a congregation, in close conjunction with its wider use, is to be found in 1 Thessalonians 4 and 5, particularly ch. 5 vv. 12-14: "Now we ask you (all), brothers, to respect those who work hard among you, who are over you in the Lord . . . and we urge you, brothers, warn those who are idle . . ."

applies to the congregation as a whole, rather than to a group within it. Furthermore, it is noteworthy that in one case where we can be quite sure that Paul is addressing a small, "mature" group within the congregation, in 1 Corinthians 8, on the issue of "weaker brothers", he does not use the term "brother/s" absolutely at all. This is despite the fact that the contrast between "brothers" absolutely and "weaker brothers" would have been natural and easy. In 1 Corinthians 10, on the other hand, an ethical matter of general congregational interest is addressed to "brothers". All in all, rather than taking "brothers" as a technical term meaning Paul's missionary associates, it seems best to understand it as a general term which can apply to any and all Christian believers, and which Paul sometimes uses to denote "the brothers (who happen to be with me)".[12]

Second, though it is true that when the term πνευματικός is used of "gifts" it is normally the gifts of speech - prophecy, teaching, etc. - that are in view, Ellis has not shown that when Paul discusses "spiritual people" he means those with "spiritual charismata". Indeed, in Corinth, where such gifts appear to have been at a premium, he describes the congregation as "σαρκίνοις": the very opposite of spiritual. On this basis we must conclude that though early Christianity may have had an "elite cadre" of travelling missionaries, there is little evidence that Paul's "family terminology" reflects this fact. Nor is there clear evidence that members of this elite were described as "spiritual" due to their gifts of inspired speech. That term had other uses.

If this is the case, then it becomes impossible to argue that the "brothers" addressed in 1 Corinthian 12-14 are any group less inclusive than the entire Corinthian assembly. It thus also becomes very difficult to argue that the various uses of πάντες in that passage can be taken at much less than face value.[13] Paul exhorts the entire congregation to "seek prophecy", fully

---

[12] This is also the conclusion reached by James Dunn, *Jesus and the Spirit*, London, 1975, p. 288. For a case similar to 1 Corinthians 8 see Galatians 6.1. See D.E. Aune, *Prophecy*, p. 402 note 37, for a critique of this view as applied to the Revelation to John.

[13] Various scholars have suggested that Paul's statements that "all" the Corinthians ought to take part in various activities are hypothetical only, along the lines of his hope that "all" would speak in tongues (14.5), or his wish that "all men" were like himself in regard to marriage (7.7.). Thus T.M. Crone, *Prophecy*, pp. 211-212, argues that "there was a definable group who regularly exercised this ministry. In principle all could prophesy, but in fact Paul does not expect all to prophesy, and only a limited number were known as prophets." Likewise Nils Engelsen (*Glossolalia*, pp. 170ff) applies this

expecting that large numbers of them may (occasionally) prophesy. This is so despite the fact that he does not think that they will all become "prophets". Prophecy is not always a matter of recognised "prophets". It is also a matter of the freedom of the Spirit of God to choose any Christian through whom to speak. The Corinthians are urged to make this theoretical position a reality in their congregational life.

This view of Paul's argument is strikingly confirmed by a detailed exegesis of 1 Cor. 14.29-31. A puzzle that most scholars have managed to avoid demands our attention. To regulate prophecy, Paul lays down that

Two or three prophets should speak, and the others should weigh carefully what is said . . . For you can all prophesy in turn (καθ' ἕνα πάντες) so that everyone may be instructed and encouraged . . .

Most commentators expend considerable effort on the instructions for "discernment of spirits" and for interruptions in verse 30, and consequently do not notice the striking contradiction between verses 29 and 31. If only two or three prophets are to speak, how can it be said that "you can all prophesy"? The passage is not addressed to any pneumatic elite. Even if it were, it is hard to imagine such a group having only two or three members.

Only three suggestions are forthcoming from the literature. Some argue that the passage should be understood as meaning "all you who are able to, i.e. who are prophets, will be able to prophesy".[14] Apart from the fact that there is no indication in the text that Paul is now addressing a limited group, a different "you all", there is still the implausibility of there being only two or three prophets to be dealt with. Perhaps the best representative of this view is Conzelmann, who says:

οἱ ἄλλοι in v 29 [sc. should be taken as] the rest of the prophets (see n. 46). For καθ' ἕνα πάντες, "all one by one," cannot mean simply everybody, but all who are considered here, all upon whom the spirit of prophecy comes. The emphasis does not lie on πάντες, all, but on "singly", i.e., that you may be understood.[15]

One can agree with Conzelmann that the emphasis is upon "singly" without removing the force of "all of you": πάντες, as I have pointed out, is

suggestion to the whole discussion, arguing that Paul does not realistically expect all or even most of the Corinthians to contribute to their meetings. But the emphatic repetition of πάντες in the passage is hard to dismiss in this way.

[14] Thus D.E. Aune says that the "all" in 1 Cor. 14 could be "all the prophets": *Prophecy*, pp. 195-7, p. 200, and notes. Likewise Engelsen, *Glossolalia*, pp. 170ff.

[15] H. Conzelmann, *op.cit.*, p. 245. See, similarly, D. Hill, *Prophecy*, p. 133, W.A. Grudem, *Gift*, pp. 237ff.

repeated several times within this verse: "you can all prophesy, so that all may learn and all be encouraged . . ." If one of these "all"s is to be limited to the prophets, there is no good reason to let the others stand! Not only so, but out of a total of eight usages of the καθ᾽ ἕνα phrase in Paul, six use ἕκαστος and could be translated "each of you singly" (1 Cor. 12.18, Ephesians 4.7, 4.16, 5.33, Colossians 4.6, 1 Thess. 2.11, 2 Thess. 1.3), Romans 12.5 has the same sense without the ἕκαστος, and this passage alone uses πάντες. It seems to me, therefore, that it would be most unwise to ignore the force of the recurrent πάντες in the passage. Paul says, and means, "you can all prophesy, one by one".[16]

The second suggestion made to overcome the apparent contradiction between "only two or three" and "all of you" is that Paul intends us to understand that anyone or everyone can prophesy over an extended period of time; not, of course, at the one meeting.[17] While this certainly does overcome the contradiction, it is not at all in harmony with the context. The passage is about what is to happen "when you gather together" (ὅταν συνέρχησθε, 14.26), and the natural sense is that these regulations and Paul's justification of them have to do with each individual instance of meeting. At each meeting there are to be two or at most three uninterpreted glossolalic episodes. At each meeting two or three prophets should speak. At that same time "the others" should judge what is said; not between meetings, or at the next meeting when the matter has been put "on notice". At each meeting, therefore, "you can all prophesy". Such must be the natural sense of the passage.

The third suggestion is that of Fee, who argues that Paul means only two or three prophets should speak before "the others weigh carefully what is

---

[16] T.C. Edwards, *A Commentary on the First Epistle to the Corinthians*, London, 1897, p. 380, is one of the few to present an argument for the strong sense of "all" here, citing Ephesians 5.33 (you are all to love your wives) as a parallel. Barrett, Bruce, Cothenet and others concur, though without detailed argumentation.

[17] Robertson and Plummer sum up the view of the overwhelming majority of older exegetes who notice the problem when they say that "you can all prophesy" means "in successive assemblies". (A. Robertson and A. Plummer, *A Critical and Exegetical Commentary on the First Epistle of St. Paul to the Corinthians*, Edinburgh, 1911, p. 322.) The same position is taken up by, among others, C.J. Ellicott, H.A. Ironside, R. St. J. Parry, J.E. McFadyen, J. Weiss, C. Hodge, F.F. Bruce and M.E. Hart, *Tongues and Prophecy*.

said".[18] This is by far the best of the three suggestions, but more can be said. My own suggestion is that, in order to fully resolve the paradox, we need to re-examine Paul's objections to Corinthian practice.

In Chapter 7 I suggested that the problem over inspired speech could be summarised as follows. The Corinthians were doing at least three things to which Paul objected. (1) They were allowing glossolalia to be widely practised in the assembly without interpretation, which Paul believed to be unhelpful to those assembled. (2) They were allowing this practice to continue even when there were unbelievers or outsiders present. (3) They were practising prophecy in a way which (in Paul's view) discouraged the congregational testing of prophetic statements, with individuals wishing to exercise prophetic gifts competing in some way with one another for opportunities to do so. In the case of (1) Paul laid down a maximum of three glossolalic episodes, and even those only if there was a reasonable expectation of an interpretation. In the case of (2) he deprecated glossolalia in favour of prophecy. In the case of (3) he limited the number of prophetic episodes, as with glossolalia, to two or three, and insisted on congregational discernment.

I argued further that the most likely explanation of (1) and (2) had to do with the combination (in the minds of the Corinthians with whom Paul is in dispute) of an elitist theology similar to Philo's view of the two stages of the philosophic life (as expounded by R.A. Horsley: cf. Chapter 2, pp. 14-15, and note 12), and a high view of the status of glossolalia (and prophecy) as an indicator of spiritual maturity. I argued that this high view of glossolalia was better explained by their own experiences of glossolalia as a phenomenon within early Christian groups than by appeals to supposed parallels from either the Jewish or the Hellenistic context. The time has now come to examine the question of elitism in more detail, so as to approach the problem of prophecy and Paul's view of its abuse in Corinth.[19]

---

[18] G.D. Fee, *The First Epistle to the Corinthians*, Grand Rapids, 1987, p. 693.

[19] It is important to emphasise that *both* glossolalia *and* prophecy are under discussion here, against the common insistence that it was predominantly glossolalia which the Corinthians valued and which Paul is revaluing. Thus even G.D. Fee, *op.cit.*, argues that it is glossolalia, far more than prophecy, with which Paul is dealing, or that he deals with prophecy primarily as a preferred alternative to glossolalia. Paul's linking of prophecy, knowledge and tongues as three things which will pass away in 13.8ff. is strong presumptive evidence that these three together were things highly valued by the Corinthians, rather than this being true of knowledge and tongues, the Corinthian

What evidence is there that Paul views elitism as a significant factor in his dispute with his converts in Corinth? The use by Paul of the terminology of childhood and maturity, "spiritual" and "psychic", has been shown by Horsley and others to point strongly in this direction. Further evidence is to be found in his citation of the presumed Corinthian slogan, "we all have knowledge" (1 Cor. 8.1) when it is clear from the following discussion, and specifically from v. 7, "but not all men have this knowledge", that the claim is not actually universal. The whole discussion of "stronger" and "weaker" brothers presupposes a claim by one group to superior status. Paul's reply, that knowledge (the elite virtue) is all very well, but that love (the communal virtue) is far superior, and indeed his insistence on the term "weaker (or stronger) brother" show him working against the elitist view (cf. later, chapter 10. 23-24). His discussion of the troubles around the Lord's Supper likewise shows us one group, materially better off than the rest, flaunting this status (11.22). Likewise his discussion of "spiritual gifts" and use of the "body" analogy is strongly oriented towards the value and participation of all members. No one ought to feel themselves outside the community (whether above it or beneath its notice, it does not matter) due to their particular charismatic endowments. God alone decides who has what gift. No one can say to the rest "I have no need of you" (v. 21); apparently less honourable members are to be treated with greater honour. All are urged to seek to contribute in the most valuable ways. Finally, it is clear that some in Corinth styled themselves "prophets", "spiritual" (2.14-16, 14.37), and made this a claim to superior status.[20]

---

favourites, but also of prophecy, which Paul proposed as an alternative (Fee, p. 643). This is evident also from Paul's concern that "the prophets, the spiritual" would deny his arguments (14.37).

[20] T.W. Gillespie, *Prophecy and Tongues*, p. 50-51, says that "there is a distribution of gifts to each member of the congregation, as opposed to a monopoly among the elite". See also J.P.M. Sweet, "A Sign for Unbelievers: Paul's Attitude to Glossolalia", *N.T.S.*, vol. 13, 1966-7, pp. 240-57, esp. pp. 240-246, and J.D.G. Dunn, *Unity and Diversity in the New Testament*, London, 1977, p. 179. See also J.H. Neyrey, "Body Language in 1 Corinthians: the Use of Anthropological Models for Understanding Paul and His Opponents", *Semeia*, vol. 35, 1986, pp. 129-170, esp. pp. 151, 155-6. In my view this corrects the emphasis of G.D. Fee, *op.cit.*, p. 577, note 36, who argues that "Paul's concern . . . is trying to place "tongues" into proper perspective, not (to) give teaching on the nature of prophecy." Paul is doing both. But the theological nature of prophecy is not the focus: its role as an indicator of "spiritual" status is. Likewise it is not fully accurate to say that "the need for diversity" is the focus of Paul's argument (Fee, p. 583,

Can elitism, then, be taken as a key factor with regard to prophecy as well? Such a suggestion yields immediate results. What Paul is objecting to in Corinthian practice is that certain prophets are simply taking up too much of the assembly's time. There may have been too many prophets wishing to speak, or there may have been a few individuals "holding the floor" for long periods. Chapter 14 verse 29 perhaps suggests the first problem, and verse 30 the second: some mixture of the two is not unlikely. Paul lays down that only two or three prophets are to speak, that their statements are to be evaluated, and that they must make way for one another. It would seem quite possible, then, that the group within the Corinthian church which saw itself as mature, as spiritual, and as having prophetic gifts, was dominating the assembly's time with prophecy as well as glossolalia, and denying that anyone had the right to evaluate their statements.[21]

The problem, then, in Paul's mind, is the use of prophecy by a "spiritual" elite and its restriction to a favoured few by a favoured few. Paul sees this as a denial of its communal nature.

Philo regularly associates the true wisdom of the philosopher with the possession of the Divine Spirit (see, for example, de Gigantibus 22), which is likewise closely linked with prophecy (i.e. Quis Rerum Divinarum Heres 259-266). The Spirit, being divine, rests only briefly upon any man, but upon the truly wise, less dominated by the flesh, the Spirit rests for much longer.[22]

600ff., note 12, unfortunately dismissing the emphasis on interdependence in Graeco-Roman parallels such as Livy 2.32, Josephus, B.J. 4.406 and to a lesser extent some of the Stoics). It is the *mutual interdependence* of diversity that is at stake in Paul's "body" metaphor. All need one another; none have independent standing.

[21] The work of J.A. Davis, *Wisdom and Spirit*, Lanham, 1984, building on the work of Horsley, shows that an interest in prophecy and things "spiritual" might well develop out of the Wisdom material. E.E. Ellis agrees: see "Prophecy in the New Testament - and Today", in Panagopoulos, *Vocation*, p. 46, where he argues that there is a strong link between prophecy and "wisdom" in the Jewish background: the wise are the inspired, and vice versa. Compare *Prophecy and Hermeneutic in Early Christianity*, Chapter 3, esp. pp. 53ff. B.A. Pearson argues that it is likely that "Sophia", as the hypostasis of divine wisdom, was often identified with the Holy Spirit in Hellenistic Judaism: see his *The Pneumatikos-Psychikos Terminology*, Missoula, 1973, pp. 36-7.

[22] Thus de Gigantibus 29-30, 48-9, 60, Quod Deus Immutabilis Sit 1.2. On the whole section above see the summary of Wolfson: "Prophecy is reserved for the refined man, the wise man, the just man, and the genuine lover of wisdom. With these qualifications of refinement, wisdom and justice any man is capable of attaining prophecy . . . there is no doubt that . . . the attainment of prophecy by those who are worthy of it is through an act of divine grace and selection." (H.A. Wolfson, *Philo*, vol. 2, pp. 47-48.)

If, based on a theology similar to Philo's, the Corinthian elitists were claiming a wisdom and a maturity not available to the less accomplished, then it would be very natural for them to claim also a virtually exclusive right to the Divine Spirit and his gifts. This would apply most especially to the gift of prophecy, pre-eminently the mark of the Patriarchs and great figures of the past.

It is also possible that the Corinthians (as is widely suggested) understood glossolalia as a form of prophecy in the wider sense of "inspired speech", but if they did so, this judgement and the consequent over-valuation of it was based on nothing in Philo. Nor, for that matter, can I see any background beyond their own Christian experience which either could or might be necessary to explain that over-valuation.[23]

With this understanding of the elitist tendencies of the Corinthian group with whom Paul is in dispute, we now return to the resolution of the contradiction between "let two or three prophets speak" and "you can all prophesy".

It has occasionally been suggested that the case for "congregational prophecy" is strengthened by the passages in which Paul refers to "prophecy" rather than "prophets". (See footnote 6, above.) Though taken in isolation the argument can hardly be conclusive, here it allows us to resolve the contradiction, and illuminates both this passage and the general context. Paul is laying down that at any one meeting, only two or three who are prophets (i.e. who claim to be, or are recognised as such) may prophesy, so that others, who do not claim the official position, but are occasionally prompted to prophesy, may do so freely. The problem to which Paul is replying would now be that certain "who think they are prophets, or spiritual" are absorbing the time of the meeting with extended prophetic performances. To curb their excesses, and to ensure that others are not excluded, Paul insists that if a revelation comes to another (regular prophet or no) then the prophet must sit down. He or she does not have exclusive rights to the assembly's attention. If this rule is followed, Paul continues, *all* will have the opportunity to prophesy, not just a prophetic few. Such a view is entirely in harmony with what we have seen above in the case of

---

[23] For the view that a fascination with ecstatic prophecy similar to Philo's underlies the Corinthian evaluation of glossolalia see B.A. Pearson, *The Pneumatikos-Psychikos Terminology*, Missoula, 1973, pp. 44-50. As was noted above, this view has serious weaknesses.

glossolalia. Those who speak in tongues are not to use their gift in ways that exclude their "less spiritual" brethren, and create distinctions of status within the community. In the same way prophets must not exercise their gift to the exclusion of those not recognised as prophets. That way everyone will have an opportunity to contribute, and everyone will be taught and encouraged. [24]

It might be objected that such a solution breaks the parallel between the cases of glossolalia and prophecy, since there is no suggestion that "recognised" glossolalists are being prohibited from dominating at the expense of those who only speak in tongues occasionally. But the objection has little force. If Paul had wished to make the parallel exact he could have used the phrase ἀνὰ μέρος that he uses in 14.27 to prescribe how prophets are to speak as well as glossolalists. Instead he chooses the strong καθ᾽ ἕνα πάντες, discussed above. Further, there was no class of "recognised" glossolalists in Paul's mind, and I have argued above that the Corinthian "elitists" used glossolalia as a mark of their status for essentially non-theological reasons. We know already, however, that Paul grants that someone may "have" prophecy (12.10, 13.2) and that some in Corinth claimed the title "prophet" (10.29, 14.37).[25] Paul is refusing to allow that they are the only ones with the right to the gift of prophecy. Certainly some are prophets, and others are not. But all should seek the higher gifts, especially that they may (on occasion) prophesy.

It is significant that a very similar view of prophecy can be shown to exist in the mid-second century work of Hermas, the "Shepherd". Jannes Reiling has shown that for Hermas, the true prophet, the man on whom the "angel of the prophetic spirit" comes, is in principle no other than any member of the Christian assembly, who all have "the divine spirit". This "modal" understanding of the work of the Holy Spirit is Hermas' own formulation,

---

[24] Thus I find myself in disagreement with A.C. Wire, *Women Prophets*, p. 146-9, who argues that Paul is attempting to limit the number of prophetic episodes. On the contrary: he is making room for more. Wire's otherwise perceptive analysis fails when she ignores v. 31, "that way you can all prophesy", and argues that "Paul wants the spiritual in Corinth to move away from communal and expressive leadership toward more individual and reflective leadership." He wants them to move from "individual elitist expressive" to "communal expressive *and* reflective".

[25] Compare also M.E. Hart, *Tongues and Prophecy*, p. 316, who notes that the parallel is not perfect anyway, because Paul discusses two or *at the most* three glossolalists, and two or three prophets (i.e. a few).

but seems to grow out of the same "congregational" view of prophecy we find in 1 Corinthians 12-14.[26]

The proposed exegesis of 1 Corinthians 14 can be further tested by examining Paul's discussion of the gift of "discernment of spirits", which is so integrally a part of the passage. Here our question is: "Who discerned?"

2. Who Discerned?

Paul's argument is as follows:

> When you come together, everyone (ἕκαστος) has a hymn, or a word of instruction, a revelation, a tongue, or an interpretation. All of these must be done for the strengthening of the church . . . Two or three prophets should speak, and the others (οἱ ἄλλοι) should weigh carefully (διακρινέτωσαν) what is said. And if a revelation comes to someone who is sitting down, the first should stop. For you can all prophesy in turn so that everyone may be instructed and encouraged . . . (14.26ff.)

The question that has divided exegetes is quite simple: who are "οἱ ἄλλοι" in v. 29? Are they "the other prophets", or are they the rest of the congregation as a whole? Though it is widely held that Paul generally gives responsibility for the judging of issues and doctrine to the congregation as a whole, many have felt constrained to argue that this case is an exception, and that here the right to judge prophetic speech is specifically delegated to those known and recognised as prophets.[27] As far as I am aware only two

---

[26] J. Reiling, *Hermas and Christian Prophecy*, Leiden, 1973, and "Prophecy, the Spirit and the Church", in J. Panagopoulos, *Vocation*, pp. 58-76. D.E. Aune is critical of the conclusions of Reiling, arguing that "the act of prophesying is inseparable from those individuals formally designated 'prophets'" (*Prophecy*, pp. 199-200). This, however, misses the force of Reiling's case. Aune is also a little misleading when he says (*Prophecy*, p. 403, footnote 39 to p. 197) that H. Paulsen is critical of Reiling's view of congregational prophecy in Hermas. While Paulsen is critical of assuming that the same view pertains to the papyrus P. Oxy 5 (apparently a commentary on Hermas), as Reiling argues, he makes only minor modifications to the emphasis of Reiling's view of Hermas himself: see notes 21-23, pp. 445-6 of his article, "Papyrus Oxyrhynchus I.5 und die ΔΙΑΔΟΧΗ ΤΩΝ ΠΡΟΦΗΤΩΝ", *N.T.S.*, vol. 25, 1978-79, p. 443 ff. On the "Shepherd" generally see now the excellent summary of R.L. Fox, *Pagans and Christians*, London, 1986, pp. 381ff, esp. p. 381 and note 22, where a date about 90 A.D. is argued for.

[27] Christophe Senft, *La première épître de Saint Paul aux Corinthiens*, Neuchatel, 1979, p. 182, suggests that the precise form of the phrase, "2 or 3 prophets . . . others", suggests "the other prophets", and says, "Leur rôle est de *diakrinein* . . ." Compare E.E. Ellis, who likewise argues that discernment is the function of prophets, *art.cit.*, in J. Panagopoulos, *Vocation*, p. 52. N.I.J. Engelsen, *Glossolalia*, pp. 170ff. Similarly D.E. Aune argues, *Prophecy*, pp. 207-8, 220-221, that despite Paul's normal view (he cites 2 Thess. 2.2., 1 John 4.1, 1 Cor. 14.12.), prophets are subject to other prophets, not to the whole congregation. More moderate is M.E. Boring, *Sayings*, p. 66: "it is not clear

arguments of substance are brought forward to support this reversal of Paul's normal view. The first is the suggestion that the διάκρισις discussed here is really a separate thing from the "gift of discernment" more generally, and is manifested, exclusively or characteristically, by prophets. Thus D.A. Carson argues that "there is no evidence that this careful weighing of the content of Christian prophecy should be confused with the gift of discerning spirits (12:20)".[28] Likewise W.A. Grudem attempts to show that there is no necessary link between 12.10 and 14.29, and likewise no necessary link between prophecy and διάκρισις.[29] While Grudem does show that there is no necessary close link, such as that between glossolalia and interpretation, his most strongly argued point, that 14.29 deals not with a particular gift, but with what the whole congregation does, is surely a false antithesis. As he himself argues (*art.cit.*, pp. 267-8), "several of the gifts Paul mentions are simply special or "highly developed" abilities which correspond to general abilities possessed by all believers". This could well be such a case. The fact remains that in both cases in which it occurs in chapters 12-14 διάκρισις is

---

whether 'the others' refers to the community as a whole or to the other prophets . . . "
See also C.M. Robeck, *art.cit.*, part 2, p. 45, which has a good survey of opinions: the position of James Dunn, *Jesus and the Spirit*, London, 1975, p. 236, and "Discernment of Spirits - A Neglected Gift" in W. Harrington, ed. *Witness to the Spirit*, Dublin, 1979, pp. 79-96, is not entirely clear. In the article, pp. 88-9 at least, he believes "the others" are the whole congregation. His "The Responsible Congregation (1 Co. 14:26-40)" in L. De Lorenzi, ed. *Charisma und Agape (1 Ko. 10-14)*, Rome, 1983, pp. 201-236, is cautious: he argues that "The most natural way to take the phrase is as a reference to the other prophets" (p. 226), but "we should not however infer from this that Paul was insisting on a matter of principle . . . Since he evidently did not envisage prophecy being confined to 'the prophets' . . . it would be unlikely that he confined the process of evaluation to the prophets. On the contrary the implication of 1 Co. 2,12-16 is precisely that *all* who have received the Spirit thereby have been given an enabling to recognize and understand the gifts of God and to make a Spirit-informed judgement on matters of the Spirit (including prophecy) . . . It may be, of course, that the particular conditions in the church at Corinth explain why in this instance Paul alludes only to the prophets when speaking of the process of evaluation." (pp. 226-7) Here I think Dunn has taken an important point in precisely the wrong direction: it is the circumstances in Corinth that make it overwhelmingly unlikely that he *is* referring primarily to the prophets.

[28] D.A. Carson, *Showing the Spirit*, p. 120. It should be noted that *Carson* (as well as Grudem, cited below) does not argue the case in order to restrict discernment to the prophets: he believes that οἱ ἄλλοι refers to the whole congregation, *op.cit.*, pp. 119ff.

[29] W.A. Grudem, *Gift*, pp. 58ff, pp. 265ff. This is part of his larger case against G. Dautzenberg's view of διάκρισις, his critique of which is quite convincing. See W.A. Grudem, "A Response to Gerhard Dautzenberg on 1 Cor. 12.10", *Biblische Zeitschrift*, vol. 22, part 2, 1978, pp. 253-270, esp. pp. 256-7., also reprinted in his *Gift*, pp. 263ff.

found in close proximity to prophecy.[30] It appears, then, that there is no simple way to argue that διάκρισις in this passage should be considered in a separate category from Paul's other usages of the term.

The second argument is that of Aune. To support the contention that it is the prophets within the congregation, not the whole congregation itself, who ought to judge prophecy, he claims that Paul's statement in 1 Cor. 14.37-8, "If anyone thinks he is a prophet or spiritual, he should acknowledge . . ." is evidence that it was prophets who exercised the ministry of discernment: Paul here demands that they do so.[31] But such a view entirely misses the strong irony in the statement, as well as the highly polemical tone. Those who claim prophetic authority or spiritual status are here put to the test. Paul knows or expects that those who do not have such pretensions will accept what he says, but he is not so sure about the "prophets" and "spirituals". Hence the veiled threat of verse 38: he who thinks himself a prophet or spiritual, but ignores what is said, will himself be ignored.

We can therefore argue that there is no strong case to be made that the διάκρισις Paul discusses here must be different from διάκρισις elsewhere in his letters. Yet in all other relevant cases he makes διάκρισις (and related terms) the prerogative of each individual or the congregation as a whole.[32] There is no single example where such a responsibility is delegated to any group within the congregation, to act on behalf of the others. It would

---

[30] Cf. M.E. Hart, *Tongues and Prophecy*, p. 329, and James Dunn, *Jesus and the Spirit*, p. 233, who argues that discernment of spirits "forms a pair with prophecy". Similar positions are taken by E. Fascher, *Prophetes*, p. 185, T.M. Crone, *Prophecy*, p. 222, and D.E. Aune, *Prophecy*, p. 220. This is not to argue that Dautzenberg is correct, or that διάκρισις has exclusively to do with prophecy, but merely that it *does* have to do with prophecy, among other things (cf. 1 Thess. 5.20-21); it can be to "determine both its source as to inspiration and its significance for the assembly". (Dunn, *Jesus and the Spirit*, London, 1975, p. 234) or to "evaluate what was said by the prophet, forming opinions about it . . . and perhaps discuss it publicly" (Grudem, *Gift*, p. 66).

[31] D.E. Aune, *Prophecy*, p. 221.

[32] See, for example, Romans 14.1, 1 Corinthians 2.14-15 (the "spiritual man" here is clearly Paul's ideal, to which all should aspire), 6.1-3, 6.5, 10.15, 11.3, 12.10, and 14.24. The suggestion of R.A. Horsley, "Wisdom of Word and Words of Wisdom in Corinth", *C.B.Q.*, vol. 39, 1977, p. 238, to the effect that the sentiment "the spiritual man judges all things" (1 Cor. 2.15) is a Corinthian statement only quoted by Paul seems to me most unlikely in the context. As T.M. Crone says, "it seems unlikely then that Paul would restrict the gift of discernment of spirits to the prophets" (*Prophecy*, p. 222, cf. p. 296). Further, if ordinary members of the congregation are to judge angels (1 Cor. 6.2-3) how likely is it that the evaluation of prophecy would be restricted to prophets only?

therefore require considerable evidence to force us to adopt such a reading here, and as we have seen, no such evidence is forthcoming.[33]

In further defence of congregational prophecy the parallel case of teachers and teaching ought to be considered. It is beyond dispute that the term "teachers" in the Acts and letters of Paul designates a fairly clearly defined group, the rough outline at least of whose duties is well known. But no-one of whom I am aware suggests that Paul's wish that all Christians be able to teach or instruct or encourage one another (Romans 14.19, 15.14, Colossians 3.16, 1 Thess. 4.8, 5.11, cf. Hebrews 5.12), is, as a result, "purely hypothetical". Yet the evidence that he expected prophecy to be widespread, alongside its "more official" form in terms of regular "prophets", is just as clear as that for what we might call "congregational teaching".[34] Nor can it be plausibly argued that the parallel drawn here is false due to prophecy's "more supernatural" nature: that is a distinction it would not have occurred to Paul to draw.

In brief, then: given that (1) elsewhere in his letters Paul regularly assigns the responsibility for evaluation of teaching, inspiration, and, indeed, most

---

[33] David Hill's comment that the change from 2nd to 3rd person in 1 Cor. 14.31 is a significant piece of evidence in favour of the prophets being in view (in J. Panagopoulos, *Vocation*, p. 109), which is the only other substantive argument known to me, seems particularly unconvincing. The most detailed case in favour of "the others" being the whole congregation is that of W.A. Grudem, *Gift*, p. 61, cf. p. 105. He cites 1 Cor 12.3, 1 Thess. 5.21. He also says, citing Godet and A.T. Robertson, that if that were Paul's meaning, he would probably have chosen οἱ λοιποί rather than οἱ ἄλλοι. Compare C.M. Robeck, *art.cit.*, part 2, pp. 45-6, who adds the consideration that "Paul does not elsewhere limit the gift of the discerning of spirits to prophets, nor does he expect to see the entire congregation as inactive in judging what is said by the prophets in their midst", and A.C. Wire, *Women Prophets*, p. 148. Similar views are held by S.D. Crane, *The Gift of Prophecy in the New Testament: An Inductive Study in the Exercise and Meaning of the Prophetic*, Diss., Princeton Theological Seminary, 1962, pp. 157 ff. The evidence of the Didache, ch. 11, where it is clearly the congregation, not other prophets, who judge prophets, is not however relevant, because it deals with a situation in which there is a shortage of prophets.

[34] Such a case makes the argument of T.M. Crone, *Prophecy*, pp. 211-212, that "there was a definable group who regularly exercised this ministry. In principle all could prophesy, but in fact Paul does not expect all to prophesy, and only a limited number were known as prophets" much less persuasive. Compare M.E. Hart, *Tongues and Prophecy*, p. 313, who thinks Romans 15.14 implies that there is "both a prophetic and a teaching ministry among members of the congregation which was in addition to the ministry of teacher and prophet. This is illustrative of the charismatic nature of the community."

other matters to the congregation as a whole; (2) Paul certainly does not believe that there ought to be a "pneumatic elite" within the congregation; (3) one group of the Corinthians would appear to have been asserting its pneumatic status, as against the remainder of the congregation, as mature believers; and (4) Paul quite expects this group, who call themselves "prophets", "spiritual",[35] to object to his teaching, it would appear highly unlikely that he would delegate the exclusive rights to the evaluation of prophetic utterance to that very group: the "other prophets". It is far more likely, on this basis, and on the basis of the general emphasis of the whole passage, that he is calling upon the entire congregation (doubtless led by those with specific gifts of discernment) to use its collective discretion as the Spirit-inspired people of God in the evaluation of prophetic claims and revelations. "The others" in 1 Corinthians 14.29, therefore, must be understood as "the rest of the congregation".

If this case is to be accepted, then the close relationship between the gifts of prophecy and discernment in Paul's thought is confirmed in another way. Both gifts are seen to exhibit the same dual nature: they are gifts that are sometimes exercised by particular specialists on behalf of the congregation (not all are prophets, to one is given prophecy, to another discernment of spirits) but they are also activities to which all may aspire, and in which all members are encouraged to join. Congregational prophecy and discernment are not the only forms the gifts take, in Paul's view, but the congregational element in them is one on which he insists, over against any attempt by any group to dominate or monopolise their exercise in the meetings of the congregation.

The final section in our answer to the question "Who prophesied? Who discerned?" has to do with the scope of Paul's exhortation to seek prophecy and take part in discernment from another point of view. Specifically what we must ask is: did he include women? At an exegetical level everything depends on the interpretation of 1 Corinthians 14.34. Is the silence here enjoined upon women absolute? If not, what are its limits? What, specifically, were women forbidden to do?[36]

---

[35] The relationship between the claim to be a prophet and the claim to "spiritual" status is discussed by W.A. Grudem, *Gift*, pp. 160-1, but he takes no account of the Philo material which so usefully links the two concepts, even if not the two terms.

[36] On this matter the best surveys of opinions known to me are those of W.H. Leslie, *The Concept of Woman in the Pauline Corpus in the Light of the Social and Religious*

3. Did women prophesy or exercise discernment?

Opinions abound, and most are not relevant here. It is now widely agreed that Paul cannot be forbidding women to prophesy, as this would contradict 1 Corinthians 11.5, where permission to prophesy is clearly implied.[37] Some argue that while they may occasionally prophesy they may not hold the office of prophet, but such a position is difficult to maintain on the basis of the available evidence.[38] It is also highly unlikely that he is confining their prophesying to "small-group prayer meetings" as opposed to the main meetings of the assembly.[39] Such a distinction reflects a view of the nature of "church" that Paul would have found incomprehensible. The older view that the churches imitated synagogue practice by segregating men and women, and that what Paul is forbidding is calling across the meeting, has had its evidential basis severely criticised at the level of synagogue practice: there seems to be no convincing evidence that either the synagogue or the early church meetings were segregated.[40] Neither, until recently, has the

Environment of the First Century, Diss., Northwestern University, 1976, esp. pp. 125ff., and more recently D.A. Carson, *Showing the Spirit*. pp. 121ff., A.C. Wire, *Women Prophets*, pp. 229ff., and R.W. Allison, "Let Women be Silent in the Churches", *J.S.N.T.* vol. 32, 1988, pp. 27-60.

[37] Among the few still resisting this conclusion are W.J. Martin, "1 Corinthians 11:2-16: an interpretation", in *Apostolic History and the Gospel*, ed. W.W. Gasque and R.P. Martin, Exeter, 1970, pp. 231-241, esp. p. 240, and A.C. Wire, *Women Prophets*, esp. pp. 152-158 and 229ff. W.A. Criswell argues that they are forbidden to speak in tongues (*The Holy Spirit in Today's World*, Grand Rapids, 1966, pp. 213ff.) but it is hard to see how such a conclusion can be drawn from the passage.

[38] Thus C.M. Robeck, *art.cit.*, part 2 p. 39, argues that "In Paul, as in Acts, women are among those who occasionally prophesy, but likewise, no woman is ever called a prophetess . . . there is no explicit evidence that any woman ever occupied the office of prophet." But I doubt that we really know what "the office of prophet" might have been in any real sense. Luke calls Anna a prophetess; clearly that does not rule out the possibility! Of course he does not present her as a Christian prophet, but in my view the point still has force. On this point see M.E. Hart, *Tongues and Prophecy*, p. 73. Philip's four daughters were well known in the sub-apostolic period for their prophesying (Eusebius H.E. 3.31, 37), and we probably ought not to put too much weight on the verbal form of the description. D. Hill, *Prophecy*, pp. 100-101, says that "the tense . . . indicates that the women exercised the gift of prophecy regularly".

[39] See D.A. Carson, *Showing the Spirit.*, pp. 122-4, and W.H. Leslie, *op.cit.*, pp. 130ff. See similarly the treatment of J.G. Sigountos and M. Shank, "Public Roles for Women in the Pauline Church: a Reappraisal of the Evidence", *J.E.Th.S.*, vol. 26, part 3, 1983, pp. 283-295, esp. p. 284: "No distinction of place is made in this passage, so its parallelism indicates that both men and women prophesied under the same circumstances."

[40] See, for criticism of the view that synagogues practised segregation, B.J. Brooten,

attempt to dismiss the problem by assigning Chapter 11.2-16 or 14.33b-35 to a post-Pauline interpolator found much favour.[41] This case can now be argued with considerable force, but I do not myself find it compelling.

The suggestion that Paul is not forbidding all women to speak, or to contribute to the meetings of the congregation, but only wives, has been advanced. On this view Paul forbids their contribution because it would involve them in unacceptable clashes of authority with their husbands.[42] But such a view has been strongly criticised by Grudem, who argues that this interpretation would find Paul allowing immature single women to speak, but forbidding their more mature married sisters to do so.[43] Another line of interpretation has been to separate the issues of Chapter 11 from those of Chapter 14, and argue that prophecy and prayer are not under consideration in the latter. According to this view, the verb λαλεῖν in this passage has the special sense "to chatter on", or similar. Paul is not forbidding meaningful contributions, but gossip or idle discussion during meetings. We are asked to presume that the Corinthian women were more prone to this than the men, though in Athens, presumably, the case was the opposite (Acts 17.21)! Though this solution is certainly possible at the level of lexicography, it does run counter to Paul's usage of the verb λαλεῖν in this chapter, and hence must be judged unlikely to be correct.[44]

Women Leaders in the Ancient Synagogue, California, 1982, pp. 103-138.

[41] See, for example, G. Dautzenberg, *Urchristliche Prophetie*, Stuttgart, 1975, pp. 257-274 and pp. 290-300, W.O. Walker, "1 Corinthians 11:2-16 and Paul's Views Regarding Women", *J.B.L.*, vol. 94, 1975, pp. 94-110, and the reply of J. Murphy-O'Connor, "The non-Pauline Character of 1 Corinthians 11.2-16?", *J.B.L.*, vol. 95, part 4, 1976, pp. 615-621. On the text of Chapter 14. 33b-35 see also J.B. Hurley, "Did Paul Require Veils or the Silence of Women?", *W.Th.J.*, vol. 35 part 2, 1973, pp. 216ff, and *Man and Woman in Biblical Perspective*, Leicester, 1981, pp. 185-6. By far the most forceful case, however, has been put forward by G.D. Fee, *op.cit.*, pp. 699ff. The more complex case of R.W. Allison, *art.cit.*, is not treated here in detail.

[42] See, for example, E.E. Ellis, "The Silenced Wives of Corinth", in *New Testament Textual Criticism: Its Significance for Exegesis*, ed. E.J. Epp and G.D. Fee, Oxford, 1981, pp. 213-220.

[43] W.A. Grudem, *Gift*, p. 247, note 24. A reasonable reply to Grudem would be either that in this particular case it is only the married women who are, in Paul's view, causing the problem, or that the vast majority of women in the congregation would be married. But what of widows?

[44] For λαλεῖν in the sense of chatter see Plutarch, Mor. 504 a, 510 c, 645 a (drunkenness), 650 d (the talkativeness of the drunken), 716 d and 727 d, 679 a, and Fragment 93 of the Moralia, where καὶ φλυάρους . . . καὶ λάλους is used of "chatterboxes" and "drivellers". Compare Diodorus Siculus 18.62.4. For Paul's own

   More plausibly, M.E. Hart has argued that women generally are restricted
from asking questions during the congregational discussion of prophecies for
the same reason that glossolalists and prophets are limited to two or three:
so that they don't take up the whole meeting.[45] For her the key to the passage
is Paul's "if they want to learn". She does not explain, however, why
(presumably male) prophets and glossolalists are permitted two or three
contributions, and women none at all.

   The interpretation that has gained most favour in recent years is not
dissimilar to Hart's view in its concern for the context of the verses in
question. This is that Paul permits women to pray and prophesy publicly, but
does not permit them to participate in the congregational testing of
prophecy.[46] While this view has the virtue of taking seriously the context of
Paul's prohibition in his discussion of glossolalia, prophecy and discernment,
it does raise another problem that is not easy to overcome. Those who put
forward such a view usually do so on the basis of an argument about the
nature of Paul's view of authority. They argue that Paul believes in a
principal of the "headship" of the male generally, and the husband
specifically, and that what he is forbidding is women speaking in a way that
would overturn that headship. He is forbidding them to sit in judgement over
prophetic statements made by men (as well as women), men who may in
fact be their own husbands.[47]

---

usage, however, which tells against the suggestion, see 1 Corinthians 14.16, 14.19, 14.29
and 14.34-5. The issue is well treated by M.E. Hart, *Tongues and Prophecy*, p. 225, and
by R.W. Allison, *art.cit.*, p. 36, who is properly critical of the mid-20th century cultural
stereotype which saw women as gossips being read into the first century context.

[45] Hart, *Tongues and Prophecy*, pp. 325ff. Cf. the threefold σιγάτω in the passage.

[46] Though this view was advanced by W.C. Klein, "The Church and its Prophets",
Anglican Theological Review, vol. 44, no. 1, p. 8., in 1962, and by M.E. Thrall in her
Cambridge Bible Commentary on 1 and 2 Corinthians, p. 102, in 1965, it seems only to
have been taken up since in the detailed treatment of J.B. Hurley, "Did Paul Require
Veils or the Silence of Women?", *W.Th.J.*, vol. 35, part 2, 1973, pp. 216ff, and *Man and
Woman in Biblical Perspective*, Leicester, 1981, pp. 162-193. Hurley has been followed
by, among others, W.A. Grudem, *Gift*, pp. 239ff, D.A. Carson, *Showing the Spirit*, pp.
129ff, and with reservations by J. Dunn, "Discernment of Spirits - A Neglected Gift", in
Witness to the Spirit, ed. W. Harrington, Manchester, 1983, p. 89. For a critique of this
view see R.P. Martin, *The Spirit and the Congregation*, p. 86.

[47] Thus J.B. Hurley, *op.cit.*, pp. 190ff., W.A. Grudem, *Gift*, pp. 253-5, and D.A.
Carson, *Showing the Spirit*, pp. 129-131. A.C. Wire, *Women Prophets*, p. 157, is the
exception here, in line with her view that Paul is silencing women absolutely. She argues
from the context of the regulation of inspired speech that it must be specifically the

The problem with such a view is that it makes a quite arbitrary distinction between the nature of the authority for prophecy and for discernment. On this view women may prophesy things which (we may presume) would occasionally override the authority of their husbands, yet they may not evaluate the prophetic utterances of their husbands, or other men. Such a case might be argued on the basis that their use of prophecy is not on their own authority, but that of God, and hence they do not overthrow the authority of their husbands.[48] Aside from the fact that the same could equally be said of the gift of discernment (and, as I have argued above, of congregational discernment more generally: both involve the work of the Spirit in the congregation, and thus it is not the women concerned who override, but the Spirit) we note that such a view is special pleading. If a wife's authority in prophecy is not her own, but the Spirit's, and that is why she may prophesy, then her husband's authority in prophecy is not his own either, and so having his prophecy evaluated by his wife is not an overturning of his authority. The same, of course, applies with their gifts of discernment.

It seems, then, that the proposal of Hurley, *et.al.*, leads to inconsistencies that are very hard to resolve. A more straightforward view is, however,

---

inspired speech of women that Paul is discussing, but then argues that Paul is forbidding *all* female speech, on a general subordinationist view.

[48] This is the view of Carson, *Showing the Spirit*, p. 130. His argument that there is only a contradiction between the woman's subordinate role and her freedom to prophesy if prophecy is seen as divinely authoritative is also logically flawed. Prophecy and discernment have similar authority. They are co-ordinate gifts, as I argued above. If a woman is free to prophesy, there is no clear reason visible in the logic of Paul's case why she ought not to be free to take part in διάκρισις. This applies to prophecy whether "official" or occasional, and to the *gift* of διάκρισις as much as to communal διάκρισις.

For the claim that prophecy and teaching are authoritative in different ways and that this explains why women may prophesy and not teach see W.A. Grudem, "Prophecy - Yes, but Teaching - No: Paul's Consistent Advocacy of Women's Participation without Governing Authority", *J.E.Th.S.* vol. 30, part 1, pp. 11-23; the critique of Moo by J.G. Sigountos and M. Shank, "Public Roles for Women in the Pauline Church: a Reappraisal of the Evidence", *J.E.Th.S.*, vol. 26, part 3, 1983, pp. 283-295, esp. pp. 285-6, seems to me to apply to the case of Grudem as well: "Certainly both teaching and prophecy were subject to scrutiny, as the example of the Bereans (Acts 17) and Paul's injunctions in 1 Corinthians 14 show. Moo . . . does not have an adequate explanation for the fact that women could do one but not another . . . both prophet and teacher were authority figures in early Christianity." The same applies, though less strongly, to the person with the gift of discernment. See also footnote 53, below.

available. The only direct evidence in the text itself as to what Paul is prohibiting is to be found in verse 35, "If they want to inquire about something, they should ask their own husbands at home; for it is disgraceful for a woman to speak in the ἐκκλησία."[49] Though it is possible that, in the context, the inquiries to which Paul is referring are actively a part of the evaluation of prophecy, the text does not require or naturally suggest that interpretation. Paul is not saying "if they have something to contribute, they should tell their husbands later" (when, of course, it might well be too late). He is saying that if they wish to learn (μαθεῖν) about anything they should ask (ἐπερωτάτωσαν) their own husbands later. Presumably the problem was that they were asking other peoples' husbands (or other people) on the spot.[50] But why should speaking to other women's husbands, or to others in the assembly, be considered shameful (αἰσχρὸν)? We should note that Paul does not merely say that it wastes valuable time, or that it interrupts the speakers; nor does he say it dishonours the woman's head. He says it is αἰσχρὸν, which is a word with powerful social connotations.[51] Why is such behaviour shameful? The answer is not difficult to find.

There existed in the Graeco-Roman world in our period a strong prejudice against women speaking in public, and especially against their speaking to other women's husbands. In a society with strictly defined gender and social roles, and a strong view of the rights of the man over his wife, such

---

[49] Thus, correctly, K. Stendahl, *The Bible and the Role of Women*, Philadelphia, 1966, pp. 29-30: "the silence here stands in contrast to 'asking questions', not to preaching, teaching, or prophesying." This is one of the few options not adequately canvassed by R.W. Allison, *art.cit.*, in his otherwise very thorough servey of options.

[50] S.C. Barton ("Paul's Sense of Place: an Anthropological Approach to Community Formation in Corinth", *N.T.S.*, vol. 32, 1986, pp. 225-246), suggests that though this is probably the way Paul read the problem in Corinth, it may not have been the whole situation. See p. 231. But Paul cannot be saying that it is disgraceful for a woman to speak in the assembly altogether, as he has earlier given implicit permission for public prayer and prophecy, so long as decorum is observed. Therefore the passage should be taken as "it is shameful for a woman to speak in the assembly (in the way specified above)". The attempt by W.A. Grudem, *Gift*, pp. 253-5, to make the (seemingly innocent) questions of the Corinthian women into disguised attempts at evaluation of prophecy, subversive of gender roles, seems to me to be too forced to be persuasive. If Paul thought their questions were an excuse for critical comments, he left no clue to that effect in the passage.

[51] See S.C. Barton, *art.cit.*, pp. 229-31.

behaviour was treated as totally inappropriate. The evidence for this view is scattered over a wide time-span in both the Greek and Roman worlds.[52]

The two most striking passages in favour of such a view are those closest in time to the New Testament. In his essay "Advice to Bride and Gröom", 31-2, Plutarch, speaking of the virtuous woman, says that

her speech . . . ought to be not for the public, and she ought to be modest and guarded about saying anything in the hearing of outsiders, since it is an exposure of herself; for in her talk can be seen her feelings, character and disposition. Pheidias made the Aphrodite of the Eleans with one foot on a tortoise, to typify for womankind keeping at home and keeping silence. For a woman ought to do her talking either to her husband or through her husband, and she should not feel aggrieved if, like the flute-player, she makes a more impressive sound through a tongue not her own.

Likewise Livy, recreating a speech of Marcus Porcius Cato for a late first-century B.C. audience, has his paragon of conservative virtue say:

If each man of us, fellow citizens, had established that the right and authority of the husband should be held over the mother of his own family, we should have less difficulty with women in general; now at home our freedom is conquered by female fury, here in the Forum it is bruised and trampled upon . . . What kind of behaviour is this? Running around in public, blocking streets, and speaking to other women's husbands! Could you not have asked your husband the same thing at home?[53]

---

[52] For this view see the references in J.J. Wettstein, *Novum Testamentum Graecum*, vol. 2, reprint of 1962, Graz, pp. 163-4. For the fifth century B.C. see Aeschylus, Septem, 230ff. (the role of women in time of preparation of war is to remain silent and stay at home), Euripides, Tro. 649ff. (Andromache tells her mother she was a proper wife to Hector, staying at home and keeping silence), Heraclid. 477 (Macaria asks not to be thought over-bold speaking publicly, since for a woman silence and staying at home are fairest), and Sophocles, Ajax 294 (Ajax repeats to Tecmessa the proverb "Woman, for women silence is a grace"). The reputation of women as gossips is mentioned in Euripides' Phoeniss. 706, and, moving to the later period, in Plautus, Aulularia 2.1.5. Rudens 4.4.70 has the slave Trachalio explain the silence of two women with the comment that "Women are always worth more seen than heard." In our period we should add the comment of Plutarch, Numa 77b, that the wise lawgiver King Numa taught Rome's women to be silent, especially in the absence of their husbands. W.H. Leslie, *op.cit.*, p. 105, notes (mistakenly) that in his Ekklesiazusae Aristophanes has his heroine put her veil on a magistrate who is trying to silence her, hand him a basket of wool, and silence him, proclaiming that women are taking over Athens. This passage, mistakenly attributed by Leslie (it is actually Aristophanes' Lysistrata, line 530ff.), is a particularly nice example of a comic reversal of normal practice.

[53] Livy, 34.2.9. Cato is speaking against the repeal of the Oppian law which strictly limited (among other things) the amount of jewellery a woman might own, the debate over which had seen Roman women lobbying in the streets. The passage is cited without detailed reference by Elisabeth Schüssler Fiorenza, *In Memory of Her*, New York, 1984, pp. 231-2. Since it is generally agreed that this speech is a free composition of Livy's

These two striking passages, as well as the other material cited above, make a highly suggestive background against which to interpret Paul's prohibition. The rights of women to pray and prophesy within the assembly may not be denied (Chapter 11), provided they maintain decorum (in this case, of hairstyle, symbolic of the order of the sexes and of their role as wives). They too have the Spirit, and may join freely in prayer (which is, after all, directed to God, and is thus unexceptionable), prophecy, through which the Spirit speaks directly to His people, and discernment, where the Spirit is also at work among the people of God, and they might well have positive contributions to make. But where there are matters that they do not understand, or on which they wish to know more, the case is different. Not only is the assembly's time limited (which was the motive for his limitation of the number of glossolalic and prophetic episodes), but to ask questions of the husbands of other women (especially as this might lead to extended discussions) would be grossly improper, and as such is not to be permitted.[54] Nor is it necessarily the case that Paul is making such a ruling absolute. He might well make exceptions for those well-known and widely respected female workers who figure in such a noteworthy fashion in his correspondence. He is certainly not saying, for example, that Priscilla may not, with Aquila, instruct Apollos, that Phoebe may not address the church in Cenchreae, or that Mary, Junia, Tryphaena, Tryphosa, Persis, Julia and others may not discuss theology with men.[55] But in reply to particular

---

own, and his opinion of Cato is high (see Livy 34.41), it seems reasonable to assume that this passage reflects conservative sentiment in our period.

[54] While the evangelistic motive is not strong here, it may not be entirely absent. It seems likely, however, that Paul's indignation is genuine, and that he shares the view of his times. To enter into a conversation with another man's husband threatens a breach of the exclusiveness of the marital relationship. It is most probably in this context that Paul argues that "they must remain in submission, as even the Law says". The alternative view which understands ὑποτασσέσθωσα as "self-controlled", in parallel with verse 33 (Hart, *Tongues and Prophecy*, p. 334, and R. and C.C. Kroeger, "An Inquiry into Evidence of Maenadism in the Corinthian Congregation", *S.B.L. Seminar Papers*, 1978, p. 336, and "Pandemonium and Silence at Corinth", in *Women and the Ministries of Christ*, eds. R. Hestenes and L. Curley, Pasadena, 1980, pp. 51ff.), can still be harmonised with my view: the women in question are to be self-controlled about when and where they ask their questions, and not breach decorum by just blurting them out to men.

[55] On the claim that prophecy and teaching are authoritative in different ways, explaining why women may prophesy and not teach see W.A. Grudem, "Prophecy - Yes, but Teaching - No: Paul's Consistent Advocacy of Women's Participation without Governing Authority", *J.E.Th.S.* vol. 30, part 1, pp. 11-23, and the critique of such views in

perceived abuses in Corinth, which both he and the Corinthians understand better than we do, he is requiring that wives with questions keep their questions for their own husbands (who, by implication, have a responsibility to answer such questions, and thus take responsibility for their wives' further education in the faith).[56]

The most likely background for such a problem, as has often been suggested, is that the overwhelming majority of ordinary women in the Hellenistic and Roman period were married early, to men considerably older than themselves, and had little or no formal education. What education they did have was strictly limited to what was perceived as their natural role: household tasks, crafts, music and such.[57] Thus it is not at all unlikely that their new-found freedom, within the assembly, to take part in congregational life and to contribute in other ways would have led to what Paul considers to be serious breaches of decorum, as they set out to understand features of teaching or prophecy for themselves. It is the availability of this interpretation which leaves me accepting the force of Fee's textual argument, but feeling no need to make use of it. I conclude, then, that Paul actively encourages women to take part in both the prophetic activity of the congregation, and the consequent communal evaluation of prophecy, providing they do not breach the common standard of decorum.

Summary

In this chapter we have discussed several of the various issues that appear to have divided Paul from his Corinthian converts on the subject of prophecy. I have argued that the major points in dispute may be understood, in parallel with the case of glossolalia, as having to do with the elitism of

---

Sigountos and Shank, *art. cit.*

[56] That husbands ought to take responsibility for the education of their wives is also suggested by Plutarch, Mor. 145 c.

[57] The objections of Sigountos and Shank, *art.cit.*, pp. 283-295, to the view that women are largely uneducated in Hellenistic culture are based on noteworthy exceptions, such as members of the ruling families, or the very wealthy. They are exceptions none the less. Even their own examples show that it such education was rigidly structured around the "woman's proper role". J.H. Leslie is correct when he says that Plutarch's evidence suggests that "there were no formal educational opportunities for Greek women in his day and that the number of educated females was relatively small" (*op.cit.*, pp. 405-6). The overwhelming majority of Corinthian women would have had (in all probability) little education of any literary sort, and almost certainly none to help them understand theology in a discussion with (educated) men.

one group within the Corinthian congregation, described by themselves (and ironically by Paul) as "spiritual". They appear to have been attempting to dominate the congregational exercise of both prophecy and its evaluation, by asserting their own elite status and their right to prophesy unhindered, and by denying the right of any they judged to be of lesser status than their own to evaluate what they said. Whether some of them also specifically denied the right of women to participate in prophecy, or, on the contrary, were women asserting their right to inquire freely about matters under discussion from whoever they chose, is an issue I have not attempted to solve. It is easy to see how either position might arise from the background suggested by such scholars as Horsley; but the required analysis will not be entered into here. Instead we will turn to the final major issue to be treated: the question of the relationship between early Christian and Hellenistic ideas of the nature of prophecy.

Chapter 11

Prophecy and Oracles in the Hellenistic World

We saw above in Chapter 8 that approaching prophecy in the Hellenistic environment of early Christianity by way of the terminology of the προφήτης word-group is unlikely to lead to useful results. Having examined some of the forms taken by early Christian prophecy, we are now in a position to ask ourselves whether any enlightening parallels can be drawn between such Christian prophecy and prophecy in the immediate environment of the early Christian groups. The problem of definition thus raises its head again. If "prophecy" was not what προφῆται did in the first century A.D., then what was it?

If, as I suggested in the first chapter, a reasonable initial definition is that a prophet is one who is believed to have access to supernatural sources of information unavailable to his or her fellows, then a working definition is not hard to form. Prophecy is the native ability or learned art of receiving and mediating information from these supposed supernatural sources. Prophets are those who have assumed a role as specialists in prophecy, or who have by accepted institutional practice been given such a specialist role.[1]

On such a simple working definition the Hellenistic world knew of many forms of prophecy. It could take the form of spontaneous dreams, dreams at incubation oracles, waking visions[2] (including "ascents to heaven"[3]), and the

---

[1] The definition of divination and prophecy proposed by D.E. Aune is essentially similar: divination is "the art or science of interpreting symbolic messages from the gods . . . oracles, on the other hand, are messages from the gods in human language, received as statements from a god . . . the term "oracle" is also used for the place where such messages are requested or received." (*Prophecy*, p. 23.)

[2] On dreams and visions see the survey of J.S. Hanson, "Dreams and Visions in the Graeco-Roman World and Early Christianity" in *A.N.R.W.*, II, vol. 23, part 2, 1980, pp. 1395-1427, and now especially the excellent and very detailed treatment of R.L. Fox, *Pagans and Christians*, London, 1986, esp. pp. 102ff.

[3] For this see especially A. Segal, "Heavenly Ascent in Hellenistic Judaism, Early Christianity and their Environment", in *A.N.R.W.*, II, vol. 23, part 2, 1980, pp. 1333-1394.

many and varied forms of technical divination.[4] In some of these forms of prophecy no specialist "prophet" was required for the reception of revelation, though the interpretation of that revelation required specialist skills. These might include phenomena as different as the anatomical knowledge of the art of the haruspex, the literary skills of the college of priests who interpreted the Sibylline books for the Roman state (and, at a lower social level, those of the χρησμολόγος), or the occult skills presumably required to run an oracle of the dead.[5] There were also forms of revelation that required no mediator or specialist knowledge or skill at all on the part of the recipient, such as "book-finding".[6]

Of all these forms of "prophecy", the one most likely to be useful for parallels with early Christian prophecy is that known as "inspiration manticism". The most common form of this is to be found in the great oracle centres of the Greek and Roman world, though there are other, less important, forms to be examined as well. It shares with early Christian prophecy the belief that revelation from the gods characteristically takes the form of statements made by persons believed to be under the influence of the god/s, who declare his/their will in a particular matter. Though early Christianity also believed in revelations in spontaneous dreams and in waking visions, as well as in other forms, we have seen above that it did not describe such revelations as prophecy.

The claim that there are close parallels between the form taken by Christian enthusiasm and prophetism and its environment, and that the parallels exist due to Christian borrowings from that cultural milieu, goes back at least to Reitzenstein. In his *Hellenistic Mystery Religions* he argued that

---

[4]   See generally R. Flacelière, *Greek Oracles*, trans. D. Garman, London, 1965, and D.E. Aune, *Prophecy*, chapter 2, p. 23ff., and R.L. Fox, *op.cit.*, pp. 168ff.

[5]   A νεκυομαντεῖον is mentioned by Diodorus Siculus 4.22.2, and another at Avernus by Strabo 5.4.5, and a ψυχομαντεῖον by Plutarch, Mor. 109 c. For a detailed survey of references to such oracles in the Graeco-Roman world (and elsewhere), see Sir James Frazer's material in T.H. Gaster, *Myth, Legend and Custom in the Old Testament*, New York, 1969, pp. 462ff.

[6]   On the phenomenon of the report of the finding of a book from the gods as a mode of revelation in the Hellenistic age see W. Speyer, *Bücherfunde in der Glaubenswerbung der Antike*, Göttingen, 1970.

No one claims that the content of early Christian ἐνθουσιασμός was borrowed from paganism; but it should no longer be disputed that its form and conception are actually appropriated . . .[7]

Such a view has, in fact, been widely disputed since Reitzenstein, specifically with reference to Christian prophecy. We might summarise the argument by suggesting that the difference between Christian prophecy and its pagan counterpart is often expressed in three main antitheses.

1. Three Antitheses

(1) Graeco-Roman prophecy is said to be predominantly ecstatic, while Jewish / Christian prophecy is said not to be.[8] (2) This frenzy or ecstasy is said to be characterised by violent seizures (of the kind examined in Chapters 6 and 7) and is claimed to be self-induced, either chemically (as is often mistakenly held of the Pythia), physically or psychologically. Jewish / Christian prophecy, on the other hand, is held to be spontaneous.[9] (3) Graeco-Roman prophecy is said to supply morally neutral information about the future, whereas Jewish / Christian prophecy is said to tell of the morally charged will of God.[10]

Whatever value these three antitheses may have in distinguishing Christian prophecy from Hellenistic popular enthusiasm generally, however,

---

[7] R. Reitzenstein, *Hellenistic Mystery Religions*, trans. J.E. Steely, from the 3rd German edition of 1926, Pittsburg, 1978, Appendix 7, "Philosopher and Prophet", p. 300. Though Reitzenstein was discussing the whole range of "enthusiastic" behaviour in early Christianity, we shall be discussing only those Christian phenomena defined in chapters 8-10 as "prophecy".

[8] See the references cited above, in Chapter 3: as was noted there this case is often made alongside a very critical evaluation of glossolalia as more ecstatic (and hence similar to non-Christian phenomena) than prophecy.

[9] See, for example, L.T. Johnson, "Norms for True and False Prophecy in First Corinthians", *American Benedictine Review*, vol. 22, 1971, p. 33. R.H. Gundry, "'Ecstatic Utterance' (N.E.B.)?", *J.Th.S.*, vol. 17 part 2, 1966, p. 307, note 2 argues that " . . . the New Testament contains no indications that glossolalia was induced artificially as in pagan religions by liquor, narcotics, frenzied dancing, rhythmic repetition of formulae, self-mutilation, or emotion-charged rituals. Prayer and the laying on of hands . . . do not easily fit into the category of techniques for the inducement of ecstatic speaking."

[10] The familiar distinction between prophecy "fore-telling" (pagan) and "telling forth" (Judaeo-Christian), criticised above, in Chapter 9, has penetrated down to the popular level. See also H. Bacht, "Wahres und falsches Prophetentum", *Biblica*, vol. 32, 1951, pp. 237-262, and L.T. Johnson, *art.cit.*, p. 33.

they have precious little value in distinguishing it from inspiration manticism in the Graeco-Roman world. We will now examine each case in turn.

Frenzied

In the case of (1), we have seen in Chapters 5-7 that there is very little evidence to suggest that oracular practice regularly involved ecstatic frenzy. Though popular writers did produce highly coloured reports of oracular practice focussing on dramatic descriptions of the emotional state of the prophetess, better informed sources produce a very different picture. The suggestion that oracles made use of narcotics has long been dismissed, and the idea that the Pythia was intoxicated by "mephitic vapours" is a total misunderstanding of our evidence.[11]

Induced, not spontaneous

With regard to (2), while it is true that some of the techniques mentioned by Gundry ("liquor, narcotics, frenzied dancing, rhythmic repetition of formulae, self-mutilation, or emotion-charged rituals") were used to produce frenzy in some forms of popular religion, *none* of them is represented in our evidence for the workings of oracle-cults. What we have seen of oracular practice, both at Delphi and Didyma, suggests a calm and aristocratic concern for detail rather than intense emotional involvement.[12] Such highly-charged expectation is far more likely to be the response of the inquirer than the priestess or προφήτης. Our information on the emotional level of early Christian meetings, on the other hand, is too slight to support Gundry's confidence that "prayer and the laying on of hands . . . do not easily fit into the category of techniques for the inducement of ecstatic speaking". That depends entirely on (a) the level of expectation and emotional intensity of the prayers in question, and (b) the emotional intensity of the early Christian experience of glossolalia. That early Christian prophecy was "spontaneous" is a statement that would require very careful definition. Were it taken to mean merely that prophecy was independent of a process of inquiry, and that it was not preceded by a period of preparation

---

[11] For a discussion of the "vapours" (πνεύματα) said to induce ἐνθουσιασμός at Delphi see Chapters 5 and 6 above, and the brief discussion below.

[12] See, for Delphi, the description in J. Fontenrose, *The Delphic Oracle*, Berkeley, 1978, pp. 224ff; for Didyma see the more speculative account of H.W. Parke, *The Oracles of Apollo in Asia Minor*, London, 1985, pp. 210-219.

and expectation, then no problems would result. In most cases, however, the statement is made in a far more polemical context: pagan prophecy is said to be self-induced in some fashion, Christian prophecy to be spontaneous. As far as I can see, such a proposition is simply not capable of historical verification or falsification. That ritual may have been used at oracle centres to bring about a mild trance state or greater receptivity to suggestion is quite possible, but it cannot be argued that this was a distinguishing factor between Christianity and its environment. It is entirely possible that early Christian inspiration likewise depended heavily on social factors. The evidence that would allow a social scientist, for example, to judge the level of "spontaneity" in early Christian prophecy, and the extent to which it might be the product of small-group dynamics, is simply not available to us.

A similar point to that made about spontaneity must be made about the suggestion that in Graeco-Roman prophecy the prophet is selected by human beings, but in Christian prophecy the prophet is selected by God. Such a statement (for which see H. Krämer, *T.D.N.T.*, vol. 6, p. 791), though probably reflecting the view of our sources, tells us little of worth and is dangerously value-laden. No doubt a Delphic official would reply that Apollo deigns to work through human choices, as he works through humans generally. Since he did continue to inspire the Pythia, we could presume he approved of her appointment. On the Christian side, while it could be argued that the claim to prophesy is a claim that one has been divinely chosen to do so, it is human beings who apply to others the title προφήτης. The more extensive claim, that "not only in choice, however, does the initiative lie with man; the whole process is, as it were, only to order . . . even the inspiration is induced by human initiative",[13] is an even worse case of theological value-judgements being imposed upon our evidence. Nothing forced Apollo to give oracles: if the omens were inauspicious, it was very dangerous to proceed. It is clear Krämer knows this from the very next sentence of his article: "Only once in Plutarch's time do we hear of a Pythia refusing to serve as the mouthpiece of the god . . ." This is an allusion to the case noted in Chapter 5 above, *Mor.* 437 d, where an attempt to force inspiration in the teeth of unfavourable omens brought on the death of the Pythia.

---

[13] H. Bacht, *art.cit.*, p. 250, cited by L.T. Johnson, *loc.cit.*; H. Krämer, *loc.cit.*

In brief, point (2) is entirely unproven, both on the Graeco-Roman side and the Christian side. Point (3) requires more detailed consideration.

Morally Neutral Prediction

There are few generalisations more firmly embedded in the discussion of our subject than that prophecy in the Biblical tradition is to be sharply distinguished from "mere pagan soothsaying". Thus, for Johnson, prophecies dealt more with ambiguous predictions concerning the future of men, than with communicating God's will to them. The prophet was less a spokesman for God than a medium of supernatural and morally neutral knowledge.[14]

We should take care to note that this distinction is highly value-laden. As D.E. Aune argues,

> while it is true that pagan oracles are only occasionally concerned with religious or moral values, that only means that divine revelation played a different social function in the Greco-Roman world generally than it did for the Jew or the Christian.[15]

It is even more important, however, that we realise that suggestion (3) is thoroughly false on two levels. A simple perusal of the corpus of known Delphic and Didymean oracles will show that a very large number indeed have to do with religious matters. If anything, the largest single group of known oracular responses have to do with the regulation of cult practices.[16] That such matters are not normally concerned with "moral" issues reflects the nature of Graeco-Roman religion as such, rather than the nature of prophecy. Furthermore, the negative value judgement attached to the claim that Graeco-Roman prophecy mediated "morally neutral knowledge" results simply from our society's adherence to the Christian tradition, in which matters of cult practice are valued below matters of personal or corporate morality. To label the Graeco-Roman oracular tradition amoral as a result is simply partisan.

It is also entirely false to state that oracles were not concerned with what we would call moral issues. In Herodotus 1.64 the people of Cyme inquired of the oracle at Didyma as to whether they should give way to extreme

---

[14] L.T. Johnson, *art.cit.*, p. 33. A better formulation, though still flawed, is that of E. Best, "Prophets and Preachers", *S.J.Th.*, vol. 12, 1959, p. 139: "Such prophecy, though concerned with the future, was not concerned with it in the redemptive sense in which we have seen the canonical prophets to be concerned."

[15] D.E. Aune, *Prophecy*, p. 21.

[16] Fontenrose argues that 210 of the 535 known Delphic oracles have to do, either directly or indirectly, with cult matters, *op.cit.*, pp. 21-9. Of the fifty oracles of Didyma he has collected, 14 likewise have to do with cult matters.

pressure and hand over certain suppliants in their temples to the Persians, thus referring a moral dilemma related to their religious obligations to the ultimate authority: Apollo himself. They were told to hand over the suppliants. One Aristodikos, mistrusting the reply, inquired a second time, and on receiving the same reply walked around the temple driving out the small birds that had taken shelter there, until a voice from within the temple ordered him to desist. When he asked why Apollo had ordered the Cymeans to do something he would not permit in his own temple (i.e. the casting out of those who had taken shelter there), he was told that Apollo had given the Cymeans false advice to bring them to disaster for daring even to ask such an immoral question. Various other stories tell of inquirers being refused responses from the god due to crimes they had committed.[17] In Herodotus 6.86 Glaukos of Sparta inquired at Delphi as to whether he ought to break an oath for financial gain. Apollo replied that in the short term such a course of action would bring benefit, but in the long term the families of oath-keepers fared better, as they avoided ancestral curses. When he begged forgiveness, he was told that tempting the god was as bad as doing the deed itself.[18] We also hear of a number of other occasions when inquirers were given moral advice, punished or forgiven: the Romans are told which gods to pray to during the second Punic War, and counselled to avoid licentiousness; the Magnesians are counselled to defend themselves in Pamphylia and avoid deceit; a priest is forgiven for violating his vow of chastity due to drunkenness, the Messenians at war with Sparta are warned about the long-term consequences of deceit, the people of Chios were "sentenced" to exile for the assassination of their king, a traitoress is pardoned because her actions had led only to the death of one fated to a bad end anyway, and those contemplating marriage are told that an oath must be fulfilled before the marriage can be entered into.[19]

---

[17] Cf. H. Krämer in G. Friedrich, ed., *T.D.N.T.*, vol. 6, 1959, E.T. 1968, p. 788: "The Delphic Oracle formulates the generally recognised standard of conduct . . ."

[18] See Pausanias 5.21.5 (refusal to pay a fine), Isocrates, Oration 6.31, Aelian, V.H. 3.43 (murder), 3.44 (desertion of friends in danger), and of Didyma, Athenaeus 26.524 b.

[19] See Livy 23.11.1-3, O. Kern, *Die Inschriften von Magnesia am Maeander*, Berlin, 1900, No. 17. Plutarch, Mor. 404 a, Pausanias 4.12.7, Plutarch, Mor. 244 e, Herodotus 6.135.2, and Aristaenetus Epist. 1.10. All these references are taken from J. Fontenrose's collection of the oracles of Delphi and Didyma, in *The Delphic Oracle*, Berkeley, 1978, pp. 244ff (Delphi) and 417ff (Didyma).

It cannot be simply asserted, then, that Graeco-Roman oracles did not pronounce on religious or moral issues. On occasion they did so; and the reason that they did not do so more often is likely to have been that people were not so often in doubt as to what was the morally correct course of action as they were as to the likely success of particular ventures, or the propriety of certain cult practices. Not only so, but few of those who were determined to carry out some immoral action were likely to consult the gods about it.

We must now ask whether it is true that the main business of oracles was the prediction of the future. Here some distinctions must be made clear. While it is true that oracular responses often had to do with things future, it is not true in the normal sense. Oracles normally answered questions as to what was the best course to be followed in a certain undertaking, or whether a particular business ought to be taken in hand at all. They dealt with the humanly unknowable consequences of actions, and hence with the choice between alternate courses of action. When they did, occasionally, produce oracles in the style of "you will soon meet a tall, dark stranger", it was inevitably because this stranger would be the god's appointed person to lead the colonizing expedition you had just inquired about.[20] In that sense they sometimes dealt with the future. But it was very rare indeed for an oracle to simply and straightforwardly predict future events. When such cases did occur, the prediction was normally made in order to suggest or confirm a particular course of action.[21] Probably the best-known example here is the

---

[20] For examples see the Magnesian oracle cited in note 19 above.

[21] On the categories of oracular response see also J. Fontenrose, *The Delphic Oracle*, Berkeley, 1978, pp. 13-20. Fontenrose distinguishes between simple commands or instructions, conditioned commands, prohibitions or warnings, statements of past or present fact, non-predictive statements about the future (i.e. promises or statements of intention), clear predictions, ambiguous predictions, and conditioned predictions. (By "conditioned" Fontenrose means a command or prediction that has a statement such as "when you see a white cow do x, or, x will happen"; he does not mean the fulfilment is conditional on some action of the receiver of the oracle.) On his analysis predictions, whether clear, ambiguous or conditioned, make up approximately 21% of legendary oracles, and less than 3% of oracles with a strong claim to historicity. For the intermediate category, which Fontenrose labels "quasi-historical", the figure is again approximately 21%. Compare the comment of R.M. Ogilvie on the Roman perspective: "it (divination) had been developed to provide answers to the question, 'Is this course of action approved by the gods?' or 'What does this sign tell us about the gods' will?' rather than 'What will happen tomorrow?' or 'Who will win the Derby?' . . ." (*The Romans and their Gods*, London, 1969, p. 55.) Precisely the same point is true of the Greek material.

famous oracle given to the Athenians when they inquired as to how they could best meet the threat of the Persian invasion. The complete capture of Attica was predicted, along with the possibility of later victories, not simply for the sake of the facts themselves, but in order to allow the Athenians to shape their plans accordingly.[22] There seems to me to be no difference whatsoever between this and Agabus' first prophecy recorded in Acts. In chapter 11.27-29 the response of the believers is to decide to take steps to help their brothers in Judaea.

There are also examples among the known corpus of oracles of what is often called conditional prophecy, where fulfilment is contingent on certain actions by the recipient of the oracle, or where the timing of the fulfilment is dependent on other events.[23] There are cases where prophets interpret past events and explain the present in terms of the past. In brief, Graeco-Roman oracles dealt with past, present and future, just as did Biblical prophecy, to the point where the knowledge of "things past, present and future" was seen as almost a defining characteristic of μάντεις.[24] See, for example, the description of Kalchas in Pindar's Sixth Olympian Oration, or the description of Teiresias in the first Nemean Ode of Pindar.

In the New Testament, on the other hand, the only two examples of prophecy explicitly so called that we have in either Acts or Paul are the two prophecies of Agabus (Acts 11.28, 21.10-11). In each case these are simple, unconditional predictions of future events, with no discernible moral content. In Chapter 9, above, I attempted to show on other grounds that for both Luke and Paul prediction was an important element in prophecy. I can see no grounds here for distinguishing between Christian prophecy and the oracles of its environment.

In summary, the suggestion that Christian and Graeco-Roman prophecy can be distinguished in terms of the theological and moral purpose of the Christian variety, and the morally neutral soothsaying of the Graeco-Roman,

---

[22] See Herodotus 7.140.2-3.

[23] See D.E. Aune, *Prophecy*, pp. 60-61, and the examples cited there. The claim that conditional oracles were unknown in the Israelite tradition (p. 142) seems to be mistaken: see Isaiah 1.18-20, 7.9(?), 30.18, 58.6-14, Jeremiah 3.12-13, 4.1-2, 7.5-15, 15.19, Ezekiel 33.1-11. Oracles of salvation conditional on repentance were common.

[24] W.C. van Unnik, "A Formula Describing Prophecy", *N.T.S.*, vol. 9, 1962-3, pp. 86-94, and "A Greek characteristic of prophecy in the Fourth Gospel", in *Text and Interpretation: Studies in the New Testament Presented to Matthew Black*, ed. E. Best and R. McL. Wilson, Cambridge, 1979, pp. 211-229.

is entirely false, as well as theologically partisan. A minority of famous oracles from Delphi have been allowed to dominate our interpretation of the evidence, and to give the impression that simply telling the future was the main activity of Graeco-Roman oracles. In fact their dominant business seems to have changed from one historical period to another; but this topic will be examined in more detail later.

All three main antitheses by which scholars have attempted to distinguish early Christian prophecy from its Graeco-Roman counterpart have been shown to be suspect. Are we forced, then, to argue, with Reitzenstein, that the form taken by Christian prophecy was in all essentials similar to the form of prophecy in its environment? I do not believe so. The remainder of this chapter will be concerned with a characterisation of Graeco-Roman oracular practice. In the confines of a single chapter I cannot hope to do justice to the whole of our evidence. The caveat expressed at the beginning of Chapter 8, that the treatment will not attempt to be exhaustive, but ought to be regarded rather as exploratory, applies most especially here. I will argue that Graeco-Roman prophecy may be characterised in terms of three main antitheses between it and Christian prophecy without distorting our evidence or prejudicing our discussion. It was, in summary, a thoroughly different phenomenon, and ought to be recognised as such.

2. Three Different Antithesis

First, although it is easily the nearest parallel to early Christian prophecy, inspiration manticism was not the dominant form taken by prophecy in the Graeco-Roman world. In the first century of our era inspired prophecy (together with spontaneous oracles) was generally believed to be very much a thing of the distant and heroic past. The dominant form taken by prophecy in the Graeco-Roman period was not inspiration manticism, but divination, which early Christianity eschewed almost totally.

Second we must briefly discuss the social structures within which prophecy operated. Where Graeco-Roman inspired prophecy was still believed to exist, it was organised in oracular shrines, with temple premises and institutionalised priesthoods, and traditionally defined relationships with surrounding communities. There were other forms of prophecy organised along other lines, but all our evidence shows that inspiration manticism characteristically took the form outlined above. Early Christian prophecy, on the other hand, as we have seen, was diverse, largely unstructured, and not particularly highly integrated into the communities within which it occurred. These communities themselves were as yet too young to have developed much institutional stability. Prophecy had no specific physical location separate from the functioning of the community as a whole, brought with it (in the New Testament period) no special privileges beyond a hearing in the community, and was not even limited to a specialist class.

Third, and partly as a consequence of its institutional nature, Graeco-Roman prophecy was characteristically a matter of answers to questions. Inquirers sought out the oracular shrine of their choice, asked their question, and received their oracle. The first evidence to suggest that early Christian prophecy ever took such a shape is to be found in Hermas, in the mid-second century, and even then Hermas treats such prophecy as illegitimate. Early Christian prophecy was characteristically spontaneous in at least this sense: one did not approach the prophet with an inquiry. The prophet addressed the congregation, without prior inquiry, in the confidence that his revelation was God's word for their need, whether or not that need had yet been perceived. Graeco-Roman prophecy knew of spontaneous oracles, but they remained very much the exception, and were, like inspiration manticism more generally, mainly confined to the legendary past.

We proceed now to a detailed consideration of each of the above three points. This will be followed by an examination of the functions of prophecy within the Graeco-Roman world, and some consideration of the distinctive ways in which early Christianity treated and understood its experience of prophecy and other forms of the miraculous.

Inspiration or Inductive Divination?

The so-called cessation of prophecy in Judaism, the belief that direct divine revelation had ceased, is a well-known and well studied phenomenon, and requires little comment here.[25] What is not so well known is that a very similar view was also widely held in the Graeco-Roman world. The evidence for this view takes two forms. First, there is strong evidence that inspired prophecy was widely believed to have been a far more common

---

[25] For a treatment of this issue see T.M. Crone, *Prophecy*, pp. 62ff, and pp. 63-67 for "exceptions"; Crone argues strongly for cessation. More interested in the continuation of prophecy in various forms is W.A. Grudem, *Gift*, pp. 24-33, though his schematisation of the full divine authority of the prophecy that had ceased, and the lesser authority of continuing prophecy, seems to me to be over-rigid. Far more detailed and less arbitrary is D.E. Aune, *Prophecy*, pp. 103ff.

phenomenon in the distant, semi-legendary past. In the immediate environment of the New Testament it was limited to a number of well-known oracular shrines. Secondly, as Plutarch's essay "On the Obsolescence of Oracles" testifies, educated Greeks of the 1st century A.D. believed that the number of such shrines had decreased markedly over the years. Nor is there any reason to think this belief incorrect; Plutarch mentions several shrines (e.g. that of Ptoan Apollo, Amphiaraus, and Tegyrae), once well known, which were no longer operating in his time, and further examples are known.[26] Of course, there were exceptions (i.e. Mopsus and Amphilochus, Mor. 434 d), and the trend was not permanent. Claros seems to have been in decline when visited by Germanicus in the early first century (Tacitus, quoted in Chapter 5, at note 34), but grew enormously in importance in the second and third centuries. Didyma also had its greatest period in the second and third centuries A.D. But in the first century most oracle centres seemed to be going through very lean times.

In this section we will examine the evidence for both these beliefs, in order to show that various types of divination, not inspiration manticism, were the dominant form of prophecy in the immediate environment of the New Testament.

From at least the fifth century B.C., and almost certainly earlier, collections of oracles circulated in the names of Sibyl and Bakis. Our sources differ extensively as to whether these names are personal names or titles, and if the latter, how many people held the titles. But the traditions attest to the belief in several ancient worthies who prophesied under the inspiration of Apollo.[27] Cicero, in his de Divinatione, mentions as persons famous for their divine inspiration Bakis, Epimenides of Crete, Cassandra, and "Marcius and Publicius", but a later reference to Marcius adds the dismissive note "whoever he may be". His dates and background were obviously as obscure to Cicero as they are to us. From the fully historical period he mentions only Socrates.[28] Plutarch tells us of the Sibyl (Mor. 397

---

[26] Pausanias 9.23.6 suggests that Ptoan Apollo was not operative later than the time of Alexander the Great. We should note that Strabo says that Dodona was virtually inoperative by this time too, and Ammon in Libya virtually deserted in his own day (Strabo 7.7.9, 17.1.43). The oracle at Patara was likewise out of action for some time; but Herodotus 1.182 says that even in his time it only operated occasionally.

[27] For extensive lists of references to these early traditions see J. Fontenrose, *The Delphic Oracle*, Berkeley, 1978, pp. 159-160.

[28] de Divinatione 1.18, 1.40, 1.50.115, 2.55.113 and 1.54.123.

a), and Pausanias knows of three different Sibyls: Herophile, "the first woman to chant oracles", who lived before the Trojan war, Demo of Cumae, and Sabbe of Israel, or Babylon, or Egypt.[29] Clearly all three belong to the legendary past: Sabbe is the most recent, and Pausanias' evidence does not even allow him to say with confidence what her nationality might have been. He knows of some other women who prophesied in a similar fashion, though they were not Sibyls, but the most recent of these, Phaennis, mentioned below, lived in the mid-third century B.C. Among men he knows of four inspired prophets, though he has himself read the oracles of only three of them: the latest of these is the legendary Bakis.[30] Clement of Alexandria refers to three different Sibyls, the most recent of which he takes to be the Jewish Sibyl.[31] Lactantius cites the Roman antiquarian Varro to the effect that there were ten Sibyls, though several of them appear to be different "versions" of Herophile, Pausanias' "first" Sibyl. The latest of Lactantius' Sibyls on whom a date can be put practised her calling in the time of Solon, a thousand years before Lactantius wrote.[32]

As we come into the historical period, however, prophetic inspiration outside the great oracular shrines becomes steadily harder to find. Dealing with the fourth century B.C., Strabo reports that in the time of Alexander the Great there was a woman of Erythrae called Athenais who was inspired like one of the ancient Sibyls. She was noted, Strabo tells us, citing Callisthenes, for pronouncing on Alexander's divine descent, but nothing else whatever is known of her.[33] Dealing with the same period, Arrian records that a certain Syrian woman, κάτοχον ἐκ τοῦ θείου γιγνομένην, regularly foretold the future, and once warned Alexander of a threat to his life.[34] Oracle stories

---

[29] Pausanias 10.12.1, cf. Plutarch Mor. 401 b.

[30] Pausanias 1.34.4.

[31] Stromata 1.108.3.

[32] Divine Institutes 1.6, ed. S. Brandt and G. Laubmann, Leipzig, 1890, reprinted 1965, pp. 20-21. It should be noted that the legends of the Sibyls exhibit a combination of wandering and permanent residency doubtless the result of attempts to reconcile varying traditions. Aune correctly notes that "The legendary inspired diviners called Sibyl and Bakis . . . functioned primarily as a means of legitimating various collections of oracles of diverse character . . .", *Prophecy*, p. 38. We have seen above that there is very little evidence to suggest that those χρησμολόγοι who handed on and made their living from such collections claimed to be inspired, either in their own right or in their choice and exposition of the oracles of Sibyl and Bakis.

[33] See Strabo, 14.1.34 and 17.1.43.

[34] Arrian, Anabasis 4.13.5-6, and compare Quintus Curtius 8.6.16.

gathered around Alexander, but Arrian notes that Aristobulos, who was present on the campaign, tells this one. Pausanias also knows of one woman named Phaennis who, though not one of the Sibyls, prophesied in a similar fashion; his evidence places her in the third century B.C.[35] In the mid-second century we know of Eunus, the Syrian slave revolutionary who led a revolt in Sicily in the second century B.C., who was discussed briefly above in Chapter 6. According to Diodorus

> He claimed to foretell the future (προλέγειν τὰ μέλλοντα), by divine command, through dreams, and because of his talent along these lines deceived many. Going on from there he not only gave oracles (ἐμαντεύετο) by means of dreams, but even made a pretence of having waking visions of the gods and of hearing the future from their own lips . . .[36]

For the late-second century we hear from Plutarch of a case in which Cybele spoke to one of her priests, one Bataces, from her sanctuary, predicting a Roman victory in the wars of Marius.[37] Bataces reported the event in Rome. It is doubtful, however, whether we should include this incident in our list, as it is a case of direct divine revelation to the priest without any process of inspiration.

From the first century B.C. Cicero is our best witness. He mentions only two occurrences from his century. He knows of one Cornelius Culleolus who spoke a prophecy under divine inspiration during the war between Sulla and Marius, c. 87 B.C. Unfortunately he gives no details whatever, and nothing further is known about the incident.[38] In his second case he tells of a Rhodian oarsman who before a battle prophesied details of the course of the fighting to come; but again, no further information is forthcoming from our sources.[39] Nothing suggests that these two persons regularly acted as prophets: as Aune points out, unsolicited oracles tended to appear in extraordinary moments of social and political crisis.[40]

---

[35] Pausanias 10.12.1f.

[36] Diodorus Siculus 34/5.2.5. It would appear that, as his reputation grew, Eunus progressed from claiming to be able to give dream oracles to a much greater claim: that, like the classical Hebrew prophets, he knew the will of the gods because he had been privileged to listen to the heavenly council in which divine decisions were made. Such a claim from one not firmly tied into the institutional structure of the Roman world was naturally highly subversive.

[37] Plutarch, Life of Marius, 17.5.

[38] Cicero, de Divinatione 1.2.4.

[39] Cicero, de Divinatione 1.31, 2.55.114.

[40] D.E. Aune, *Prophecy*, p. 66. Here we have a partial explanation for the paradox of the greatest prevalence of Christian prophecy coinciding with the low ebb of

Popular writers of the late-first century B.C. tell a similar story. In the histories of both Diodorus Siculus and Dionysius of Halicarnassus divination of various sorts abounds. But I can find in these writers only one case of inspired divination outside the great oracular centres.[41] Prophecy is a matter of astrology,[42] incubation,[43] the analysis of the entrails of sacrificial animals,[44] watching the flight of birds,[45] and the interpretation of prodigies and portents.[46] A distinction is observable between the interpretation of unsolicited signs (auspicia oblativa) such as prodigies and lightning strikes, and the interpretation of signs specifically searched for (auspicia impetrativa), such as malformations of the liver of sacrificial animals, but in both cases it is quite clear that it is inductive divination with which we are concerned.[47]

Graeco-Roman inspiration manticism. We might argue that while the mid-first century was a time of far lower social stress for the mainstream of society, the intense group identification of the early Christians, the related alienation from mainstream society, and the consequent threat of persecution provided ideal conditions within the Christian sub-culture for a revival of spontaneous prophecy. However this speculation ignores the cause and effect relationship: our sources suggest that prophetic phenomena had as much to do with creating the sub-culture as with maintaining it, so the puzzle remains.

[41] This is the case of Nevius, discussed below in note 47. One possible further exception to this generalisation is one reference in Diodorus Siculus 18.1.1 to the commonplace idea that is possible for people to know something of the future at the point of death. This concept has been touched on above in Chapter 9, at note 59, and other references have been cited there. But it hardly constitutes a serious exception to the general case.

[42] For astrology, whether Greek, Roman or Chaldaean, see Diodorus Siculus 1.53.8, 2.29.2, 2.31.2, 13.12.6, 15.80.3, 17.112.3, 19.55.7 and 21.1.3.

[43] For incubation see Diodorus Siculus 1.53.8, 5.74.5. We should note here that Cicero puts dreams and inspired oracles together as his two examples of natural divination, apparently on the basis that their reception requires no particular skill (though of course their interpretation may). See de Divinatione, 1.4.12, 1.6.12, 1.20, 1.33, and 2.11.

[44] For the interpretation of the entrails of sacrificial animals see Diodorus Siculus 1.53.8, 2.29.2, 5.31.3, 13.97.4, 15.85.1, 20.29.3, 22.13.2-5, and Dionysius of Halicarnassus 4.40.2, 8.89.5, 9.12.2.

[45] For divination using the flight of birds see Diodorus Siculus 1.87.7, 2.29.2, 5.31.3, and Dionysius of Halicarnassus 3.70.1ff.

[46] For the interpretation of prodigies as an important role of mantics see Diodorus Siculus 2.29.2, 13.86.2, 17.10.1, 17.18.1, 17.16.4-7, and Dionysius of Halicarnassus, 3.47.3, 4.2.2, 4.59.3ff, 5.54.3, 8.89.5, 9.12.2, 12.16.5, and 16.1.3.

[47] Of the ancient authors known to me, Dionysius of Halicarnassus is the only one who does not seem totally consistent in distinguishing between inspired and inductive divination. Even in his writings the distinction is only ignored once, if then. This is the case of one Nevius, a figure from early Roman history, who is described as particularly gifted in divination (A.R. 3.70ff). As a youth he first attempted divination when some of the pigs he was minding went astray. He prayed to some local heroes for assistance,

For the late-first century A.D. we have the evidence of Plutarch. In his de
Defectu Oraculorum (Mor. 421 b) Plutarch has Cleombrotus talk of a
recluse living near the Persian Gulf who was inspired to prophesy (εἰς δὲ
μαντικὴν ἐνεπνεῖτο . . . καὶ προεθέσπιζε) once a year. The point of the
discussion, however, is the extreme rarity of such persons: Cleombrotus had
to travel virtually to the ends of the earth to find the man, and the story of
their meeting, and what Cleombrotus learned from him, amazes the other
participants in the dialogue. Plutarch was a Pythian priest and knew well the
distinction between normal technical divination and that highest form of
inspired knowledge based on "an understanding and awareness of the actual
conversation of the gods". He summarised what must have been the view of
the majority, at least of the educated classes, when he said that "heaven
consorts directly with but a few, and rarely."[48]

In the mid-to-late second century, Lucian tells us that Alexander, later of
Abonouteichos, practised all kinds of charlatanry in the early stages of his
career, but nowhere suggests that he claimed to be inspired to speak oracles.
His oracular activity began only when he settled down and built his shrine to
Glykon/Asclepius. But we can finish by returning to Pausanias. Having gone
through his list of ancient inspired prophets, he finishes by saying:

> These are the women and men who, down to the present day, are said to have been the
> mouthpiece by which a god prophesied. But time is long, and perhaps such things may
> occur again.[49]

He knows of no inspired mantics in recent times:

---

offering to dedicate to them the largest bunch of grapes in the vineyard. On finding the
pigs he realised he did not know how to find the largest bunch, prayed for guidance, and
κατὰ δαίμονα divided the vineyard in two, wait for omens, and continued the process
until the correct bunch was located, and he was able to make his offering. Here direct
inspiration and inductive divination go hand in hand. The question this single apparent
exception raises is whether the phrase κατὰ δαίμονα is really strong enough to force us
to say that Dionysius has here given up on the distinction. Regardless of this, however,
Nevius still does not constitute an exception to the generalisation that inspired prophecy
was a matter of the distant past, as his life is dated by Dionysius during the time of
Tarquinius Superbus, earlier than 570 B.C.

[48] Plutarch, de Genio Socratis, Mor. 593 c-d. The only example he gives (other than
Socrates) is the Homeric figure of Helenos the Trojan. Though Plutarch's argument in
the de Defectu Oraculorum would most directly to the decline of oracular shrines, many
of the reasons he gives would function equally well as explanations of the decline of
inspired prophecy as such.

[49] Pausanias 10.12.11.

Except those whom they say Apollo inspired of old (μανῆναι . . . τὸ ἀρχαῖον) none of the seers uttered oracles, but they were good at explaining dreams and interpreting the flight of birds and the entrails of victims.[50]

Only two types of figure have been suggested as exceptions to this general rule: the θεομάντεις mentioned by Plato, and the "Eurycleis" or "πύθονες" mentioned in Acts and by Plutarch.[51] On the θεομάντεις, D.E. Aune correctly notes that "Plato does not provide an example of the kind of oracular speech which characterised the inspired diviners whom he so briefly discussed."[52] Plato in fact gives no actual cases of such people at all, and the paucity of references in the lexica makes it most unlikely that this term was used in our period to indicate inspired diviners.[53] As to the "Eurycleis", or πύθονες, our evidence is extremely scanty. The original Eurycles, the eponym for the phenomenon, is known to us primarily from oblique references in the late fifth and fourth centuries. Aristophanes says that he had written some of his plays and had them published through other playwrights, speaking "like Eurycles" through other people.[54] Plato likewise uses Eurycles as a metaphor: in his Sophist he described a certain philosopher by a comparison with Eurycles because he taught a standard but was unable to live up to it.[55] Eurycles' internal spirit was likewise said to contradict what he himself said. Still in the fourth century, a fragment of Philochorus tells us that such people were called ἐγγαστρίμυθοι, and that they were commonly women who summoned up the spirits of the dead.[56]

---

[50] Pausanias 1.34.4. The only clear exception to this of which I am aware is Pausanias' mention of the oracle of Dionysius at Amphiclea, where he believes a priest, called a πρόμαντις, still speaks under inspiration (ἐκ τοῦ θεοῦ κάτοχος) in his own time. (See Diodorus Siculus 10.33.11, which (with Pausanias) was briefly discussed in Chapter 6 above: Plutarch Mor. 109 b also knows of this and also calls him πρόμαντις.)

[51] For Eurycles see Aristophanes, Wasps 1019-1020, Plato's Sophist 252 c, and Plutarch, Mor. 414 e, where such people are discussed; from Plutarch's comment that they are now called πύθονες we presume that they are known at this time, but as will become clear, we have precious little direct evidence.

[52] D.E. Aune, *Prophecy*, p. 39.

[53] The only pre-Christian or contemporary references to θεομάντεις I have been able to locate are in the works of Plato himself. The use of the term in Apology 22c and Meno 99 c would seem to indicate that Plato simply means diviners who are inspired (i.e. not technical diviners), as opposed to a special class of such diviners. E.R. Dodds makes a similar suggestion, *The Greeks and the Irrational*, Berkeley, 1951, p. 88 note 46.

[54] Aristophanes, *loc.cit.*

[55] Plato, Sophist, 252 c.

[56] Philochorus, fragment 192, cited in the Suda. See C. Müller, *Fragmenta Historicorum Graecarum*, Frankfurt, 1975 (reprint), vol. 1, p. 416, or A. Adler, ed.,

They are likewise mentioned in the Hippocratic corpus, though again only
by way of comparison with something else: the symptoms of a certain
disease will occasionally lead to the patient's stomach giving off a noise like
that of those called ἐγγαστρίμυθοι.[57] The feminine article given to the term
again makes it clear that women are in view.

The next usage of the term ἐγγαστριμῦθος comes with its adoption by
the Septuagint as its regular translation for the Hebrew *ob*. The best known
case here is the "witch of Endor" consulted by Saul: the link to Philochorus'
claim that ἐγγαστρίμυθοι were often women who summoned the dead is
clear, and may be the basis of the translation. From the Septuagint comes the
use of the term by Philo and Josephus for some types of pagan divination.[58]

In the mid-first century, Erotianus Grammaticus, commenting on the
passage from the Hippocratic corpus cited above, says that those that
Hippocrates calls ἐγγαστρίμυθοι are called πύθονες by some. Similarly
Plutarch, discussing the nature of Delphic inspiration, says it is absurd to
suggest that the God enters the body of his προφήτης, as in the case of
πύθονες, which he says is the name given in his time to those earlier called
"Eurycleis".[59] It is clear from these statements that such people do exist in
the mid-to-late first century: there would be no point in saying that their
name has changed otherwise. Neither writer, however, gives any examples,
and they betray no particular interest in the phenomenon for its own sake.
Similarly Pollux the Grammarian, writing somewhere in the mid-second
century, merely notes the word as one compound among several of the term
for stomach.[60]

Lucian likewise seems to know of the phenomenon, but as with so much
of our evidence, his reference to it is by way of comparison, not a
description of the thing itself. In his "Lexiphanes", a satire about a man
obsessive in his Atticism, and addicted to obscure archaisms, he attempts to
cure the sufferer with a potion that will make him burp up his literary
vocabulary so that he can speak normally. On swallowing the potion, the

---

Suidae Lexicon, Stuttgart, 1928-1938.

[57] Hippocrates, Epidemiae 5.62-63.

[58] See, for example, Philo, de Somniis 1.220, and Josephus, A.J. 6.327ff (the only time
he uses the term, taking it directly from the LXX version of the story of Saul and the
witch of Endor, 1 Sam. 28).

[59] Erotianus Grammaticus, Fragment 21, cited in Foerster, "Πύθον", in G. Friedrich, ed.,
T.D.N.T., vol. 6, 1959, E.T. 1968, p. 917ff, and Plutarch, Mor. 414e.

[60] Julius Pollux, Onomasticon 2.168, ed. W. Dindorf, Leipzig, 1824.

sufferer cries out that he has swallowed an ἐγγαστριμῦθος; the meaning is, of course, that his voice is changing.[61] The Historia Alexandri Magni, 1.4.12, written in perhaps the third century A.D., though incorporating earlier material, mentions ἐγγαστρίμυθοι along with interpreters of horoscopes, signs and dreams, Magi and other mantics. From this time the term seems to fall out of common use in secular writers. A computerised search of the Thesaurus Linguae Graecae finds no further usages outside the scholiasts until the Byzantine lexicographers. The term does, however, become common in ecclesiastical literature, as the standard term for witches and mediums. When we come to the late lexicographers and scholiasts, they add virtually nothing to our understanding of the terms. They do clearly equate "Eurycleis", πύθονες, ἐγγαστρίμυθοι, ἐγγαστρίμαντεις and στερνόμαντεις, but they give no concrete examples of such people.[62]

We are faced, then, with an extraordinary situation. It is clear that ἐγγαστρίμυθοι are found from the fifth century B.C. through to the second century A.D., but over this whole time-span, only two actual cases are known to us: the original Eurycles, and the "girl with a Pythonic spirit" in Acts 16.16. Many of the writers cited above think the phenomenon sufficiently well-known to use it as a parallel for other phenomena, or as a joke; none of them thinks it worthwhile to cite actual cases. It may be that what we are dealing with here is the disdain of the educated for popular superstition; that could well be argued, for example, of the comments of Plutarch. If this is the case, then the ἐγγαστρίμυθοι may give us another glimpse into that "spiritual underworld" of which Morton Smith spoke. But it is at best a glimpse, and a hazy one at that; aside from the comments of Plutarch contrasting Delphic theology with beliefs about such people, we know no more about them than the little we are told by Philochorus and Acts. It would appear, then, that outside the great oracle centres, and with the exception of the ἐγγαστρίμυθοι, who remain something of a puzzle, there was virtually no inspiration manticism known in the first century A.D. If the ἐγγαστρίμυθοι were common, as might be argued from our evidence, they appear not to have been taken seriously by the educated levels of

---

[61] Lucian, Lexiphanes 20.

[62] See the Scholia on the passages of Aristophanes and Plato cited above, and Hesychius (M. Schmidt, *Hesychii Alexandrini Lexicon*, Amsterdam, 1965, reprinted from the edition of 1858, place not given), and the Suda, under the terms ἐγγαστρίμαντις, ἐγγαστριμῦθος, Εὐρυκλῆς, πύθων, and στερνόμαντις.

Graeco-Roman society. It is not clear how we should assess the importance of the ἐγγαστρίμυθοι in the immediate cultural environment of the New Testament. The dominant form taken by prophecy in the Graeco-Roman period, however, according to our evidence, was not inspiration manticism, but inductive divination.

The argument can now be taken two stages further. Even at the great shrines inspiration manticism was not the only form of divination. We have seen above, in Chapter 8, that in the Hellenistic period the oracle of Ammon at Siwah used a form of inductive divination based on ancient Egyptian practice. At Dodona, likewise, a form of lot-oracle was used. At the oracle of Amphiaraus in Boeotia and at Patara in Asia Minor incubation, more closely related to inspiration (but still separate), was the technique.[63] The oracle of Trophonius used a form of waking vision[64]central only at the oracles of Apollo, such as Delphi, Didyma and Claros. But even in the case of Delphi, the best known of all ancient oracles, scholars are still divided as to whether inspiration was the only, or even the main form of divination.

Finally it must be borne in mind that in the first century A.D. even these few great shrines were far less important than they had been in the fifth and fourth centuries. The most striking case is Delphi itself. As we saw above in Chapter 6, Lucan's Pharsalia represents the oracle as being inoperative in the mid-first century B.C. Though such a conclusion can be supported from Juvenal, Satires 6. 553-6 (quoniam Delphis oracula cessant), and some of the scholiasts, the case has been doubted, because, it is argued, such a cessation of operations is not mentioned by Plutarch.[65] There is, however, some ambiguous evidence in Plutarch which might support such a case. First there is the general consideration that from approximately 200 B.C. a Delphic law made it mandatory for the Pythia to be a woman of fifty or

---

[63] See, arguing that a form of lot-oracle was actually more common than inspired manticism, D.E. Aune, *Prophecy*, p. 25, 30, and cf. Amandry, *La mantique apollonienne à Delphes*, Paris, 1950, p. 29ff. See also T.M. Crone, *Prophecy*, pp. 28ff. Strongly opposed to such a view is J. Fontenrose, *op.cit.*, pp. 219-223.

[64] For full discussion of incubation oracles see E.J. and L. Edelstein, *Asclepius: a Collection and Interpretation of the Testimonies*, 2 vols, 1945. Cicero thought incubation was a form of natural, not inductive divination, as was pointed out above, in note 43.

[65] See F.M. Ahl, *Lucan, an Introduction*, Cornell University Press, London, 1976, cited in Chapter 6, note 35, for the supporting evidence. Joseph Fontenrose is one who denies the probability of such a closure, but he seems to be dealing exclusively with events in the time of Nero.

more. Yet we know that in Plutarch's time the Pythia was again a young, unmarried woman.[66] Here is clear evidence of a serious break in institutional continuity at some point, though we do not know when. Further, in Mor. 409 c he says that the presence of the god is the cause of Delphi's recent and unspecified change of fortune. He argues that

To us the god grants clearer, stronger and plainer evidence than this (sc. nature miracles) by bringing about after a drought, so to speak, of earlier desolation and poverty, affluence, splendour and honour.

It is not at all clear, however, to what misfortune Plutarch is referring. Cicero's evidence is much more precise. In his de Divinatione he twice refers to the fact that in his time the Oracle is either in a serious decline or not functioning at all. Thus he says that

at present its glory has waned because it is no longer noted for the truth of its prophecies . . . possibly, too, those subterranean exhalations which used to kindle the soul of the Pythian priestess with divine inspiration have gradually vanished in the long lapse of time . . . but explain the decadence of the oracle as you wish . . .

In the second half of the essay, he says that

the main question is this: Why are Delphic oracles (of which I have just given you examples) not uttered at the present time and have not been for a long time?[67]

What we do not know is how long this state of affairs lasted. We know that under Nero the oracle was operating again, but we do not know at what level.[68] Perhaps Plutarch's evidence deals only with a period of decline after Nero's altercation with the oracle, or perhaps it is meant to describe the century or more between the dramatic date of Appius Claudius' visit and Plutarch's own time: we cannot be sure. What we can say is that the first century A.D. was not a period in which oracles were abundant and prestigious.

Strabo provides us with our only evidence for the likely social causes of this decline. He says that

Among the ancients both divination in general and oracles were held in greater honour, but now great neglect of them prevails, since the Romans are satisfied with the oracles of Sibylla, and with the Tyrrhenian prophecies obtained by means of the entrails of animals,

---

[66] For the Delphic law and its origins in the seduction of one particular Pythia by Echecrates, envoy of Ptolemy Philopator, see Diodorus Siculus 16.26.6. For the practice in Plutarch's day see Mor. 405c-d.

[67] Cicero, de Divinatione 1.19, 2.57.

[68] See Dio Cassius 62.14.2, Lucian, Nero 10.

flight of birds, and omens from the sky; and on this account, also, the oracle at Ammon has been almost abandoned, though it was held in honour in earlier times . . . [69]

This is extremely valuable evidence, especially when combined with the suggestion of H.W. Parke,[70] that in the Hellenistic period the dominance of Delphi declined markedly, but smaller local shrines grew in importance, some to rival Delphi itself. The establishment of the Pax Romana, the decline of independent action among the Greek states, possible aping of Roman manners: we could speculate about all of these. Aune argues that

> The decline of the great oracle centres may have been caused by the changed political situation of the Greek city-states . . . When the old oracle-shrines began to increase again in popularity, it was not delegations from various Greco-Roman cities who came to consult the gods, as in the classical period, but rather individuals with more private problems and concerns.[71]

While the suggestion that there was a major change in the function of oracles from dealing with public matters to dealing with private matters is an over-generalisation - the oracle had always dealt with both kinds of inquiries, and continued to do so - there can be no doubt that Aune's point about changed social conditions is correct. Plutarch summarises the matter:

> I am well content with the settled conditions prevailing at present, and I find them very welcome, and the questions which men now put to the god are concerned with these conditions. There is, in fact, profound peace and tranquillity; war has ceased, there are no wanderings of peoples, no civil strifes, no despotisms, nor other maladies and ills in Greece requiring many unusual remedial forces . . . there is nothing complicated or secret or terrible, but the interrogations are on slight and commonplace matters, like the hypothetical questions in school: if one ought to marry, or to start on a voyage, or to make a loan; and the most important consultations on the part of States concern the yield from crops, the increase of herds, and public health . . .[72]

In the Graeco-Roman environment of the New Testament, then, inspiration manticism was something of a rarity. Inductive divination, in its many and varied forms, was much more common. The New Testament, on the other hand, knows of only one attempt to determine the will of God by inductive means: the selection of Matthias as Judas' replacement in Acts

---

[69] Strabo 17.1.43, noted above.

[70] *Greek Oracles*, London, 1967, p. 121ff.

[71] D.E. Aune, *Prophecy*, p. 24. Of course, private questions had been asked before: see for some examples *Fouilles de Delphes*, vol. 3, part 1, 560, c. 360 B.C., Pausanias 4.24.2, Plutarch, Mor. 116 c, 245 c, 315 f, 409 f, Diodorus Siculus 8.17.1, Herodotus 1.85.2, 5.92, 6.86, 9.33.2, Xenophon, Cyropaedia 7.2.19, 20.

[72] Plutarch, Mor. 408c

1.15-26. It can hardly be chance that this lone case of inductive divination falls before Pentecost.

Inductive divination was practised in the Graeco-Roman world in an extraordinary variety of forms. We have seen that it may have been practised at Delphi, and most certainly was practised at Dodona and other oracular shrines, in some cases as the predominant form of divination.[73] Outside the recognised shrines it reigned supreme. Rome had its colleges of augurs, delegated to watch the skies for lightning and listen for thunder. In the mid-first century B.C. a Roman senator even published an almanac on the meanings of thunder on different days.[74] The state also maintained the college of fifteen who, when directed, consulted and interpreted the Sibylline volumes. Also influential, though less official, were those μάντεις who were sometimes employed by the Imperial family, or other notables.[75]

At a less exalted level were the various technical diviners whom we might class as self-employed, or in private practice. These included χρησμολόγοι (for whom see Chapter 8), the "astrologers, augurs, Isis-seers and dream-interpreters" mentioned by Cicero as haunting the crowds in the Circus,[76] necromancers,[77] perhaps ἐγγαστρίμυθοι like the girl in Acts, and

---

[73] Dice was the method at the oracle of Herakles on the Bura river, Pausanias 7.25.10, and at Termessos (W.R. Halliday, *Greek Divination, a Study of its Methods and Principles*, Chicago, 1967, pp. 213ff.). Drawing lots was also used in Italy, Livy 21.62.5.

[74] Nigidius Figulus' almanac is known to us only from the Greek translation of John the Lydian, and may be based on either Etruscan or Mesopotamian models. Nigidius was well qualified to write on the topic: he was an antiquarian of some note, and had himself written on the theory of divination.

[75] For example see Suetonius, Nero 34.4, for Magi hired by Nero, and cf. Pliny N.H. 30.5, for astrologers, similarly. Compare Tacitus, Annals 2.28 for the hiring of local necromancers under Tiberius.

[76] Cicero, de Divinatione 1.58. Compare Lucian's satire of astrology, the Astrologia, and the serious work of Ptolemy Tetrabyblos. Extispicy is so common that it seems unnecessary to give multiple references: see, for one comment, Pausanias 6.2.4. For dream interpreters see also Theophrastus, Character 16, and for details see the extant works of Artemidorus.

[77] Strabo, 16.2.39, and Varro, cited by Augustine, City of God 7.35. The Strabo passage would appear to be cited (without reference) by A.D. Nock as the list of the prophets of all the cultures known to Posidonius *(Conversion*, Oxford, 1933, p. 79), though Nock does not mention Strabo and the passage does not quote Posidonius. Though the point of the passage is that Moses is cited as the founding μάντις of Judaism, alongside Teiresias, Amphiaräus, Trophonius, Orpheus, Musaeus, Zalmoxis/Decaeneus, Achaecarus, the Gymnosophists, the Magi, the Chaldaeans and the Tyrrhenian ὡροσκόποι, it is intriguing, as Nock points out, that the author appears to be unaware of the claims of the Biblical prophets.

the many and varied diviners who used containers of water[78] or mirrors[79] to produce visions. Divination covered the full scale from the commonplace (such as the interpreting the flight of birds: see above) to the exotic (such as the burning of pieces of coal on the flat of an axe by Persian μάγοι).[80]

Beyond this there were also the places where anyone could go where oracular dreams or visions were to be had. In many of these places no intermediary was needed at all: the oracular potencies of the place itself were all that was necessary. Incubation and waking vision were, as we have argued above, common methods of divination. The oracle of Trophonius is one of the best known cases, though here there were professionals to help you make sense of your experience. At Pharae in Achaea, on the other hand, having prayed and made a donation at the statue in the market place, one blocked one's ears and walked out of town. Outside, one unblocked them, and took as oracular the first thing one heard.[81] There were likewise shrines where dice could be thrown, with tables of data to allow the enquirer to determine the meaning of the response.[82] Finally, there were doubtless many people with a store of their own experience to draw on, who could interpret for themselves the omens they encountered. Dio Chrysostom mentions certain women who, in areas around shrines, would pick up clods of earth, and by estimating their weight come to conclusions about the answers to their questions.[83]

Technical divination was, we have seen, the dominant form of prophecy in the immediate environment of the New Testament. Within early Christianity, by contrast, prophecy was defined in terms of inspired speech. Dreams and visions were also accepted as means of revelation, but prophecy as defined by Luke and Paul excluded all forms of inductive divination absolutely.

---

[78] Λεκανομάντεις and ὑδρομάντεις according to Strabo, *loc.cit.*, and mentioned also by Varro, again cited by Augustine, *loc.cit.*, who claim these arts were of Persian origin. Augustine claims that if blood was used instead of water, the spirits of the dead were conjured up. This category of divination is also common in the magical papyri, though without the use of blood, so far as I am aware.

[79] See Apuleius, Apology 13 and 42. Occasionally mirrors and water were used in combination: see Pausanias 7.21.12.

[80] Pliny, N.H. 36.142.

[81] Pausanias 7.22.2-3, and similarly 9.11.7.

[82] See note 72, above.

[83] Dio Chrysostom, Discourse 13.1-2.

The Social Context of Prophecy

We have seen above that in the first-century world inspired prophets were believed to have existed in ancient times independent of fixed shrines and established structures. In the fully historical period, however, inspiration manticism (and much technical divination as well) was characteristically to be found in such fixed shrines. Such a place was usually called a χρηστήριον or μαντεῖον.[84] Depending on the prestige of the individual shrine it might have extensive temples and other buildings. The Temple of Apollo at Didyma is one of the most splendid examples. If one had need of an oracle there was no problem as to where they were to be found.

The picture in the historical period had changed in other ways as well. The legends tell of solitary figures moving from place to place, and (usually) settling at a site which later became one of the historical shrines.[85] The reality faced by the visitor was an institutionalised priesthood, with set (though differing) hierarchical structures and complex rituals of approach.[86] The greater oracles were, in the main, self-governing communities, and their relationships with the states surrounding them were complex. One only has to think of the Alcmaeonid patronage of Delphi during the time of the Peisistratid tyranny in Athens and the Phocian domination of the oracle during the fourth century to see the differing possibilities inherent in such a situation. Didyma, on the other hand, was throughout its history closely linked with the neighbouring city of Miletus, and the great majority of its officials were drawn from the Milesian aristocracy, as we saw in Chapter 8. Claros was torn between Notion and Colophon.[87]

It must be obvious that such a picture of prophecy as a social phenomenon is totally different from the picture of early Christian prophecy

---

[84] See, for examples, Diodorus Siculus, 4.2.1, 4.10.7, 4.82.1; Plutarch, Mor. 292 e, 361 e, 378 d, 402 b, 403 a, etc., and Philo, Legatione 78. For μαντεῖον see Plutarch Mor. 208 f, 397 d, 402 d, Diodorus Siculus 9.31, 10.14.3, 11.14.3,4, etc. See also Dionysius of Halicarnassus A.R. 12.16.1 and Dio Chrysostom 10.28.

[85] See the accurate comment of D.E. Aune, *Prophecy*, p. 37: "Many Sibylline legends depict the prophetesses, not as wandering aimlessly, but as travelling from oracle to oracle. Eventually they are depicted as settling permanently at a particular oracle sanctuary. The Greek association of oracular activity with sites which possessed oracular potencies appears to have exerted a magnetic attraction on the Sibylline traditions."

[86] For the priesthoods see Chapter 8. For the rituals required before one could approach the oracle of Trophonius, for example, see Pausanias 9.39.7. For the (simpler) ritual at Delphi see Plutarch, Mor. 347 d.

[87] See H.W. Parke, *The Oracles of Apollo in Asia Minor*, London, 1985, p. 112.

drawn in Chapters 9 and 10 above. Part of this difference is due to the basic distinction between the wider Graeco-Roman world, and the phenomenon of early Christianity within that world. There was never any likelihood that early Christianity would set up prophetic shrines: in its first two centuries it did not even have special buildings for its congregational meetings. But even granted the differences in social context, it is clear that early Christianity conceived of the place of prophecy within the community very differently from the way it was understood within its environment. As I suggested above, in Chapter 9, prophecy had no specific physical location separate from the functioning of the community as a whole, brought with it no special privileges beyond a hearing in the community, and was not even limited to a specialist class.

So much is clear, and requires little further comment. The consequences of these facts for prophetic procedure, however, are very significant. Graeco-Roman prophecy was fundamentally a matter of answers to questions, while early Christian prophecy was not. This is our third major point.

Response Oracles and Unsolicited Prophecy

There is no clear case in the New Testament where prophetic revelation comes as a result of deliberate inquiry.[88] Prophecy is characteristically spontaneous in that sense. The Graeco-Roman world knew of spontaneous oracles, but they were, along with inspiration manticism more generally, overwhelmingly a phenomenon of the legendary past. This point is, however, obscured by Aune. He argues that "unsolicited oracles" were a well-known category of revelation, consisting mainly of unsolicited dreams, legitimation (or recognition) oracles, and predictions of doom.[89] That dreams were considered a medium of spontaneous revelation in this period is not to be disputed: they occur in both the wider Graeco-Roman world and within early Christianity. The question here is whether oracles were given spontaneously in this period.

---

[88] Though there is some evidence that revelations came at times when Paul, for example, had been considering serious decisions (e.g. Acts 16.6-10: see P. Bowers, "Paul and Religious Propaganda in the First Century", *Nov.T*, vol. 22 part 4, 1980, pp. 316-323), there is no direct evidence that revelation had been sought. Not even 2 Corinthians 12.7-9 constitutes such a case: the saying "My grace is sufficient for you" etc. constitutes a spontaneous oracle; Paul had asked for his "thorn" to be removed, not for an oracle about it. On this passage see also D.E. Aune, *Prophecy*, pp. 249-50.

[89] D.E. Aune, *Prophecy*, pp. 66ff.

The evidence he cites for his contention can be divided into three sections. First there are some twenty-eight Delphic pronouncements which can lay some claim to being unsolicited.[90] On closer examination, however, we find that only six of these come from the fifth century or later, and of these six only one is later than the late third century B.C. (Parke and Wormell no. 469, 228 A.D.). A case could perhaps be made that one or two of them were actually unsolicited. None is certainly so.[91] Aune argues that:

Although many of these oracles are probably spurious, they could have produced their desired effect and been accepted as authentic by the ancients only if they had been patterned after genuine models . . . In one of his Pythian dialogues Plutarch observed that "the Pythian priestess is accustomed to deliver some oracles on the instant, even before the question is put." This kind of clairvoyant oracular response cannot be regarded as an unsolicited oracle since the oracle is given in response to a question, which, though unexpressed, is miraculously known to the god speaking through the medium. Most of these clairvoyant oracular responses are either mythical or fraudulent attempts to enhance the reputation of a particular oracle sanctuary.[92]

Such an argument, which is almost certainly correct, does not affect Aune's main case, for he is interested first and foremost in the literary structure of oracles, as becomes clear from the first half of his statement

---

[90] D.E. Aune, *Prophecy*, footnote 101 to p. 66, p. 365.

[91] The criteria for suggesting that an oracle may have been unsolicited appear to be simply that no particular occasion for the visit to the oracle is given in our sources, and no question, but only the response. Some more definite criteria are needed if we are to establish reasonably clearly that these oracles were in fact unsolicited. The oracles in question are:
1) Parke/Wormell no. 101, (=Fontenrose, Q.153): Herodotus 8.114.1, probably legendary, dated about 480 B.C.
2) Parke/Wormell no. 114 (=Fontenrose, Q 174): Thucydides 1.134.4, Diodorus Siculus 11.45.8, Plutarch Mor. 560 e. See Fontenrose p. 325. In an inquiry about other matters (Diodorus only) the Spartans were told, post 476 B.C., how to redress a case of ritual pollution. In all the other sources no occasion is discussed at all.
3) Parke/Wormell no. 162, (=Fontenrose, H.8): Thucydides 5.32.1. In 421 B.C. the Athenians are instructed to return the people of Delos to their home. Fontenrose (p. 247) suggests plausibly that the Athenians inquired as to how they could improve matters after a run of misfortunes, and were given the above reply.
4) Parke/Wormell no. 258 (=Fontenrose, Q.207): Pausanias 8.11.10. In 362 B.C., Epaminondas is told that he should beware of the sea. We have no further details.
5) Parke/Wormell no. 431 (=Fontenrose. Q 245): somewhere pre-240 B.C. Attalos (later of Pergamon) is told he will become a king. Diodorus Siculus 34/5.13, Pausanias 10.15.3.
6) Parke/Wormell no. 469 (=Fontenrose, Q.258): in A.D. 228 an otherwise unknown philosopher named Themistokles is commended as a good and fortunate man.
[92] D.E. Aune, *Prophecy*, pp. 66-67.

quoted above. But since we are primarily concerned with the historical question of whether such oracles actually occurred in the first century, the second half of his statement is crucial. What evidence is there of genuinely unsolicited oracles in the historical period? The second part of Aune's case, the evidence he cites from Lucian's *Alexander* ceases to be relevant, as it would be very hard to argue that these oracles, part of Alexander's propaganda for his shrine, ought to be treated as genuine. This leaves, in the third category of Aune's case, (1) two oracles, one a dream oracle and the other a literary fiction, reported in Philostratus' *Life of Apollonius*, (2) several spontaneous oracles recognising Alexander the Great as son of Zeus or Ammon, (3) the oracles of C. Culleolus and the unnamed Rhodian oarsman reported by Cicero, (4) Cleombrotus' inspired prophet from the region of the Persian gulf, *if* his oracles were spontaneous, and if he is not a total literary fiction, (5) the otherwise unknown woman who "practised some form of divination" during the famine of A.D. 7, reported in Cassius Dio 55.31 (cited by Aune, *Prophecy*, p. 43 note 245), *if* her divination was inspired rather than inductive, (6) the unknown individual (cited by Aune, *Prophecy*, p. 43) who predicted the fiery end of the world at Rome under Marcus Aurelius, and (7) four oracles known to us from non-literary evidence. These are one possibly unsolicited oracle of Hermes Trismegistos from 168 B.C.,[93] the Delphic oracle to Attalos I of Pergamon, noted above, from somewhere prior to 240 B.C., one fragmentary inscription of Didyma's προφήτης Ulpius Athenagoras, between 177 and 300 A.D., and one other, Posidonius of Didyma, treated below. On the oracles to Attalos and Ulpius, H.W. Parke notes that

This kind of oracle whereby the oracle addressed an enquirer immediately on his entry to the sanctuary before his question had been put is more a legendary happening than one of authenticated history . . . an address of this sort to Cypselus the Tyrant may be genuine, and it was made the model for a similar address to Attalus I of Pergamum, which is probably mythical. This last is the only example falling within fully historical periods . . . nowhere does a parallel exist for Apollo greeting his own prophet with a spontaneous oracle. The idea seems to be a fantastic piece of self-advertisement on behalf of Ulpius, even if he contrived or connived at some actual performance of the sort.[94]

There does seem to be one other parallel, however, for the concept of Apollo greeting his prophet with an oracle, though it is not clear whether it was unsolicited. This fourth inscription, not mentioned by either Aune or

---

[93] Aune, *Prophecy*, p. 73, is properly cautious about whether it is actually unsolicited.

[94] H.W. Parke, *The Oracles of Apollo in Asia Minor*, p. 88.

Parke, is an epigram for Posidonius the προφήτης, commemorating his appointment as προφήτης, and recounting an oracle in his favour, apparently given as he took up his office. The date of the inscription is not certain, but if the Posidonius in question is the same man as the Posidonius who features as προφήτης in two other Didymean inscriptions, it must be from either the late-first century B.C. or the early-first century A.D.[95] Unfortunately the inscription does not provide sufficient detail to allow us to be sure either of the date, or of the spontaneity of the oracle in question. That Apollo could greet his προφήτης as he took office, however, is not as extraordinary as Parke seems to think.

In summary, from the immediate environment of the New Testament, the first centuries B.C. and A.D., we have *at most* 6 cases (numbers 3, 4, 5 and 6 above, and the inscription of Posidonius) of unsolicited and inspired prophecy known from our evidence. If Cleombrotus' inspired prophet did not really exist, or answered questions, and Cassius Dio's unknown woman practised some kind of inductive divination, rather than claiming to be inspired, and if Posidonius' oracle was not unsolicited, then we have only three. We certainly have nothing to compare with Alexander's unsolicited oracle of A.D. 166, "Phoebus the unshorn wards off the deadly cloud of plague", which Alexander had widely publicised.[96] It was clearly intended for public consumption: our three certain examples were either delivered to people gathered at oracular shrines, or to particular individuals in person. Clearly the evidence is that the form overwhelmingly taken by inspired prophecy in the Graeco-Roman world of the New Testament was that of answers to questions. The early Christian view that inspired prophecy came to the prophet unsolicited would therefore most probably strike the non-Christian as extraordinary. If they believed it, it might suggest one of two things. Either among the Christians the great old days of inspired prophecy had begun again, or (if Aune's suggestion, relating unsolicited oracles to times of social crisis, is correct) some great crisis was imminent.

---

[95] The inscription is discussed by L. Robert in *Hellenica*, vol. XI-XII, pp. 456ff., citing T. Wiegand, *Didyma, 2. Teil: Die Inschriften*, Berlin, 1958. I have been unable to locate this inscription in *Didyma Inscriptions*, though the other two Posidonius inscriptions are to be found there.

[96] D.E. Aune, *Prophecy*, p. 67.

Summary

We have seen that there are at least three major ways in which early
Christian prophecy differed from prophecy (broadly defined) in the
Hellenistic world. Early Christian prophecy was conceived of as inspired;
"technical divination" was eschewed. The vast majority of cases of prophecy
in the Hellenistic world, on the other hand, was precisely in the field of
technical divination. Early Christian prophecy was "charismatic" in the
sociological sense; it was unstructured and variable in form. Hellenistic
inspired prophecy was thoroughly institutionalised. Finally, early Christian
prophecy was unsolicited, while Hellenistic prophecy (whether inspired or
inductive) was overwhelmingly a matter of answers to questions.[97] Having
established, then, that prophecy in the Hellenistic and Roman world and
prophecy within early Christianity are in at least these three respects very
different phenomena, we turn now to the question of the social functions of
oracles and prophecy in the Graeco-Roman world.

3. The Social Functions of Oracles and Prophecy

I argued above, in Chapter 10, that it was not possible to provide a simple
answer to the question of the function of Christian prophecy. It is difficult,
though not impossible, to do the same for prophecy in the Hellenistic world,
though for very different reasons. The first is that our only real sources of
information as to the social functions of oracles come from the literary
tradition and (to a lesser extent) from epigraphic and papyrological records
of oracular responses. The historical value of the literary tradition is much
disputed.[98] Rather than become embroiled in this debate, I propose simply to
use the tradition as it stands as a rough indication of what people *expected*

---

[97] If time and space permitted, I would add the consideration of a fourth major way in
which early Christian prophecy differed from inspired manticism in its environment. To
"Where and when?", "What?" and "Who?" we could add "How?", and discuss the
differing theories of inspiration of early Christianity and its world. Though both
"cultures" used the term πνεῦμα or πνεύματα for the agent of inspiration, early
Christianity saw πνεῦμα as non-material and personal, whereas the Hellenistic world at
large conceived of πνεῦμα as material and impersonal. But the full consideration of this
point is simply not possible within the constraints of this piece of work.

[98] See, for example, the dispute as to the historicity of the tradition of Delphic oracles
between J. Fontenrose, *The Delphic Oracle*, Berkeley, 1978, and his reviewers,
particularly Brenk, in *Gnomon*, vol. 52, 1980, pp. 700ff, Walcot, in *Greece and Rome*,
vol. 27, 1980, p. 104, and Robertson, in *Phoenix*, vol. 36, 1982, pp. 358ff; the criticisms
of this last reviewer are particularly trenchant.

of oracles, supplementing this where possible from the relatively safer epigraphic and papyrological evidence.

The second reason is simply that oracles had been a part of the Greek world for approximately seven hundred years by the time the New Testament was being written, and during this period they had exercised, as far as we can see, many differing functions. With these two constraints in mind, I suggest that the following is a reasonable sketch of the changing functions of oracles.

In the archaic and classical periods the Delphic oracle acted as an adviser in colonial policy and as both an adviser and arbitrator in interstate relations. It was also open to private individuals, though it is hard to know whether this effectively meant only the wealthy and powerful. It was the ultimate international authority on cult matters. In the Hellenistic period it had to share all these functions with the burgeoning local shrines in other places, often under the patronage of the new royal elites of the "Successor Kingdoms". Didyma was, of course, the most successful of these. In this period the oracles often acted as guarantors of a kind of neutrality, with their declarations that various states were ἄσυλος. Didyma and Miletus received this privilege themselves in the late third century B.C., and many more such decrees in favour of other cities followed. The oracles arbitrated on border squabbles and on questions of citizenship for mercenaries hired to settle such disputes. They acted as guarantors of treaties, and gave reassuring oracles after earthquakes.[99] For the second century B.C. we have a particularly rich supply of oracular responses from Didyma. There are matters of public cult, matters of professional concern to builders in the Temple itself, matters of private concern (success or failure in a dancing career, or in animal training in the case of a circus performer), matters of private cult and the fulfilment of vows, public cult and the declaration that certain people were to be commemorated as heroes, and the explanation of prodigies and disasters.[100]

There seems to me to be no evidence that the role of oracles in local and interstate politics declined until the beginning of the Roman period, and even the decline in this period was gradual. The impression that under the Pax Romana interstate politics among the subject states came to an end is

---

[99] H.W. Parke, *The Oracles of Apollo in Asia Minor*, London, 1985, p. 58, p. 61f, p. 66f.
[100] H.W. Parke, *op.cit.*, pp. 75ff.

misleading. Local governments still made and altered treaties, redefined their relationships, and fell into disputes. The real change was that in most, but not all, cases these disputes were confined to the political level by the threat or presence of Roman military force. Over time, of course, local politics became more and more integrated with the wider world, but the tradition of local autonomy went very deep, and remained central to the governing of the Roman empire for the whole of the period with which we are concerned, and beyond. In the meantime the tradition of private inquiry continued and, if anything, grew in importance. By the late-first and early-second century, matters had reached the state described by Pausanias and Plutarch: Delphi was no longer consulted about great matters of state because the Romans had their own methods, and private inquiries predominated, though not to the exclusion of state business of other kinds. Plutarch's satisfaction with this state of affairs is well illustrated by Mor. 408, quoted above. But it must be emphasised that international delegations to Delphi were still known within Plutarch's memory, as Mor. 438 a demonstrates, and such visitors were sometimes important enough (or rare enough?) to risk falsifying the omens to please them!

So much, then, for the great oracle-centres. What do we know of the small-town oracles, the local shrines that the ordinary man or woman might visit? The answer is, very little, and that only for Egypt, where a reasonable number of oracular questions have survived on papyrus. We cannot be certain whether this sample of oracular business is representative, though there is no strong reason to think otherwise. We find here evidence of two main oracular techniques, both clearly forms of inductive divination. The first is the random selection of an answer from a collection, similar in principle to the Chinese "I Ching". The second is the writing of the question with a positive and a negative response on two pieces of papyrus, one of which is then selected, again at random (by the inquirer or an officiating priest: we do not know which) from a container of some kind.[101] The questions that survive are very much of a personal day-to-day nature. On this Horsley has aptly commented that

---

[101] The former method, which is known to us in a later developed form as the "Sortes Astrampsychi", has been touched upon in Chapter 5, above, and is fully discussed in G. Horsley, ed., *New Documents Illustrating Early Christianity*, vol. 2, North Ryde, 1982, pp. 37-44, with full references. The latter method is illustrated in "P. Carlsberg 24: Question to an Oracle", by A. Bülow-Jacobsen, *Z.P.E.*, vol. 57, 1984, pp. 289-293.

It is important not to confuse what is common in human experience with the banal. Questions about marriage, going on a journey, and advancing in one's career, figure largely in the surviving examples; but each was of importance for the particular individual who importuned the god. For all their lack of context these brief documents illustrate common concerns of the time. Personal and domestic matters are to the fore . . .[102]

There is thus some measure of overlap between what we know of the inquiries made at the small local oracles, and those at the great centres.

In summary, then, what can be said about the functions of inspiration manticism and prophecy more generally? First and most importantly, Delphi and the other great oracle centres acted as guardians and expositors of the dominant religious consensus. Nearly forty percent of recorded oracles have to do with cult regulations. If we were to add to this total those oracles concerned with colonisation, from the seventh and sixth centuries B.C., many of which may be legendary developments from inquiries to do with the cultic side of colonisation, the figure reaches fifty-two percent.[103] Alternatively, if we allow more historical value to these oracles we could argue that in a period of social stress due to population pressures (and other factors) the oracle acted to legitimise and promote colonising activities in order to relieve the tensions in society and re-integrate marginalised groups. In either case, of course, its function was socially integrating. Secondly, the oracles sometimes acted as arbitrators both at a public and private level, settling, for example, questions of royal inheritance, and pronouncing on alliances and truces. In the Hellenistic period they seem to have acted as mediators between competing forces within society (in this case the city-states and the military power of the Successor Kingdoms) in order to limit the potential for conflict, by way of declarations of ἀσυλία. Thirdly, oracles acted as sources of information on topics on which there could be no certain human knowledge, such as whether children were legitimate, where one should settle and live, and occasionally on what portents and prodigies might mean. Fourthly, oracles acted in the field of personal decision-making as a social mechanism to limit the anxiety caused by the unpredictability of human affairs. Events might appear chaotic, meaningless, or even perverse, but the gods, speaking through their oracles, were to be relied upon. Oracles thus served the very important social and psychological function of helping

---

[102] G.H.R. Horsley, *op.cit.*, p. 38.

[103] See, for the statistics, J. Fontenrose, *op.cit.*, pp. 23ff. The suggestion that "colonisation inquiries" may originally have been purely cultic is my own.

to maintain the sense of order within the world-view of those who inquired of them.

At the level of the social and political aspirations of the ruling elites of the Greek πόλεις which maintained oracular institutions, oracles served as another field for political aggrandisement and euergetism. But nothing in this had to do with their specific religious function as institutions for making known the will and decisions of the gods. At this level they remained institutions for defending, articulating and interpreting the dominant consensus, both religious and social. They are thus a good example of what Lewis describes as "central mediation".[104]

There are doubtless parallels that might be drawn between some features of the above characterisation and features of early Christian prophecy. But it seems to me that the caution expressed in Chapter 9, above, is still appropriate. We know too little about early Christian prophecy, and it was itself too varied a phenomenon, for statements about its social functions to be more than guesses.

4. Final Questions

Given all of the above, it is appropriate that we reflect for a minute over the comparison with which we have been engaged. Was inspiration manticism really the appropriate form of prophecy to compare with early Christian prophecy? Perhaps it would have been more meaningful to compare it with the unstructured, "underground" forms of manticism, most strikingly exemplified by people like Eunus, the Syrian slave rebel? He, for example, claimed (like several of the Hebrew prophets) to be privy to the "council of the gods". Surely it is here, it might be suggested, on the margins of Graeco-Roman society and in movements with eastern origins, that we ought to look for our parallel phenomena, rather than in the institutional mainstream of the Graeco-Roman world. We have already seen, however, in Chapters 6 and 7, that there are very few parallels to be had for inspired speech in the religious background of our period. Comparing the divination of early Christianity, relying predominantly on inspiration, with that of the Hellenistic world, predominantly technical, is even less likely to yield overall parallels than the method we have followed. Further, we know too little about the role of diviners in the "spiritual underworld" of the Hellenistic period to make the comparison useful. The fact that inspiration

---

[104] I.M. Lewis, cited by D.E. Aune, *Prophecy*, p. 20.

manticism has provided us with more contrasts than parallels need not prove that we have framed our quest for parallels poorly. Rather it proves that even the closest parallel between early Christian prophecy and prophecy in its environment is still a distant one.

What little we do know about popular prophecy in the Hellenistic period raises one final contrast between the two fields. This contrast has to do with the way the Hellenistic world and Pauline Christianity organise their concepts of the miraculous, and particularly their concepts of the person divinely empowered. A.B. Kolenkow has shown how, in the Greek and Roman world, miracle and prophecy are seen as closely related. Both powers commonly occur in the one person.[105] Divinatory techniques were very similar to magic, diviners are commonly thought of as having power to work miracles (especially miracles - or at least extraordinary feats - of healing), and oracles give responses to do with healing.[106] In the Jewish world the claim to be a prophet is often supported by the display of signs and wonders. Kolenkow shows how Josephus adds the motif of the "combination of powers" to passages from the Old Testament. Josephus likewise reports on several "sign-prophets" - a tell-tale designation![107] In the Gospels the miracles of Jesus lead to his being described as a prophet.[108] In Acts Ananias' vision leads him to Saul, whom he heals. Dreams and visions, signs and wonders are the active proof of the power of the eschatological Spirit.[109] We should also note that in both the Jewish world and the wider Hellenistic world the prophet (whether he be Jewish προφήτης or Hellenistic μάντις) is often said to have insight into the hearts of men beyond the natural: indeed, he can claim to know "all things", or even "things past, present and future".[110] All of this is good and useful. But we

---

[105] A.B. Kolenkow, "Relationships between Miracle and Prophecy in the Greco-Roman World and Early Christianity", *A.N.R.W.*, II, 31, part 2, pp. 1470-1506, esp. pp. 1472-3.

[106] A.B. Kolenkow, *art.cit.*, pp. 1473-1478.

[107] A.B. Kolenkow, *art.cit.*, pp. 1482-1483, and see P.W. Barnett, "The Jewish Sign-Prophets, A.D. 40-70: their Intentions and Origin", *N.T.S.*, vol. 27, 1980, pp. 679-697.

[108] A.B. Kolenkow, *art.cit.*, pp. 1480ff, 1491, 1492.

[109] A.B. Kolenkow, *art.cit.*, pp. 1495ff.

[110] See A.B. Kolenkow, *art.cit.*, and the two important articles of W.C. van Unnik, "A Formula Describing Prophecy", *N.T.S.*, vol. 9, 1962-3, pp. 86-94, and "A Greek characteristic of prophecy in the Fourth Gospel", in *Text and Interpretation: Studies in the New Testament Presented to Matthew Black*, ed. E. Best and R. McL. Wilson, Cambridge, 1979, pp. 211-229. These articles, also cited above, seem to me to represent

should note that in Luke an important narrowing of the range has occurred. While visions, healings and miracles continue to occur, the προφήτης does not perform them. His role, though broad by comparison with that allotted him by Paul, has been limited to inspired speech. Visions and wonders are no longer characteristic of the prophet.

In Paul this tendency has gone even further. While Luke, as we saw in Chapter 3, includes virtually all inspired speech under the heading of prophecy, Paul distinguishes glossolalia, words of wisdom, words of knowledge and prophecy properly so called. The prophet and the worker of miracles are different people, with differing χαρίσματα. Doubtless the one person may exercise several of these gifts at different times, but for Paul, it would appear, that does not obliterate the distinction to be made between them.[111] The only traditional link that he maintains is that between prophecy and the inspired insight into the hearts of men that lies behind 1 Corinthians 14.24-25.

Now in terms of the combination of phenomena there is little difference between the New Testament and its world. Prophecy and miracles are claimed in both: certain people within early Christianity profess to practise both. It is at the conceptual level that they differ. What has brought Paul (and to a lesser extent Luke) to so analyse and dissect the work of the Spirit?

Here I think there are two related points to be made. First, in Paul this analysis must be seen as related to his theology of the church as a body with interdependent members. If each member is to have a contribution to make, it becomes necessary to distinguish what those differing contributions might be. Thus gifts normally lumped together are separated and dispersed - conceptually at least - among the congregation. Secondly, and in the same context, we may see Paul's aim as polemical. It is in 1 Corinthians 12-14 that Paul's analysis is taken to the greatest lengths, and we have seen that he is there dealing with opponents who wish to concentrate in their own hands several of the more prestigious χαρίσματα. Paul is therefore at pains (once again) to separate and disperse them. Luke stands half way between Paul and the normal view of the Hellenistic world, and if, as I would argue, he is

---

a very promising way forward in terms of parallels between early Christianity and its environment.

[111] The point is noted by W.H. Mare, "Prophet and Teacher in the New Testament Period", *B.E.Th.S.*, vol. 9, no. 3, 1966, pp. 143, 144 and 147.

a companion of Paul, it is not unlikely that his view has been somewhat influenced by Paul's.

Even if, then, we were to attempt to parallel early Christian prophecy within the world of Hellenistic divination more generally, we would find that the social context within which it was exercised was so different as to fundamentally alter the conception of the role of the prophet. No longer is he the independent figure of power. Now he is one member among many in a community in which all have the same Spirit - and potentially the same gifts - as he has. He has no specialist skills, and no particular privileges beyond a hearing - a critical one - in the gathering of the community. Thus is the power of the prophet/miracle-worker subordinated to the good of the community.

We have seen that, though several of the attempts that have been made to distinguish Christian prophecy from its Hellenistic counterpart have failed, none the less the two phenomena are very different things. We have seen that though there are a few parallels which mean that we can use the term "prophecy" of phenomena in both "cultures", none the less there was no likelihood that anyone at the time would have been confused, or would have thought the phenomena similar in detail. Likewise it seems most unlikely that any of the Corinthians could have brought with them into their Christianity Hellenistic views about the nature of prophecy, without the matter being much clearer than it is in our evidence. There is nothing in 1 Corinthians comparable to Hermas' polemic against Christian divination. There is no evidence to suggest, then, that the views of Paul's opponents in Corinth on the nature of prophecy are based on Hellenistic models. Once again it seems far more likely that the problems between Paul and his converts are due to the kinds of factors - spiritual elitism and exclusivism - analysed above in Chapters 9 and 10.

Chapter 12

Conclusions

This thesis set out to investigate a widely-held hypothesis made up of two main components. The first was that early Christian inspired speech (both glossolalia and prophecy) was a phenomenon closely related to inspired speech in the religions of the wider Graeco-Roman world. The second component was that this similarity, and the resultant crossover of ideas from the pre-Christian religious experience of the Corinthians to their new Christian situation, went a long way towards explaining how Paul and his Corinthian converts had come into conflict over inspired speech. It was also supposed to provide the interpretative key for several crucial passages in his debate with them, as recorded in 1 Corinthians.

In the case of early Christian glossolalia I have argued that no convincing parallels whatsoever have been found within the traditions of Graeco-Roman religion, as they were known in the environment of the New Testament, whether it be at the level of terminology, phenomena or concept. Whether or not γλώσσαις λαλεῖν is a Pauline coinage, its use as technical terminology for a form of inspired speech has no parallels in Greek literature. Specifically, the use of the noun γλῶσσα for obscure and archaic language provides no useful parallel, despite claims to the contrary. Γλῶσσα in this sense is a rare technical term of academic grammarians, not a common usage. The phrase γλώσσαις λαλεῖν is Christian, and arose from the belief, all but universally held within early Christianity, that glossolalia was the gift of speaking in human (or possibly heavenly) languages (γλῶσσαι) which one had not learned. The phenomenon itself is described by Luke and Paul (as well as later writers) as a form of inspired speech, which has the appearance of language (and which might well be taken for a foreign language). As a medium of revelation it was "interpreted" for the benefit of others. Such a phenomenon is, despite the multitude of claims to the contrary, unique within the religions of the Hellenistic and Classical periods. Revelatory speech in those periods was believed to take an archaic and poetic form, not, as I have shown, a form analogous to foreign languages. The "interpretation" that some oracles were believed to need was at the level of metaphor and imagery, not the linguistic level. Other forms of inspired speech than the oracular were known in the environment of early Christianity, but the attempts to demonstrate that they were analogous to glossolalia have been shown to be unconvincing. In particular the claim that Dionysiac cult included a form of inspired speech known as "Bacchic tongues" has been found to be baseless. Likewise the idea that the Hellenistic world believed in "divine languages" has been shown to be a false trail in terms of parallels, as there is no suggestion in any of our evidence that such languages were available to humans as a form of prayer or a medium of revelation. Divine languages (when they were believed in, for the belief was far from universal) were simply the languages in which the gods or daimons conversed with one another. Finally, at the conceptual level, since inspired speech in the Hellenistic world does not appear to have taken a form analogous to foreign languages, it is hardly surprising to learn that it was not conceived of in that fashion.

We have seen that the nearest parallels for early Christian glossolalia are to be found in two passages from Jewish literature with strong apocalyptic colouring. None the less, these constitute a far from certain basis for any theory that glossolalia was a common phenomenon in some sections of Judaism. They both deal with the concept of angelic languages, and the attempt to interpret glossolalia in such terms has, as I have shown, little support in our evidence. Neither work can be convincingly shown to be pre-Christian. There would appear to be very little link between the Hellenistic concept of divine languages and the Jewish belief in angelic languages. If glossolalia is, as G. Dautzenberg suggests, the peculiarly Christian form of the virtually universal phenomenon of ecstatic speech, then it must be emphasised that this peculiarly Christian form is very peculiar indeed. I suggest, however, that "ecstatic speech" is a term too laden with undefined connotations to be really useful. We need to take great care that we mean by it what our evidence means by the term ἐκστατικός, or else define the term ourselves and stick to our definition. Atypical, religiously motivated speech took varying forms in Hellenistic religion. Glossolalia is very different from the others, terminologically, phenomenologically, and conceptually.

Perhaps the most that could be said for the hypothesis that Paul's problems with his Corinthian converts have a background in Hellenistic religion is that the Corinthians may have held, from their pre-Christian experience, that divine inspiration was an overwhelming phenomenon, not to be resisted, and endowing one with a spiritual status beyond the ordinary. But R.A. Horsley has argued persuasively that the second half of this claim could just as easily be based on a form of Hellenistic-Jewish "Wisdom speculation", and the belief that the inspiration of divine powers is overwhelming is a fairly minimal parallel. It is certainly not sufficient to support the hypothesis with which we are concerned.

The case of early Christian prophecy was not as straightforward as that of glossolalia. At the level of terminology we saw that, while the term προφήτης was used in common, it meant substantially different things to the early Christians and to their non-Christian neighbours. The background to the early Christian usage is to be found in the Septuagint version of the Old Testament, not in the Graeco-Roman world. Beyond that point, the terminology of early Christian prophecy has very little in common with that of Hellenistic prophecy. Terms that are crucial to the Hellenistic view, such as μάντις, πρόμαντις, κατοχή, and so on, are simply not used by the early Christians to describe their own experience of prophecy. The reason is not hard to find. From their earliest days Christian prophecy and miracle-working were in conflict with divination and miracle-working in their environment - Simon Magus! - and the early Christians followed the example of Greek-speaking Judaism in differentiating themselves as clearly as possible from their competitors in their use of terminology.

In terms of phenomena, early Christian experiences of prophecy themselves may or may not have been similar to experiences of inspired manticism in the Hellenistic world. We do not really know, because we have no first-hand descriptions of those experiences on which to draw. What can be said is that the social forms taken by prophecy, broadly defined, were very different. The early Christian groups we have examined had no priestly hierarchies, no consciously formalised prophetic ritual beyond a few simple rules of procedure (and even those seem to have been more honoured in the breach than the observance), no oracular places, and no procedure for securing an oracle should one be required. Some of these differences have to do with the phenomena of the early Christian form of prophecy itself, while others have to do with wider matters, such as the role of the prophet within his community. But either way, prophecy in early Christianity took a very different overall form from that which it took in the wider Hellenistic world.

This is also evident at the conceptual level. It is clear that messages from the gods were believed to come in very different forms in the two cultures. This was not exclusively so, of course, as Judaism, the Hellenistic world and early Christianity all believed in oracular dreams and visions. But Christianity had an implicit definition of "the prophetic" which was lacking in the wider world, and that definition seems to have been restricted to the reception and proclamation of verbal messages. For the early Christians, these messages were prophecy. Dreams, visions, and other forms of revelation were just that - other forms of revelation. Inductive divination, common in both the Judaic and Hellenistic traditions in varying forms, was, for early Christianity, simply beyond the pale.

Were it not for the constraints of space in a thesis such as this I would also have argued in detail that the agent of inspiration - πνεῦμα, in all three cultures - was conceived of very differently by the Hellenistic world and by the Judaeo-Christian world. But I think enough has been said to show that the concepts of prophecy in the Hellenistic world and in early Christianity were very different.

With the collapse of its basis of evidence in the Hellenistic world, I argued that the hypothesis that similarities between Hellenistic and early Christian inspired speech explained much of Paul's conflict with the Corinthians over the matter must be abandoned. It therefore became necessary to suggest alternative reasons for the fact that the focus of the dispute between Paul and the Corinthians was on inspired speech. I argued that there were quite adequate reasons for believing that the Corinthian valuation of glossolalia was based on its status within early Palestinian Christianity (as John Chrysostom had suggested), understood against the background of the kind of "Wisdom" speculation described by R.A. Horsley. I showed that those Corinthians who believed themselves to have reached the stage of "maturity" (and who described themselves as "spiritual" and "prophets", no longer mere "children"), made the practice of glossolalia, with little regard for its interpretation, a mark of this elite status. They likewise attempted to limit the practice of prophecy, and its evaluation, to those whom they believed were sufficiently mature to take part. Against such a background as this, Paul's reply makes good sense. He argues that prophecy, not glossolalia, is a sign for believers, and that uninterpreted glossolalia was at best a negative sign, for unbelievers. The central theme of his polemic (the superior value of prophecy, which edifies the congregation, over glossolalia, which unless interpreted for the benefit of all, edifies only the speaker) likewise fits this context well. Most important of all, I showed that Paul argued that prophecy was subject to the evaluation of the whole of the congregation, not merely the will of a self-appointed spiritual elite.

It was not possible to treat every verse which had been interpreted in the light of the hypothesis in equal depth. For example, I have not attempted a full explanation or exegesis of the "cursing of Jesus" in 1 Corinthians 12.3. But I have shown that there are at least two alternative readings of the "gongs and cymbals" metaphor of 13.1, and W.W. Klein has shown that in any case χαλκός is not a term used of the musical instruments characteristic of pagan enthusiastic worship. It is rarely, if ever, used of musical instruments at all. Likewise there are better explanations for Paul's statement that tongues are a sign for unbelievers than that he means that tongues (as a common form of inspired speech) are the kind of sign unbelievers will recognise as evidence of divine activity. The comment attributed by Paul to the unbeliever who overhears uninterpreted glossolalia, μαίνεσθε, can clearly take the negative connotation, "you are all crazy", and I have shown that this seems to be the best interpretation. Finally, the connection between Paul's rebuke to the Corinthian women and the inspired speech issue has been broken by the recognition that it is not glossolalia, prophecy, speech in general or Bacchanalian shouting that Paul is forbidding. Rather he forbids the breaching of decorum by Corinthian women, who, now able to participate in congregational meetings, have begun publicly to ask questions of, and strike up discussions with, men with whom they have no socially acceptable relationship in the semi-public context of the Christian meeting.

What, then, has been achieved? The misleading hypothesis that a familiar Hellenistic experience of, and a set of beliefs about, inspired speech carried over into the life of the Corinthian congregation has been refuted. The connections between the issues of feminine decorum, spiritual elitism and inspired speech have been shown to be less direct than is often argued. Several cruxes of interpretation in Acts (2.4ff., 2.16ff., 10.44ff., 19.6ff.) and Paul (1 Corinthians 12.10, 12.30, 13.1-13, 14.2-5, 6-12, 20-25, 27-32,

33b-36 and 37ff.) have been interpreted along new lines, and these new interpretations have been shown to make up a coherent though complex picture. Against a theological background most probably drawn from speculations within Hellenistic Judaism, and with the example of Paul and (perhaps) the other early apostles in mind, some among the Corinthians began to value and practise glossolalia as a sign of elite spiritual status. They likewise began to restrict the practice of prophecy to their own number, dominating the congregational meetings, and claiming that only they (the spiritual, the mature, the prophets) had the right to evaluate prophetic utterances. It is against this position, one based on a mixture of Christian experience, Hellenistic-Jewish popular philosophy and a partial view of his own teaching, that Paul directs his attack in 1 Corinthians 12-14.

These conclusions in themselves may be sufficient. It is my hope, however, that a little more than that has been achieved. I would hope that along the way something more has been learnt of what Jannes Reiling aptly characterises as the "abundant life of the Spirit" - its pitfalls and its potential - as it took shape in the formative years of early Christianity.[1]

---

[1] J. Reiling, *Hermas and Christian Prophecy*, Leiden, 1973, p. 175.

Bibliography.

Ahl, F.M., *Lucan, an Introduction*, London, 1976.

Allen, T.W., W.R. Halliday and E.E. Sikes, *The Homeric Hymns*, Oxford, 1936.

R.W. Allison, "Let Women be Silent in the Churches (1 Cor. 14.33b-36): what did Paul really say, and what did it mean?", *J.S.N.T.* vol. 32, 1988, pp. 27-60.

Amandry, P., *La mantique apollinienne à Delphes*, Paris, 1950.

Arnold, C.E., *Ephesians: Power and Magic; the Concept of Power in Ephesians in light of its Historical Setting*, Cambridge, 1989.

Athanassakis, A.N., *The Homeric Hymns*, Baltimore, 1976.

Aune, D.E., "Herm. Man. 11.2: Christian False Prophets Who Say What People Wish to Hear", *Journal of Biblical Literature*, vol. 97, 1978, pp. 103-4.

"The Problem of the Genre of the Gospels", in *Gospel Perspectives*, vol. 2, ed. R.T. France and D. Wenham, Sheffield, 1981, pp. 9-60.

Prophecy in Early Christianity and the Ancient Mediterranean World, Grand Rapids, 1983.

"Magic in Early Christianity", *Aufstieg und Niedergang der römischen Welt*, Teil II, vol. 23, part 2, 1980, pp. 1507-1557.

"The Apocalypse of John and Graeco-Roman Revelatory Magic", *N.T.S.* vol. 33, 1987, pp. 481-501.

Bacht, H., "Wahres und falsches Prophetentum", *Biblica*, vol. 32, 1951, pp. 237-262.

Baker, D.L., "The Interpretation of 1 Corinthians 12-14", *Evangelical Quarterly*, vol. 46, 1974, pp. 224-234.

Barnett, P.W., "The Jewish Sign-Prophets, A.D. 40-70: Their Intentions and Origin", *New Testament Studies*, vol. 27, 1980, pp. 679-697.

Barrett, C.K., *The First Epistle to the Corinthians*, London, 1968.

A Commentary on the Second Epistle to the Corinthians, 2nd Edition, London, 1973.

Barton, S.C., "Paul's Sense of Place: an Anthropological Approach to Community Formation in Corinth", *New Testament Studies*, vol. 32, 1986, pp. 225-246.

Beare, F.W., "Speaking with Tongues: a Critical Survey of the New Testament Evidence", *Journal of Biblical Literature*, vol. 83, part 3, 1964, pp. 229-246.

Behm, J., "Glossa", in *Theological Dictionary of the New Testament*, vol. 1, ed. G. Kittel, pp. 719-727.

Berchman, R.M., "Arcana Mundi: Prophecy and Divination in the *Vita Mosis* of Philo of Alexandria", *S.B.L. 1988 Seminar Papers*, Atlanta, 1988, pp. 385-423.

Best, E., "Prophets and Preachers", *Scottish Journal of Theology*, vol. 12, 1959, pp. 129-150.

"The Interpretation of Tongues", *Scottish Journal of Theology*, vol. 28, no. 1, 1975, pp. 45-62.

Betz, H.D., *Lukian von Samosata und das Neue Testament*, Berlin, 1961.

Plutarch's Theological Writings and Early Christian Literature, Leiden, 1975.

"The Formation of Authoritative Tradition in the Greek Magical Papyri", in B.F. Meyer and E.P. Sanders, eds., *Jewish and Christian Self-Definition*, vol. 3, London, 1982, pp. 161-170.

The Greek Magical Papyri in Translation, vol. 1, Chicago, 1986.

Black, M., *The Book of Enoch, or, 1 Enoch*, Leiden, 1985.

Blenkinsopp, J., "Prophecy and Priesthood in Josephus", *Journal of Jewish Studies*, vol. 25, 1974, pp. 239-262.

Boardman, J., *Athenian Red-Figure Vases, The Archaic period*, Norwich, 1975.

Böhlig, A. and Wisse, F., trans., "The Gospel of the Egyptians", in *The Nag Hammadi Library in English*, ed. J.M. Robinson, Leiden, 1977, pp. 195-205.

Boring, M.E., *Sayings of the Risen Jesus: Christian Prophecy in the Synoptic Tradition*, Cambridge, 1982.

"What Are We Looking For?: Toward a Definition of the Term 'Christian Prophet'", *Society for Biblical Literature Seminar Papers*, Missoula, 1973, pp. 142-154.

Bornkamm, G., *Early Christian Experience*, London, 1969.

Bowers, P., "Paul and Religious Propaganda in the First Century", *Novum Testamentum*, vol. 22, no. 4, 1980, pp. 316-323.

Brandt, S. and Laubmann, G., eds., *Lactantius*, Leipzig, 1890, reprinted 1965.

Brenk, F.E., *In Mist Apparelled: Religious Themes in Plutarch's Moralia and Lives*, Leiden, 1977.

Bruce, F.F., *Paul: Apostle of the Free Spirit*, Exeter, 1977.

1 and 2 Corinthians, London, 1971.

Bülow-Jacobsen, A., "The Archiprophetes", *Papyrologica Bruxellensia*, vol. 19, part 4, ed. J. Bingen and G. Nachtergael, Brussels, 1979, pp. 124-131.

"P. Carlsberg 24: Question to an Oracle", *Zeitschrift für Papyrologie und Epigraphik*, vol. 57, 1984, pp. 289-293.

Cagnat, R., ed., *Inscriptiones Graecae ad Res Romanas Pertinentes*, vol. 1, Paris, 1911.

Callan, T., "Prophecy and Ecstasy in Greco-Roman Religion and in 1 Corinthians", *Novum Testamentum*, vol. 27, 1985, pp. 125-140.

Campenhausen, H. von, *Ecclesiastical Authority and Spiritual Power in the Church of the First Three Centuries*, trans. J.A. Baker, Stanford, 1969.

Carson, D.A., *Showing the Spirit: a Theological Exposition of 1 Corinthians 12-14*, Sydney, 1987.

Cerny, J., "Egyptian Oracles", in in *A Saite Oracle Papyrus from Thebes*, ed. R.A. Parker, Providence, 1962, pp. 35-48.

Chadwick, H., ed., *Origen: Contra Celsum*, Cambridge, 1965.

Priscillian of Avila, Oxford, 1976.

Charles, R.H., *The Apocrypha and Pseudepigrapha of the Old Testament in English*, vol. 2, Oxford, 1913.

Charlesworth, J.H., *The Pseudepigrapha and Modern Research*, Missoula, 1976.

ed., *The Old Testament Pseudepigrapha*, vol. 1, London, 1983.

Colin, M., *Fouilles de Delphes*, vol. 3, part 1, Paris, 1922.

Conzelmann, H., *Die Apostelgeschichte*, 2nd edition, Tübingen, 1972.

A Commentary on the First Epistle to the Corinthians, trans. J.W. Leitch, Philadelphia, 1975.

Cothenet, E., "Les prophètes chrétiens comme exégètes charismatiques de l'écriture", in *Prophetic Vocation in the New Testament and Today*, ed. J. Panagopoulos, Leiden, 1977, pp. 77-107.

Crane, S.D., *The Gift of Prophecy in the New Testament: an Inductive Study in the Exercise and Meaning of the Prophetic*, unpublished thesis, Princeton Theological Seminary, 1962.

Cranfield, C.E.B., *The Gospel according to St. Mark*, Cambridge, 1963.

Crone, T.M., *Early Christian Prophecy: a Study of its Origin and Function*, Baltimore, 1973.

Currie, S.D., " 'Speaking in Tongues': Early Evidence Outside the New Testament Bearing on '*Glossais Lalein*' ", *Interpretation*, vol. 19, 1965, pp. 274-294.

Dannemann, R., review of D.L. Tiede, *The Charismatic Figure as Miracle Worker*, *Journal of Biblical Literature*, vol. 93, 1974, pp. 129-130.

Daris, S., *Spoglio Lessicale Papirologico*, vol. 3, Milan, 1968.

Dautzenberg, G., "Glossolalie", *Reallexikon für Antike und Christentum*, vol. 11, 1981, cols. 225-246.

    Urchristliche Prophetie, Stuttgart, 1975.

Davis, J.A., *Wisdom and Spirit: an Investigation of 1 Corinthians 1.18-3.20 Against the Background of Jewish Sapiental Traditions in the Greco-Roman Period*, Lanham, 1984.

Delling, G., *Worship in the New Testament*, trans. P. Scott, London, 1962.

Diercks, G.F., *Novatianus, Opera quae supersunt*, Turnhout, 1972.

Dindorf, W., ed., *Iulii Pollucis, Onomasticon*, Leipzig, 1824.

Dodd, C.H., *The Interpretation of the Fourth Gospel*, Cambridge, 1953.

Dodds, E.R., *The Greeks and the Irrational*, Berkeley, 1951.

    "Supernormal Phenomena in Classical Antiquity", in *The Ancient Concept of Progress and Other Essays*, Oxford, 1973, pp. 156-210.

    Euripides, Bacchae, 2nd edition, Oxford, 1960.

Dollar, G.W., "Church History and the Tongues Movement", *Bibliotheca Sacra*, vol. 120, October 1963, pp. 316-321.

Doughty, D.J., "The Presence and Future of Salvation in Corinth", *Zeitschrift für die neutestamentlishe Wissenschaft*, vol. 66, 1975, pp. 61-90.

Dunn, J.D.G., *Jesus and the Spirit*, London, 1975.

    Unity and Diversity in the New Testament, London, 1977.

    "Discernment of Spirits - a Neglected Gift", in *Witness to the Spirit*, ed. W. Harrington, Dublin, 1979, pp. 79-96.

    "Prophetic 'I'-sayings and the Jesus Tradition: the Importance of Testing Prophetic Utterances Within Early Christianity", *New Testament Studies*, vol. 24, 1977-78, pp. 175-198.

    "The Responsible Congregation (1 Co. 14:26-40)" in *Charisma und Agape (1 Ko. 10-14)*, ed. L. De Lorenzi, Rome, 1983, pp. 201-236.

Edelstein, E.J. and L., *Asclepius: a Collection and Interpretation of the Testimonies*, 2 vols, Baltimore, 1945.

Edwards, T.C., *A Commentary on the First Epistle to the Corinthians*, London, 1897.

Ellis, E.E., *Paul's Use of the Old Testament*, Grand Rapids, 1957.

    "The Role of the Christian Prophet in Acts", in *Apostolic History and the Gospel*, ed. W.W. Gasque and R.P. Martin, Exeter, 1970, pp. 55-67, reprinted in *Prophecy and Hermeneutic in Early Christianity*, Grand Rapids, 1978, pp. 129-144.

    "Wisdom and Knowledge in 1 Corinthians", *Tyndale Bulletin*, vol. 25, 1974, pp. 82-98.

"Prophecy in the New Testament Church - and Today", in *Prophetic Vocation in the New Testament and Today*, ed. J. Panagopoulos, Leiden, 1977, pp. 46-57.

Prophecy and Hermeneutic in Early Christianity, Grand Rapids, 1978.

"The Silenced Wives of Corinth", in *New Testament Textual Criticism: its Significance for Exegesis*, ed. E.J. Epp and G.D. Fee, Oxford, 1981, pp. 213-220.

Engelsen, N.I.J., *Glossolalia and Other Forms of Inspired Speech According to 1 Corinthians 12-14*, unpublished thesis, Yale, 1970.

Evans, E., *Tertullian, Adversus Marcionem*, Oxford, 1972.

Fascher, E., *Prophetes: Eine sprach- und religionsgeschichtliche Untersuchung*, Giessen, 1927.

Feldman, L.H., "Prophets and Prophecy in Josephus", *J.Th.S.* vol. 41 no. 2, 1990, pp. 386-422.

Fiorenza, E.S., *In Memory of Her*, New York, 1984.

Flacelière, R., *Greek Oracles*, trans. D. Garman, London, 1965.

Fontenrose, J., *The Delphic Oracle*, Berkeley, 1978. See also the reviews of Brenk, in *Gnomon*, vol 52, 1980, pp. 700ff, Walcot, in *Greece and Rome*, vol. 27, 1980, p. 104, and Robertson, in *Phoenix*, vol. 36, 1982, p. 358ff.

Didyma: Apollo's Oracle, Cult, and Companions, Berkeley, 1988.

Foerster, W., "Python", in *Theological Dictionary of the New Testament*, ed. G. Friedrich, vol. 6, 1959, E.T. 1968, pp. 917ff.

Friedrich, G., et.al., "Prophetes", in *Theological Dictionary of the New Testament*, ed. G. Friedrich, vol. 6, 1959, E.T. 1968, pp. 828ff.

Fraenkel, E., *Aeschylus Agamemnon*, Oxford, 1962.

Fuller, R.H., "Tongues in the New Testament", *American Church Quarterly*, no. 3, 1963, pp. 162-8.

Gaster, T.H., *Myth, Legend and Custom in the Old Testament*, New York, 1969.

Georgi, D., *Die Gegner des Paulus im 2 Korintherbrief*, Neukirchen, 1964.

Gillespie, T.W., *Prophecy and Tongues: the Concept of Christian Prophecy in the Pauline Theology*, unpublished thesis, Claremont Graduate School and University Centre, 1971.

"A Pattern of Prophetic Speech in First Corinthians", *Journal of Biblical Literature*, vol. 97, no. 1, 1978, pp. 74-95.

Goold, G.P., *Catullus*, London, 1983.

Green, E.M.B., *Evangelism in the Early Church*, London, 1970.

I Believe in the Holy Spirit, Grand Rapids, 1975.

Greeven, H., "Propheten, Lehrer, Vorsteher bei Paulus", *Zeitschrift für die neutestamentliche Wissenschaft*, vol. 44, 1952, pp. 1-43.

Grosheide, F.W., *Commentary on 1 Corinthians*, London, 1954.

Grudem, W.A., *The Gift of Prophecy in 1 Corinthians*, Lanham, 1982.

"1 Corinthians 14.20-25: Prophecy and Tongues as Signs of God's Attitude", *Westminster Theological Journal*, vol. 41, No.2, Spring 1979, pp. 381-396.

"A Response to Gerhard Dautzenberg on 1 Cor. 12:10.", *Biblische Zeitschrift*, vol. 22, part 2, 1978, pp. 253-270.

"Prophecy - Yes, but Teaching - No: Paul's Consistent Advocacy of Women's Participation without Governing Authority", *Journal of the Evangelical Theological Society*, vol. 30, part 1, pp. 11-23.

Gundry, R.H., " 'Ecstatic Utterance' (N.E.B.)?", *Journal of Theological Studies*, vol. 17, part 2, 1966, pp. 299-307.

Güntert, H., *Von der Sprache der Götter und Geister: bedeutungs-geschichtliche Untersuchungen zur homerischen und eddischen Göttersprache*, Halle, 1921.

Haenchen, E., *The Acts of the Apostles, A Commentary*, trans. B. Noble, G. Shinn and R. McL. Wilson, Oxford, 1971.

Halfmann, H., *Die Senatoren aus dem östlichen Teil des Imperium Romanum bis zum Ende des 2.Jh. n. Chr.*, Göttingen, 1979.

Halliday, W.R., *Greek Divination, a Study of its Methods and Principles*, 1913, reprinted, Chicago, 1967.

Halton, T., "Stylistic Device in Melito, *Peri Pascha*", in *Kyriakon*, ed. P. Granfield and J.A. Jungmann, Münster, 1970, vol. 1, pp. 249-255.

Hanson, J.S., "Dreams and Visions in the Graeco-Roman World and Early Christianity" in *Aufstieg und Niedergang der Römischen Welt*, Teil II, vol. 23, part 2, 1980, pp. 1395-1427.

Harnack, A. von, *Über das gnostische Buch Pistis Sophia*, Texte und Untersuchungen zur altchristlichen Literatur 7.2, Leipzig, 1891.

Harrisville, R.A., "Speaking in Tongues: a Lexicographical Study", *Catholic Biblical Quarterly*, vol. 38, 1976, pp. 35-48.

Hart, M.E., *Prophecy and Speaking in Tongues as Understood by Paul and at Corinth, with Reference to Early Christian Usage*, unpublished thesis, Durham, 1975.

Harvey, A.E., "The Use of Mystery Language in the Bible", *Journal of Theological Studies*, vol. 31, 1980, pp. 320-336.

Haykin, M., "The Fading Vision? The Spirit and Freedom in the Pastoral Epistles", *Evangelical Quarterly*, vol. 57, no. 4, 1985, pp. 291-305.

Heberdey, R., ed., *Tituli Asiae Minoris*, vol. 3, Vienna, 1941.

Heine, R.E., "A Note on Lucan's *Bellum Civile* 5.79-81", *Classical Bulletin*, vol. 54, January, 1978, pp. 44-45.

"A Note on Lucan's *Bellum Civile* 5.121", *Classical Bulletin*, vol. 54, January, 1978, p. 45.

Hennecke, E., *New Testament Apocrypha*, ed. W. Schneemelcher, vol. 2, 1964, E.T. 1965, 1974.

Henrichs, A., "Greek Maenadism from Olympias to Messalina", *Harvard Studies in Classical Philology*, vol. 82, 1978, pp. 121-160.

Héring, J., *The First Epistle of St. Paul to the Corinthians*, trans. A.W. Heathcote and P.J. Allcock, London, 1962.

Hill, D., trans., "The Ascension of Isaiah", from the German of J. Flemming and H. Duensing, in E. Hennecke, *New Testament Apocrypha*, ed. W. Schneemelcher, vol. 2, 1964, E.T. 1965, 1974, pp. 642-663.

"Christian Prophets as Teachers and Instructors in the Church", in *Prophetic Vocation in the New Testament and Today*, ed. J. Panagopoulos, Leiden, 1977, pp. 108-130.

New Testament Prophecy, Richmond, 1979.

Hoehner, H.W., "The Purpose of Tongues in 1 Corinthians 14:20-25", *Walvoord, a Tribute*, ed. D.K. Campbell, Chicago, 1982, pp. 53-66.

Hollander H.W. and de Jonge, M., *The Testaments of the Twelve Patriarchs, a Commentary*, Leiden, 1985.

Horner, G., *Pistis Sophia*, London, 1924.

Horsley, G.H.R., ed., *New Documents Illustrating Early Christianity*, vol 2, North Ryde, 1982.

Horsley, R.A., "Pneumatikos vs. Psychikos: Distinctions of Spiritual Status among the Corinthians", *Harvard Theological Review*, vol. 69, 1976, pp. 269-288.

"Wisdom of Word and Words of Wisdom in Corinth", *Catholic Biblical Quarterly*, vol. 39, 1977, pp. 224-239.

" 'How can some of you say there is no resurrection of the dead?' Spiritual Elitism in Corinth", *Novum Testmentum*, vol. 20, 1978, pp. 202-231.

House, H.W., "Tongues and the Mystery Religions of Corinth", *Bibliotheca Sacra*, vol. 140, part 558, 1983, pp. 134-150.

Hull, J.M., *Hellenistic Magic and the Synoptic Tradition*, London, 1974.

Hunter, H.H., "Tongues-Speech: a Patristic Analysis", *Journal of the Evangelical Theological Society*, vol. 23, part 2, 1980, pp. 125-137.

Hurd, J.C., *The Origins of 1 Corinthians*, London, 1965.

Hurley, J.B., "Did Paul Require Veils or the Silence of Women?", *Westminister Theological Journal*, vol. 35, part 2, 1973, pp. 190-220.

Man and Woman in Biblical Perspective, Leicester, 1981.

Isaacs, M.E., *The Concept of Spirit: A Study of Pneuma in Hellenistic Judaism and its Bearing on the New Testament*, London, 1976.

Isbell, C.D., "Glossolalia and Propheteialalia: a Study of 1 Corinthians 14", *Wesleyan Theological Journal*, vol. 10, 1975, pp. 15-22.

Jeremias, J., "Sabbathjahr und neutestamentliche Chronologie", *Zeitschrift für die neutestamentliche Wissenschaft*, vol. 27, 1928.

Johanson, B.C., "Tongues, A Sign for Unbelievers?: a Structural and Exegetical Study of 1 Corinthians XIV. 20-25", *New Testament Studies*, vol. 25, pp. 180-203.

Johnson, L.T., "Norms for True and False Prophecy in First Corinthians", *American Benedictine Review*, vol. 22, 1971, pp. 29-45.

Käsemann, E., "The Cry for Liberty in the Worship of the Church", in *Perspectives on Paul*, London, 1969, pp. 122-137.

Commentary on Romans, trans. G.W. Bromiley, Grand Rapids, 1980.

Kaibel, G., ed., *Epigrammata Graeca*, repr. Hildesheim, 1965.

Kees, H., "Der berichtende Gottesdiener", *Zeitschrift für ägyptische Sprache und Altertumskunde*, vol. 85, 1960, pp. 138-143.

Keilbach, W., "Zungenreden", in *Religion in Geschichte und Gegenwart*, 3rd edition, vol. 6, 1962, cols 1940-1941.

Kerenyi, C., *Dionysos; Archetypal Image of Indestructible Life*, trans. R. Manheim, London, 1976.

Kern, O., *Die Inschriften von Magnesia am Maeander*, Berlin, 1900.

Klein, W.C., "The Church and its Prophets", *Anglican Theological Review*, vol. 44, no. 1, January 1962, pp. 1-17.

Klein, W.W., "Noisy Gong or Acoustic Vase? A Note on 1 Corinthians 13.1", *New Testament Studies*, vol. 32, 1986, pp. 286-288.

Kleinknecht, H., "Pneuma", in *Theological Dictionary of the New Testament*, vol. 6, ed. G. Friedrich, 1959, E.T. 1968, pp. 332-359.

Knox, W.L., *Hellenistic Elements in Primitive Christianity*, London, 1944.

Kolenkow, A.B., "Relationships between Miracle and Prophecy in the Greco-Roman World and Early Christianity", *Aufstieg und Niedergang der römischen Welt*, II.23.2, 1980, pp. 1470-1506.

Krämer, H., et.al., "Prophetes", in *Theological Dictionary of the New Testament*, ed. G. Friedrich, vol. 6, 1959, E.T. 1968, pp. 781ff.

Kraemer, R.S., "Ecstasy and Possession. The Attraction of Women to the Cult of Dionysus", *Harvard Theological Review*, vol. 72, 1979, pp. 55-80.

Ecstatics and Ascetics: Studies in the Functions of Religious Activities for Women in the Greco-Roman World, unpublished thesis, Princeton University, 1976.

Kroeger, R. and C.C., "An Inquiry into Evidence of Maenadism in the Corinthian Congregation", *Society for Biblical Literature Seminar Papers*, 1978, pp. 331-338.

"Pandemonium and Silence at Corinth", in *Women and the Ministries of Christ*, ed. R. Hestenes and L. Curley, Pasadena, 1980 (?), pp. 49-55.

Kydd, R., "Novatian's *De Trinitate*, 29: Evidence of the Charismatic?", *Scottish Journal of Theology*, vol. 30, 1977, pp. 313-318.

de Labriolle, P., *Les sources de l'histoire du Montanisme*, Fribourg, 1913.

Lafaye, G., ed., *Inscriptiones Graecae ad Res Romanas Pertinentes* vol. 4, Paris, 1927, reprinted Rome, 1964.

Lampe, G.W.H., "Grievous Wolves (Acts 20.29)", in *Christ and Spirit in the New Testament*, ed. B. Lindars and S.S. Smalley, Cambridge, 1973, pp. 253-268.

Lane, E.N., *Corpus Monumentorum Religionis dei Menis*, vol. 3, Leiden, 1976.

Latte, K., "The Coming of the Pythia", *Harvard Theological Review*, vol. 33, 1940, pp. 9-18.

Leslie, W.H., *The Concept of Woman in the Pauline Corpus in the Light of the Social and Religious Environment of the First Century*, unpublished thesis, Northwestern University, 1976.

Lohse, E., "Pentecost", in *Theological Dictionary of the New Testament*, vol. 6, ed. G. Friedrich, 1959, E.T. 1968, pp. 50-53.

Lutz, C.E., "Musonius Rufus, the Roman Socrates", *Yale Classical Studies*, vol. 10, 1947, pp. 3-147.

McCabe D.F. and Plunkett, M.A., *Didyma, Inscriptions*, The Institute for Advanced Study, Princeton, 1985, unpublished.

McDonald, J.I.H., "Some Comments on the Form of Melito's Paschal Homily", *Studia Patristica*, vol. 12, ed. E.A. Livingstone, Berlin, 1971, pp. 104-112.

MacDonald, W.G., "Glossolalia in the New Testament", *Bulletin of the Evangelical Theological Society*, vol. 7, Spring, 1964, pp. 59-68.

MacGorman, J.W., "Glossolalic Error and its Correction: 1 Corinthians 12-14", *Review and Expositor*, vol. 80, 1983, pp. 389-400.

McLeod, W.E., "Oral Bards at Delphi", *Transactions and Proceedings of the American Philological Association*, vol. 92, 1961, pp. 317-325.

MacMullen, R., *Enemies of the Roman Order*, Cambridge, Mass., 1966.

Paganism in the Roman Empire, New Haven, 1981.

Mann, C.S., Appendix 3 to J. Munck, *The Acts of the Apostles*, New York, 1967.

Manson, T.W., "The Corinthian Correspondence (1)", in *Studies in the Gospels and Epistles*, ed. M. Black, Manchester, 1962, pp. 190-209.

Mare, W.H., "Prophet and Teacher in the New Testament Period", *Bulletin of the Evangelical Theological Society*, vol. 9, no. 3, 1966, pp. 139-148.

Marshall, I.H., "The Significance of Pentecost", *Scottish Journal of Theology*, vol. 30, 1977, pp. 347-369.

The Acts of the Apostles, Leicester, 1980.

Martin, R.P., *The Spirit and the Congregation*, Grand Rapids, 1984.

Martin, W.J., "1 Corinthians 11:2-16: an Interpretation", in *Apostolic History and the Gospel*, ed. W.W. Gasque and R.P. Martin, Exeter, 1970, pp. 231-241.

Mason, H.J., *Greek Terms for Roman Institutions*, Toronto, 1974.

Meeks, W.A., *The First Urban Christians*, New Haven, 1983.

Méhat, A., "L'enseignement sur <<les choses de l'ésprit>>", *Revue d'histoire et de philosophie religieuses*, vol. 63, no. 4, 1983, pp. 395-415.

Merkelbach, R., ed., *Die Inschriften von Kalchedon*, Bonn, 1980.

Metzger, B.M., "Methodology in the Study of the Mystery Religions and Early Christianity", in *Historical and Literary Studies, Pagan, Jewish and Christian*, Leiden, 1968.

Meyer, R., et.al., "Prophetes", in *Theological Dictionary of the New Testament*, ed. G. Friedrich, vol. 6, 1959, E.T. 1968, pp. 812ff.

Miguens, E., "1 Cor 13:8-13 Reconsidered", *C.B.Q.* vol. 37, 1975, pp. 76-97.

Mills, W.E., *A Theological / Exegetical Approach to Glossolalia*, Lanham, 1985.

Mortley, R.J., *From Word to Silence*, 2 vols, Bonn, 1986.

Müller, C., *Fragmenta Historicorum Graecarum*, Frankfurt, 1975 (reprint).

Müller, U.B., *Prophetie und Predigt im Neuen Testament*, Gütersloh, 1975.

Murphy-O'Connor, J., "The non-Pauline Character of 1 Corinthians 11.2-16?", *Journal of Biblical Literature*, vol. 95, part 4, 1976, pp. 615-621.

Neyrey, J.H., "Body Language in 1 Corinthians: the Use of Anthropological Models for Understanding Paul and His Opponents", *Semeia*, vol. 35, 1986, pp. 129-170.

Nock A.D. and Festugière, A.J., *Hermes Trismégiste*, Paris, 1972.

Ogilvie, R.M., *The Romans and their Gods*, London, 1969.

Orr W.F. and Walker, J.A.R., *1 Corinthians*, New York, 1976.

Oster, R., "Numismatic Windows into the Social World of Early Christianity: a Methodological Inquiry", *Journal of Biblical Literature*, vol. 101, 1982, pp. 195-223.

Oulton, J.E.L. and Chadwick, H., *Alexandrian Christianity*, vol. 2, London, 1954.

Painter, J., "Paul and the Pneumatikoi at Corinth", in *Paul and Paulinism*, ed. M.D. Hooker and S.G. Wilson, London, 1982, pp. 237-250.

Parke, H.W., *Greek Oracles*, London, 1967.

The Oracles of Apollo in Asia Minor, London, 1985.

"The Temple of Apollo at Didyma", *Journal of Hellenic Studies*, vol. 106, 1986, pp. 120-131.

Parke, H.W. and Wormell, D.E.W., *The Delphic Oracle*, Oxford, 1956.

Patrick, J., trans., "Origens Commentary on the Gospel of Matthew", *The Ante-Nicene Fathers*, vol. 10, ed. A. Menzies, reprinted Grand Rapids, 1969.

Paulsen, H., "Papyrus Oxyrhynchus 1.5 und die ΔΙΑΔΟΧΗ ΤΩΝ ΠΡΟΦΗΤΩΝ", *New Testament Studies*, vol. 25, 1978-9, pp. 443-453.

Pearson, B.A., *The Pneumatikos-Psychikos Terminology in 1 Corinthians*, Missoula, 1973.

Peisker, C.H., "Prophet", in *New International Dictionary of New Testament Theology*, ed. C. Brown, Grand Rapids, 1978, vol. 3, pp. 75-92.

Perler, O., *Méliton de Sardes sur la pâque*, Paris, 1966.

Phillips, J.B., *The New Testament in Modern English*, London, 1972.

Picard, C., *Ephèse et Claros*, Paris, 1922.

Pieper, J., *Love and Inspiration*, trans. R. and C. Winston, London, 1964.

Poythress, V., "The Nature of Corinthian Glossolalia: Possible Options", *Westminster Theological Journal*, vol. 40, 1977, pp. 130-135.

Preisigke, F., *Wörterbuch der griechischen Papyrusurkunden*, vols. 2 and 3, Berlin, 1925 and 1931.

Price, S.R.F., "Delphi and Divination", in *Greek Religion and Society*, ed. P. Easterling and J. Muir, Cambridge, 1985, pp. 128-154.

Reiling, J., "The Use of *pseudoprophetes* in the Septuagint, Philo and Josephus", *Novum Testamentum*, vol. 13, 1971, p. 147-156.

    Hermas and Christian Prophecy, subtitled "A Study of the Eleventh Mandate", Supplement to Novum Testamentum, vol. 37, Leiden, 1973.

    "Prophecy, the Spirit and the Church", in *Prophetic Vocation in the New Testament and Today*, ed. J. Panagopoulos, Leiden, 1977, pp. 58-76.

    "Marcus Gnosticus and the New Testament: Eucharist and Prophecy", from *Miscellanea Neotestamentica*, vol. 1, ed. T. Baarda, A.F.J. Klijn and W.C. van Unnik, Leiden, 1978, pp. 161-179.

Reitzenstein, R., *Poimandres*, Leipzig, 1904.

    Hellenistic Mystery Religions, trans. J. Steely, Pittsburgh, 1978.

Richardson, W., "Liturgical Order and Glossolalia in 1 Corinthians 14.26c-33a", *New Testament Studies*, vol. 32, 1986, pp. 144-153.

Riesenfeld, H., "Note Supplémentaire sur I Cor. XIII", *Coniectanea Neotestamentica*, vol. 12, 1948, pp. 50-53.

Ridderbos, H.N., *Paul: an Outline of his Theology*, Grand Rapids, 1975.

Robeck, Jr., C.M., "The Gift of Prophecy in Acts and Paul", *Studia Biblica et Theologica*, vol. 5, no. 1, 1975, pp. 15-38; vol. 5, no. 2, pp. 37-54.

    "Irenaeus and 'Prophetic Gifts'", in P. Elbert, ed., *Essays on Apostolic Themes*, Massachusetts, 1985, pp. 104-114.

    "Canon, *Regula Fidei*, and Continuing Revelation in the Early Church", in J.E. Bradley and R.A. Muller, eds., *Church, Word and Spirit: Historical and Theological Essays in Honor of Geoffrey W. Bromiley*, Grand Rapids, 1987, pp. 65-91.

    Prophecy in Carthage: Perpetua, Tertullian and Cyprian, Cleveland, 1992.

Robert, L., "Inscriptions de Didyme et de Milet", *Hellenica* XI-XII, 1960, pp. 440-489.

Roberts, P., "A Sign - Christian or Pagan?", *Expository Times*, vol. 90, no. 7, April, 1979, pp. 199-203.

Robertson, A. and Plummer, A., *A Critical and Exegetical Commentary on the First Epistle of St. Paul to the Corinthians*, Edinburgh, 1911.

Robertson, A.T., *A Grammar of the Greek New Testament in the Light of Historical Research*, Nashville, 1934.

Robertson, O.P., "Tongues: Sign of Covenantal Curse and Blessing", *Westminister Theological Journal*, vol. 38, no. 1, 1975, pp. 43-53.

Rogers, C.L., "The Gift of Tongues in the Post Apostolic Church", *Bibliotheca Sacra*, vol. 122, part 486, 1965, pp. 134-143.

Rollins, W.G., "De Pythiae oraculis", in *Plutarch's Theological Writings and Early Christian Literature*, ed. H.D. Betz, Leiden, 1975, pp. 103-130.

Ruef, J., *Paul's First Letter to Corinth*, London, 1977.

Sandmel, S., *Philo's Place in Judaism*, augmented edition, Ktav, New York, 1971.

"Palestinian and Hellenistic Judaism and Christianity: The Question of the Comfortable Theory", *Hebrew Union College Annual*, vol. 50, 1979, pp. 137-148.

Schmidt, C., ed., *Pistis Sophia*, translated and with notes by V. Macdermot, Leiden, 1978.

Schmidt, M., ed., *Hesychii Alexandrini Lexicon*, Amsterdam, 1965, reprinted from the 1858 edition, no place given.

Schmithals, W., *Gnosticism in Corinth*, trans. J.E. Steely, Nashville, 1971.

Paul and the Gnostics, trans. J.E. Steely, Nashville, 1972.

Schwyzer, E., ed., *Dialectorum Graecarum Exempla Epigraphica Potiora*, Leipzig, 1923.

Scott, W., *Corpus Hermeticum*, vol. 1, London, 1924.

Segal, A.F., "Heavenly Ascent in Hellenistic Judaism, Early Christianity and their Environment", in *Aufstieg und Niedergang der römischen Welt*, Teil II, vol 23 part 2, 1980, pp. 1333-1394.

Senft, C., *La première épître de Saint Paul aux Corinthiens*, Neuchatel, 1979.

Sigountos, J.G. and Shank, M., "Public Roles for Women in the Pauline Church: a Reappraisal of the Evidence", *Journal of the Evangelical Theological Society*, vol. 26, part 3, 1983, pp. 283-295.

Smit, J.F.M., "Two Puzzles: 1 Corinthians 12.31 and 13.3: a Rhetorical Solution", *N.T.S.* vol. 39, 1993, pp. 246-264.

Smith, D.M., "Glossolalia and Other Spiritual Gifts in a New Testament Perspective", *Interpretation*, vol. 28, 1974, pp. 307-320.

Smith, M., "Pauline Worship as Seen by Pagans", *Harvard Theological Review*, vol. 93, part 1-2, 1980, pp. 241-249.

"Prolegomena to a Discussion of Aretalogies, Divine Men, the Gospels and Jesus", *Journal of Biblical Literature*, vol. 90, 1971, pp. 174-199.

Smith, W.D., "So-called Possession in Pre-Christian Greece", *Transactions and Proceedings of the American Philological Association*, vol. 96, 1965, pp. 403-426.

Souter, A., *The Text and Canon of the New Testament*, London, 1913.

Speyer, W., *Bücherfunde in der Glaubenswerbung der Antike*, Göttingen, 1970.

Spittler, R.P., *The Testament of Job: Introduction, Translation, and Notes*, unpublished Ph.D. thesis, Harvard University, 1971.

"The Testament of Job", in J.H. Charlesworth, ed., *The Old Testament Pseudepigrapha*, London, 1983, pp. 829-868.

Squires, J.T., *The Plan of God in Luke-Acts*, Cambridge, 1993.

Stewart, Z., ed., *A.D. Nock: Essays on Religion and the Ancient World*, vol. 1, Oxford, 1972.

Sweet, J.P.M., "A Sign for Unbelievers: Paul's Attitude to Glossolalia", *New Testament Studies*, vol. 13, 1966-7, pp. 240-57.

Stendahl, K., *The Bible and the Role of Women*, Philadelphia, 1966.

"Glossolalia and the Charismatic Movement", in *God's Christ and His People*, ed. J. Jervell and W. Meeks, Oslo, 1977, pp. 122-129.

Tabbernee, W., *The Opposition to Montanism from Church and State*, unpublished Ph.D. thesis, Melbourne University, 1978.

Talbert, C.H., "Paul's Undertanding of the Holy Spirit: the Evidence of 1 Corinthians 12-14", *Perspectives in Religious Studies*, vol. 11, no. 4, 1984, pp. 95-108.

Talbert, R.J.A., *The Senate of Imperial Rome*, Princeton, 1984.

Taylor, A.E., *Plato: the Man and His Work*, London, 1926.

Taylor, V., *The Gospel According to St. Mark*, 2nd edition, London, 1966.

Theissen, G., *The Social Setting of Pauline Christianity*, Edinburgh, 1982.

Thiselton, A.C., "The 'Interpretation' of Tongues: a New Suggestion in the Light of Greek Usage in Philo and Josephus", *Journal of Theological Studies*, vol. 30, 1979, pp. 15-36.

"Realised Eschatology at Corinth", *New Testament Studies*, vol. 24, 1977-78, pp. 510-526.

Thomas, R.L., "Tongues . . . will Cease", *Journal of the Evangelical Theological Society*, vol. 17, 1974, pp. 81-89.

Thrall, M.E., *The First and Second Letters of St. Paul to the Corinthians*, Cambridge, 1965.

Tiede, D.L., *The Charismatic Figure as Miracle Worker*, Missoula, 1973.

Toussaint, S.D., "First Corinthians Thirteen and the Tongues Question", *Bibliotheca Sacra*, vol. 120, October 1963, pp. 311-316.

Trocmé, E., *Le 'Livre des Actes' et l'histoire*, Paris, 1957.

Tschiedel, H.J., "Ein Pfingstwunder im Apollonhymnus", *Zeitschrift für Religions- und Geistesgeschichte*, vol. 27, 1975, pp. 22-39.

Tugwell, S., "The Gift of Tongues in the New Testament", *Expository Times*, vol. 84, no 5, 1973, pp. 137-140.

Turner, M., "Spiritual Gifts Then and Now", *Vox Evangelica*, vol. 15, 1985, pp. 7-64.

Turner, N., *Christian Words*, Edinburgh, 1980.

van der Horst, P.W., "Hellenistic Parallels to the Acts of the Apostles (2.1-47)", *Journal for the Study of the New Testament*, vol. 25, 1985, pp. 49-60.

"The Role of Women in the Testament of Job", *Nederlands Theologisch Tijdschrift*, vol. 40, no. 4, 1986, pp. 273-289.

Van Haelst, J., *Catalogue des papyrus littéraires juifs et chrétiens*, Paris, 1976.

van Unnik, W.C., "A Formula Describing Prophecy", *New Testament Studies*, vol. 9, 1962-63, pp. 86-94.

"A Greek characteristic of prophecy in the Fourth Gospel", in *Text and Interpretation: Studies in the New Testament Presented to Matthew Black*, ed. E. Best and R. McL. Wilson, Cambridge, 1979, pp. 211-229.

"The Meaning of 1 Corinthians 12.31", *Novum Testamentum* vol. 35, part 2, 1993, pp. 142-159.

Vermes, G., *The Dead Sea Scrolls in English*, Harmondsworth, 1968.

Vieilleux, A., trans., *Pachomian Koinonia*, vol. 2, Kalamazoo, 1981.

Walker, W.O., "1 Corinthians 11:2-16 and Paul's Views Regarding Women", *Journal of Biblical Literature*, vol. 94, 1975, pp. 94-110.

Wedderburn, A.J.M., "Romans 8.26 - Towards a Theology of Glossolalia?", *Scottish Journal of Theology*, vol. 28, 1975, pp. 369-377.

Wessely, C., ed., *Griechische Zauberpapyri von Paris und London*, Vienna, 1888.

Wettstein, J., *Novum Testamentum Graecum*, vol. 2, Graz, reprint of 1962.

Whittaker, C.R., "The Delphic Oracle; Belief and Behaviour in Ancient Greece - and Africa", *Harvard Theological Review*, vol. 58, no. 1, 1965, pp. 21-47.

Wicker, K., "De defectu oraculorum", in *Plutarch's Theological Writings and Early Christian Literature*, ed. H.D. Betz, Leiden, 1975, pp. 131-180.

Wilkinson, T.L., "Tongues and Prophecy in Acts and 1st Corinthians", *Vox Reformata*, no. 31, Nov. 1978, pp. 1-20.

Williams, C.G., *Tongues of the Spirit*, Cardiff, 1981.

"Glossolalia as a Religious Phenomenon: Tongues at Corinth and Pentecost", *Religion*, 1975, pp. 320-338.

"Ecstaticism in Hebrew Prophecy and Christian Glossolalia", *Studies in Religion*, vol. 3, no. 4, 1974, pp. 320-338.

Williams, C.S.C., *A Commentary on the Acts of the Apostles*, London, 1964.

Wilson, R.R., "Prophecy and Ecstasy: a Reexamination", *Journal of Biblical Literature*, vol. 98, 1979, pp. 321-337.

Wintermute, O.S., "The Apocalypse of Zephaniah", in J.H. Charlesworth, ed., *The Old Testament Pseudepigrapha*, London, 1983, pp. 497-515.

Wire, A.C., *The Corinthian Women Prophets: a Reconstruction through Paul's Rhetoric*, Minneapolis, 1990.

Wolfson, H.A., *Philo, Foundations of Religious Philosophy in Judaism, Christianity and Islam*, Cambridge, 1947.

Index of Modern Authors.

Index of Greek Words and Phrases.

Index of Ancient Sources.

Subject Index